Task-based Language Learning and Teaching

D1570544

Task-based Language Learning and Teaching

Rod Ellis

OXFORD

UNIVERSITY PRESS

Acknowledgements

There have been many inputs into the writing of this book. I am grateful to Martin Bygate for inviting me to participate in a series of colloquiums on task-based learning at the American Association of Applied Linguistics and the Annual TESOL Convention as these first gave me the idea for a book that would bring together the various perspectives on tasks. I am indebted to the comments provided by various readers of the first draft. Four of these were anonymous, chosen by the Press, but I could guess who two of them were. Henry Widdowson read a number of chapters with his usual critical acumen. Three other reviewers kindly accepted my invitation to read specific chapters. Merrill Swain commented in detail on Chapters 4, 5, and 6 and then engaged in an e-mail exchange that helped me to understand sociocultural theory more deeply. Cathie Elder read Chapter 9 and enabled me to avoid a number of faux pas, which as a non-member of the language testing community I would have otherwise made. Mike Rost read Chapter 10 and helped me shape its purpose more clearly. I have responded to most of the comments provided by these reviewers, sometimes revising chapters quite extensively in the light of their suggestions. Thus, to use a fashionable term, this book is a co-construction, although, of course, I alone accept the responsibility for its failings.

I am also indebted to the University of Auckland for the sabbatical leave that made it possible to finish the book, to Showa Women's University in Tokyo for the large and peaceful office where the final writing took place and, above all, to my wife and children for their patience with my absences from them.

The author and publisher are grateful to those who have given permission to reproduce the following extracts and adaptations of copyright material:

Cambridge University Press for:
p. 11 'Same or Different' from *Keep Talking* (1984) by Friederike Klippel ©.
p. 47 Extract from *Cognition and Second Language Instruction* (2001) by Peter Robinson (ed.).
p. 143 'Materials for focused communications tasks' from *Grammar Practice Activities* (1988) by Penny Ur.

Dr N. S. Prabhu for:
p. 213 Extract from *Second Language Pedagogy* (1987) by Dr N. S. Prabhu.

Macmillan, Oxford and the authors for:
p. 219 'The theme generator' from *Planning Classwork* (1994) by Sheila Estaire & Javier Zanón.

Pearson Education for:
p. 288 'Tasks and language performance assessment' from *Researching Pedagogic Tasks, Second Language Learning, Teaching and Testing* (2001) by M. Bygate, P. Skehan and M. Swain (eds.)

University of Michigan Press for:
p. 12 'Lesson 1' from *Pyramids, Structurally Based Tasks for ESL Learners* (1987) by Madden and Reinhart.

Preface

I decided to write a book about task-based learning and teaching for a number of reasons. One is my personal commitment to a form of teaching that treats language primarily as a tool for communicating rather than as an object for study or manipulation. It is clear to me that if learners are to develop the competence they need to use a second language easily and effectively in the kinds of situations they meet *outside* the classroom they need to experience how language is used as a tool for communicating *inside* it. 'Task' serves as the most obvious means for organizing teaching along these lines. Another reason is my interest in and knowledge of second language acquisition research (SLA). 'Task' has served as both a research instrument for investigating L2 acquisition and also as a construct that has been investigated in its own right. Thus 'task' has assumed a pivotal position in SLA. A third, and probably the most important reason for writing this book, is my wish to see SLA develop not just as an autonomous discipline (and I think it clearly has moved in this direction in the last decade) but also as an applied area of study. SLA began with firm links to language teaching back in the 1960s and I would like to see these links maintained. The study of 'tasks' serves to bring SLA and language pedagogy together. It is a construct they have in common and thus is the ideal means for establishing bridges between the two fields.

This book attempts to examine 'task' from a variety of different perspectives. I have deliberately chosen not to present a personal view of tasks but to strive for a rounded, balanced account of how tasks have figured in both SLA and language pedagogy. I have, however, largely limited myself to psycholinguistic accounts of tasks, as these are what I know and understand best. However, in the last chapter, I do acknowledge the need for perspectives provided by education and critical pedagogy to be considered. Of course, there is no such thing as a truly objective and balanced account of tasks. Inevitably, my own particular thinking on tasks creeps in.

This is not a 'how to' book (although I can see the need for such a book). A practitioner looking for clear guidance about how to conduct task-based research or teaching may be disappointed. It is a book *about* task-based research and teaching. It seeks not to instruct but to illuminate, and hopefully to challenge. It attempts to identify the problems as well as the advantages of task-based teaching. In *SLA Research and Language Teaching* (Ellis 1997a) I argued, drawing on Stenhouse (1975), that the goal of theory and research in SLA is not to direct teachers how to teach but rather to advance a number of 'provisional specifications' that teachers can then try out, adapting them to their own particular teaching contexts. It is in this spirit that this book is written.

1 Tasks in SLA and language pedagogy

Introduction

Second language acquisition (SLA) researchers and language teachers both seek to elicit samples of language use from learners. In the case of researchers these samples are needed to investigate how second language (L2) learning takes place. In the case of teachers, these samples serve as the means by which learners can be helped to learn and as evidence that successful learning is taking place. Furthermore, both researchers and teachers recognize that the samples they elicit can vary according to the extent to which learners focus on using language correctly as opposed to simply communicating a message. For example, samples elicited by means of blank-filling exercises are likely to reflect the learners' attention to accuracy whereas samples elicited by means of some kind of communicative activity are more likely to reflect how learners use the L2 for message conveyance.

Increasingly, both researchers and teachers acknowledge the need to elicit samples of language use that are representative of how learners perform when they are not attending to accuracy. Such samples, it is believed, provide evidence of learners' ability to use their L2 knowledge in real-time communication. SLA researchers recognize the importance of such samples for documenting how learners structure and restructure their **interlanguages** over time. Teachers recognize that unless learners are given the opportunity to experience such samples they may not succeed in developing the kind of L2 proficiency needed to communicate fluently and effectively. The question arises, then, as to how these samples of meaning-focused language use can be elicited. The means that both have employed are 'tasks'.

Tasks, then, hold a central place in current SLA research and also in language pedagogy. This is evident in the large number of recent publications relating to task-based learning and teaching (for example, Willis 1996; Skehan 1998; Lee 2000; Language Teaching Research Vol. 4.3, 2000; Bygate *et al.* 2001). These publications raise many issues. What exactly is a task? Can tasks be designed in such a way that they predetermine language use? How does L2 learning take place as a product of performing tasks? What is task-based language pedagogy? How can language courses be constructed around tasks? How can tasks be used to assess what learners can do in the L2? These are the questions this book seeks to address. It will examine the theories of language acquisition and use that have informed research into tasks. It will also discuss the principles and practice of task-based language pedagogy, and the extent to which these are underwritten by research.

This chapter will begin by examining a number of definitions of a 'task', and discuss the important distinction between 'unfocused' and 'focused' tasks. A framework for describing tasks is developed and applied to the description of actual tasks. The second half of the chapter examines tasks from the perspective of SLA research and of language pedagogy, providing an overview of the key issues.

Defining a 'task'

What exactly is a 'task'? How does a 'task' differ from other devices used to elicit learner language, for example, an 'activity', or an 'exercise', or 'drill'. It should be acknowledged from the start that in neither research nor language pedagogy is there complete agreement as to what constitutes a task, making definition problematic (Crookes 1986: 1), nor is there consistency in the terms employed to describe the different devices for eliciting learner language. Figure 1.1 provides a number of definitions of task, drawn from both the research and pedagogic literatures. These definitions address a number of dimensions: (1) the scope of a task, (2) the perspective from which a task is viewed, (3) the authenticity of a task, (4) the linguistic skills required to perform a task, (5) the psychological processes involved in task performance, and (6) the outcome of a task.

Scope

A broad definition, such as that provided by Long (1985), includes tasks that require language, for example, making an airline reservation, and tasks that can be performed without using language, for example, painting a fence. However, more narrow definitions, such as those of Richards, Platt, and Weber (1985) and Nunan (1989) define task as an activity that necessarily involves language. Given that the overall goal of tasks, in both research and teaching, is to elicit language use, as suggested by Crookes' (1986) definition, there seems little sense in extending the term to include language-free activities. Therefore, in this book, we will be concerned only with tasks whose successful completion involves language.

Differences regarding scope involve another important distinction, which is more central to the role tasks have played in research and teaching. Should the term 'task' be restricted to activities where the learners' attention is primarily focused on message conveyance or should it include any kind of language activity including those designed to get learners to display their knowledge of what is correct usage? Long (1985), Richards, Platt, and Weber (1985), Nunan (1989), and Skehan (1996a) clearly wish to restrict the use of term to activities where meaning is primary. Breen (1989), however, adopts a broader definition that incorporates any kind of language activity, including 'exercises'. His definition seems synonymous with the term 'activity'. Given the importance that is currently attached to meaning-focused communication both in theories of L2 acquisition and of language pedagogy, there is a clear need for a term to label devices that elicit this type of language use. I will adopt the narrower definition, then. 'Tasks' are activities that call for primarily meaning-focused language use. In contrast, 'exercises' are activities that call for primarily form-focused language use. However, we need to recognize that the overall purpose of tasks is the same as exercises—learning a language—the difference lying in the means by which this purpose is to be achieved.

It might be objected that this distinction is somewhat simplistic. As Widdowson (1998) has pointed out, learners will need to pay attention to both meaning and form in both tasks and exercises. For example, learners involved in 'making an airline reservation' will need to find the linguistic forms to explain where they want to fly to, what day and time they want to fly, what kind of ticket they want, etc. Also, learners completing a blank filling exercise designed to practise the use of the past simple and present perfect tenses in English will need to pay attention to the meanings of sentences to determine which tense to use. Widdowson argues that what distinguishes a task from an exercise is not 'form' as opposed to 'meaning', but rather the *kind* of meaning involved. Whereas a task is concerned with 'pragmatic meaning', i.e. the use of language in context, an exercise is concerned with 'semantic meaning', i.e. the systemic meanings that specific forms can convey irrespective of context. However, it is precisely this distinction that the terms 'form-focused' and 'meaning-focused' are intended to capture, so Widdowson's objection is more one of terminology than substance.

The distinction between meaning-focused and form-focused is also intended to capture another key difference between an exercise and a task relating to the role of the participants. Thus, a 'task' requires the partici-pants to function primarily as 'language users' in the sense that they must employ the same kinds of communicative processes as those involved in real-world activities. Thus, any learning that takes place is incidental. In contrast, an 'exercise' requires the participants to function primarily as 'learners'; here learning is intentional. In short, as Widdowson (1998) notes, there is a fundamental difference between 'task' and 'exercise' according to whether linguistic skills are viewed as developing through communicative activity or as a prerequisite for engaging in it. However, when learners engage in tasks they do not always focus on meaning and act as language users. Nor indeed is this the intention of tasks. While a task

1 **Breen** (1989)
   A task is 'a structured plan for the provision of opportunities for the refinement of
   knowledge and capabilities entailed in a new language and its use during
   communication'. Breen specifically states that a 'task' can be 'a brief practice exercise'
   or 'a more complex workplan that requires spontaneous communication of meaning'.

2 **Long** (1985)
   A task is 'a piece of work undertaken for oneself or for others, freely or for some
   reward. Thus, examples of tasks include painting a fence, dressing a child, filling out a
   form, buying a pair of shoes, making an airline reservation, borrowing a library book,
   taking a driving test, typing a letter, weighing a patient, sorting letters, taking a hotel
   reservation, writing a cheque, finding a street destination, and helping someone across
   a road. In other words, by "task" is meant the hundred and one things people *do* in
   everyday life, at work, at play, and in between. "Tasks" are the things people will tell you
   they do if you ask them and they are not applied linguists'.

3 **Richards, Platt, and Weber** (1985)
   A task is 'an activity or action which is carried out as the result of processing or
   understanding language, i.e. as a response. For example, drawing a map while listening
   to a tape, and listening to an instruction and performing a command, may be referred to
   as tasks. Tasks may or may not involve the production of language. A task usually
   requires the teacher to specify what will be regarded as successful completion of the
   task. The use of a variety of different kinds of tasks in language teaching is said to
   make teaching more communicative … since it provides a purpose for classroom
   activity which goes beyond practice of language for its own sake'.

4 **Crookes** (1986)
   A task is 'a piece of work or an activity, usually with a specified objective, undertaken
   as part of an educational course, at work, or used to elicit data for research'.

5 **Prabhu** (1987)
   A task is 'an activity which required learners to arrive at an outcome from given
   information through some process of thought, and which allowed teachers to control
   and regulate that process'.

6 **Nunan** (1989)
   A communicative task is 'a piece of classroom work which involves learners in
   comprehending, manipulating, producing, or interacting in the target language while
   their attention is principally focused on meaning rather than form. The task should also
   have a sense of completeness, being able to stand alone as a communicative act in its
   own right'.

7 **Skehan** (1996a)
   A task is 'an activity in which: meaning is primary; there is some sort of relationship to
   the real world; task completion has some priority; and the assessment of task
   performance is in terms of task outcome'.

8 **Lee** (2000)
   A task is '(1) a classroom activity or exercise that has: (a) an objective obtainable only
   by the interaction among participants, (b) a mechanism for structuring and sequencing

interaction, and (c) a focus on meaning exchange; (2) a language learning endeavor that requires learners to comprehend, manipulate, and/or produce the target language as they perform some set of workplans'.

9 Bygate, Skehan, and Swain (2001)
'A task is an activity which requires learners to use language, with emphasis on meaning, to attain an objective.'

Figure 1.1: Examples of definitions of a 'task'

requires a learner to act *primarily* as a language user and give focal attention to message conveyance, it allows for peripheral attention to be paid to deciding what forms to use. Also, when performing a task, learners' focal attention may switch momentarily to form as they temporarily adopt the role of language learners. Thus, the extent to which a learner acts as language user or language learner and attends to message or code when undertaking tasks and exercises is best seen as variable and probabilistic rather than categorical.

Perspective

Perspective refers to whether a task is seen from the task designer's or the participants' point of view. This is relevant to the distinction between meaning-focused and form-focused. A task may have been designed to encourage a focus-on-meaning but, when performed by a particular group of learners, it may result in display rather than communicative language use. As Hosenfeld (1976) has pointed out, learners are adroit at redefining activities to suit their own purposes. Thus the 'task-as-workplan' may or may not match the 'task-as-process' (Breen 1989). Do we decide whether an activity is a 'task' by examining the intention of the task designer, i.e. the task-as-workplan, or the learners' actual performance of the task, i.e. the task-as-process? Most of the definitions in Figure 1.1 (Richards, Platt, and Weber 1985; Prabhu 1987; Breen 1989; Nunan 1989; Lee 2000) adopt the task-designer's perspective and I will do likewise: a task is, to use Breen's (1989) term, a 'workplan' that is intended to engage the learner in meaning-focused language use.[1] Of course, a task can be successful, i.e. it actually results in meaning-focused communication; or unsuccessful, i.e. it results in learners displaying their knowledge of language; or, as is often the case, it can be more or less successful/unsuccessful. One of the goals of task-based research is to establish whether the predictions made by designers are actually borne out.

The instructions, or what Bachman and Palmer (1996) call 'rubric', are an essential part of the task workplan. They specify what the purpose of the task is, i.e. its outcome, and what the participants need to do to reach an outcome. They constitute what Lee (2000) calls 'a mechanism for structuring and sequencing interaction' as the participants perform the task. The task rubric, then, creates the context for the participants to function as language users.

Authenticity

Authenticity concerns whether a task needs to correspond to some real-world activity, i.e. achieve situational authenticity. The examples that Long (1985) provides indicate that for him a task must be real-world.[2] 'Painting a fence', 'dressing a child', 'borrowing a library book', etc. are activities that occur in day-to-day living. The 'survival tasks', for example, filling in various kinds of official forms, which are common in 'second' (as opposed to 'foreign') language classes, are further examples of real-world tasks. However, there are many tasks that have been used by both researchers and teachers which are patently not real-world. For example, telling a story based on a series of pictures, describing a picture so someone else can draw it, identifying the differences in two pictures, deciding where to locate buildings on a map are all activities that language learners are unlikely to ever carry out in their lives. Such tasks, however, can be said to manifest 'some sort of relationship to the real world' (Skehan 1996a) in that they could possibly occur outside the classroom but more especially because the kind of language behaviour they elicit corresponds to the kind of communicative behaviour that arises from performing real-world tasks. For example, in a picture-drawing task, the participants will need to negotiate their way to a shared understanding by asking questions and clarifying meanings—aspects of interactional authenticity. The definition of task that informs this book will include tasks that are both situationally authentic and/or seek to achieve interactional authenticity.

Language skill

Most of the definitions in Figure 1.1 do not explicitly address what linguistic skills are involved in performing tasks. Long's examples make it clear that a task can involve both oral and written activities, for example, 'making an airline reservation', and 'writing a cheque'. Bygate *et al.*'s (2001) definition is intended to apply to written as well as oral tasks. Richards, Platt, and Weber (1985) explicitly state that a task 'may or may not involve the production of language', giving an example of a listening task, 'drawing a map while listening to a tape'. Presumably, too, they would allow that tasks can be directed at reading. However, the literature on tasks, both research-based and pedagogic (for example, Ur 1981; Klippel 1984;

Day 1986; Crookes and Gass 1993a and 1993b; Bygate, Skehan, and Swain 2001), assumes that tasks are directed at oral skills, particularly speaking. Of course, the materials for the task may also involve some reading and, if a planning stage is involved, learners may also be required to write, but the assumption is that the task itself is performed orally. In this book, 'task' will be used to refer to activities involving any of the four language skills. However, as the main purpose of the book is to provide an overview of task-based research and pedagogy to date, the contents will reflect the emphasis placed on oral tasks.

Cognitive processes

One of the more interesting differences in the definitions provided in Figure 1.1 concerns the nature of the processes involved in task performance. Richards, Platt, and Weber (1985) explicitly refer to 'processing and understanding *language*' and, quite naturally, this concern for language underlies several of the other definitions. Nunan (1989), for example, talks about tasks involving learners in 'comprehending, manipulating, producing, or interacting in the target language'. However, there is a cognitive as well as a linguistic dimension to tasks.

Prabhu's (1987) definition is alone in calling attention to the cognitive processes entailed by tasks. He talks about tasks involving 'some process of thought'. For Prabhu, tasks should ideally involve learners in 'reasoning'—making connections between pieces of information, deducing new information, and evaluating information.[3] While such a definition is well-suited to the kinds of tasks that Prabhu himself prefers, for example, working out a schedule of a visit based on railway timetables, it is probably too exclusive. There are many information- and opinion-sharing activities that are commonly seen as 'tasks' that do not involve reasoning, for example, spotting the difference between two pictures, although they may well involve other cognitive skills, for example, perceptual skills.

Tasks, however, clearly do involve cognitive processes such as selecting, reasoning, classifying, sequencing information, and transforming information from one form of representation to another. One of the limitations of both SLA research and language pedagogy is that insufficient attention has been paid to the cognitive dimension of tasks. It seems reasonable to suppose that there will be a relationship between the level of cognitive processing required and the kind of structuring and restructuring of language that tasks are designed to bring about. As Craik and Tulving (1975) have pointed out, retention depends on the 'elaborateness of the final encoding', with material more likely to be remembered when information is more deeply processed. Robinson (2001) suggests that tasks vary in their complexity according to the cognitive demands placed on learners and distinguishes what he calls 'resource-directing' factors, for example, +/– reasoning demands, and 'resource-depleting' factors, for example, whether or not a secondary task accompanies the primary task. There is a clear need, then, to acknowledge the cognitive dimension of a task in any definition.

Outcomes

One feature of tasks in which most of the definitions in Figure 1.1 concur is that they result in some clear outcome, other than simply the use of language; that is, the outcome of a task can be judged in terms of content. Thus, a narrative task based on pictures can be judged according to whether the learners have told the story successfully, i.e. have included all the main events and no 'false' events. Similarly a spot-the-difference task involving pictures can be evaluated according to whether the learners have successfully identified all the differences. The idea of a definite outcome or what Crookes (1986) calls 'a specified objective' is an essential feature of a task.

It is useful to distinguish between the 'outcome' and the 'aim' of a task. 'Outcome' refers to what the learners arrive at when they have completed the task, for example, a story, a list of differences, etc. 'Aim' refers to the pedagogic purpose of the task, which is to elicit meaning-focused language use, receptive and/or productive. This distinction is important. It is possible to achieve a successful outcome without achieving the aim of a task. For example, learners performing a spot-the-difference task based on pictures may successfully identify the differences by simply showing each other their pictures, but because they have not used language to identify these differences the aim of the task will not have been met.

In fact, tasks involve a sleight of hand. They need to convince learners that what matters is the outcome. Otherwise, there is a danger that the learners will subvert the aim of the task by displaying rather than using language. However, the real purpose of the task is not that learners should arrive at a successful outcome but that they should use language in ways that will promote language learning. In fact, the actual outcome of a task may be of no real pedagogic importance. For example, whether learners successfully identify the difference between two pictures is not what is crucial for language learning. It is the cognitive and linguistic processes involved in reaching the outcome that matter. Thus, although in one sense, and certainly from the learners' perspective it is correct to claim that 'the assessment of task performance is in terms of task outcome' (Skehan 1996a), in another, perhaps more important sense, is not. Ultimately the assessment of task performance must lie in whether learners manifest the kind of language use believed to promote language learning.

The definitions in Figure 1.1 and the preceding discussion reflect a general, decontextualized view of what a task is. Bygate, Skehan, and Swain (2001: 11) have rightly pointed out that 'definitions of task will need to differ according to the purposes for which tasks are used'. They suggest, for example, that somewhat different definitions are needed for pedagogy and research and, further, that definitions will need to vary depending on what aspect of pedagogy or research (teachers and teaching; learners and learning; testing) are at stake. They propose a 'basic, all-purpose definition' (the one included in Figure 1.1) and then show how this can be modified to reflect the different purposes of tasks. For example, if the purpose is 'testing' in the context of 'language pedagogy' they suggest the following definition:

> A task is an activity which requires learners to use language, with the emphasis on meaning, to attain an objective, and which is chosen so that it is most likely to provide information for learners and teachers which will help them in their own learning.

Bygate, Skehan, and Swain are obviously correct that what constitutes a task is to some extent variable but there is also a need for a generalized definition (as, indeed, their own 'basic definition' recognizes) that can serve to identify the essential commonalities in tasks, irrespective of their actual use. It is such a definition that the next section seeks to provide.

Criterial features of a task

The following criterial features of a task can be identified:

1 A task is a workplan.
   A task constitutes a plan for learner activity. This workplan takes the form of teaching materials or of ad hoc plans for activities that arise in the course of teaching (see Note 1). The actual activity that results may or may not match that intended by the plan. A task, therefore, may not result in communicative behaviour.
2 A task involves a primary focus on meaning.
   A task seeks to engage learners in using language pragmatically rather than displaying language. It seeks to develop L2 proficiency through communicating. Thus, it requires a primary focus on meaning. To this end, a task will incorporate some kind of 'gap', i.e. an information, opinion, or reasoning gap. The gap motivates learners to use language in order to close it. The participants choose the linguistic and non-linguistic resources needed to complete the task. The workplan does not *specify* what language the task participants should use but rather allows them to choose the language needed to achieve the outcome of the task. However, as we have seen from the preceding discussion, a task creates a certain semantic space and also the need for certain cognitive

processes, which are linked to linguistic options. Thus, a task *constrains* what linguistic forms learners need to use, while allowing them the final choice. As Kumaravadivelu (1991: 99) puts it, tasks 'indicate' the content but 'the actual language to be negotiated in the classroom is left to the teacher and the learner'. However, as we shall shortly see, one type of task can be designed in such a way as to predispose learners to use a *specific* linguistic form, for example, a particular grammatical structure. This task type is discussed below. Even in this kind of task, however, the final choice of what resources to use is left up to the learner.

3 A task involves real-world processes of language use.

The workplan may require learners to engage in a language activity such as that found in the real world, for example, completing a form, or it may involve them in language activity that is artificial, for example, determining whether two pictures are the same or different. However, the processes of language use that result from performing a task, for example, asking and answering questions or dealing with misunderstandings, will reflect those that occur in real-world communication.

4 A task can involve any of the four language skills.

The workplan may require learners to: (1) listen to or read a text and display their understanding, (2) produce an oral or written text, or (3) employ a combination of receptive and productive skills. A task may require dialogic or monologic language use. In this respect, of course, tasks are no different from exercises.

5 A task engages cognitive processes.

The workplan requires learners to employ cognitive processes such as selecting, classifying, ordering, reasoning, and evaluating information in order to carry out the task. These processes influence but do not determine the choice of language; they circumscribe the range of linguistic forms a user will need to complete the task but allow the actual choice of forms to remain with the learner.

6 A task has a clearly defined communicative outcome.

The workplan stipulates the non-linguistic outcome of the task, which serves as the goal of the activity for the learners. The stated outcome of a task serves as the means for determining when participants have completed a task.

Figure 1.2 provides examples of language teaching activities. The extent to which these activities can be called 'tasks' can be determined by evaluating whether they satisfy the criterial features of a task given above.

Activity 1, 'A dangerous moment', is the kind of task favoured by sociolinguists who wish to elicit samples of vernacular language use. They argue that people are more likely to talk spontaneously when they are recounting a traumatic experience. This activity has all the characteristics of a task. (1) The workplan specifies what the two participants in the task are supposed

Activity 1
A dangerous moment

Student A

Have you ever been in a situation where you felt your life was in danger? Describe the situation to your partner. Tell him/her what happened. Give an account of how you felt when you were in danger and afterwards.

Student B

Listen to your partner tell you about a dangerous moment in his/her life. Draw a picture to show what happened to your partner. Show him/her your picture when you have finished it.

Activity 2
The same or different?

Work with a partner. Take it in turn to describe your pictures. Does your partner have the same picture as you or a different one? Ask your partner questions about his/her picture if you are not sure.

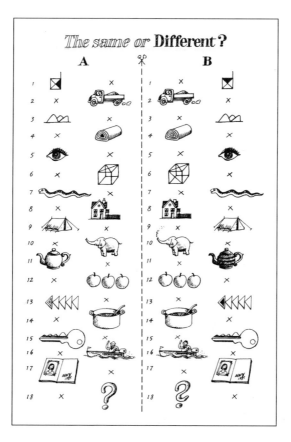

Activity 3
New students

Lesson 1

Here are some information cards for four new students in Level 2 at the English Language Academy. Some information is missing from them. Listen to the conversation and write in the missing information about the new students.

New Students

Name: *Gabriela*

Country: *Portugal*

Birth date: *8/25/50*

Married ☑

Single ☐

Occupation: *doctor*

Interest and hobbies:

reading & photography

Name: *Samuel*

Country: _____

Birth date: *2/4/65*

Married ☐

Single ☐

Occupation: *student*

Interest and hobbies:

classical music

Name: *Kuniko*

Country: *Japan*

Birth date: _____

Married ☐

Single ☐

Occupation: _____

Interest and hobbies:

volleyball & swimming

Name: _____

Country: *Morocco*

Birth date: _____

Married ☐

Single ☐

Occupation: *doctor*

Interest and hobbies:

_____

Complete the following summary about Kuniko:

Kuniko is _____ Japan. She was born on _____. She _____ married. She _____ Japanese. She is a student and she _____ to play volleyball and swim.

Now find out the same information about some of your classmates by interviewing each other. Complete an information card for each classmate you interview.

Activity 4
Asking for help

Work in pairs. One student looks at card A. The other looks at card B. Practise the conversation.

Card A

You are a student. You want your friend to help you with some homework.

A Check if B is busy.
B _____
A Ask him/her to help you.
B _____
A Try to persuade him/her.
B _____
A Thank him/her.

Card B

You are a student. Your friend wants you to help him/her with homework. You are not keen.

A _____
B Tell him/her you are not doing anything.
A _____
B Refuse. Give a reason.
A _____
B Agree reluctantly.
A _____

Activity 5
Going shopping

Look at Mary's shopping list. Then look at the list of items in Abdullah's store.

Mary's shopping list
1 oranges   **3** flour   **5** biscuits
2 eggs   **4** powdered milk   **6** jam

Abdullah's store
1 bread   **5** Coca Cola   **9** curry powder
2 salt   **6** flour   **10** biscuits
3 apples   **7** mealie meal flour **11** powdered milk
4 tins of fish **8** sugar   **12** dried beans

Work with a partner. One person be Mary and the other person be Abdullah. Make conversations like this:

Mary   Good morning. Do you have any flour?
Abdullah   Yes, I do.

or

Mary   Good morning. Do you have any jam?
Abdullah   No, I'm sorry, I don't have any.

Figure 1.2: Examples of language learning activities

to do. However, it is relatively unstructured as no input is provided so Student A is required to conceptualize the propositional content for him/herself. (2) The primary focus is obviously on meaning. (3) Student A (the speaker) has to use his/her own linguistic resources to talk about the dangerous moment while Student A is free to ask questions. (4) The language use elicited by the task corresponds to a natural communicative event, i.e. telling people about our noteworthy personal experiences. (5) The task involves oral language use. (6) The cognitive operations involved are relatively simple in that Student A can call on a ready-made schema of the dangerous moment which will provide a structure for his/her account of it. (7) The requirement that Student B draws a picture of what happened provides for a clear outcome of the task.

Activity 2, 'The same or different', is a popular language teaching activity and has also been used quite widely in research (for example, Samuda and Rounds 1993). The activity requires learners to describe their pictures with sufficient precision to enable their partners to decide whether they are holding the same or different pictures. It displays all the features of a 'task'. (1) It takes the form of a 'workplan' designed to elicit interaction between learners working in pairs. (2) The focus is primarily on meaning—describing the content of the pictures. (3) The participants choose the linguistic resources to use, i.e. there is no attempt to tell them how to describe the pictures or how to conduct the interaction, although the nature of the task may predispose them to use particular forms. (4) The activity is clearly artificial but the kind of language it elicits may correspond to that found in normal communication, for example, attempting to give clear information about something so somebody can identify it. (5) The performance of the activity entails oral language use. (6) The pictures vary in the ways in which they differ, calling on different cognitive operations. For example, the pictures in (A) differ according to which sector of the square is blacked in, whereas the pictures in (B) differ with regard to the presence or absence of a feature. (7) The participants have to state whether each pair of pictures is the same or different, which provides a definite outcome for the activity.

Activity 3, 'New students' (Madden and Reinhart 1987), entails three separate activities. The first requires students to listen to some information about four people and fill in missing information on forms. The second requires students to fill in the missing words in a short written passage. The third asks students to ask their classmates questions in order to fill in forms. The first activity satisfies the defining characteristics of a task. (1) It constitutes a workplan. (2) The focus is on meaning. (3) The learners have to make their own selection of what words to use, as opposed to being provided with, say, multiple choice answers. (4) The kind of language behaviour required is artificial but related to natural language use. (5) It is a listening activity. (6) It involves the cognitive process of identifying specific information. (7) There is a definite outcome, i.e. the completed forms. The third activity similarly functions as a task, in this case, though, an interactive one involving speaking.

The second activity in 'New students', however, seems more like an exercise. In this case, the workplan focuses learners' attention primarily on grammatical form as most of the blanks in the text require function words like 'from' or 'is' rather than content words. Except for the words needed to fill in the blanks, the learners have no choice over the linguistic resources to be used. It is difficult to see how filling in blanks in a passage manifests 'some sort of relationship to the real world'. Finally, the only outcome is the completed passage, i.e. the outcome cannot be established separately from the language that is produced. Of course, the fact that this activity is an exercise does not denigrate its worth as a language-learning activity. Indeed, theoretical grounds can be found for including exercises alongside tasks, a teaching strategy quite widely favoured (see, for example, Estaire and Zanon's (1994) proposals for developing a task-based curriculum).

Activity 4, 'Asking for help', is an example of a cue-card activity (for example, Revell 1979). This has some of the features of a task. For example, it provides a workplan for an oral interaction and, to some extent at least, the participants are free to choose the linguistic resources, i.e. they decide how to request help, refuse, persuade, etc. Also, the resulting interaction may bear some resemblance to an authentic conversation. However, the intended primary focus is on form rather than meaning—the meanings of the utterances are given so that all the learners have to do is find the linguistic forms to encode the stated functions. Also, the only outcome is the performance of the activity itself; the oral interaction does not result in an outcome to show that the activity has been completed. This kind of cue-card activity, while of potential value for practising language, does not constitute a task.

Activity 5, 'Going shopping', is even more obviously an exercise. The workplan requires learners to attend to form—the use of 'any' and 'some' in questions and replies; it asks them only to substitute items in sentences they are given; it is not likely to lead to the kind of language use found in the real world; it is cognitively undemanding; and the outcome of the activity does not involve a definite product. However, as Johnson (1982) has shown, exercises like this can easily be made more task-like by splitting the information. Thus, if Student A had Mary's shopping list and Student B the list of items in Abdullah's store, the resulting 'gap' would require a focus on meaning. The participants could be left to choose their own linguistic resources by removing the model sentences. Finally, a definite outcome could be introduced by requesting the students to write down what items Mary was able to buy.

The discussion of these five language-learning activities, which are representative of the kinds of workplans found in teaching materials, demonstrates the essential differences between a task and an exercise. Moreover, the discussion shows that some language-teaching activities cannot easily be classified as a 'task' or an 'exercise' as they manifest features of both.[4] We have also seen that it may be possible to make an activity more task-like by making adjustments to the way it is designed.

The discussion also indicates that some of the criteria are more important for judging whether an activity is a task than others. The key criterion is (2), the need for a primary focus on meaning. As Stern (1992: 202) has pointed out, 'a task stops being communicative only if the choice of activity has been prompted by purely linguistic considerations'. Also important are (3), (4), and (7). In contrast, (1), (5), and (6) would seem to apply to all kinds of teaching materials, including exercises. The following, then, is the definition of a task that will inform this book:

> A task is a workplan that requires learners to process language pragmatically in order to achieve an outcome that can be evaluated in terms of whether the correct or appropriate propositional content has been conveyed. To this end, it requires them to give primary attention to meaning and to make use of their own linguistic resources, although the design of the task may predispose them to choose particular forms. A task is intended to result in language use that bears a resemblance, direct or indirect, to the way language is used in the real world. Like other language activities, a task can engage productive or receptive, and oral or written skills, and also various cognitive processes.

Next we will consider two general types of tasks and the difference between them.

Unfocused and focused tasks

Unfocused tasks of the kind illustrated in Figure 1.2 may predispose learners to choose from a range of forms but they are not designed with the use of a specific form in mind. In contrast, focused tasks aim to induce learners to process, receptively or productively, some particular linguistic feature, for example, a grammatical structure. Of course this processing must occur as a result of performing activities that satisfy the key criteria of a task, i.e. that language is used pragmatically to achieve some non-linguistic outcome. Therefore, the targeted feature cannot be specified in the rubric of the task. Focused tasks, then, have two aims: one is to stimulate communicative language use (as with unfocused tasks), the other is to target the use of a particular, predetermined target feature. Such tasks are of obvious use to both researchers and teachers. Researchers often want to know whether learners are able to perform some specific feature they are investigating in a communicative context. Teachers may want to provide learners with the opportunity to practise a specific feature under real operating conditions.

There are two main ways in which a task can achieve a focus. One is to design the task in such a way that it can only be performed if learners use a particular linguistic feature. Activity 1, 'Find the picture', in Figure 1.3 is an example of such a task. This requires one learner to describe the picture indicated so that his/her partner can identify which picture it is from the same set. To achieve this, the learner has to use prepositions of place. For example, in the first set in Activity 1, the speaker will have to use the preposition 'on' to distinguish it from the other two pictures. Loschky and Bley-Vroman (1993) refer to this kind of focused task as a 'grammatical task'. However, it is not easy to design such tasks. This is because learners can always use communication strategies to get round using the targeted feature. For example, a learner who did not know or could not recall the preposition 'on' could always say, 'The ball—not in, not by the side of the box'. It is easier to force learners to process a specific feature in a comprehension task.

The second way of constructing a focused task is by making language itself the content of a task. In unfocused tasks the topics are drawn from real life or perhaps from the academic curriculum that students are studying. However, it is also possible to make a language point the topic of a task. For example, in Activity 2 in Figure 1.3 the topic is prepositions of time. Learners use the data supplied to complete a table by classifying the time phrases into those that use 'in', 'on', and 'at'. They then try to work out a rule to describe how these prepositions are used. This kind of activity, which I have called 'consciousness raising (CR) tasks' (Ellis 1991), is a task rather than an exercise because it requires learners to talk about the data together. This talk, like talk about any other topic, involves the exchange of information and ideas and is, therefore, meaning-centred. Focused tasks are discussed in detail in Chapter 5.

The design features of tasks

Irrespective of whether a task is unfocused or focused it will manifest certain design features. In this section we will examine a framework for examining these.

As Wright (1987) suggests, tasks are comprised of two principal elements: 'input data', and 'instructional questions' that invite learners to operate on the input in some way. He argues that tasks cannot be described in terms of 'output' because tasks can only have a 'discourse potential', a point I have already acknowledged by following Breen (1989) in distinguishing task-as-workplan and task-as-process, and by insisting that a task is defined as a workplan. Nunan (1989: 48) identifies three components of

Activity 1
Find the picture

Student A
Work with a partner. Describe the picture marked with an arrow so your partner can find it.

Student B
Work with a partner. Listen to your partner. Write down the letter of the picture he/she describes. Then describe your picture marked with an arrow.

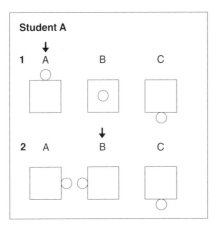 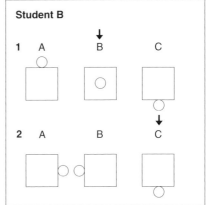

Activity 2
Prepositions of time

1 Underline the time expressions in this passage.

   I made an appointment to see Mr. Bean at 3 o'clock on Tuesday 11th February to discuss my application for a job. Unfortunately, he was involved in a car accident in the morning and rang to cancel the appointment. I made another appointment to see him at 10 o'clock on Friday 21st February. However, when I got to his office, his secretary told me that his wife had died at 2 o'clock in the night and that he was not coming into the office that day. She suggested I reschedule for sometime in March. So I made a third appointment to see Mr. Bean at 1 o'clock on Monday 10th March. This time I actually got to see him. However, he informed me that they had now filled all the vacancies and suggested I contact him again in 1998. I assured him that he would not be seeing me in either this or the next century.

2 Write the time phrases into this table.

AT	IN	ON
3 o'clock		

3 Make up a rule to explain when to use 'at', 'in' and 'on' in time expressions.

Figure 1.3: Examples of focused tasks (Ellis 1998: 48)

tasks: input, activities (corresponding to Wright's instructional questions), and goals, which he defines as 'the vague general intentions behind any given learning task'.

Table 1.1 outlines the task framework that informs this book. The framework is somewhat more complex than that proposed by either Wright or Nunan. As in Nunan's framework, I include 'goal', the general purpose of the task. This can be specified in terms of what aspect(s) of communicative competence the task is intended to contribute to. Canale (1983) distinguishes four aspects: linguistic competence, sociolinguistic competence, discourse competence, and strategic competence. Tasks can potentially contribute to the development of all four with particular tasks designed to emphasize specific aspects of communicative competence. Or the goal can be specified in terms of linguistic skills or the rhetorical mode (description, argument, directions, etc.) the task is intended to elicit.

Whereas Wright and Nunan both identify 'input' as a task component, I distinguish two separate components—'input' and 'conditions'. This reflects the need to distinguish between the kind of input data that a task provides, for example, whether it is verbal or non-verbal or both, and the way in which the data are presented, for example, whether the data are split among the task participants or shared by them. These constitute two quite distinct task variables. Thus, a task may have the same input, for example, a set of pictures telling a story, but different conditions, for example, the pictures could be seen by all the participants or they could be divided up among them. Likewise, a task could have different input, for example, a set of pictures vs. a written story, but the same condition, for example, the information was split. As we will see in subsequent chapters, input and conditions have both been found to have an effect on task performance.

'Procedures' concern the methodological options available to researchers and teachers for implementing tasks. They may or may not be mentioned in what Wright calls the 'instructional question' or Nunan the 'activity'. Consider the final task in Activity 3 in Figure 1.2. The participants are asked to interview their fellow classmates in order to fill in forms about them. Thus, the instructions do specify the procedure of working in pairs. However, there are other choices available, which are not referred to in the instructions. For example, a teacher using this task could decide to give the students time to plan the questions they would need to ask. Such procedures are independent of both the input and the conditions of the task. One of the goals of current task-based research is to investigate what effect varying the procedures for using a task has on task performance (see Chapter 4).

Finally, the framework includes the 'predicted outcomes' of a task. Neither Wright nor Nunan include this component as both consider it impossible to say what the outcome of a task will be. With respect to 'product outcomes' this is clearly not the case. As we have already seen, tasks must have clear, specifiable product outcomes in order to qualify as tasks. Thus, the intended product outcome of the final activity in Activity 3 in Figure 1.2 is, fairly obviously, a set of completed forms. In the case of 'process outcomes', i.e. what actually transpires when participants perform a task, it is much more difficult to make predictions as the language and cognitive behaviour elicited by a task are to a considerable extent depen-dent on the particular participants and cannot be reliably predicted. Nevertheless, predictions can and have been made. For example, we might predict that participants performing the final task in Activity 3 will 'ask questions', although we cannot be sure whether they will produce target-like questions, for example, 'What is your name?', or employ interlanguage structures, for example, 'What your name is?'. In fact, one of the goals of task-based research is to establish what language and cognitive processes are likely to occur when input, conditions, and procedures are systemat-ically varied. In language pedagogy, too, tasks are devised with the expec-tation that they will generate specific process outcomes. It would seem important, therefore, to include 'predicted outcomes' as a component in any descriptive framework.

Let us now apply this framework to the description of Activity 2 in Figure 1.2. The 'goal' of such a task might be that of 'developing the students' oral ability to describe objects precisely'. The 'input' consists of pairs of pictures, some of which are the same and some of which differ in minor details. The 'conditions' for this task involve the provision of different sets of pictures to pairs of students; the information, therefore, is split. The methodological 'procedures' involve the use of pair work. Note that this is not a necessary procedure for it would also be possible to do this task in lockstep, with the teacher holding one set of pictures and the rest of the class the other. Finally, the predicted outcomes are: (1) a written statement saying whether each pair of pictures is the same or different (the product outcome), and (2) descriptions of the pictures, probably involving the use of locative expressions such as 'at the top' or 'inside' (the process outcome).

A framework such as that in Table 1.1 has a number of uses. First, it allows for the systematic description of different tasks. Second, it provides a basis for identifying the various options for designing tasks. Third, it can assist in the identification of different task types and their classification (see Chapter 7). These uses are of importance to both researchers and teachers for without a clear idea of what a particular task consists of neither research nor teaching can be carried out efficiently.

We have now, at some length, defined what a task is and offered a frame-work for describing the features of different tasks. We have established the object of our enquiry. It is now time to sketch out how tasks have been employed in research and pedagogy as a preliminary for the more detailed investigation of tasks in the chapters that follow. The unifying theme of both sections is the relationship between task and language use on the one hand, and language use and language development on the other.

Design feature	Description
1 Goal	The general purpose of the task, e.g. to practise the ability to describe objects concisely; to provide an opportunity for the use of relative clauses.
2 Input	The verbal or non-verbal information supplied by the task, e.g. pictures; a map; written text.
3 Conditions	The way in which the information is presented, e.g. split vs. shared information, or the way in which it is to be used, e.g. converging vs. diverging.
4 Procedures	The methodological procedures to be followed in performing the task, e.g. group vs. pair work; planning time vs. no planning time.
5 Predicted outcomes:	
Product	The 'product' that results from completing the task, e.g. a completed table; a route drawn in on a map; a list of differences between two pictures. The predicted product can be 'open', i.e. allow for several possibilities, or 'closed', i.e. allow for only one 'correct' solution.
Process	The linguistic and cognitive processes the task is hypothesized to generate.

Table 1.1: A framework for describing tasks

Tasks in SLA research

The use of tasks in SLA has been closely linked to developments in the study of second language acquisition (SLA). In the early years of SLA (the late sixties and seventies), researchers were primarily concerned with describing how learners acquired an L2, documenting the order and sequence in which the grammar of a language was acquired (for example, Dulay and Burt 1973; Hakuta 1976; Cancino *et al.* 1978), and the types of oral interactions in which child and adult language learners participated (for example, Wagner-Gough 1975; Hatch 1978b). Over the years, SLA has become more theory-oriented with researchers seeking to test specific hypotheses based on theories of L2 acquisition. Tasks have played an important role in both the early descriptive research and the later more theoretically based research. Also, tasks have become a focus of research in their own right.

In early descriptive research, the main goal was to examine how learners acquired an L2 naturalistically, i.e. without formal instruction. The primary data for this research consisted of the spontaneous speech that learners used when they tried to converse in the L2. However, such data were often difficult to collect and did not always afford examples of the particular linguistic features the researchers wished to investigate. For this reason, it was often supplemented with data collected by asking the learners to perform various kinds of tasks. These tasks were intended to elicit communicative samples of learner language, which could then be carefully analysed to plot how learners' use of specific linguistic features changed over time. For example, in a study of three classroom learners carried out between 1979 and 1982 (Ellis 1984 and 1985), I collected both samples of naturally occurring speech in the classroom and samples of speech elicited by means of 'What's Wrong Cards', where the learners talked with their teacher about a set of pictures.

The kind of instrument I used involves what Corder (1973) describes as 'clinical elicitation'. The purpose of such instruments is to collect general language data. They contrast with other kinds of instruments designed to elicit samples of language containing specific linguistic features. For example, the Bilingual Syntax Measure (BSM) (Burt, Dulay, and Hernandez 1973) was used to elicit a number of morphological features such as plural -*s* and regular past tense -*ed*. Learners were shown a series of pictures and then responded orally to questions about them. The BSM, then, serves as an early example of a focused task. However, the exercise-like nature of this task, together with the test-like way in which it is performed may result in form-focused rather than meaning-focused language use.[5] Other instruments, such as the sentence imitation test used by Cancino *et al.* (1978), are even more obviously exercises.

A question of considerable importance—and one that was soon asked—was whether the data collected by means of clinical and experimental elicitation devices were similar to or different from naturally occurring data. The study of variability in learner language tackled this question and constituted the first attempt to investigate the relationship between tasks, language use, and L2 acquisition. In this respect, Tarone's work (see Tarone 1979; 1982; 1983a) is seminal. Tarone was able to show that learners do vary in their use of language according to the type of activity they are engaged in. Adapting Labov's stylistic continuum, she argued that learners possess a continuum of styles. At one end of this continuum is the 'vernacular style', where learners attend to meaning rather than form. This is manifest in naturally occurring speech. At the other end is the 'careful style', where learners attend primarily to form. This can be tapped by means of experimental elicitation devices such as a grammaticality judgement test. In between, there is an indeterminate number of other styles which can be studied through data collected by a range of devices from tasks to test-like exercises. A number of studies carried out in the eighties testified to the variability in learners' performance of specific grammatical features depending on the kind of instrument used to collect data (for example, Beebe 1980; Ellis 1987;

Tarone and Parrish 1988). This research has contributed to our understanding of the variables that affect task performance.

Whereas variability research was directed at investigating learner
production, another branch of SLA research in the eighties focused on the
input to which learners were exposed and the kinds of interactions learners participated in. In this respect the work of Krashen (1981, 1985, 1994)
and Long (1981, 1983a, 1996) is of particular importance. Krashen has
advanced the Input Hypthesis, which claims that language acquisition is
input-driven; that is, learners acquire an L2 incidentally and subcon-
sciously when they are able to comprehend the input they are exposed to.
He suggests that input becomes comprehensible when it is contextually
embedded and is roughly tuned to the learners' level or proficiency. Long's
Interaction Hypothesis places a similar emphasis on the role of input but
claims that the 'best' input for language acquisition is that which arises
when learners have the opportunity to negotiate meaning in exchanges
where an initial communication problem has occurred, as in this example
of an interaction between two learners:

Hiroko	A man is uh drinking c-coffee or tea with uh saucer of the uh coffee set is uh in his uh knee
Izumi	In him knee
Hiroko	uh on his knee
Izumi	Yeah
Hiroko	on *his* knee
Izumi	So sorry, on *his* knee

(Gass and Varonis 1989: 81)

In early versions of the Interaction Hypothesis (Long 1981 and 1983),
Long emphasized the role that meaning negotiation of this kind played in
providing comprehensible input. More recently (Long 1996), he has
suggested that meaning negotiation can contribute to acquisition in other
ways—through the negative feedback that learners receive by means of
recasts, i.e. interlocutor reformulations of learner utterances that contain
errors, and through the opportunities to reformulate their own erroneous
utterances in a more target-like way. These theories have led to research
that utilizes tasks to investigate which kind of input—unmodified,
premodified, or interactionally modified—works best for comprehension
(for example, Pica, Young, and Doughty 1987); which kind of input works
best for language acquisition (for example, Doughty 1991; Ellis, Tanaka, and
Yamazaki 1994; Loschky 1994); and, more recently, the effect of negative
feedback on acquisition (for example, Mackey and Philp 1998; Ayoun 2001).

The Input and Interaction Hypotheses have also motivated several
studies where the focus of the research was the tasks themselves. The goal
of this research was to identify 'psycholinguistically motivated task characteristics' which 'can be shown to affect the nature of language produced

in performing a task in ways which are relevant to SL processing and SL learning' (Crookes 1986). In particular, researchers wanted to find out which tasks were most likely to lead to the kind of meaning negotiation hypothesized to promote language acquisition. In this research, then, the dependent variables were derived from the interactions that resulted when learners performed different tasks. Researchers investigated a variety of task variables such as whether the information exchange required by a task was one-way or two-way (Long 1980; Pica and Doughty 1985a), whether the input was shared or split (Newton 1991), whether the outcome of a task was closed or open (Crookes and Rulon 1985), and whether it was divergent or convergent (Duff 1986). Other research focused on the nature of the learner's participation in a task, examining whether tasks performed in small groups or in lockstep with a teacher led to greater meaning negotiation (Pica and Doughty 1985b), and the effects of such variables as the learner's proficiency and gender on meaning negotiation (for example, Yule and McDonald 1990; Pica, Holliday, Lewis, Berducci and Newman 1991).

Not all task-based research has been motivated by the Input and Interaction Hypotheses, however. A number of recent studies have drawn on Vygotskian accounts of language learning. These view all learning as socially constructed. When L2 learners have the opportunity to interact with other users of the language, for example, a teacher, a native speaker, or another learner, they are able to perform functions in the language which they can not perform by themselves. With time and practice they internalize these functions, learning to perform them independently. In this way, learning involves a progression from the inter- to the intra-mental as learners shift from object and other regulation to self-regulation. Vygotskian theory also emphasizes how learners shape the goals of any activity to suit their own purposes. Recently, this theoretical perspective has led to task-based studies that investigate 'scaffolding' and 'collaborative dialogue', the supportive interactions that arise when learners communicate with others (for example, Donato 1994; Swain and Lapkin 1998; Swain 2000a) and also to studies that demonstrate how the task-as-workplan is interpreted and reshaped by learners in actual performance (Coughlan and Duff 1994). There have also been attempts to show how learners and native speaker interlocutors vary in the way they perform a single task depending on the learners' developmental stage (Aljaafreh and Lantolf 1994).

Other recent task-oriented research has been based on theories of language competence and of speech production. Skehan (1996a, 1998a) has suggested that language competence is comprised of both lexis, including fixed and formulaic expressions such as 'I don't know', and grammatical rules. Native speakers make use of these two different types of knowledge by means of a 'dual processing system', drawing on both lexicalized and grammatical processing but varying in which type they rely on in a given activity according to the communicative pressure they experience and their need to be precise. Skehan argues that when required to perform spontaneously L2 learners are likely to depend on lexicalized processing. This leads him to suggest that it may be possible to identify the task conditions and procedures that lead learners to place a differential emphasis on fluency, i.e. performance free of undue pauses and false starts, complexity, i.e. the use of a wide range of grammatical structures, and accuracy, i.e. the correct use of grammatical structures. Variables so far investigated (see Skehan 1998b, and Skehan and Foster 2001 for reviews) include a number of input features of tasks, for example, familiarity of the information and degree of structure, of task procedures, for example, whether the task was to be performed dialogically or monologically, and whether there was time made available for planning, and of the product outcome, for example, how complex this is.

Other researchers have based their research on Levelt's model of speech production (Levelt 1989). This identifies three stages in speech production: (1) conceptualization, when the purpose and semantic content of a message is determined; (2) formulation, when the speaker maps grammatical and phonological features onto the preverbal message; and (3) articulation, when the phonetic plan produced by (2) is converted into actual speech. Wendel (1997) has used this model to distinguish two types of planning—strategic or off-line planning, i.e. the planning that takes place when learners are given time to plan a task prior to performing it, and online planning, i.e. the planning that occurs while learners are actually performing the task. Thus, strategic planning, according to Wendel, involves conceptualization. Online planning, in contrast, is directed at formulation and articulation, and manifests itself through monitoring. Bygate (1996) also utilizes Levelt's model to account for the effect that asking learners to repeat a task has on task performance.

The task-based research reviewed above involved the use of unfocused tasks. However, there have also been a number of studies that have investigated focused tasks. Newton and Kennedy (1996), for example, provide evidence to suggest that it is possible to predict the linguistic forms that will be used when particular tasks are performed. They found that the discourse genre, i.e. description vs. persuasion, elicited by tasks influenced the linguistic forms used. Bygate (1999b) has also demonstrated that the processing involved in performing a narrative and an argumentation task led to learners making different linguistic choices. Also, varying a task condition, i.e. shared vs. split information, influenced learners' choice of linguistic forms. Nobuyoshi and Ellis (1993) and Takashima and Ellis (1999) demonstrated that it may be possible to push learners into using a particular grammatical form (past tense) if they receive requests to clarify utterances containing an error in this structure. These studies, then, demonstrated that task procedures can be manipulated to induce the use of specific features.

Other studies have investigated consciousness-raising tasks. Fotos and Ellis (1991) and Fotos (1994) set out to examine whether the grammatical understanding that resulted from learners performing a CR task was as good as that resulting from traditional grammatical explanations provided by a teacher. They also examined whether the quality of meaning negotiation that results from such tasks was comparable to that derived from unfocused tasks. In both respects, the results were encouraging. The CR tasks used in these studies led to a good understanding of the target grammar points and resulted in plentiful meaning negotiation.

More recently, researchers have turned their attention to how participants in a task temporarily suspend attention to meaning in order to focus on form. By switching attention to form during the performance of a task teachers can incorporate form-focused instruction into meaning-focused instruction methodologically, rather than through task-design as in the ways described above. This branch of task-based research has been motivated by findings from SLA which indicate that even after years of content-based instruction learners fail to acquire full grammatical and sociolinguistic competence (Swain 1985), and also by developments in SLA theory that stress the importance for acquisition of conscious 'noticing' of forms in the input (Schmidt 1990; 1994). A temporary focus-on-form can be achieved in a number of ways—when teachers respond to learner errors (Lyster and Ranta 1997), when they draw learners' attention to the usefulness of specific forms in the task they are performing (Samuda 2001), or when learners collaboratively try to solve some linguistic problem in order to complete a task (Swain and Lapkin 1998). A key question is whether such shifts detract from the overall communicativeness of a task, but studies to date (for example, Lyster and Ranta 1997 and Ellis, Basturkmen, and Loewen 2001) suggest that this does not happen.

This bird's eye view of SLA research involving tasks shows a development from a time when tasks were viewed simply as instruments for investigating SLA to the present where tasks are now seen as objects of enquiry in their own right. It also demonstrates the wide range of theoretical perspectives that now inform task-based research—variability theory, the Input and Interaction Hypotheses, socio-cultural theories of learning, theories of language competence and of speech production, and theories relating to the role of conscious attention to form. These theories are considered in subsequent chapters. The next five chapters examine task-based research in SLA and the theories that have informed this research. Chapter 2 focuses on research based on listening tasks. Chapter 3 looks at research that examines tasks in relation to the kinds of interaction they lead to. Chapter 4 is concerned with the effect that varying task variables has on learner production. Chapter 5 deals with focused tasks. Chapter 6 looks at tasks from the perspective of socio-cultural theory.

The fact that tasks have become objects of enquiry in their own right is testimony to the pedagogical orientation of much of the later research. 'Task' is a pedagogical unit that can be used as a basis for designing language courses (Long and Crookes 1992). By specifying what tasks are to be used course designers can create blueprints for the kinds of language use that will foster language development. But this requires information upon which to base the design of individual tasks and their sequencing into a programme of instruction. This is what the research aims to provide— drawing on the theoretical constructs provided by SLA to motivate the enquiry. But how have tasks been used in language pedagogy? We turn now to consider the other side of the coin.

Tasks in language teaching

Like researchers, language teachers, materials writers, and course designers have not been slow to recognize the value of tasks. However, they have differed considerably in the use they have made of them. Some methodologists have simply incorporated tasks into traditional language-based approaches to teaching. Others, more radically, have treated tasks as units of teaching in their own right and have designed whole courses around them. These two ways of using tasks can be referred to respectively as *task-supported language teaching* and as *task-based language teaching*. In both cases, tasks have been employed to make language teaching more communicative. Tasks, therefore, are an important feature of *communicative language teaching* (CLT). We will begin, then, by considering CLT and the roles that tasks play in it.

Communicative language teaching

CLT aims to develop the ability of learners to use language in real communication. Brown and Yule (1983) characterize communication as involving two general purposes—the interactional function, where language is used to establish and maintain contact, and the transactional function, where language is used referentially to exchange information. CLT, then, is directed at enabling learners to function interactionally and transactionally in an L2. In this respect, however, the goal of CLT is not so different from that of earlier methods such as the audiolingual or oral-situational method, which also claimed to develop the ability to use language communicatively. CLT, however, drew on very different models of language. Thus, whereas the earlier methods were based on a view of language as a set of linguistic systems (phonological, lexical, and grammatical), CLT drew on a functional model of language (Halliday's) and a theory of communicative competence (Hymes').[6] To adopt Widdowson's (1978) terms, whereas structural approaches to teaching focus on *usage*, i.e. the ability to use language correctly, communicative language teaching is directed at *use*, i.e. the ability to use language meaningfully and appropriately in the construction of discourse.

In fact, though, CLT is not a monolithic and uniform approach. Howatt (1984) distinguishes a 'weak' and a 'strong' version. The former is based on the assumptions that the components of communicative competence can be identified and systematically taught. In this respect, a weak version of CLT does not involve a radical departure from earlier methods as it still reflects what White (1988) refers to as a Type A approach to language teaching, i.e. an approach that is interventionist and analytic. Thus, instead of (or, perhaps in addition to) teaching learners the structural properties of language, a weak version of CLT proposes they be taught how to realize specific general notions such as 'duration' and 'possibility', and language functions such as 'inviting' and 'apologizing'. The weak version of CLT is manifest in the proposals for *notional/functional syllabuses* developed by Wilkins (1976) and Van Ek (1976).

In contrast, a strong version of CLT claims that 'language is acquired through communication' (Howatt 1984: 279). That is, learners do not first acquire language as a structural system and then learn how to use this system in communication but rather actually discover the system itself in the process of learning how to communicate.[7] The strong version of CLT, therefore, involves providing learners with opportunities to experience how language is used in communication. This approach reflects what White (1988) has called a Type B approach, i.e. an approach that is non-interventionist and holistic. It is evident in Krashen and Terrell's (1983) Natural Approach and also in proposals for teaching centred on the use of tasks (Candlin 1987).

The distinction between a weak and a strong version of CLT parallels the distinction between task-supported language teaching and task-based language teaching. The weak version views tasks as a way of providing communicative practice for language items that have been introduced in a more traditional way. They constitute a necessary but not a sufficient basis for a language curriculum. The strong version sees tasks as a means of enabling learners to learn a language by experiencing how it is used in communication. In the strong version, tasks are both necessary and sufficient for learning. We will now explore these two ways of viewing tasks in language teaching in greater depth.

Task-supported language teaching

Teaching based on a linguistic content, whether this is specified in structural terms as a list of grammatical features or in notional/functional terms as in the weak version of CLT, has traditionally employed a methodological procedure consisting of present–practise–produce (*PPP*) (see Gower and Walters 1983 for a detailed account of this standard procedure). That is, a language item is first presented to the learners by means of examples with or without an explanation. This item is then practised in a controlled manner using what we have called 'exercises'. Finally opportunities for using the item in free language production are provided. It is in this 'production' stage that tasks have been employed. Implicit in PPP is the idea that it is possible to lead learners from controlled to automatic use of new language features by means of text-manipulation exercises that structure language for the learner followed by text-creation tasks where learners structure language for themselves (Batstone 1994).

The view of language learning that underlies this approach to language teaching has been criticized on a number of grounds. PPP views language as a series of 'products' that can be acquired sequentially as 'accumulated entities' (Rutherford 1987). However, SLA research has shown that learners do not acquire a language in this way. Rather they construct a series of systems, known as interlanguages, which are gradually grammaticized and restructured as learners incorporate new features. Furthermore, research on developmental sequences has shown that learners pass through a series of transitional stages in acquiring a specific grammatical feature such as negatives, often taking months or even years before they arrive at the target form of the rule. In other words, L2 acquisition is a 'process' that is incompatible with teaching seen as the presentation and practice of a series of 'products'.

There are practical problems with PPP as well. Clearly, the production stage calls for 'grammar tasks', i.e. tasks that will elicit the feature that is the target of the lesson (see p. 17). However, as we have already seen, it is not easy to design tasks that require learners to use a targeted structure, as learners can always fall back on their strategic competence to circumvent it. One way out of this problem is to make it clear to the learners that they must use the targeted structure when they perform the task. However, this would encourage the learners to focus primarily on form with the result that the task then ceases to be a task as it has been defined in this chapter, and becomes instead an exercise.

However, despite these criticisms and problems and despite the doubts as to whether PPP can deliver what it promises, i.e. the ability to use the structures taught in real communication, it has proved highly durable. Skehan (1996b) suggests that this is because it affords teachers procedures for maintaining control of the classroom, thus reinforcing their power over students and also because the procedures themselves are eminently trainable.

It would be wrong, however, to characterize task-supported language teaching entirely in terms of PPP. It can take other forms. For example, Brumfit (1979) has suggested changing the sequence of stages in PPP, beginning with the production stage and following up with the presentation and practice stages only if learners demonstrate their inability to use the targeted feature during the production stage. In this scheme, the task comes first and serves a diagnostic purpose. However, the problem remains that presenting and practising features learners have failed to use correctly in production may not result in their acquisition if the learners are not developmentally ready to acquire them.

A better alternative might be to view the language curriculum as consisting of two separate, unrelated strands, one of which follows traditional lines and the other which is task-based (see, for example, Allen's 1984 proposals for a syllabus with a variable focus). No attempt is made to use tasks to target specific linguistic features. Here tasks are seen not as a means by which learners acquire new knowledge or restructure their interlanguages but simply as a means by which learners can activate their existing knowledge of the L2 by developing fluency. This is clearly a lesser goal for tasks, as they do not replace exercises, but one that is compatible with a 'process' view of language acquisition. Many of the early handbooks of tasks for teachers (for example, Winn-Bell Olsen 1977; Byrne and Rixon 1979) explicitly acknowledge that tasks are supplementary.[8]

Task-based language teaching

Task-based language teaching constitutes a strong version of CLT. That is, tasks provide the basis for an entire language curriculum. We should note, however, that task-based teaching is not the only way of achieving a strong version of CLT. Stern (1992) offers a comprehensive classification of 'communicative activities' that includes field experiences, classroom management activities, inviting guest speakers, talking on topics related to the students' private life and on substantive topics drawn from other subjects on the school curriculum (as in immersion programmes), and what he calls 'communicative exercises', i.e. tasks. These are arranged in descending order with those closest to communicative reality at the top and those furthest removed at the bottom. Clearly, a strong version of CLT can be realized in a variety of ways, not just by tasks. Nevertheless, tasks can function as a useful device for planning a communicative curriculum, particularly in contexts where there are few opportunities for more authentic communicative experiences, for example, many FL situations.

One of the attractions of a task-based approach is that it appears to blur the traditional distinction between syllabus, i.e. a statement of what is to taught, and methodology, i.e. a statement of how to teach. This distinction still underlies the weak version of CLT, where the syllabus is 'communicative', i.e. a list of notions and functions, but the methodology is traditional and non-communicative, i.e. PPP.[9] Weak CLT, like earlier structural approaches, is content-driven, methodology being tacked on as a way of 'mediating' the syllabus (Widdowson 1990). In contrast, a task-based curriculum involves 'an integrated set of processes involving, among other things, the specification of both what and how' (Nunan 1989: 1). In fact, it could be argued that 'methodology becomes the central tenet of task-based pedagogy' (Kumaravadivelu 1993) in that no attempt is made to specify what the learners will learn, only how they will learn.

Despite these arguments, it is still useful to draw a distinction between the design of the syllabus and the choice of methodology in task-based teaching, as Skehan (1996a) has argued. Designing a task-based curriculum involves making decisions about what tasks learners will *do* (a question of selection) and, then, the order in which they will perform these tasks (a question of grading). Then, there are decisions to be made regarding the specific methdological procedures for teaching each task. Skehan (1996a) suggests that these can be organized in terms of pre-task, during-task, and after-task choices. Thus, whereas task-based teaching prescribes teaching methodology in broad terms, i.e. as 'fluency' rather than 'accuracy' (Brumfit 1984), there remains a whole range of micro-options to choose from. In this book, then, we will follow Skehan in continuing to distinguish between syllabus and methodology in task-based teaching. Indeed, such a distinction is implicit in Figure 1.4, which distinguishes 'procedures'— a matter of methodology, from 'input' and 'conditions'—a matter of design.

So far, we have discussed task-based teaching as if it constituted a unified approach. In fact, a number of rather different approaches to using tasks in language pedagogy can be identified. We will now briefly consider these.

Perhaps one the earliest proposals for task-based teaching is that associated with *humanistic language teaching*. Humanistic principles of education emphasize the achievement of students' full potential for growth by acknowledging the importance of the affective dimension in learning as well as the cognitive. Humanistic approaches encourage learners to recognize their feelings and put them to use by caring for and sharing with others, thereby increasing their own self-esteem and their motivation to learn. Moskowitz (1977) gives examples of what she calls 'humanistic exercises' for language learning,[10] which, in fact, have all the characteristics of tasks as we have defined them here. For example, 'Identity Cards' asks students to pin on cards that give some personal information about themselves, for example, 'three adjectives that describe you'. The students circulate while the teacher plays some music. When the music stops they choose a partner and talk about the information written on their cards. Moskowitz discusses the 'affective' and 'linguistic' purposes of such tasks. One of the affective purposes of 'Identity Cards' is 'to warm up a new group of students' while the linguistic purpose is 'to practise asking and answering questions'. There is no attempt to focus students' attention on the linguistic purpose, however. Moskowitz envisages these humanistic tasks as supplementing and reinforcing traditional materials, i.e. as contributing to task-supported language teaching. However, a more radical idea might be to structure an entire course around such tasks. Curran's (1972) 'counseling language learning' can be seen as an attempt to construct a task-based method that incorporates humanistic principles.

A very different approach to task-based teaching is that embodied in the 'procedural syllabus' proposed by Prabhu (1987). Prabhu instituted an innovative curriculum project in secondary schools in southern India whereby the structural-oral-situation method, which was the predominant method at that time, was replaced by a task-based method. He devised a series of meaning-focused activities consisting of pre-tasks, which the teacher completed with the whole class, followed by tasks where the students worked on similar activities on their own. These tasks provided a basis for what Prabhu calls 'meaning-focused activity' that required students to understand, convey, or extend meaning, and where attention to language forms is only incidental. Thus, whereas Moskowitz's tasks are affective in orientation, Prabhu's tasks are primarily cognitive. For example, in one task the students were asked to find, name, and describe specific locations on a map. In his book, *Second Language Pedagogy*, Prabhu discusses the different kinds of tasks he used in the project, the syllabus, and the methodological procedures the teachers followed.

A third approach to task-based teaching is the 'process syllabus' advocated by Breen and Candlin. Whereas the procedural syllabus provides a specification of the tasks to be used in the classroom, the process syllabus is constructed through negotiation between the teacher and the students. Breen (1987), for example, envisages a curriculum where learners carry out their own needs analysis, find and choose content appropriate to their needs and interests, plan procedures for working in the classroom, and reflect on and evaluate every aspect of the teaching-learning process. In this approach to teaching, then, there is no a priori syllabus. Rather the syllabus is constructed as the course is taught. The teacher, however, can call on a set of 'curriculum guidelines' (Candlin 1987), which specify the range of options available to the participants. Task is the chosen unit for constructing the process syllabus because it constitutes a concept that both teachers and students can easily understand. However, as we have already seen, Breen's (1989) definition of task (see Figure 1.1) is broader than the one that informs this book as it incorporates both form-focused and meaning-focused activities. Breen disputes the value of this distinction at the level of task-as-workplan, arguing that what really counts is the task-as-process, i.e. the actual processes that result from the performance of a task.

Finally, tasks can be designed with a metacognitive focus for learner-training purposes. This can be achieved by constructing tasks that help learners to become aware of, reflect on, and evaluate their own learning styles and the strategies they use to learn. For example, Ellis and Sinclair (1989) offer a number of tasks aimed at making learners more effective and self-directed in their approach to learning an L2. For example, in one task learners fill in a questionnaire designed to help them understand what kind of language learner they are. In such tasks, language learning becomes the content that is talked about, an idea also proposed by Breen (1985). An alternative way of introducing a metacognitive dimension to tasks is to have learners appraise the tasks they are asked to perform by consciously asking such questions as 'Why should I do the task?', 'What kind of task is this?', and 'How should I do the task?' (Wenden 1995). Here there are no learning-training tasks per se but rather learning training is integrated into content tasks.

A key pedagogical issue is how a task can be fitted into a cycle of teaching. Various proposals have been advanced (for example, Estaire and Zanon 1994; Willis 1996). Willis, for example, envisages a 'task cycle' consisting of three broad phases: (1) pre-task, (2) task, and (3) language focus. There are opportunities for attention to form in all three phases. In the pre-task phase one option is for the teacher to highlight useful words and phrases. The task phase ends with a 'report' where the learners comment on their performance of the task. In the final phase, learners perform consciousness-raising and practice activities directed at specific linguistic features that occurred in the input of the task and/or in transcripts of fluent speakers doing the task. SLA researchers have begun to investigate the possibility of learners attending to form *during* the actual performance of the task (see p. 26).

These various approaches to task-based teaching reflect the issues that figure prominently in current discussions of language pedagogy—the role of meaning-based activity, the need for more learner-centred curricula, the importance of affective factors, the contribution of learner-training, and the need for some focus-on-form. Task-based pedagogy provides a way of addressing these various concerns and for this reason alone is attracting increasing attention.

Tasks have also been used in communicative language testing (Morrow 1979). For example, the Royal Society of Arts' examination in the 'Communicative use of English as a Foreign Language' (see Davies *et al.* 1999 for a brief description) required candidates to undertake a number of oral tasks in pairs and then evaluated their performances in terms of a set of criteria described at three levels of proficiency. More recently, the use of tasks in performance-testing has been advocated (McNamara 1996). Proposals for the development of task-based tests for assessing specific purpose language ability have been advanced (see, for example, Bachman and Palmer 1996 and Douglas 2000). Skehan (1998a, 2001) has also discussed how tasks might be used in tests of general language proficiency.

Chapters 7 to 9 consider task-based pedagogy and assessment, drawing on the contents of the preceding chapters that investigated tasks in SLA research. Chapter 7 looks at different ways in which tasks have been classified and discusses their use in course design, including ways in which a focus-on-form can be incorporated into the design of a task-based course. Chapter 8 considers the methodology of using tasks, describing the pre-task, during-task, and post-task options available to teachers. Chapter 9 considers the use of tasks for assessing L2 ability and development.

Conclusion: on the relationship between researching and teaching tasks

The relationship between an area of research such as SLA and language pedagogy is a complex one (see Ellis 1997a). Certainly, a positivist view of the relationship, where researchers demonstrate the most effective means for achieving pre-determined aims, is neither desirable nor tenable (Carr and Kemmis 1986). However, research does have the capacity to inform language pedagogy in a variety of ways, for example by subjecting existing pedagogical practices to critical scrutiny and sometimes by suggesting new ideas which teachers can experiment with in their own classroom, i.e. by providing what Stenhouse (1975) has called 'provisional specifications'.

The relationship between research and pedagogy is strengthened when practitioners of both work with shared constructs. Arguably, such is the case where tasks are concerned. Pica (1997) identifies a number of different kinds of relationship between research and pedagogy, suggesting that one of the strongest is that of 'compatibility', i.e. a sharing of mutual interests.[11] She suggests that tasks constitute one of the best examples of this relationship. Both teachers and researchers are concerned to find those tasks that work best for learning. In particular, they both grapple with the need to design tasks that draw learners' attention to L2 forms and structures as well tasks that promote fluency. Here then is an area where 'SLA and pedagogy are interdependent pursuits' (van Lier 1994: 341). One of the purposes of this book is to demonstrate the nature of the interdependence.

Notes

1 Of course, teachers sometimes improvise tasks 'on the hoof'. However, the distinction between 'task-as-workplan' and 'task-as-process' still applies in such cases. The 'task' that the teacher invents is the workplan—in this case the plan is in the mind of the teacher; the 'task' that the students perform may or may not match the teacher's workplan.
2 In fact, Long makes a careful distinction between what he calls 'target-tasks', which are real-world of the kind referred to in his definition in Figure 1.1, and 'pedagogic tasks', which he suggests can be derived from target tasks. This distinction is considered further when Long's proposals for designing a task-based syllabus are examined in Chapter 7.

3 Discussions of tasks in content teaching have given attention to cognitive processes. Doyle (1983), for example, draws on work in psychology to analyse the cognitive operations involved in different academic tasks, distinguishing memory tasks, procedural or routine tasks, comprehension or understanding tasks, and opinion tasks. Similarly, Mohan's (1986) analysis of tasks in content-based language teaching employs a cognitive framework.

4 Nunan (1989: 11) also recognizes that it is not always easy to distinguish a task from an exercise and argues that 'making decisions will always be partly intuitive and judgemental'. However, the use of a set of criterial features such as those proposed in this chapter provides a way of assessing with some rigour to what extent an activity is a task.

5 The extent to which the BSM elicits communicative language use is a matter of controversy. Certainly, Larsen-Freeman (1976) found that the results obtained from its use did not entirely match those obtained from other more obviously communicative activities.

6 Brumfit and Johnson (1979) published a collection of papers entitled 'The Communicative Approach to Language Teaching' that began with extracts from seminal papers by Halliday and Hymes.

7 The strong view of CLT finds a direct correlate in discourse theories of L2 acquisition. Hatch (1978b) for example claimed that linguistic competence develops as a product of learners learning how to participate in conversations in the L2.

8 Winn-Bell Olsen (1977), for example, suggests that her 'communication starters' can be used 'to provide an occasional change of pace' (p. xii).

9 Of course, it may be possible to implement a notional/functional syllabus by means of a communicative methodology by constructing tasks that focus on specific language uses. The extent to which it is possible to adopt a communicative methodology in the realization of an itemized syllabus (structural or notional) is a matter of argument. Widdowson (1990) argues that it is perfectly feasible. I would suggest that it is very difficult given the problems of designing effective focused tasks.

10 Subsequently, Moskowitz referred to humanistic tasks as 'humanistic communication activities' (Moskowitz 1982).

11 The other relationships between researchers and teachers that Pica (1997) discusses are 'coexistence', as evident in SLA research based on Universal Grammar and work in pedagogical grammar, 'collaboration', as in action research studies, and 'complementarity', as in research directed at improving immersion education in Canada.

2 Tasks, listening comprehension, and SLA

Introduction

In Chapter 1 we noted that task-based research has been primarily concerned with production tasks, especially speaking tasks. However, the definition of tasks on p. 16 acknowledged that tasks can involve any of the four language skills. In this chapter, we will focus on listening tasks. Such tasks are of special interest to both researchers and teachers. For researchers they provide a means of investigating learners' ability to process specific linguistic features. Focused tasks can be devised by 'seeding' the input with the targeted feature and designing the task in such a way that the product outcome can only be achieved if the learners are successful in processing the targeted feature. Thus, listening tasks provide an excellent means for measuring whether learners have acquired the feature in question. Further, listening tasks can be devised to facilitate the acquisition of the targeted feature. For example, the input can be 'modified' to enable learners to process the feature and thereby create the conditions for acquisition. Listening tasks, then, provide a means of investigating the effect of different kinds of input modification. For teachers, listening tasks provide the obvious starting point for a task-based course designed for low-proficiency learners. Simple listening tasks can be devised that can be performed with zero competence in the L2 (see, for example, the beginner tasks described in Prabhu 1987) and that thus cater to the 'silent period', which characterizes the early stages of acquisition for some learners (Krashen 1981). They provide a non-threatening way of engaging beginner learners in meaning-centred activity and, thereby, of developing the proficiency that, later on, can be used in production tasks. Also, of course, like researchers, teachers can use listening tasks to present the students with input enriched with specific features they wish to target.

Researchers have been interested in two main questions: (1) 'What effect do the properties of the task have on learners' comprehension?', and (2) 'What effect do the properties of the task have on L2 acquisition?'. Underlying these two questions are the two different functions of listening—listening-to-comprehend and listening-to-learn. An important issue, then, is to what extent the kinds of processes involved in comprehending and learning from input are the same or different. We will begin, therefore, with an illustration of tasks directed at these two types of listening and then move on to consider each type in depth.

Two types of listening: an example

Figure 2.1 illustrates the two types of listening. In Task 1 learners are given the names of three well-known singers and asked to state the kind of music they are famous for. To do this they will need to draw on their encyclopaedic knowledge. The listening task requires them to listen to short biographies of the three singers to check whether they are correct. In this task, then, learners are required to listen-to-comprehend by making use of their schematic knowledge. Task 2 makes use of the same listening texts but is designed to focus learners' attention on a specific grammatical feature—the simple past tense. Here the learners are required to listen carefully to distinguish between the past and present forms of verbs. The purpose is to help them 'notice' the past tense morphological markers of regular and irregular verbs. These forms are unstressed and in the stream of speech lack saliency and so are often not attended to. In these materials, listening-to-comprehend and listening-to-notice are tackled separately. Many listening

---

Task 1
Listening-to-comprehend

1   Do you know these musicians? Say what kind of music each one is famous for.

Johnny Cash   _____
Frédéric Chopin   _____
Ella Fitzgerald   _____

2   Now listen carefully and check if you were right.

Task 2
Listening-to-notice

Listen again. Fill in the missing words.

a   Johnny Cash _____ his first song when he was 12. In his twenties he _____ a number of country and western albums for Sun Records. Later he _____ with Bob Dylan for Columbia Records. Now, he _____ in the United States with his second wife.

b   Frédéric Chopin _____ one of the most famous classical composers of the early 19th century. He _____ piano concerts all over Europe. Unfortunately, he _____ while still young. His *Nocturnes* _____ to be very popular.

c   Ella Fitzgerald _____ her career in a singing context in Harlem. She _____ Chick Webb's band and _____ several hits. Later her *Songbird* albums _____ her one of the most famous jazz singers of the 20th century. Ella was also very kind and religious. People _____ Ella as a person as well as a singer.

Figure 2.1: Great musicians (Ellis and Gaies 1999)

tasks, of course, require learners to engage in both types of listening at the same time.

Listening-to-comprehend

There is now a broad consensus among applied linguists that listening is an active rather than a passive skill. Andersen and Lynch (1988), for example, view listeners as 'active model builders' rather than 'tape recorders'. Rost (1990) suggests that listening involves 'interpretation' rather than 'comprehension' because listeners are involved in hypothesis-testing and inferencing, not just decoding what is said. Similarly, Brown (1995) argues that listening is a process by which listeners construct 'shared mutual beliefs' rather than 'shared mutual knowledge'. How then do listeners engage actively in the process of constructing shared beliefs? To answer this question we will examine a number of key aspects of listening.

The listener's role

Goffman (1981) distinguishes three different listener roles. There are listeners whose participation is not ratified and who therefore function as 'overhearers'. In contrast, there are listeners whose participation is ratified, who function either as 'addressees', i.e. they are being directly addressed by the speaker, or as 'hearers', i.e. they are not being directly addressed. Imagine a live television programme where members of the audience are invited to put questions to a panel of experts. The person who asks the question becomes the 'addressee' while the other members of the audience are the 'overhearers', because the answer to the question has not been designed for them and they are not ratified as listeners. The real 'hearers' are the viewers in front of the television sets. How they all behave as listeners in these different roles will differ considerably.

   In task-based teaching the participants are all ratified as listeners and thus there is little opportunity for learners to function as overhearers.[1] However, tasks can be distinguished according to whether the role they require students to perform is that of addressee or hearer. For example, a note-making lecture task where there is no opportunity for students to interact positions them as hearers. Here the lecturer addresses the class in general, i.e. there is no specific addressee.[2] In contrast, an interactive lecture task treats some students as addressees, i.e. the ones that ask questions, and others as hearers, i.e. the ones who do not take up the opportunity to interact. Tasks performed in pairs inevitably position the participants as addressees. However, tasks performed in groups are more complex, as students can variably take on the roles of addressee and hearer.

A participant's role as listener influences comprehension. Schober and Clark (1989) in a study of native-speaker listeners found that addressees were much more efficient at performing an object identification task than hearers. To a large extent, this was because the addressees were able to interact with the speakers and, thereby, to construct a common perspective and control the pacing of new information. In contrast, the hearers were entirely dependent on the speakers' ability to predict what, how and when information should be supplied.

Listening purpose

In some cases, the purpose for listening is determined by the text itself. For example, we will probably listen carefully to a set of directions to try to understand them fully. However, in other contexts, the purpose for listening to a text is more indeterminate. For example, we could have very different purposes for listening to a radio broadcast of a political speech— to evaluate to what extent the views expressed correspond to our own, to obtain information for an essay we have to write, or simply to find out when it ends because we are interested in the programme that follows. In fact, even if the text constrains the purpose for listening quite narrowly, it is usually possible for us to establish our own different purpose. Clearly, the purpose we establish for listening to a text will influence both what we listen for and how we actually listen.

In Chapter 1 we saw that tasks are workplans that seek to specify how learners will respond. In other words, a workplan for a listening task must explicitly or implicitly provide learners with a purpose for listening. A lecture task, for example, might require that students listen in order to take detailed notes (for example, Dunkel 1988). However, as we also saw in Chapter 1, the task-as-workplan may or may not correspond to the task-as-process. One reason why this is the case should now be clear. Even though the task specifies the purpose for listening, individual listeners may choose to establish their own purpose. Thus, a student might respond to the lecture task by only writing down new information.

The ability of learners to set their own 'tasks' in this way suggests that researchers need to investigate how individual students react to the tasks they have been asked to perform. Kumaravadivelu (1991) undertook such an investigation, examining the transcripts of two pairs of students performing a task and subsequently interviewing the participants. He uncovered ten sources of mismatch between the teacher's intention and the learners' interpretation of task. These included 'pedagogic', i.e. the participants' perceptions of the goals of the task, 'strategic', i.e. the strategies the participants use to reach an outcome, and 'attitudinal', i.e. the participants' attitudes towards the nature of L2 learning and teaching. However, this kind of study is rare. To date, researchers have typically evaluated learners' performance on a task solely in terms of the outcome specified by the task.

The utilization of schematic knowledge

Language users make use of their knowledge of the world to help them comprehend texts.[3] Research in cognitive psychology has shown that learners possess schemata, i.e. mental structures that organize their knowledge of the world which they draw on in interpreting texts. For example, Andersen, Reynolds, Schallert, and Goetz (1977) showed that when readers are given different titles, 'A Prisoner Plans his Escape' vs. 'A Wrestler in a Tight Corner', they interpret an identical text quite differently, in accordance with their particular title.

There is a general distinction between content and formal schemata. The former are structures that organize our knowledge of the world. The latter are structures that represent our knowledge of the different ways in which textual information can be organized. Andersen and Lynch (1988) distinguish three types of content schemata: (1) general factual knowledge, (2) local factual knowledge, and (3) socio-cultural knowledge. For example, understanding a newspaper headline like 'Saddam Slams Door on Hopes for Peace' involves knowing who Saddam is (general knowledge); knowing that Saddam expelled American members of a United Nations inspection team from Iraq (local factual knowledge); and knowing that slamming doors is generally perceived negatively in English-speaking cultures (socio-cultural knowledge). Formal schemata include mental representations of (1) micro-rhetorical structures such as adjacency pairings, for example, knowing that an invitation is likely to be followed by either a refusal or an acceptance, and (2) macro-rhetorical structures, for example, the problem–solution pattern described by Hoey (1983).

Listeners, like readers, use these schemata to comprehend a text in three major ways: (1) interpretation, (2) prediction, and (3) hypothesis testing. Interpretation involves recognizing key lexical items that activate an appropriate schema. Prediction occurs on the basis of the initial interpretation. For example, listeners who activate a content schema for weather forecasting will be able to predict that there will be information relating to both the kind of weather (whether there will be sun, rain, or snow) and the temperature (both minimum and maximum). They will also be able to predict how the information in the forecast will be structured, for example, information about the current state of the weather will precede information about future weather. Hypothesis testing involves further processing of the language of the text in order to confirm/disconfirm predictions. In cases where they are disconfirmed, new schemata are invoked and the process of prediction and hypothesis testing continues. The processes of interpretation, predicting, and hypothesis testing do not necessarily occur sequentially. They are dynamic and can be carried out in parallel.

This account of listening constitutes a 'top-down' model. That is, comprehension is seen as primarily the result of the schemata the listener brings to a text. It contrasts with a 'bottom-up' model of listening, which emphasizes listeners' ability to identify linguistic constituents (sounds, lexical items, and sentence structures) in a text and use these to derive ideational and interpersonal meanings. However, as Richards (1990) has argued, listening involves processing at a variety of levels, including both the activation of schemata and constituent identification. Indeed, top-down processing can only be carried out effectively if language users are able to recognize linguistic constituents automatically, thus making time available for higher order processing involving schemata. McLaughlin and Heredia (1996) point out:

> Some tasks require more attention; others that have been well-practised require less. The development of any complex cognitive skill involves building up a set of well-learned, efficient procedures so that more attention demanding processes are freed up for new tasks.

Thus, language users who have difficulty in processing a text linguistically may not be able to engage effectively in top-down processing. This of course is the position that many L2 learners find themselves in, as illustrated in the following comment by a Chinese learner of English:

> Sometimes when I come across a word which I remembered I had learned recently but I just forgot its meaning, I would think of it hard and this affected my listening to the following sentences.
> (Goh 2000: 63)

Goh found that this problem was especially acute with low-ability learners. It derives from the fact that learners have a limited capacity to process language and thus experience difficulty in attending to form and meaning at the same time (see Chapter 5 for a fuller discussion of this point).

Several studies point to the need for bottom-up processing. Buck (1991) has shown that if learners fail to adjust the interpretation they derive from a top-down approach by monitoring incoming information they experience serious communication problems. Tsui and Fullilove (1998) found that in a listening examination in Hong Kong, those learners with higher scores were better than learners with lower scores at comprehending texts where the schema initially activated by the text was not congruent with the rest of the text. In other words, the learners with higher scores were better at adjusting their initial interpretation of such texts. These studies provide evidence for an interactive model of listening (see below).

It should be noted, however, that the terms 'top-down' and 'bottom-up' are somewhat vague as it is neither clear exactly what is meant by 'higher' and 'lower' levels of processing nor is it possible to say in what ways these processes interact (Flowerdew 1994b). Also, the above account of listening explains listening-to-comprehend but it does not follow that the same processes are involved in listening-to-learn, where top–down processing may contribute little. This is a point we will examine later in this chapter.

The utilization of contextual knowledge

Listeners also make use of contextual information, i.e. information that is available to them in the situation in which they are functioning as listeners. Listeners with limited language proficiency, in particular, are likely to rely on contextual clues. L2 learners have been found to benefit from comprehension-based teaching methods, i.e. methods that do not require them to speak or write the L2, at least in the initial stages of the course, and that enable them to relate what they hear to the here-and-now (Potovosky 1974; Asher 1977).

Clearly, listeners make use of contextual clues in conjunction with their schematic knowledge. That is, they use the information available from the situational context to help them activate a relevant schema. For example, children develop schemata as a result of the routine nature of the events that comprise their lives, for example, the events associated with feeding, bathing, and dressing. They use the clues available to them in a particular situation to activate a schema. These clues in conjunction with the schema help them to interpret utterances addressed to them and to map words onto referents, as illustrated by Ferrier (1978). Thus, the use of contextual information to comprehend a message testifies further to the top-down nature of listening. When listeners are able to infer what is meant by attending to context and can activate a relevant schema there is little need for them to attend closely to what is actually said. Again, though, this accounts for listening-to-comprehend, not listening-to-acquire.

Many standard tasks incorporate contextual clues. For example, Brown's (1995) map task required speakers to describe a route that was marked on their maps but not on the listeners' maps. The task was complicated by the fact that the interlocutors' maps differed in a number of key features. Brown documents how the language users in this study used the contextual information to establish a 'search field' to relate what they heard to places and objects shown on the map. Brown notes that they were usually successful even though the information available to them was strikingly underspecified.

The collaborative construction of a mental model

In the case of interactive listening tasks, listeners have the opportunity to provide feedback to speakers on whether they have understood. According to Brown (1995), listeners are successful in comprehending what speakers are saying when they are able to construct a shared 'mental model' of what is being talked about. Such a model is best achieved collaboratively. Brown (1995: 218) describes how,

> ... participants in a conversation in which information is being exchanged do not simply swop utterance tokens that contain information. They spend a good deal of time ensuring that the other speaker is made aware of their own relevant information state, in trying to ensure that the other speaker adopts the same perspective on information and in attempting to relate the new information which they have just been made aware of to existing information.

Brown sees listening as an interactive process, with the listener contributing as much as the speaker to the achievement of understanding.

Conversational participants vary enormously in their ability to engage in this interactive process. Children below the age of seven, for example, generally fail to signal when they have not understood a message (Patterson and Kister 1981). Furthermore, as Brown's (1995) research shows, even older learners are not always skilled at assessing message quality and identifying what information they need to overcome problems. Indeed, it may not always be socially or culturally appropriate for listeners to display their non-understanding. Aston (1986) points out that what he calls 'trouble-shooting procedures' may sometimes jeopardize an interaction from a social point of view. There are limits on the extent to which listeners can risk the goodwill of their interlocutors by insisting that their comprehension problems are resolved! These limits may be extreme in some cultures. For example, in formal situations Japanese listeners may not feel able to show their lack of comprehension, let alone seek clarification. For such learners, the kinds of referential communication tasks used by researchers and teachers (Yule 1996) may require listener behaviour that is not acceptable in many real-life situations.

Whereas collaboration is self-evidently a feature of interactive listening tasks, it is less clear that it plays a role in non-interactive listening tasks, where by definition there is no opportunity for listeners to intervene verbally. This may be one reason why non-native speakers often report difficulty in understanding lectures (Flowerdew and Miller 1996). However, even non-interactive lecturers need to be responsive to non-verbal signals provided by listeners, for example, obvious signs of inattention. The shift from highly formal lectures read from a prepared text to more informal lectures employing a conversational style (Flowerdew 1994) may have been motivated by the need to involve listeners more fully in the process of information exchange.

An interactive model of listening comprehension

To conclude this section we will briefly outline the kind of interactive model of listening that informs current research. The term 'interactive' is here used with two meanings. First, it refers to the interaction of bottom-up processing, where the listener attends to acoustic-phonological information by decoding words and other constituent structures in the stream of speech, and top-down processing, where the listener processes language in meaningful chunks by utilizing schemata and contextual information. For example, in Task 1 in Figure 2.1 learners need to identify and decode the key words in the texts that tell them what kind of music each musician is famous for and use this to test predictions based on their schematic knowledge. Interaction in this sense views listening as a complex set of mental actions performed simultaneously and cyclically. It also assumes that listeners need access to both automatic decoding skills and higher-order strategies for processing input.

'Interactive' also refers to the social processes of collaboration that listeners enter into to ensure a degree of convergence between their schematic world and that of the speaker. These processes are evident in all communication but become highly visible when listeners need to signal a lack of understanding and where their comprehension problems lie. We have noted that these collaborative processes are most evident in interactive listening tasks but that they also arise in non-interactive tasks. Communication can only take place when there is interactive engagement of one kind or another. In interactive tasks it is overt while in non-interactive tasks it is largely covert. It is by means of these collaborative processes that listeners control the pace at which they receive information and thus cope with the need to process information 'online' as it is heard.

Listening-to-learn

We have hinted that the processes involved in listening-to-comprehend and listening-to-learn are different. In fact, such a claim is controversial. Krashen (1985; 1994) has argued that the 'fundamental principle' of L2 acquisition is that 'acquisition', i.e. the subconscious process of internalizing new linguistic forms and their meanings, will occur automatically if learners receive comprehensible input. According to Krashen's Input Hypothesis, learners need (1) access to comprehensible input and (2) a low affective filter that makes them open to the input in order to acquire. Krashen identifies two primary ways in which input is made comprehensible. Speakers employ 'simplified registers' when speaking to learners. These registers ensure that the input is 'roughly tuned', i.e. pitched at a level that enables the learner to understand but also containing some linguistic forms that the learner has not yet acquired. Secondly, listeners can use contextual information to help them decode input containing unknown linguistic forms and thereby comprehend and acquire them.

The idea that comprehension is crucial for acquisition also underlies Long's Interaction Hypothesis (Long 1983a; 1996), which we will consider in greater detail in Chapter 3. Here it will suffice to simply state two of claims of the early version of this hypothesis: (1) comprehensible input is necessary for acquisition, and (2) modifications to the interactional structure of conversations which take place in the process of negotiating solutions to communication problems help to make input comprehensible to the learner. This hypothesis has informed a number of studies involving tasks.

There are a number of objections to the central claim advanced by Krashen and Long, namely that acquisition will occur naturally if learners understand what is said to them. One obvious objection is that neither Krashen nor Long specify what they mean by 'comprehension'. As Andersen and Lynch (1988) point out, comprehension involves degrees of understanding. At one end of the continuum is total non-comprehension, i.e. the listener is unable to segment the continuous stream of speech, while at the other is successful comprehension, i.e. the listener has attended to the message fully and is able to construct a coherent interpretation. Intermediate levels of comprehension arise when the listener can hear words but cannot fully understand them and when the listener is able to hear and understand but has 'switched off'. A key question, not addressed by either Krashen or Long, is what degree of comprehension is necessary for acquisition to take place.

Other applied linguists have pointed out that there is a theoretical need to distinguish input that functions as intake for comprehension and input that functions as intake for learning. White (1987), for example, argues that the kind of simplified input that works well for comprehension may be of little value for acquisition because it deprives learners of essential information about the target language. This is not a strong argument, however, because it views simplified registers as static. In fact, research has shown that such registers become progressively more complex in accordance with the language proficiency of the learners (see, for example, Henzl 1979). It would seem likely, then, that simplified input does not totally deprive learners of the input that is crucial to acquisition but rather gradually and systematically supplies them with input that is more and more linguistically complex. If one assumes that this input is one step ahead of learner, then, it may serve as the ideal source of input that Krashen claims it to be.

A stronger criticism of the Input Hypothesis can be found in Sharwood Smith's (1986) argument that there are two ways of processing input, one involving comprehension and the other acquisition. He argues that acquisition only occurs when learners discover that their original surface structure representation of the input does not match the semantic representation required by the situation. It will not occur if learners rely purely on top-down processing by utilizing non-linguistic input, as extensive bottom-up processing is also needed. In other words, comprehension is necessary but not sufficient for acquisition to take place. Færch and Kasper (1986) offer a similar view, arguing that interactional input modifications will only lead to acquisition if learners recognize that a 'gap' in understanding is the result not of the interlocutor's failure to make herself understood but of the learner's own lack of linguistic knowledge. They also point out that not all communication problems, even when fully negotiated, will contribute to acquisition.

A further challenge to the position adopted by Krashen comes from work on the role of consciousness and attention in language acquisition. Krashen has consistently argued that acquisition is a subconscious process, i.e. learners are not aware of what they attend to in the input and are not aware of what they acquire. Schmidt (1990, 1994, 2001), however, has argued persuasively that attention to input is a conscious process. Furthermore, he claims that attention and its subjective correlates *noticing*, i.e. registering formal features in the input, and *noticing-the-gap*, i.e. identifying how the input to which the learner is exposed differs from the output the learner is able to generate, are essential processes in L2 acquisition:

> The allocation of attention is the pivotal point at which learner-internal factors (including aptitude, motivation, current L2 knowledge, and processing ability) and learner-external factors (including the complexity and the distributional characteristics of input, discoursal, and interactional context, instructional treatment, and task characteristics) come together. What then happens within attentional space largely determines the course of language development, including the growth of knowledge (the establishment of new representations), fluency (access to that knowledge), and variation.
> (Schmidt 2001)

Schmidt refers to his own experience as a learner of Portuguese in Brazil to demonstrate the importance of attention, showing that in nearly every case new forms that appeared in his spontaneous speech were consciously attended to previously in the input (Schmidt and Frota 1986). He also draws on a wide body of research in SLA and cognitive psychology to support his central contention that little (possibly no) learning of new linguistic material from input is possible without attended processing.

There are, of course, the important questions concerning what 'attended processing' actually consists of and whether any learning is possible without it. Schmidt (2001) draws on the work of Posner (1994) and Tomlin and Villa (1994) in distinguishing three sub-systems of attention. Attention as 'alertness' refers to motivation and readiness to learn. Here he makes the point that noticing and acquisition are not dependent on learner intention, i.e. involuntary noticing can occur. This is an important point where tasks are concerned because it allows for learners' attention to be influenced through the design of the task. 'Orientation' concerns the general focus of attention, for example, whether on meaning or on form, which can also be influenced by the design of the task (see Chapter 5). Schmidt suggests that orientation plays a role in both facilitating and inhibiting processing. In the case of the former it causes certain stimuli to be attended to at the expense of others. In the case of the latter, it helps learners to avoid interference by attention-capturing information that is not relevant to their orientation. 'Detection' refers to the cognitive registration of stimuli that allows for the further processing of information. It is here that controversy exists both regarding whether detection involves awareness and whether it requires only global attention, for example, general attention to form, or more specific attention, for example, attention to a specific aspect of language. With regard to the first of these controversies, Schmidt (2001) distinguishes a strong and weak form of the noticing hypothesis. The strong form, which reflects his earlier position, states that 'there is no learning whatsoever from input that is not noticed', while the weak form, indicative of his current position, allows for representation and storage of unattended stimuli in memory but claims that 'people learn about the things they attend to and do not learn much about the things they do not attend to'. On the second issue, Schmidt argues that attention needs to be specifically directed. As he puts it, 'nothing is free'.

Schmidt's position is clearly incompatible with that of Krashen. However, as Schmidt (2001) points out, a role for consciousness can fairly easily be incorporated into the Interaction Hypothesis if it is assumed that one of the principal functions of interactional modifications is to draw the learners' conscious attention to the linguistic properties of the input and how these differ from the properties of the learners' output. In fact, the later version of the Interaction Hypothesis, to be discussed in Chapter 3, makes just this claim.[4]

Information-processing models of L2 acquisition also distinguish the processes responsible for comprehension and acquisition. Robinson (1995), in a review of these models, identifies two general types. He characterizes filter models as viewing information being processed serially and attention as selective. In contrast, he sees capacity models as allowing for the parallel processing of information with the possibility of allocating attention to two tasks simultaneously. It should be clear that the model of listening espoused in this chapter is of the capacity model type. According to this, the listener is credited with the capacity to attend simultaneously to both message and to code. Thus, this model allows for the dual processing needed for comprehension and acquisition. There are, however, constraints on individuals' ability to perform two tasks concurrently—in particular, the extent to which the task can draw on processes that have been automatized. Wickens and Carswell (1997) point to three possibilities of combining tasks: (1) the tasks will be performed as well in tandem as singly; (2) the level of performance of one task will decline when it is performed together with another task; and (3) the tasks will require serial processing, requiring attention to be shifted from task to task rather than performing them at the same time. The important question, then, is 'What happens when learners are asked to attend to meaning and form?'

An important study by VanPatten (1990) has addressed this question. This study asked learners to listen to a text in Spanish under four conditions. In one task, the learners were instructed to listen for content only. In a second task they listened for content and the word *inflación*, making a check mark each time it occurred. In the third task they listened for content and checked each time they heard the definite article *la*. In the fourth task they listened for content and checked each time they heard the verb morpheme *-n*. VanPatten reports a significant difference on the comprehension scores (derived from asking students to recall the text) for tasks one and two on the one hand and tasks three and four on the other. There was no difference between the scores for tasks one and two or for tasks three and four. In other words, when the learners attended to form, their comprehension suffered. VanPatten concludes that meaning and form compete for learners' attention and that only when learners can understand input easily are they able to attend to meaning. VanPatten's results were replicated in a study based on a reading text by Wong (2001).

This discussion of the processes involved in listening-to-comprehend and listening-to-learn raises a key question for task-based researchers, 'Can learners successfully acquire the L2 as a result of carrying out listening comprehension tasks?'. It is to this question that we now turn.

Researching listening tasks

Tasks can be interactive or non-interactive. We will refer to these respectively as or *reciprocal* or *non-reciprocal* (Ellis 2001). Non-reciprocal tasks correspond to what is generally understood as listening tasks. That is, learners listen to a text without any opportunity to interact, for example, when learners listen to directions about what route to follow and mark in the route on the map. Reciprocal tasks are tasks that require a two-way flow of information between a speaker and a listener, for example, the production tasks in Figure 1.2.

However, the distinction between non-reciprocal and reciprocal tasks is best seen as continuous rather than dichotomous. That is, there can be degrees of opportunity for participants to interact in a task. At one end of the continuum are listening tasks that do not permit the learners any opportunity to interject whatsoever if they do not understand although, of course, they may still be able to signal their interactive engagement non-verbally. At the other end are speaking tasks that can only be successfully accomplished if the participants interact to ensure mutual understanding. In between are tasks that provide the learners with some negotiation rights but these are restricted, for example, an interactive lecture where students have the opportunity to interrupt the lecturer.

We will only consider research that has investigated tasks towards the non-reciprocal end of this continuum. Included in this category are tasks that allow some limited response from the listener. Two types of non-reciprocal tasks will be examined. *Listen-and-do tasks* require learners to listen to verbal input and show their understanding by performing actions. They figure in research that has investigated the effects of modifying input on comprehension and acquisition. They also figure extensively in the pedagogic literature on task-based teaching. *Academic listening tasks* require learners to listen to a lecture and show their understanding in some way, typically by taking notes. They are also of interest to both researchers and teachers. Again, researchers are interested in the relationship between the lecture input and learners' comprehension and acquisition, while teachers employ such tasks to develop learners' academic language proficiency. These task types will be described in more detail below.

Listen-and-do tasks

The listen-and-do tasks we will consider here result in a definite product. For example, Pica, Young, and Doughty (1987) used a task that required learners to listen to directions for choosing and placing objects on a small board illustrating an outdoor scene. In this case, the product was the board with the objects as they were positioned at the end of the task. Loschky (1994) used three listen-and-do tasks: (1) a 'still-life task' involving arrangements of pictures of everyday objects such as pens and rulers, (2) a 'map task' showing a bird's eye view of streets bordered by various locations such as parks and train stations, and (3) a 'shapes task' which presented diagrams of various geometrical shapes. In each case, the learners heard a description and had to find the object and number it on their picture sheets. Ellis, Tanaka, and Yamazaki's (1994) 'kitchen task' (see Figure 2.2) required learners to listen to directions about where to place various objects in a matrix picture of a kitchen. The objects were depicted in small numbered pictures. The product outcome of the task was the matrix picture of the kitchen with the numbers of the small pictures entered in different locations.

Listen-and-do tasks of the kind used in these studies can be described using the framework outlined in Chapter 1 (see Table 1.1 on p. 21):

1 Goal

Listen-and-do tasks promote listening for close understanding and they can also be used to teach new linguistic forms if these are embedded in the input.

2 Input

The task input consists of both verbal information in the form of directions or descriptions, and non-verbal information in the form of physical objects, pictures, maps, or diagrams. The verbal information can be simplified in various ways (see below). The speed of the oral directions can also be varied.

3 Conditions

The information is split, with one participant holding all the information to be communicated. The task, therefore, is one-way. However, the conditions can be varied according to whether the listeners are allowed to interact with the speaker or not.

4 Procedures

Listen-and-do tasks can be performed with the whole class where the teacher is the speaker and the learners are the listeners, as in Loschky (1994) and Ellis, Tanaka, and Yamazaki (1994). Alternatively, they can be performed in pairs or small groups, as in Pica, Young, and Doughty (1987). The directions/descriptions can be given just once or repeated.

5 Predicted outcomes

Listen-and-do tasks provide opportunities for the processes involved in both listening-to-comprehend and listening-to-learn. The non-linguistic product of a listen-and-do task is a physical action and/or a non-verbal device on which the learners have entered information.

Listen-and-do tasks are a particularly useful tool for SLA researchers for a number of reasons. First, the products of such tasks afford a record of how well individual learners have understood the input. Thus, the task provides a built-in measure of comprehension thus obviating the need to develop a separate measure.

Second, the directions/descriptions can be constructed to test particular hypotheses about how input, in its various forms, affects comprehension and acquisition. The tasks in the studies referred to above were designed to investigate the differential effect of 'baseline', 'premodified', and 'interactionally modified' input on task performance. Baseline input was derived by asking native speakers to perform the task with other native speakers. The data from these interactions was then used to construct descriptions which learners would listen to without the opportunity to interact. Premodified input was prepared by adapting the baseline input, based on the kinds of modifications native speakers make when communicating with

L2 learners. Interactionally modified input was produced when learners were allowed to request clarification of baseline input. Examples of the directions used in Ellis, Tanaka, and Yamazaki (1994) are shown in Figure 2.2. The directions differ in three major respects: (1) quantity, i.e. the number of words in each direction, (2) redundancy, i.e. the repetition of content words in each direction, and (3) complexity, i.e. the extent to which each direction contains subordinate constructions. For example, in Pica, Young, and Doughty (1987), the interactionally modified directions were longer and more redundant than the baseline directions with the premodified directions intermediate. With regard to grammatical complexity, the interactionally modified and baseline directions were almost the same while the premodified directions were the simplest.

Third, the input can be designed so that it contains linguistic forms that the learners do not yet know, i.e. 'focused tasks' can be designed. For example, in Loschky (1994) learners were exposed to Japanese locative expressions and also to new vocabulary. Ellis, Tanaka, and Yamazaki (1994) pre-tested their learners in order to identify a number of lexical items that they did not yet know. These items were then incorporated into the directions used in the task (see the items in bold in Figure 2.2). In this way, it was possible to investigate what effect the different kinds of input had on the learners' acquisition of these items.

Research based on listen-and-do tasks has been directed at investigating the claims of the Input and Interaction Hypotheses; in particular how properties of modified input affect learner comprehension and acquisition. Rather than examine each of the studies separately, we will consider a number of general conclusions that can be drawn from them.

All the studies have found that interactionally modified input assists comprehension, as measured by learners' ability to do the tasks. Pica, Young, and Doughty (1987) found that interactionally modified input resulted in better comprehension than premodified input. Loschky (1994) also found that it led to better comprehension overall than premodified input. However, the interactionally modified input functioned more effectively than baseline input in only one of the three tasks he used. Ellis, Tanaka, and Yamazaki (1994) found that in their kitchen task the group receiving interactionally modified input comprehended the directions better than both the baseline and premodified groups. Interestingly, both Loschky, and Ellis, Tanaka, and Yamazaki failed to find consistent evidence that premodified input works better for comprehension than baseline input, a result that is rather counterintuitive.[5]

These studies all involved older learners, i.e. adolescents or adults. Ellis and Heimbach (1997) used a listen-and-do task with ten children aged five to six years old learning English as an L2 on an American military base in Japan. The task required the children to locate the picture card depicting a particular insect or a bird and place it in the correct position on a board. It

Baseline

Can you find the **scouring pad**? Take the scouring pad and put it on top of the counter by the sink—the right side of the sink.

Premodified

Can you find the **scouring pad**? A scouring pad—'scour' means to clean a dish. A scouring pad is a small thing you hold in your hand and you clean a dish with it. Take the scouring pad and put it on top of the counter by the sink—on the right side of the sink.

Interactionally modified

A   Can you find the **scouring pad**? Take the scouring pad and put it on top of the counter by the sink—the right side of the sink.

B   One more time.

A   OK. Can you find the scouring pad? Take the scouring pad and put it on top of the counter by the sink—the right side of the sink.

B   What is a scouring pad?

A   Scouring pad is uh … you hold it in your hand and you wash dishes with it. OK?

D   Once again.

A   Once again? Can you find the scouring pad? Take the scouring pad and put it on top of the counter by the sink—the right side of the sink.

C   One more time.

A   One more time. Can you find the scouring pad? Take the scouring pad and put it on top of the counter by the sink—the right side of the sink.

C   What is a scouring pad?

A   Scouring pad? Uh, small, and it's … you use it in the sink and you wash dishes with it. You hold it in your hand and you can wash dishes and it takes little bits of food off a dish, to scrub and wash a dish. You understand?

C   Where do I put it?

A   Ah, you put it on the counter, uh, on the right side of the sink, the right side of the sink.

D   What is a counter?

A   Counter, a counter is a flat place to work. You can cut vegetables on the counter, you can work on the counter. A place to work in the kitchen. The counter is very long.

D   One more time.

A   One more time. Can you find the scouring pad? Take the scouring pad and put it on top of the counter by the sink—the right side of the sink.

Figure 2.2: Examples of baseline, premodified, and interactionally modified directions (Ellis, Tanaka, and Yamazaki 1994)

was carried out first in pairs and then in groups, with the teacher giving the descriptions of the insects and birds in both cases. The children were allowed to negotiate as much as they wanted. Ellis and Heimbach found that with the pairs procedure only three of the ten children made any attempt to negotiate with the teacher. In the group procedure there was more interaction but four of the children still declined to say anything. Overall, the children's comprehension in the pair condition was only 28%. In the group condition it was much higher (68%). This study bears out the general finding that young children are reluctant to engage in meaning negotiation (see p. 44). However, it also suggests that this problem may be partly overcome if several children work together in a group. This study also confirms that when meaning negotiation does take place it facilitates comprehension.

On the face of it, then, these studies provide convincing evidence that learners comprehend better when they can interact with their interlocutors. There is, however, a problem. The time taken to complete a task in the interactive condition is much greater than the time taken in the baseline or premodified input conditions, for as Loschky (1994: 313) has pointed out, 'increased time is an inherent difference between negotiated and unnegotiated interaction'. This, in fact, proved to be the case in all the studies we have considered. For example, in Ellis, Tanaka, and Yamazaki's (1994) Saitama study, the task took 45 minutes in the interactive condition but only ten minutes in the premodified condition. We cannot be certain, then, what it is about interactionally modified input that helps comprehension. Does it work because it enables learners to sort out misunderstandings and construct a shared mental model of the task, as suggested by Brown (1995)? Or does it work simply because learners have more time to process input? Ellis and He (1999) set out to answer this question in a study similar to those reported above except, in this case, the amount of time allocated to the premodified and interactionally modified groups was the same. This was achieved by repeating the premodified directions so they took up the same length of time as that required in the interactionally modified condition. In this study there was no statistically significant difference in the comprehension scores of the two groups, suggesting that the crucial factor in the earlier studies may have been time rather than condition. The effectiveness of interactionally modified input may derive from the additional time that it gives learners to process modified input.

Another question of interest is whether interactionally modified input works best for those learners who are directly involved in meaning negotiation as 'addressees' or whether it works equally well for learners who act as 'hearers'. Pica (1992) reports a study that examined this question. The study had three groups: (1) negotiators, who had opportunities to actively negotiate, (2) observers, who observed the negotiators but did not themselves negotiate, and (3) listeners, who performed the task later, listening to the teacher read directions based on the interactionally modified input but with no opportunity to interact. The comprehension scores of the three groups were not significantly different. Ellis, Tanaka, and Yamazaki (1994) found no relationship between the number of times individual learners in the Tokyo study interacted with the teacher and their comprehension scores. Ellis and Heimbach (1997) also found no relationship between these two variables in the case of children interacting in a group with the teacher. These studies, then, suggest that L2 learners can benefit from inter-actionally modified input even if they themselves do not elicit it. That is, where comprehension is concerned it does not seem to matter whether the learners are 'addressees' or 'hearers'. However, as Pica (1992) suggests, this may depend on the listening ability of the learners. When she examined individual learners she concluded that whereas the opportunity to interact did not benefit those with a high level of comprehension ability it was helpful for those with lower levels.

Finally, we need to note that giving learners the opportunity to interact can sometimes lead to input that overloads them with the result that comprehension is impeded rather than facilitated. A number of studies (for example, Chaudron 1982; Ehrlich, Avery, and Yorio 1989) have shown that over-elaborated input can have a negative effect on comprehension. However, the results of the Saitama study did not bear this out. Ellis (1995) found that every direction in this study was comprehended better by the interactionally modified than by the premodified group. As we will now see, however, this was not the case where acquisition was concerned.

A number of the studies discussed above also considered the relationship between modified input and acquisition. This was possible because the input used in these studies had been designed to contain items that the learners had not yet acquired. These studies addressed two questions. The first concerned what kind of input—baseline, premodified, or interactionally modified—worked best for acquisition. The second asked what specific properties of modified input were important for acquisition.

With regard to the first question the results are somewhat mixed. Loschky (1994) found no effect for the type of input. That is, the baseline, premodified, and interactionally modified groups performed at the same level on a sentence verification test designed to measure the extent to which the learners had learned the target grammatical structure (Japanese locative particles) and on a vocabulary test designed to measure whether they were able to retain new words that had been included in the descriptions. Ellis and He (1999) also found that premodified and interactionally modified input worked equally effectively for vocabulary acquisition—there was no baseline group in this study. In contrast, Ellis, Tanaka, and Yamazaki (1994) found a very clear effect for type of input. Thus, in the Tokyo study, the interactionally modified group acquired more new words than the premodified group, which in turn acquired more than the baseline group.

This result was obtained in a post-test administered immediately after the treatment. In later post-tests, however, the advantage for the interactionally modified group over the premodified group disappeared. Ellis, Tanaka, and Yamazaki suggest that this may have been because the students in the premodified group made efforts to learn the new words after the first post-test. One of the differences between Loschky (1994) and Ellis and He (1999) on the one hand and Ellis, Tanaka, and Yamazaki (1994) on the other was that in the former studies the target words were presented initially to all the learners either in writing or orally, while in the latter study the learners were entirely dependent on the directions for any learning that took place. It is possible that a brief presentation of the target items followed by premodified input in a task format works as effectively as interactionally modified input for acquiring new words.

To address the second question, Ellis (1995) analysed the modified input used in the Saitama study with a view to determining what it was in the input that enabled the learners to learn some of the new words much more easily than others. In the case of premodified input, he found that two factors were significantly correlated with acquisition scores in the immediate post-test: (1) range, defined as the number of different directions that a target item appeared in, and (2) length of direction, i.e. the number of words in the direction that first introduced a target word. In other words, learners remembered best those words that occurred in many different directions and in longer directions. In the case of interactionally modified input, range also proved important. However, length of direction no longer had a positive effect. In fact, the analysis showed that learners were less likely to remember words when the negotiation led to very long definitions. For example, the target item 'stove' was defined very succinctly, i.e. 'A stove is a hot place for cooking', with a resulting level of acquisition of 83%. In contrast, 'scouring pad' was defined lengthily (see Figure 2.2) and was poorly acquired (25%). Thus, although this study did not find that over-elaborate input had a negative effect on comprehension, it did show that over-elaborate input was detrimental to vocabulary acquisition. Ellis was also able to show that although interactionally modified input led to higher levels of vocabulary acquisition than premodified input overall it was less efficient. That is, in terms of words acquired per minute of input (wpm), premodified input worked much better, for example, 0.25 wpm as opposed to 0.13 wpm in the immediate post-test. Finally, Ellis found that the number of negotiations that individual students took part in was not related to their vocabulary acquisition scores. There were learners who did not negotiate at all but who achieved relatively high levels of word acquisition. In this respect, then, the results for acquisition mirrored those for comprehension.

What was the relationship between comprehension and acquisition in these studies? We have seen earlier that there are theoretical grounds for believing that listening-to-comprehend and listening-to-learn involve different processes. To what extent do these studies support such a claim? Loschky's study found that interactionally modified input aided comprehension but not acquisition, suggesting that the two were not strongly related. In fact, the correlations between the different measures were very low and non-significant in this study. Loschky concludes that it is not possible to posit a linear relationship between comprehension and acquisition. This conclusion is in part borne out by Ellis (1995). He found only a weak correlation between comprehension and acquisition scores on the immediate post-test. However, he did find a much stronger and statistically significant correlation between the comprehension scores and scores on a picture-word matching task administered two and a half months later. This test made use of the same materials used in the experimental treatment. Clearly, the relationship between comprehension and acquisition is complex. Comprehending a message does not guarantee acquisition of new word meanings, as Krashen (1985) has recognized. Also, it would seem that it is not necessary to comprehend a complete message in order to acquire a new word embedded in it. The strength of the relationship may depend on how acquisition is measured; if the measure directly taps into the same context in which the items were initially experienced, the relationship may be stronger.

Finally, these studies show that individual learners vary in their ability to comprehend and acquire from modified input in listening tasks. We have already seen some evidence of this. Children and adults do not benefit equally from opportunities to negotiate meaning. Individual learners vary in their preparedness to negotiate. We can also expect variables such as language aptitude to impact on how learners perform. Nagata, Aline, and Ellis (1999) examined the relationship between measures of language aptitude on the one hand and measures of comprehension and vocabulary acquisition on the other. They gave the kitchen task to a group of Japanese college students in the premodified condition. They measured the students' language aptitude using various tests from the Modern Language Aptitude Battery (Carroll and Sapon 1959) and Pimsleur's Language Aptitude Battery (Pimsleur 1966). The results showed that differences in the learners' inductive ability to identify the functions of grammatical forms, their ability to memorize the meanings of words in an unknown language, and their ability to associate phonological and graphological forms were all significantly related to how well they understood the premodified directions. Interestingly, somewhat different aptitude factors seemed to be involved in the acquisition of new words. Ability to memorize word meanings in an unknown language and the ability to learn new phonetic sounds were the important factors where acquisition was concerned. This study only investigated premodified input. Further research is needed to investigate the aptitude factors related to learners' comprehension and acquisition in baseline and interactive conditions.

To sum up, listen-and-do tasks provide an excellent tool for investigating hypotheses drawn from SLA theory. This kind of task has been found to be effective in generating meaning negotiation in adolescent and adult learners but less effective with young children. When the tasks do provide an opportunity for meaning negotiation, comprehension is enhanced, although this may simply be because of the additional processing time such tasks afford the learner. Also, it may not be necessary for learners to function as negotiators themselves as long as they have access to the modified input secured by other negotiators. Negotiated input runs the risk of becoming over-elaborate with consequent negative effects on acquisition. In fact, where acquisition is concerned, premodified input may turn out to be as efficient as interactionally modified input. Indeed, in one study (Ellis 1995) it was shown to be more efficient. The research also suggests that listening-to-comprehend and listening-to-acquire are different processes in that the relationship between comprehension and acquisition scores does not appear to be very strong. Finally, it is likely that individual learner factors, such as language aptitude, are involved in comprehending and acquiring from oral input.

A word of caution is in order, however. These studies were primarily concerned with the acquisition of vocabulary and, in general, they measured whether acquisition had occurred only receptively. We cannot be certain that the conclusions reached will apply to other aspects of language, for example, grammatical features, nor do we know if the same results would have been obtained if the measures involved language production.

We will conclude this section by evaluating the effectiveness of listen-and-do tasks for vocabulary learning. Laufer and Hulstijn (2001) propose that task effectiveness is determined by the learners' level of 'involvement', which determines the extent to which words processed incidentally are retained. Involvement is operationalized in terms of three constructs: (1) need, a motivational factor that concerns the extent to which the task requirements create a need to process a word; (2) search, a cognitive factor concerning whether learners engage in trying to find the meaning of the word by consulting a dictionary or another authority such as a teacher; and (3) evaluation, a cognitive factor that relates to what learners do with a word they have encountered to establish its semantic and formal properties. Laufer and Hulstijn suggest that these three factors can be used to assess the 'task-induced involvement load' of different tasks. Table 2.1 compares the premodified and interactionally modified versions of the kitchen task in Ellis, Tanaka, and Yamazaki (1994). We can see that the premodified version of the task, which involves 'need' but not 'search' or 'evaluation', is assessed as posing a smaller task-induced involvement load than the interactionally modified version, which involves both 'need' and 'search' but not 'evaluation'. From this, it can be predicted that the interactionally modified version would result in greater vocabulary learning,

Task	Need	Search	Evaluation
Premodified version of task	Yes—learners need to process the words to understand the directions	No—learners have no opportunity to consult a dictionary or the teacher	No—the task does not require any manipulation of the target words
Interactionally modified version	Yes—learners need to process the words to understand the directions	Yes—learners are able to request clarification of the teacher	No—the task does not require any manipulation of the target words

Table 2.1: An evaluation of the two versions of the kitchen task in terms of task-induced involvement load

which Ellis, Tanaka, and Yamazaki (1994) found to be the case. However, it should be noted that tasks that involve 'search' are likely to take more time than tasks that do not and that, as we saw above, the different learning outcomes of the two versions of the task are explicable in terms of time-on-task.

Academic listening tasks

Academic listening tasks all have the same basic format; they consist of a lecture on some academic topic during which the learners are required to take notes. In the eyes of some readers such activities may not constitute 'tasks' in the widely used sense of this term.[6] However, such a view is mistaken, as academic listening tasks meet all the key criteria for a task discussed in Chapter 1. They require learners to focus primarily on meaning in order to achieve a clearly defined outcome, i.e. a set of notes. Learners have to use their own linguistic resources to process the lecture input and to produce the notes, i.e. they cannot simply write down what they hear. Academic listening tasks engage a variety of cognitive processes, for example, identifying how the content is structured; selecting which point to record in the notes. The 'taskness' of academic listening tasks is indisputable.

Listening to lectures and taking notes is 'a time honored tradition in academe' (Dunkel, Mishra, and Berliner 1989) and, in the eyes of some researchers, lecturing constitutes the most important medium of education at university level (Flowerdew 1994b). It is not surprising, therefore, to find that lectures have been studied in some depth by researchers and educators interested in language for academic purposes. However, they are not normally considered by second language acquisition researchers, an exception being Chaudron.

Much of the research has focused on describing the discourse features of lectures. This has addressed such issues as the linguistic differences that result from lecturing style, for example, interactive vs. non-interactive lecturing styles; the discourse structure of lectures, for example, the extent to which particular groups of L2 learners are able to identify the different parts of a standard discourse pattern such as the problem-solution-evaluation pattern, as in Tauroza and Allison (1994); interpersonal features, for example, how 'definitions' are handled in lectures; and lexico-grammatical features, for example, the technical and semi-technical vocabulary used in subject-specific lectures. Our concern here, however, is not with this descriptive research (see Flowerdew 1994 for an excellent summary). Instead, we will focus more narrowly on research that has examined lectures as input to a note-taking task. This research is still quite limited.

We will begin by describing academic listening tasks using the framework from Chapter 1 (see Table 1.1 on p. 21).

1 Goal

The goals of an academic listening task are (1) to develop students' ability to comprehend an academic lecture and (2) to provide practice in taking notes that will be comprehensible to the note-taker when read some time later.

2 Input

The input consists of the lecture itself together with any non-verbal aids, for example, diagrams, maps, and charts that are presented on a handout, the chalk board, or an overhead transparency. This input can vary in a variety of ways.

3 Conditions

Academic listening tasks are clearly one-way, although as Flowerdew (1994b) has observed, a more informal, interactive listening style is becoming increasingly favoured. The note-taking itself can be unguided or guided when the students are given an outline of the lecture to complete.

4 Procedures

The students may be given training in how to write notes, using the techniques described by Rost (1990); they may be taught how to 'topicalize' by writing down a word or phrase to represent a proposition in the lecture, to 'schematize' by inserting a diagram to represent a series of propositions or to employ 'hierarchy cuing' by labelling points as main points, supporting points, and examples, etc. Note-taking can also be either concurrent, i.e. undertaken online as students listen to the lecture, or spaced, i.e. undertaken retrospectively during pauses in the lecture.[7]

5 Predicted outcome

The product outcome of an academic listening task is a set of notes that provide a record of the content of the lecture. As we will see this product can be subsequently analysed in a variety of ways.

Describing academic listening tasks in this way makes clear the very large number of variables that can impact on the performance of such tasks. Clearly, the nature of the *input* is likely to affect the quality of the notes. For example, Chaudron and Richards' (1986) study of the effects of macro-markers, for example, 'Now getting back to our main point ...', and micro-markers, for example, 'Well ...', 'Then ...', and 'On the other hand ...', showed that L2 learners comprehended a lecture more fully when the former were present than either the latter or a mixture of the two types. Similarly, options relating to the conditions of the task and the actual procedures followed in implementing the task are likely to influence both the learners' notes and their comprehension of the lecture. It is likely, for example, that if L2 learners have the opportunity to control the speech rate of the material they are listening to, their comprehension will improve considerably. Noting the complexity of the variables involved, Rost (1990: 126) points out, 'it is unlikely that we will find consistent correlations between note quality ... and listener performance on tests'.

The research has focused on the relationship between note-taking and comprehension of lecture content. In contrast to the research on listen-and-do tasks, no attempt has been made to examine to what extent or in what ways listening to lectures contributes to the acquisition of an L2. Clearly, though, academic listening tasks offer a useful potential mechanism for investigating how input influences language acquisition. Like listen-and-do tasks, they allow the researcher to systematically manipulate input variables such as speech rate and discourse structure in order to study how these affect acquisition.

Note-taking can facilitate comprehension of a lecture in two ways (Di Vesta and Gray 1972). According to the *encoding hypothesis*, taking notes serves as a way of organizing lecture content while listening and thus of enhancing comprehension. It helps to activate the learners' attentional mechanisms and to stimulate the cognitive processes of coding, integrating, synthesizing, and transforming information (Dunkel 1988). It can be thought of, therefore, as a device that promotes the kind of deep processing believed to be important for learning (Craik and Lockhart 1972). According to the *external storage hypothesis*, note-taking results in a record of the content of a lecture which can be subsequently referred to and which thus promotes long term retention and ease of recall. Having notes to refer to enables learners to rehearse the content and also may aid reconstruction of memory. These hypotheses have sometimes been seen as competing. However, research which has investigated the effects of note-taking and note-reviewing on native speaking students' comprehension and recall of lecture content has failed to find conclusively in favour of either (see Chaudron, Lubin, Sasaki, and Grigg 1986, and Dunkel 1988 for reviews of the L1 studies). It may be better, therefore, to view the encoding and external storage hypotheses as mutually compatible rather than as competing.

The L2 research based on academic listening tasks has addressed two issues: (1) the nature of the notes taken by L2 learners and (2) the effects of note-taking on comprehension. We will now examine the findings of this research.

An issue of considerable importance is the quality of notes taken by L2 learners. Given that L2 learners frequently report problems in listening to lectures (Flowerdew and Miller 1996), it can be expected that they will also have difficulty in taking notes. Indeed, as Chaudron, Loschky, and Cook (1994) point out, the dual tasks of listening and taking notes may overburden the language-processing mechanisms of many L2 learners with the result that each task interferes with the other.

The available research suggests that L2 students do indeed experience problems in taking notes. Dunkel (1988), for example, reports that many of the L2 learners she studied adopted the strategy of 'writing down as much as possible'. Their notes included numerous structure words such as articles and prepositions with the result that although they used more words or notations overall than L1 note-takers they encoded fewer information units. However, Clerehan (1995), in a study that compared the notes taken by eight native speakers, three bilinguals, and eighteen non-native speakers found that non-native speakers' notes were on average much shorter than the other two groups, i.e. 232 words as opposed to 442 and 438.[8] This difference was reflected in the amount of information the three groups of students were able to encode in their notes. Whereas the native-speakers and the bilinguals hardly missed any points from the lecture, the non-native speakers missed many high-level and low-level points. Clerehan observed that if one element in a hierarchical sequence in the lecture was missed then often the whole sequence was missed. Hansen (1994) also found that the two L2 note-takers she investigated missed points at all hierarchical levels in the lecture and also that they sometimes wrote down wrong information. On the surface, then, these studies contradict each other. However, the difference may reflect a difference at the input level of the tasks. In Dunkel's study, the input consisted of a short, specially prepared video-taped lecture on the evolution of Egyptian pyramids. In both Clerehan's and Hansen's studies the input took the form of genuine lectures. Perhaps many L2 learners do strive to adopt a strategy of 'writing down as much as possible' when the input allows them to do so but when faced with input that is demanding they struggle (and often fail) to create a full and accurate set of notes. The important point is that either way their notes are less than satisfactory.

In an attempt to identify the key dimensions in the notes taken by ninety-eight adult ESL students when they listened to three seven-minute mini-lectures, Chaudron, Loschky, and Cook (1994) first coded the notes using a number of measures of quantity, for example, number of words, and quality, for example, number and proportion of high order information as opposed to low order information in the text, and then submitted the scores obtained to a principal components factor analysis. This revealed three main factors. Factor 1 emerged as a 'quantity-organizational factor', with heavy loadings for number of words and outlining. Factor 2 had loadings for frequency of use of diagrams and was thus characterized as 'representational simplicity'. In contrast, factor 3 reflected 'elaborateness' with a loading only for verbatim notes. This kind of analysis, while obviously very exploratory, is useful in that it might provide a way of characterizing the different styles of note-taking employed by individual L2 learners.

A number of issues concerning the relationship between note-taking and comprehension have been investigated. One issue is whether taking notes works better for comprehension than just listening. Dunkel, Mishra, and Berliner (1989) found no difference in the scores obtained from tests measuring comprehension of main points and specific details between L2 students who took notes and those who just listened. Chaudron, Loschky, and Cook (1994) found no difference in the comprehension test scores between those students who were allowed to retain their notes after the lecture and those who were asked to hand them in. In this study, however, all the students took notes. One possible reason for these studies failing to find an expected relationship between taking–retaining notes and comprehension may be that the notes were lacking in quality, as discussed above. It is reasonable to assume that notes will only assist comprehension if they are complete, accurate, and well-written.

The key issue, then, is the relationship between note quality and comprehension. Dunkel (1988) used multiple regression analysis to try to identify what specific characteristics of the notes taken by both L1 and L2 students predicted scores on comprehension tests measuring understanding of main concepts and details. She concluded that the key variables were: (1) terseness, i.e. the ratio between the number of information units encoded and the number of words used in the notes, and (2) answerability, i.e. the extent to which the notes included information relating to the test items. Chaudron, Loschky, and Cook (1994), however, found few significant correlations between their measures of note-taking and comprehension scores. In general, the correlations were stronger for those students who were allowed to keep their notes. This study, then, failed to find any support for the encoding hypothesis and provided only limited support for the external storage hypothesis. Clerehan (1995: 151) found that even though the notes produced by the non-native speakers were inferior to those produced by the native speakers the former did as well as the latter in an examination at the end of the course and concluded 'it is obviously possible for students to make up for poor notes'. To date, then, the research has not convincingly demonstrated what qualitative aspects of L2 learners' notes are important for comprehension or retention of information.

There are two possible reasons for this. One is that the effectiveness of note-taking cannot be considered in absolute terms but depends on the style and form of the lecture. Thus, Chaudron, Loschky, and Cook (1994) conclude the report of their own rather inconclusive study with a call to examine qualitative aspects of note-taking in relation to the input supplied by the lecture. The second reason is that individual learners may vary in what kind of notes work best for them. Dunkel (1988: 271) makes the obvious point that 'the notion that there is a single, unitary (or universal) note-taking method that is effective for all groups of students does not find support'. Dunkel, Mishra, and Berliner (1989) report that L2 note-takers with better memories, not surprisingly, achieved higher comprehension scores than those with more limited memory spans.

To sum up, academic listening tasks have been studied in order to examine the quality of the notes taken by L2 learners and to investigate what effect note-taking has on comprehension and information retention. There is clear evidence that in many cases L2 learners' notes are incomplete and inaccurate in comparison to the notes taken by native speakers. However, the research to date has not been able to demonstrate conclusively whether note-taking aids or impedes comprehension of a lecture or what qualities in notes are important for comprehension. The effectiveness of note-taking is likely to vary as a product of the particular lecture, i.e. depending on such variables as the lecturing style and discourse structure of the lecture, and also as a product of individual learner differences such as language proficiency and memory ability.

To date no attempt has been made to explore how academic listening tasks contribute to language acquisition. However, we can use Laufer and Hulstijn's (2001) method for measuring 'task-induced involvement load' (see above) to predict their effectiveness for vocabulary learning. Academic listening tasks clearly create a 'need' for learners to process words in the input. There is limited opportunity for 'search' even in an interactive task. Arguably, though, they create opportunities for 'evaluation' as learners have to use the words they hear in their notes. Potentially, then, academic listening tasks serve as a means by which learners can expand their vocabulary.

Conclusion

We will conclude this chapter by considering what the research based on listening tasks has contributed to theory (as it concerns both listening and language acquisition), research methodology, and language pedagogy.

Theoretical considerations

In general, the research reported in this chapter lends support to the interactive model of listening outlined on p. 45. Academic listening task research, for example, has shown that when learners lack relevant schemata their ability to take notes and comprehend a lecture suffers. It has also shown that L2 learners are at a disadvantage in comparison to native speakers when it comes to taking notes, probably because of difficulties in processing oral input rapidly. This research, then, broadly bears out the claim that effective listening involves both top-down and bottom-up processing. L2 learners, it appears, may be disadvantaged in both respects when listening to lectures. The research based on listen-and-do tasks lends support to the other claim of the interactive model, namely that comprehension is successful when listeners are able to construct a shared 'mental model' of what is being talked about. One way of achieving such a model is by negotiating meaning to ensure understanding but another way may be through exposure to premodified input.

The research also supports the contention that listening-to-comprehend and listening-to-learn involve separate processes. Those studies based on listen-and-do tasks that examined both comprehension and language acquisition did not find a close relationship between the two. Comprehension could occur without acquisition and acquisition could sometimes take place even though learners had not fully comprehended the input.

Finally, the task-based listening research has contributed to our understanding of how specific input properties affect comprehension and language acquisition. Clearly redundancy in input aids both comprehension and acquisition. However, input that becomes excessively redundant as a result of over-elaboration may have a negative impact on acquisition. However, much work remains to be done to tease out the macro and micro properties of oral discourse that influence learning outcomes.

Methodological considerations

Listening tasks, whether of the listen-and-do kind or the academic listening kind, offer a promising tool for investigating the micro processes involved in comprehending and language acquisition. This is because they allow the researcher to control and to experimentally manipulate the nature of the oral input the learners will be exposed to. In this way, it is possible to test specific hypotheses relating to how input affects learning outcomes. There is, of course, a danger that the input becomes artificial, thus making it impossible to extrapolate results to real-life situations. One of the criticisms often levelled at research based on academic listening tasks is that it has typically been based on video-presented mini-lectures rather than actual lectures. There is an obvious need to balance tightly-designed experimental research with ethnographic research of academic lectures as advocated by Benson (1989).

A further methodological problem that has received little attention is the need to obtain information about how learners view a task. The point has been made earlier that the task-as-workplan may not conform to the personal task that an individual learner constructs for him/herself. In none of the studies reported in this chapter was any attempt made to establish how individual learners responded to the tasks they were set. For example, the research based on academic listening tasks did not investigate what learners thought they were doing when they were taking notes or even if they thought that taking notes was a useful activity.

Pedagogic considerations

The research based on listen-and-do tasks has shown that such tasks are effective both as listening comprehension devices and as a means of presenting new linguistic material to students. It also suggests that where acquisition is concerned premodified input can be as effective as interactionally modified input. This finding is encouraging for the many language learners who have no or very limited opportunities to interact in the L2. Ellis, Tanaka, and Yamazaki's (1994) study also demonstrates that even Japanese learners, who are culturally resistant to interacting in a whole-class task, can be encouraged to do so by a task that can only be completed successfully through interaction. The research based on academic listening tasks was undertaken with a very specific pedagogic purpose in mind—to improve the teaching of note-taking skills. Even though the results afford few definite proposals they offer a number of 'provisional specifications' (Stenhouse 1975) that teachers can experiment with in their own classrooms. Perhaps the most important contribution of this area of research to date is to warn against simplistic ideas about what constitutes effective note-taking.

As Dunkel (1991) noted, listening in an L2 has received relatively little attention by researchers despite its obvious importance both as a skill in its own right and as one of the primary sources of language acquisition. This chapter has demonstrated that tasks can serve as an effective methodological tool for investigating both theoretical and pedagogically relevant aspects of listening. It also shows the importance of distinguishing listening-to-comprehend and listening-to-learn.

Notes

1 Of course, it is possible to create a situation that caters for overhearers, for example, when learners are performing a task in a small group a learner from another group could be asked to 'sit in'.
2 In effect, I am claiming that when the person being addressed is anonymous, the listening role is closer to that of 'hearer' than 'addressee'.
3 Anderson and Lynch (1988) suggest that there is a close relationship between listening and reading ability. They cite a study by Neville (1985) which found a strong correlation between native-speaker children's cloze reading and listening scores. Readers and listeners, they claim, employ an underlying 'language processing skill' to build an interpretation of a text.
4 However, there may be limitations regarding what is 'noticed' as a result of meaning negotiation. Færch and Kasper (1986) point out that comprehension problems may stimulate learning of 'higher-level L2 material', for example, pragmatic knowledge, but may be much less effective where low-level rules, for example, morphological features, are concerned. Sato's (1988) study of the effects of opportunities for interaction on the acquisition of morphological features of English by two Vietnamese children lends support to this claim.
5 In Loschky (1994), the baseline and premodified groups comprehended equally well. Ellis, Tanaka, and Yamazaki (1994) actually reported two studies, the Saitama Study and the Tokyo Study. They found that the premodified group comprehended better than the baseline group in the Tokyo study but were the same in the Saitama study. Pica, Young, and Doughty (1987) do not report any comparisons between the premodified and the interactionally modified groups' comprehension.
6 One of the readers of an earlier draft of this chapter commented: 'I am not convinced this section, i.e. the one dealing with academic listening tasks, has any place in a book of the current title'. However, I can see no reason why academic listening tasks should be excluded nor were any given by this reader.
7 Rost (1994: 98) reports a study that used 'spaced' summaries to investigate L2 learners' comprehension of video-taped mini-lectures. The tape was paused at 'logical breaks in the text after approximately four minutes, six minutes, and ten minutes'. Two minutes was allotted to summary writing at each pause. Rost argues that this task provides a window for viewing how learners construct interpretations of lectures *while* they are listening.
8 In a later study, Dunkel and Davis (1994) found that the notes taken by native speakers contained more words than those taken by non-native speakers. Dunkel's (1988) study, therefore, appears to be the odd one out.

3 Tasks, interaction, and SLA

Introduction

In the last chapter we looked at non-reciprocal tasks that involved listening. In this chapter we will consider reciprocal tasks that require learners to engage in interpersonal interaction. Such tasks are viewed as devices for generating interaction involving L2 learners and through this interaction affecting the course of acquisition. Because interaction has been seen as central to the course of acquisition in SLA, the study of how task design and implementation affects interaction affords important insights into the potential relationship between task and acquisition. An understanding of this relationship is of potential value to both course design and language-teaching methodology.

This relationship between task and acquisition, then, is an indirect one. To understand it we need to explore the relationship between task and language use on the one hand and language use and language acquisition on the other. With regard to the relationship between task and language use, three major avenues of enquiry have been explored: (1) the negotiation of meaning, (2) communicative strategies, and (3) communicative effectiveness. These constructs are considered in the next section followed by a discussion of the theoretical claims concerning the place of these constructs in L2 acquisition. Finally, we will consider the task-based research these claims have given rise to. No attempt will be made to examine focused tasks, i.e. tasks that attempt to incorporate some focus on form, in this chapter as these will be considered separately in Chapter 5.

The study of learner interaction

Maintaining a conversation is often effortful for learners because they lack both the linguistic resources to understand what is said to them and to make themselves understood. In this section we will begin by examining the devices they use to negotiate meaning when there is a breakdown in understanding and also the communicative strategies they employ to overcome their own linguistic deficiencies in order to say what they want to say. Finally, we will consider how communicative effectiveness can be achieved. As we will see later in this chapter, researchers have examined all three aspects of interaction in studying the relationship between task design and task performance.

The negotiation of meaning

Working with conversational data collected from non-native speakers per-forming a number of different tasks with native speakers, Long (1981) found that native speakers engaged in modification of both their input, for example, by using simpler grammar and vocabulary, and the interactional structure of the conversations, for example, by requesting clarification, and noted that the latter was more common. In fact, modified interaction occurred even when there was no input modification. Long (1983b) sug-gested that native speakers employ two sets of interactional strategies. One set is directed at avoiding conversational trouble. Strategies belonging to this set include relinquishing topic control to the learner, selecting salient topics, treating topics briefly, and checking that the addressee has compre-hended. The second set consists of what Long calls 'tactics' for repairing trouble when it arises. Strategies in this set include requesting clarification, confirming comprehension, and tolerating ambiguity. Some interactional features, such as stressing key words, decomposing topic-comment con-structions, and repeating utterances, serve both purposes.

Subsequent work has focused on the specific strategies interlocutors employ to cope with problems of understanding. In general, more attention has been paid to the strategies used to resolve rather than prevent problems. Varonis and Gass (1985), for example, developed a model to account for discourse where non-understandings take place. See Figure 3.1.

Trigger	**Resolution**
T	I R RR

T = trigger (i.e. the utterance which causes misunderstanding)

I = indicator (i.e. of misunderstanding)

R = response

RR = reaction to response

Example:

S1	And your what is your mmm father's job?	
S2	My father now is retire.	T
S1	retire?	I
S2	yes	R
S1	Oh, yes.	RR

Figure 3.1: Proposed model for non-understandings
(Varonis and Gass 1985: 74)

The discourse work done to resolve such non-understanding sequences has become known as the *negotiation of meaning*. Researchers have tended to focus on a fairly narrow set of strategies used in these sequences, using counts of these as measures of the extent to which different tasks promote negotiation. Four strategies in particular have figured in the research:

1 Comprehension checks—any expression designed to establish whether the speaker's own preceding utterance has been understood by the addressee, for example, 'I was really chuffed. Know what I mean?'

2 Clarification requests—any expression that elicits clarification of the preceding utterance, for example,

A I was really chuffed.
B *Uh?*
A Really pleased.

3 Confirmation checks—any expression immediately following the preceding speaker's utterance intended to confirm that the utterance was understood or heard correctly, for example,

A I was really chuffed?
B You were pleased?
A Yes.

4 Recasts—defined by Long (1996: 436) as an utterance that rephrases an utterance 'by changing one or more of its sentence components (subject, verb, or object) while still referring to its central meanings', for example,

A I go to cinema at weekend.
B *You went to the* cinema. What did you see?
A 'Gladiators'. It was great.

Recasts resemble confirmation checks but, as Oliver (2000) has pointed out, they are not identical. Some recasts do not perform the function of confirmation checks (as when one speaker corrects another speaker even though no communication problem has arisen). Also, not all confirmation checks take the form of recasts (as when one speaker paraphrases rather than reformulates what another speaker has said). Recasts are further considered in Chapter 5 in the context of implicit feedback.

In all these examples it is the meaning of A's utterances that is being negotiated. That is, the sequences involve a language problem—the meaning of 'chuffed' or the time the learner is referring to. However, similar sequences can arise when a knowledge problem arises, for example,

A Then we visited Kyoto, the capital of Japan.
B The capital?
A Well, the old capital.

Rulon and McCreary (1986) have coined the term *negotiation of content* to refer to this kind of negotiation. However, it is not always easy to distinguish the negotiation of meaning and content nor, indeed, to identify utterances that unambiguously perform these different discourse functions. For example, in the above example, we do not know for sure whether B is questioning whether Kyoto is the capital of Japan or whether B is requesting confirmation that she has heard the word 'capital' correctly.

Two kinds of negotiation of meaning and content can be identified, depending on whether the source of the communication problem lies in something the learner has said or something that the learner's interlocutor has said, i.e. whether the learner is playing an initiating or responding role in the exchange. In the example below, A (a learner) is led to reformulate her initial utterance, producing a more grammatical version of it, as a result of B's clarification request. Thus, this kind of exchange provides an opportunity for what Swain (1985) has called *pushed output*, i.e. output that reflects what learners can produce when they are pushed to use the target language accurately and concisely, for example,

A I go cinema.
B You what?
A I went cinema.

In the following example, B (a learner) does not understand what A has said and responds with a confirmation check, leading A to add the word 'yesterday' to make it clear she is referring to the past, not the future. This kind of negotiation helps learners to achieve *comprehensible input*, i.e. input that they can understand.

A I went to see a great movie.
B You are going?
A Yesterday, I went to see a great movie.

As we will see, both types of negotiation have been hypothesized to be important for language acquisition. Of course, if both the interlocutors in such exchanges are language learners, negotiation can provide them with both comprehensible input and opportunities for pushed output.

Various typologies of more specific interactional strategies have also been developed. For example, Rost and Ross (1991) provide a framework for classifying different kinds of listener response moves during the negotiation of meaning. The framework is summarized in Figure 3.2. Rost and Ross also suggest that the strategies have different effects on the continuation of the discourse. For example, a lexical or global reprise typically results in a repetition or rephrasing of an entire utterance or segment. It is possible, therefore, that because different strategies result in different types of language use they have a differential effect on language acquisition.

General response strategy	Specific types
1 Global questioning strategies	**a** Global reprise, i.e. the listener asks for a repetition, rephrasing, or simplification of the preceding utterance or simply states he/she has not understood.
	b Continuation signal, i.e. an overt signal that the listener has understood.
2 Local questioning strategies	**a** Lexical reprise, i.e. a question referring to a specific word in the preceding utterance as in 'What does X mean?', or repeating a word or phrase with a rising intonation.
	b Fragment reprise, i.e. a question referring to a specific part of the preceding utterance but without identifying a specific lexical item.
	c Lexical gap, i.e. a question about a specific word or term used previously that the listener has understood but cannot recall.
	d Positional reprise, i.e. a reference to a specific position in the preceding utterance as in 'I don't understand the last part.'
3 Inferential strategies	**a** Hypothesis testing, i.e. the use of specific questions to verify whether an inference about what the speaker has said is correct.
	b Forward inference, i.e. a question that elaborates on a previously given piece of information.

Figure 3.2: A typology of clarification requests (Rost and Ross 1991)

We will see shortly that there are strong theoretical grounds for investigating the negotiation of meaning. In particular, the distinction between strategies that contribute to comprehensible input and those that lead to opportunities for pushed output is theoretically important. However, the theoretical status of more detailed taxonomies such as that of Rost and Ross is more uncertain. Such taxonomies are essentially descriptive with no basis in theory. For example, there does not seem to be any theoretical reason for distinguishing the different kinds of local questioning strategies. A further problem is that they are derived from the analysis of a particular data set and, therefore, may not be generally applicable. The important discourse strategies are those that (1) can be shown to be general in nature, and (2) can be theorized to contribute to acquisition.

Communication strategies

Whereas the discourse strategies associated with the negotiation of meaning are listener-oriented, *communication strategies* are typically viewed as speaker oriented—they constitute what Kasper and Kellerman (1997: 2) describe as 'a form of self-help that did not have to engage the interlocutor's support for resolution'.[1] Speakers employ them when they have to communicate meanings for which they lack or cannot access the requisite linguistic knowledge. Communication strategies, therefore, are seen as compensatory in nature.

A variety of speaker strategies have been identified, using a similar approach to that found in the study of the negotiation of meaning. That is, learners are asked to perform a referential task, such as describing a picture or diagram. Their speech is then transcribed and subsequently analysed in order to identify and define the communication strategies they employed. Most of the strategies so identified relate to lexis, although, potentially they can apply to any linguistic problem, i.e. phonological, grammatical, or pragmatic. Examples of the communication strategies that have been identified are:

1 Reduction strategies: where the learner gives up a topic or abandons a specific message
2 Achievement strategies: where the learner decides to keep the original communicative goal and attempts to compensate for insufficient means for achieving it. These include:
   a approximation, for example, 'worm' is substituted for 'silkworm'
   b paraphrase, for example, 'it sucks air' is substituted for 'vacuum cleaner'
   c word coinage, for example, substituting 'picture place' for 'gallery'
   d conscious transfer, i.e. the deliberate use of the L1, for example, by literally translating an L1 expression.
   e appeals for assistance
   f mime.

Tarone (1981) provides an extended list of communication strategies. As in the negotiation of meaning research, the strategies so identified have tended to proliferate, with more and more elaborate taxonomies being developed.

Færch and Kasper (1983), however, usefully locate such communication strategies within a general model of speech production. In this psycholinguistic account, communication strategies are seen as part of the planning stage; they are called upon when speakers experience some kind of problem with their initial plan that prevents them from executing it. Bialystok (1990) offers a somewhat different psycholinguistic account. She suggests that communication strategies can be distinguished according to whether they are 'knowledge-based' or 'control-based'. The former involve the speaker adjusting the content of a message by exploiting knowledge of a concept, for example by providing a definition or paraphrase. The latter involve maintaining the original content of the message and manipulating the means of expression by going outside the L2, for example by using the L1 or mime.

A third psycholinguistic model of communication strategies, somewhat similar to Bialystok's, is that developed in the Nijmegen Project (Kellerman, Bongaerts, and Poulisse 1987; Poulisse 1990; Kellerman 1991). The model rests on two archistrategies (general approaches to solving a communicative problem) labelled 'conceptual' and 'linguistic'. Conceptual strategies involve the manipulation of the concept to be communicated. There are two broad types. Analytic strategies involve the identification of features of a referent and are reflected in circumlocution, description, and paraphrase. Holistic strategies involve the substitution of a superordinate, subordinate, or coordinate term for the term that is problematic. The distinction between analytic and holistic strategies is continuous rather than dichotomous. Linguistic strategies involve the manipulation of the language by recourse to the L1 or through morphological creativity. The model is summarized in Figure 3.3. Kellerman (1991) claims that these distinctions reflect differences in mental processing.

A key issue in the study of communication strategies is what motivates learners to use one type of strategy rather than another. Poulisse (1997) suggests that learners seek to conform to two general principles of communication—the principle of clarity and the principle of economy (see Leech 1983). The former requires speakers to be informative and clear while the latter requires them to be brief and economical. The problem facing learners is that they do not always have access to the language needed to be brief and economical, for example, they may not know the L2 word to label a referent. Thus, they may need to sacrifice economy in order to achieve clarity, for example, by using a circumlocution. However, Poulisse argues that learners do try to adhere to the two principles and this motivates their choice of

Archistrategies	Communication strategies	
Conceptual	1	Analytic (circumlocution, description, and paraphrase)
	2	Holistic (the use of a superordinate, coordinate, or subordinate term)
Linguistic	1	Transfer (borrowing, foreignizing, and literal translation)
	2	Morphological creativity, e.g. the use of 'representator' in place of 'representative'.

Figure 3.3: A typology of communication strategies
(based on Poulisse 1990: Chapter 7)

strategies. For example, they are likely to first try using their L1 (which satisfies both principles) and only subsequently apply other strategies involving providing progressively more information, for example, through approximation, word coinage, and paraphrase until they have achieved their goals. If a choice has to be made between being clear and saving effort, learners weigh up the importance of the goal, sometimes opting for clarity and sometimes for economy, for example, by avoiding the problem.

Communication strategies are an important component of *strategic competence*, i.e. the competence required to make effective use of one's linguistic and pragmatic resources. As such they warrant our careful attention, as one of the frequently stated goals of task-based instruction is to develop learners' strategic competence (see Willis 1996). However, there are some obvious weaknesses in the approach that has been adopted to the study of communication strategies. First, as Kasper (Kasper and Kellerman 1997) points out, it has been largely restricted to learners' attempts to convey referential meanings. With a few exceptions, such as Rampton (1987), researchers have neglected the communication strategies learners employ to deal with problems relating to their actional and relational goals and to the need to reconcile these two types of goals in intercultural communication, i.e. to deal with problems of a pragmatic nature. Second, by emphasizing just the compensatory aspect of strategic competence, researchers have adopted an overly narrow view of strategic competence. Bachman (1990) sees strategic competence as central to all communication. He characterizes it as meta-cognitive in nature; it is involved in such complex operations as determining communicative goals, assessing communicative resources, planning communication, and executing communication. It enables learners to integrate their encyclopaedic knowledge and language competence in performance. Such a conceptualization is obviously much richer and is closely related to the notion of communicative effectiveness, to which we now turn.

Communicative effectiveness

Clearly, the extent to which participants in a task engage in the negotiation of meaning and make use of communication strategies will affect their overall communicative effectiveness. Yule (1997) has developed a model of *communicative effectiveness* for referential communication that incorporates two broad dimensions—the 'identification-of-referent' dimension and the 'role-taking' dimension.

Speakers need to be able to identify and encode the referents they wish to communicate about. This ability is particularly important in referential tasks of the 'spot-the-difference' kind but is also important in any task that calls for an exchange of information, for example, narrative tasks. Yule suggests that speakers need three kinds of ability: (1) the perceptual ability needed to notice specific attributes of a referent; (2) the comparison ability needed to distinguish one referent from another; and (3) the linguistic ability needed to encode the referent in a way that distinguishes it from other referents. Yule notes that SLA researchers have been concerned only with (3) but that the successful performance of a task also rests on (1) and (2). For example, learners may fail to perform a 'spot-the-difference' task effectively not because they lack the necessary linguistic resources but because they fail to identify the specific attributes of a referent that need to be communicated. Yule also makes the important point that it should not be assumed that L2 learners possess effective referential communication skills in speaking in their L1.

The role-taking dimension concerns the ability of the participants to take account of their communicative partners in order to achieve intersubjectivity. This also involves a number of different abilities: (1) the ability to recognize the importance of the other speaker's perspective; (2) the ability to make inferences about the other speaker's perspective; (3) the ability to take these inferences into account when encoding a message; and (4) the ability to attend to feedback from the other speaker and to monitor output accordingly. These skills are as much social and cognitive as they are linguistic. They underlie learners' use of interactional strategies, both for negotiating meaning and for communicating problematic concepts.

The study of communicative effectiveness requires an analysis of communicative outcomes. This can be undertaken globally by examining whether the participants successfully accomplish the task. For example, in a 'spot-the-difference' task the researcher can establish whether the participants have successfully identified the differences between the two visual displays. This approach, however, will only work with closed tasks, i.e. tasks that have just one or a limited number of correct answers and, in case of failure to reach the required outcome, offers no information about the source of the problem. Yule and Powers (1994), therefore, propose a framework for the micro-analysis of communicative outcomes based on how specific referential problems are solved. This framework is shown in Figure 3.4.

A model of communicative effectiveness is of enormous promise for the study of tasks. It affords a means for examining the interactions that arise out of a task in relation to the outcome achieved. Such an approach is highly compatible with the definition of a task provided in Chapter 1, which emphasized the outcome-orientedness of tasks. It is also an approach that will resonate with teachers as it provides a basis for determining whether a particular task 'works' in the sense that students can achieve a satisfactory outcome—perhaps the most obvious way of assessing the appropriateness of task selection. However, the model of communicative effectiveness presented above is limited in that it relates only to referential communication. Also, disappointingly, it has received relatively little attention from researchers.

1   No problem: a referential problem exists but is not identified.

2   Non-negotiated solutions:
  a   Unacknowledged problem: a problem is identified by the receiver but not acknowledged by the sender.
  b   Abandon responsibility: a problem is acknowledged by the sender, but responsibility is not taken for solving it.
  c   Arbitrary solution: a problem is acknowledged by the sender who solves it arbitrarily, ignoring the receiver's contribution.

3   Negotiated solutions:
  a   Other-centred solution: the sender tries to solve the problem based on the receiver's (and the sender's) perspective.
  b   Self-centred solution: the sender tries to solve the problem by making the receiver's perspective fit the sender's.

Figure 3.4: Communicative outcomes
(Yule and Powers 1994)

Interaction and language acquisition

The frameworks outlined above can be used to answer the question, 'How does the design of a task affect the kind of interaction that occurs when it is performed?'. As we have seen, this question can be answered by considering how the design of a task affects the negotiation of meaning, the use of communication strategies, and communicative outcomes. In due course, we will consider each of these. However, in order to make the link between tasks and language acquisition it is necessary to consider first how opportunities to interact affect acquisition. It is to this question that we will now turn by examining a number of interactionist theories that have addressed the roles of the negotiation of meaning, communication strategies and communicative effectiveness in language acquisition.

Interactionist theories view language learning as an outcome of participating in discourse, in particular face-to-face interaction. Brown (1968: 287), commenting on how children acquire their first language (L1), observed:

It may be as difficult to derive a grammar from unconnected sentences as it would be to derive the invariance of quantity and number from the simple look of liquids in containers and objects in space. The changes produced by pouring back and forth, by gathering together and spreading apart are the data that most strongly suggest the conversation of number and quantity.

In other words, interaction is important for language learning because the 'pouring back and forth' that it entails serves as the principal means by which children discover how units of language can be gathered together and spread apart. A second quotation, from Hatch (1978b: 404), goes a step further by suggesting that the process of learning how to interact entails the process of learning grammar:

> One learns how to do conversations, one learns how to interact verbally, and out of this interaction syntactic structures are developed.

This perspective—that conversation is in some way the matrix of language learning—informs all interactionist theories.

The Interaction Hypothesis

We considered the *Interaction Hypothesis* briefly in Chapter 2. Here we will examine it in greater detail, considering how it has evolved since its inception.

Initially, the Interaction Hypothesis proposed that comprehensible input that arises when the less competent speaker provides feedback on his/her lack of comprehension assists acquisition (see Long 1983a). As so formulated, however, the hypothesis is very restricted. It deals only with exchanges where the 'less competent speaker' is placed in the position of responding to the 'more competent speaker' and it views language acquisition as entirely input-driven. However, the hypothesis has been subsequently extended to take account of discourse exchanges where the initial problem, i.e. the trigger, arises in the speech of the less competent speaker and where learner production as well as input is given a constitutive role in language acquisition. In this respect, the work of Teresa Pica has been seminal.

Pica (1992 and 1994) proposes that opportunities to negotiate meaning assist language learners in three principal ways. First, as Long and others have claimed, they help learners to obtain comprehensible input. As we saw in Chapter 2, there is considerable empirical support for the claim that negotiation facilitates comprehension. Pica suggests that one way in which this takes place is when the conversational modifications that arise through negotiation break down or segment the input into units that learners can process more easily. In this way, learners are able to attend to L2 form, a view endorsed by Schmidt (2001) in his account of the role that attention plays in L2 acquisition (see Chapter 2). Second, Pica suggests that negotiation provides learners with feedback on their own use of the L2. When more competent interlocutors respond to less competent speakers they frequently attempt to reformulate what they think they meant in ways that provide very specific feedback on a problem item. For example, in this exchange from Pica (1994) the L2 learner received feedback on how to pronounce 'closed', something that was obviously problematic to her:

| NNS | the windows are crozed |
| NS | the windows have what? |

NNS   closed
NS   crossed? I'm not sure what you're saying there.
NNS   windows are closed
NS   oh the windows are closed oh OK sorry.

Finally, Pica argues that negotiation prompts learners to adjust, manipulate, and modify their own output. In this respect, exchanges where the more competent speaker requests clarification of the less competent speaker seem to work best. Learners are pushed into producing output that is more comprehensible and therefore more target-like. Thus, in the example above, the learner is pushed into improving her pronunciation of 'closed'. Swain (1985; 1995) has claimed that such output contributes to language acquisition.

The Interaction Hypothesis, then, suggests a number of ways in which interaction can contribute to language acquisition. In general terms, it posits that the more opportunities for negotiation (meaning and content) there are, the more likely acquisition is. More specifically, it suggests: (1) that when interactional modifications lead to comprehensible input via the decomposition and segmenting of input acquisition is facilitated; (2) that when learners receive feedback, acquisition is facilitated; and (3) that when learners are pushed to reformulate their own utterances, acquisition is promoted. These claims provide a basis for investigating tasks. Tasks that stimulate negotiation and through this provide comprehensible input and feedback and push learners to reformulate are the ones that will work best for acquisition. The relevant properties of tasks, then, are those that have these psycholinguistic outcomes.

However, the Interaction Hypothesis is limited in a number of respects and has attracted considerable criticism. Some of this criticism has to do with identifying when negotiation actually takes place and what the outcomes of it are. These deal with whether the Hypothesis can be investigated reliably. Other criticisms have challenged the validity of the Hypothesis. We will briefly consider these various criticisms.

As Aston (1986) has pointed out, the forms used to realize the topic management functions associated with meaning negotiation, for example, confirmation checks and requests for clarification, can also be used to realize entirely different functions in conversational discourse. Consider the example in Figure 3.1 on p. 70. What exactly is S1 doing when he says 'retire'? Varonis and Gass (1985) assume that he is performing a confirmation check. However, it is possible that S1 heard and understood what S2 said. In fact, S1 may simply be repeating 'retire' as a conversational continuant, i.e. as an expression of interest or to encourage a speaker to say more. It is possible therefore that the exchange in Figure 3.1 does not involve any negotiation of meaning at all. Furthermore, it is not always possible to tell whether the 'response' move in negotiation exchanges signals a successful resolution in the sense that comprehension has been achieved. Hawkins (1985) asked two adult non-native speakers to perform a number of information-gap tasks, identified instances where they produced what were apparent responses signalling comprehension and then collected retrospective data by asking them whether in fact they had comprehended. She reports that the learners often admitted they in fact had not understood. Thus, what appear to be negotiation sequences may in fact not be and what seem to be successful outcomes may just be a pretence.[2]

Gass and Varonis (1994) and Polio and Gass (1988) have also found that sometimes negotiation does not lead to native speakers comprehending non-native speakers. They found that the success of negotiation in this respect depends in part on the strategic abilities of the NNSs and in part on whether they, rather than the NSs, take the lead role in accomplishing the task. When the NS leads, for example, by asking questions to elicit information from the NNSs, comprehension suffers.

In addition, there is uncertainty as to whether comprehending input contributes to acquisition. This concerns the validity of the Interaction Hypothesis. In Chapter 2, we noted that comprehension is not a monolithic phenomenon but highly differentiated, reflecting a continuum of understanding. We also noted that whereas comprehension can be achieved by means of top-down processing based on world knowledge and inference from context, language acquisition requires bottom-up processing involving attention to linguistic forms. In other words, comprehending input need not necessarily either facilitate or promote acquisition.

This objection, however, applies more to the early version of the Interaction Hypothesis, which stressed the role of comprehensible input in language acquisition, than to the later version, according to which interaction also contributes to acquisition by providing feedback and pushing learners to modify their output. Even here, however, there is a problem. Whereas it is fairly easy to see how interaction can show learners how utterances are segmented into parts thus facilitating the acquisition of syntax, it is less clear how it can contribute to the acquisition of morphological features, particularly when these are redundant. Consider the following exchange:

NNS   I go cinema.
NS   Uh?
NNS   I go cinema last night.
NS   Oh, last night.

Here the NNS is pushed into clarifying her initial utterance, which is not marked for time. She responds by adding a lexical marker of past time reference ('last night') and the conversation proceeds. Thus, successful communication takes place without the learner needing to modify her output by incorporating the past tense marker. This example demonstrates the need to distinguish between pushed and **modified output,** showing that not all pushed output is in fact modified.

Evidence of the failure of modified interaction to promote morphological acquisition comes from Sato's (1986) longitudinal study of the acquisition of English by two Vietnamese children aged 10 and 12 years. Sato found that even though they engaged in frequent negotiated sequences with native speakers they failed to acquire the English morphological markers of past tense. She suggests that this might have been because the interactional support they were given enabled them to communicate past time reference effectively without using tense markers. In other words, meaning negotiation obviated the need for the learners to either attend to past tense forms in the input or to use them in their own output.

More generally, there is very little research to show that meaning negotiation actually leads to grammatical development of any kind. Braidi (1997: 164) argues that researchers have failed to show that interaction promotes the acquisition of grammar because researchers have tended to focus on the nature of the interaction rather than on the grammatical structures. She proposes that a number of specific questions need to be addressed: 'Are the required grammatical features available in the interaction?', 'Does the structure of negotiated interaction enhance the accessibility of particular features for the learner?', and 'How does the variability of interactional input affect the acquisition of these features?'. However, studies that have been able to show that meaning negotiation facilitates grammar acquisition are beginning to appear. Mackey (1999), for example, found that learners who took part in negotiated interaction showed greater developmental gains in English question forms than learners who did not do so.

There is also some evidence to support the claim that pushed output promotes language acquisition. Nobuyoshi and Ellis (1993), in a small-scale study, showed that two adult learners who reformulated their deviant utterances as a result of negotiation subsequently improved their accuracy of past tense use. Ellis and Takashima (1999) also found that pushed output aided classroom learners' acquisition of past tense forms. However, Van den Branden (1997) found that pushing child learners to modify their output through negotiation had no significant effect on subsequent syntactical complexity or grammatical accuracy. Thus, the acquisitional significance of pushed output remains to be shown (but see Chapter 6 where research by Swain is discussed in the light shed by sociocultural theory on tasks).

Another criticism of the Interactional Hypothesis concerns its limited scope. The hypothesis addresses the role of repair sequences, assuming that it is these that are crucial for acquisition, but, in fact, there is much more to interaction than such sequences. Learners can acquire from exchanges that proceed smoothly without any communication problem. Wells (1985: 398), for example, has argued that interaction is central to understanding how children acquire their mother tongue. He emphasizes the importance of 'intersubjectivity of attention'. He shows that caretakers (those responsible for looking after children) utilize a variety of devices for achieving intersubjectivity, only some of which concern repair work. For example, they frequently help children to talk about topics they have nominated by means of various extending devices. These push the children to communicate even though no breakdown occurs.

Finally, we should note a danger in the way the Interaction Hypothesis has been used in task-based research. As we have seen, interactional modification involves the use of various topic-contingency devices such as comprehension checks and requests for clarification. One way of quantifying the amount of negotiation that takes place in a conversation resulting from a task, then, is to count the number of utterances performing these discourse functions. However, as van Lier (1996) has pointed out, counting units in this way will not necessarily account for those qualitative aspects of discourse that are important for acquisition. He elaborates an analogy from Vygotsky taken from Wertsch (1985): dividing water into its constituent elements of oxygen and hydrogen will not improve our understanding of how it can be used to put out a fire. For van Lier, quantifying isolated features in order to perform statistical comparisons masks rather than aids understanding of how interaction contributes to acquisition. The atomistic approach to evaluating interaction, which the Interaction Hypothesis has encouraged, treats discourse as a static product to be analysed and the parts classified, rather than as holistic, collaborative, and dynamic (see also Nunan 1992 for a similar argument).[3] For this reason, van Lier and others have suggested that a more appropriate approach would be one that provides for the intense examination of 'pieces of talk'. This is the approach of researchers in the Vygotskian tradition (see Chapter 6).

Despite these problems, the Interaction Hypothesis has assumed a central place in SLA research and has much to offer task-based research. It offers a theoretical basis and a set of clearly defined discourse categories for analysing the interactions that arise in the performance of a task. While it may be dangerous to evaluate tasks solely in terms of the quantity of meaning negotiation they give rise to, there are solid grounds for believing that tasks that afford opportunities for this kind of discourse work will contribute to the acquisition of at least some aspects of language.

Communication strategies and language acquisition

Whereas strong claims have been advanced regarding the usefulness of meaning negotiation for facilitating language acquisition, considerable uncertainty exists about the role of communication strategies. In general, communication strategies are seen as important for understanding L2 communication rather than explaining acquisition. However, a number of

researchers have suggested ways in which such strategies might aid acquisition, particularly lexical acquisition. Corder (1978) suggests that achievement strategies will foster acquisition but that avoidance strategies will not,
a view endorsed by Færch and Kasper (1980). They suggest that learners
may incorporate some of the strategic solutions to problems into their
interlanguage systems. Tarone (1980) argues that all strategies may be
beneficial in that they help learners negotiate their way to the correct target language forms. Communication strategies may also assist acquisition
by helping to keep the conversation going, thus securing more input for
learners. Kasper and Kellerman (1997) suggest that communication strategies are also an important vehicle for producing pushed output, which, as
we have seen, some researchers claim contributes to acquisition. More
specifically, they suggest that they help to develop semantic connections in
the learner's mental lexicon and skill in word formation. Skehan (1998a)
adopts a very different stance, however, arguing that learners who are
adept in using communication strategies to overcome their linguistic problems may fossilize because they do not experience any communicative need
to develop their interlanguage knowledge resources. This is analogous to
the position Sato (1986) adopted with regard to the role of meaning
negotiation in the acquisition of verb morphology (see p. 84).

Of course, language acquisition involves more than the development of
linguistic competence. Even if communication strategies do not contribute
to linguistic competence they may contribute to the development of strategic competence. Schmidt's (1983) case study of Wes, a Japanese painter
acquiring English naturalistically in Hawaii, found that although his
linguistic competence failed to develop over a number of years, his strategic
competence advanced considerably to the point where Wes was able to
carry out complex business negotiations and give lectures in English.
Indeed, one of the specific goals of task-based teaching is to develop learners' strategic competence in order to make them more communicatively
effective using the linguistic resources already at their disposal.

Communicative effectiveness and language acquisition

The relationship between communicative effectiveness and language acquisition has not been explicitly addressed. This perhaps is the result of the different foci of referential communication research and traditional L2 acquisition
research. Yule (1997) notes that where the former has been concerned with
such aspects of language use as pragmatic function, communicative effectiveness, and the development of ability, the latter has addressed linguistic form
(in particular, accuracy of use) and acquisition stages.

As the above discussion of communication strategies suggests, one possible position is that communicative effectiveness and language acquisition
are complementary rather than mutually reinforcing. That is, learners may

opt to emphasize communicative effectiveness or language acquisition when performing a task, trading off one for the other. Such a view is supported by processing models of language acquisition (Robinson 1995) and by research which shows the difficulty learners have in attending simultaneously to meaning (a requisite for communicative effectiveness) and to form (a requisite for acquisition). See, for example, VanPatten (1990) and Wong (2001). Further evidence of a trade-off between communicative effectiveness and language acquisition can be found in Foster and Skehan's research on tasks, for example, Foster and Skehan 1996. This provides evidence that tasks that promote fluency do so at the expense of complexity and/or accuracy and vice versa. This research is considered in detail in Chapter 4.

However, alternative positions can be advanced. If communicative effectiveness is measured in terms of communicative outcomes (see Figure 3.4), it seems self-evident that 'negotiated solutions' will lead to more interaction and thus more input and output than 'no problem acknowledged' or 'non-negotiated solutions' and, thus in broad terms, will be more beneficial for language acquisition. The relationship between communicative ability and language acquisition can be seen as two-way—the more language learners acquire, the more communicatively effective they become, while the more effective they are as communicators, the more opportunities for language acquisition they will be able to obtain for themselves.

Investigating tasks: a review of the L2 research

We will now turn to examine the research that has investigated the interactions that tasks give rise to, drawing on the three theoretical perspectives outlined in the previous section. There is now a substantial body of research that has investigated the relationship between interaction and comprehension–acquisition, addressing such issues as the difference between NS–NNS and NNS–NNS conversations, the difference between teacher-fronted and small group interactions, and the effects of learner variables such as proficiency level, age, gender, and interlocutor familiarity on interaction (see Ellis 1994 and Ondarra 1997 for reviews). Most of these studies made use of tasks. Here we will focus quite narrowly on those studies that have specifically addressed the effect of task factors on interaction. Our concern will be with reciprocal referential tasks, i.e. tasks that require two or more people, at least one of whom is an L2 learner, to exchange information with each other. We will examine a number of task variables that have been found to impact on the amount of meaning negotiation, the use of communication strategies, and communicative effectiveness. The variables to be considered relate to what Skehan (1998b) calls 'task features', i.e. variables relating to the goal, type of input, or conditions of a task (see Figure 1.4 in Chapter 1), and 'task implementation', i.e. variables relating to task procedures. These will be considered separately.

Task features

The task variables that we will consider here are: (1) required vs. optional information exchange, (2) types of required information exchange, (3) expected task outcome, (4) topic, (5) discourse domain, and (6) cognitive complexity. The assumption that underlies the approach to be followed is that through investigating tasks 'it ought to be possible to build up a multi-dimensional classification, organizing tasks in terms of their potential for second language learning on the basis of psycholinguistically motivated dimensions' (Long and Crookes 1987).

Required vs. optional information exchange

A common distinction made in language pedagogy is between *information gap tasks* and *opinion gap tasks*.[4] These differ from each other in a number of ways: (1) as the labels for these tasks suggest, information gap tasks involve an exchange of information while opinion gap tasks involve learners in going beyond the information given by supplying their own ideas; (2) in an information gap task the information provided is split, i.e. the learners do not all have the same information while in an opinion gap task it is shared; (3) in information gap tasks information exchange is *required* (that is, learners cannot complete the task unless they exchange the information) whereas in opinion gap tasks it is *optional*. From a psycholinguistic point of view, the crucial difference appears to be the last of these. Therefore, we will refer to this distinction with the labels 'required information exchange' and 'optional information exchange' (cf. Pica, Kanagy, and Falodun 1993).

It should be noted that, in fact, many tasks are compound in nature, that is, they consist of a first part involving information exchange (with the information split either one way or two way) followed by a second part involving opinion-giving. For example, Newton (1991) investigated a medical task which in one of its formats required learners to first exchange information about four candidates for a heart transplant (a required information task) and then to use the information to choose who should get a heart transplant (an optional information task). This kind of compound task is often referred to as a 'jigsaw task'.

In a series of studies, Doughty and Pica found that small group work in language classrooms only resulted in more negotiation work than teacher-fronted lessons when the task was of the required information type. Pica and Doughty (1985a) found that when they compared performance on an optional information exchange task there was no difference, mainly because there was little negotiation in either participatory condition. However, in Pica and Doughty (1985b) they used a required information exchange task and found that there was significantly more modified interaction in group work than in a teacher-fronted lesson. Doughty and Pica

concluded that the crucial factor determining the amount of meaning negotiation was the task type rather than participatory organisation. Pica and
Doughty (1985b: 246) comment 'neither a teacher-fronted nor a group
format can have an impact on negotiation as long as these tasks continue
to provide little motivation for classroom participants to access each
other's views'.

Newton's (1991) study provides a means of comparing the effects of
required information exchange tasks and optional information exchange
tasks on conversational modifications. Newton found almost double the
quantity of negotiation in tasks where the information provided was split
among the learners when compared to tasks where the information was
shared. In this study, the topic of the tasks, a potentially confounding factor
in some studies, was held constant. Interestingly, Newton (1993) went a
step further and investigated which kind of task resulted in greater gains in
vocabulary. In accordance with the claims of the Interaction Hypothesis, he
found that although there was substantial learning of vocabulary in both
types, there was slightly more in the split information tasks. However, he
concluded that both shared and split information tasks were able to create
the necessary conditions for vocabulary learning.

Foster (1998) compared the amount of negotiation that occurred when
learners performed required and optional information exchange tasks in
both pairs and in groups. She found that, irrespective of tasks, there was
more negotiation in the pairs than in the groups. However, the required
information exchange tasks more consistently elicited negotiation than the
optional information exchange tasks, i.e. the range of the students' negotiation scores was narrower. Foster concluded that overall the best context
for negotiation was one involving dyads performing a required information
exchange task. Similar results were obtained for modified output, although
in this case there were very few instances even in the best circumstances.
This study was unique in that data were collected when the learners
performed the tasks in their normal classroom situation as opposed to a
more experimental setting, although it is possible that because the teacher
was also the researcher the learners did not respond to the tasks as they
normally did.

Finally, a study by Nakahama, Tyler, and van Lier (2001) found that
although a required information exchange task resulted in more negotiation
exchanges, as defined by Varonis and Gass (1985), these exchanges were
rather mechanical, centring on lexical items. In contrast, the interactions
derived from a conversation task, where there was no required information
exchange, resulted in greater negotiation of global problems, for example,
problems relating to anaphoric reference and interpretation of an entire
utterance, significantly longer and more complex turns and wider use of
discourse strategies, for example, paraphrase. The authors conclude that the
conversational activity offered 'a larger range of opportunities for language

use' (ibid. 401) than the information gap task. They also note that, contrary to the claims of other researchers, the participants in their study struggled to communicate by means of 'negotiation in the broader sense' when completing the conversation task. This study is important because it indicates that although required information exchange tasks are effective in instigating meaning negotiation, other types of task may afford opportunities for different kinds of language use that may assist language acquisition.

Information gap: one-way vs. two-way tasks

One-way tasks and *two-way tasks* are required information exchange tasks that are distinguished in terms of whether the information to be shared is split one-way , i.e. held by a single person or between two or more people. The listen-and-do tasks that we considered in Chapter 2 are one-way tasks (with the teacher holding all the information to be communicated). The same-or-different task in Figure 1.2 in Chapter 1 is an example of a two-way task. In the case of one-way tasks the burden of completing the task successfully is placed on the participant who holds the information, although other participants can contribute by demonstrating when they comprehend and when they do not.[5] In contrast, in two-way tasks all the participants are obligated to participate in order to complete the task.

Long (1980) compared the interactional adjustments that occurred in NS–NS and NNS–NS dyads on two sets of tasks. The first set consisted of (1) a narrative task, (2) giving instructions, and (3) discussing the supposed purpose of the research. They are all one-way tasks, classified by Long as '– information exchange'. The second set consisted of (4), a conversation task, and (5) and (6), communication games. They were all two-way and thus '+ information exchange'. Long found that in the one-way tasks the NSS–NS dyads did not engage in significantly more meaning negotiation than the NS–NS dyads but in the two-way tasks there were significantly more confirmation checks, comprehension checks, and clarification requests in the NNS–NS dyads. In other words, NSs were much more likely to modify their interaction to take account of NNSs' comprehension problems in two-way tasks than in one-way tasks.

A number of studies, however, have failed to show that two-way tasks promote more negotiation than one-way tasks. Gass and Varonis (1985) compared the NNS–NNS interactions resulting from a describe-and-draw task and a jigsaw listening task, which required participants to share information in order to work out who had committed a robbery. They found that more indicators of non-understanding occurred in the one-way task, although the difference was not significant. Jauregi (1990, reported in Ondarra 1997) also found that a one-way task (describe-and-draw) produced more negotiation work than a two-way task that involved talking about future plans.

What conclusions can we reach? Long (1989: 13) feels confident enough of the research results to claim that 'two-way tasks produce more negotiation work and more useful negotiation work than one-way tasks'. However, such a conclusion might be premature given that two studies to date do not bear out this conclusion. Furthermore, no study to date has actually investigated whether any difference in learning results from the use of one-way and two-way tasks. Also, the distinction between one-way and two-way tasks may not be as straightforward as it sounds. Gass and Varonis (1985), for example, suggest that it is continuous rather than dichotomous. As we will see later, task implementation variables can also impact on the kind of interaction that takes place in one-way tasks, making them more or less interactive.

Task outcome: open vs. closed tasks

Another dimension that has received attention is the open/closed distinction. *Open tasks* are those where the participants know there is no predetermined solution. Many opinion gap tasks, for example, tasks involving making choices, surveys, debates, ranking activities, and general discussion (see Ur 1981) are open in nature because learners are free to decide on the solution. Open tasks obviously vary in their degree of 'openness', for example a task that allowed learners freedom to choose the topics to discuss is more open than a task that stipulates the topic-information.[6] *Closed tasks* are those that require students to reach a single, correct solution or one of a small finite set of solutions. Information gap tasks, for example, 'same-or-different' (see p. 11), are typically closed in nature. However, the open/closed distinction does not entirely match the split/shared distinction. Thus, it is possible to conceive of tasks that are both open–split and open–shared and also closed–split and closed–shared. For example, a task that required learners to plan a new town by filling in a map and then compare their plans in order to decide on the best plan could be described as open–split, whereas a task that required learners to discuss the viability of a town plan given to them and make changes to it is clearly shared–open. An example of a closed–split task might be 'Find the thief', where learners are first each given information about the possible culprit which they must exchange in order to work out who the thief was. The same task could also be performed in a shared information condition.

Long (1989) presents a rationale for the use of closed tasks. He argues that closed tasks are more likely to promote negotiation work than open tasks because they make it less likely that learners will give up when faced with a challenge. In the case of open tasks such as 'free conversation' tasks there is no need for students to pursue difficult topics. They can treat topics briefly and switch topic if necessary. Furthermore, there is no need for them to provide or incorporate feedback. In short, open tasks remove the need to make an effort to communicate. In contrast, closed tasks, Long argues, require students to persevere to make themselves understood, resulting in greater precision and more language recycling. This, Long suggests, is good for acquisition.

Long cites a study by Duff (1986) in support of his claim. This compared the negotiation work resulting from *divergent tasks*, for example, discussing the pros and cons of television, where students were assigned different viewpoints on an issue and had to defend their position and refute their partner's, and *convergent tasks*, for example, deciding what items to take on to a desert island, which required students to agree on a solution to a problem. Duff found that the convergent tasks resulted in more turns per task, more questions and more confirmation checks than divergent tasks although not all these differences were statistically significant. Interestingly, however, divergent tasks produced more words and greater utterance complexity than the convergent tasks. Duff concluded that overall the convergent tasks resulted in more comprehensible input than the divergent tasks but that the divergent tasks led to more output. Thus, the results of Duff's small-scale study (there were only four dyads) do not clearly show that convergent tasks are more effective in promoting meaning negotiation. Also, contrary to Long's citation of this study, it was not designed to address the open vs. closed distinction, as both the divergent and convergent tasks used were open in nature, i.e. they allowed multiple solutions. The divergent/convergent distinction is best seen as a sub-category of open tasks.

A number of other studies speak more directly to the open/closed distinction. Crookes and Rulon (1985) compared the feedback supplied by a native-speaker interlocutor to learners in three tasks: a free conversation task (open), a closed one-way information gap task, and a closed two-way information gap task . They found that feedback was more frequent in the closed tasks than in the open task. Berwick (1990) investigated a number of different tasks performed by Japanese college students. These included a free discussion task (open) and two reconstruction tasks involving Lego (closed).[7] His very detailed analyses included some relevant to the present discussion, which focuses on meaning negotiation. He found that in general the closed tasks led to more clarification requests, more comprehension checks, more confirmation checks, more self-expansions, and more self-repetitions than the open discussion task. In other words, the closed tasks resulted in more extensive meaning negotiation than the open task. Newton (1991), in the study we have already referred to, also found that the quantity of negotiation was greater in his closed tasks. Thus the tasks characterized as two-way–closed produced the most negotiation. However, the one-way–open tasks led to discourse characterized by longer turns. Manheimer (1995) compared Spanish L2 learners' performance on an open task where students had to decide whose life should be saved from a crashing plane and a closed task involving the solution to a mystery murder. He found that the learners displayed more incorporation of input into their own speech, i.e. modified output, and greater overall sentence complexity in the closed task.

Although the quantity of research comparing the effects of open and closed tasks on learner discourse is still limited, the results are encouraging. All the studies to date show that closed tasks result in more negotiation than open tasks. From the perspective of the Interaction Hypothesis, therefore, it would appear that closed tasks are more likely to promote acquisition. However, it is worth bearing in mind that closed tasks may be less beneficial if other aspects of discourse that may be important for acquisition, for example, the opportunity to produce long turns, are considered.[8]

Topic

It is reasonable to suppose that the topic of a task will also impact on learners' propensity to negotiate meaning. However, a problem facing researchers interested in this dimension is identifying general categories for classifying topics that can be theoretically linked to task performance. Clearly, the topic variable is likely to interact with learner variables, with individual learners differing in which topics they find conducive to negotiate about.

Obvious factors to consider are topic familiarity and topic importance. Gass and Varonis (1984) investigated the effects of topic familiarity on four advanced learners of English performing the same task with different topics. As might be expected, they found that the learners' familiarity with the topic had a clear effect on comprehension. It also influenced the amount of negotiation work that took place, with the less familiar topic leading to less negotiation. Zuengler and Bent (1991) compared performance on tasks that differed with regard to the relative importance of the topic to the learners. They found that when the topic held little importance to the interactants, for example, talking about food, the learners functioned as active 'speakers' and the native speakers as active 'listeners' but the roles were reversed when the topic was important, for example, talking about a topic in their shared field of expertise, with the native speakers becoming more dominant. These studies suggest that topic familiarity and topic importance have an influence on the interaction that results from a task.

It is also possible that topic can have an effect that is independent of learner factors, i.e. that certain kinds of topics will predispose all learners to negotiate more than others. Newton (1991), for example, compared the number of negotiating questions on tasks that had an identical design but differed in topic. Two of his tasks had a zoo topic and another two a medical topic. Newton suggests that these topics differed with regard to the kind of information that needed to be exchanged: human-ethical in the case of the medical topic, and objective-spatial in the case of the zoo topic. Newton found that the zoo topic resulted in a significantly greater number of negotiating questions when performed by adult ESL learners of mixed sex and ethnicity. Lange (2000) also found topic to be a crucial factor in determining the amount of talk produced by intermediate learners. In mixed information-opinion gap tasks with identical designs, she found that learners were more motivated to talk about which prisoner should be granted parole than which candidate should get a heart transplant operation. Clearly, though, firm conclusions are not yet possible regarding the effect of topic on learner interaction.

Discourse mode

Clearly, discourse mode is likely to affect the particular linguistic forms a learner uses in performing a task. For example, a task involving description of an object or place is likely to result in the use of present tenses while a storytelling task will lead more naturally to the use of past tenses. This is a point we will take up in the next chapter. Here we will concern ourselves only with the effect of discourse mode on signals of meaning negotiation.

There are few studies that have addressed this variable directly. In a number of studies already mentioned the discourse mode variable is confounded with other variables. For example, Berwick's tasks, which we considered in relation to the open/closed distinction, also involved a difference in discourse mode. Where his open discussion task involved 'conversation', the two Lego tasks required 'directions'. The results he reported, then, could equally be interpreted as reflecting differences in discourse mode. Berwick (1993) recognizes this. He reanalysed data from five tasks—the three tasks mentioned earlier and also two other tasks, one of which consisted of a lecture about how to use a word processing program and the other a demonstration of how to use a laptop computer. A factor analysis produced three factors. The first factor, which Berwick labelled 'collaborative', had loadings for the two tasks that involved collaborative exchanges without any shared concrete point of reference, i.e. the free discussion task and the Lego task performed with the learners back to back. It was these tasks that produced discourse rich in meaning negotiation. The second factor, labelled 'experiential', had loadings for the two tasks where contextual support was available, i.e. the laptop demonstration task and the Lego task where the learners sat face to face. The third factor was labelled 'didactic'. The two computer tasks loaded on this factor. The tasks loading on the second and third factor resulted in less meaning negotiation. Berwick's study suggests that the type of discourse a task affords can influence the extent to which learners negotiate for meaning.

This conclusion is also supported by a study by Pica, Lincoln-Porter, Paninos, and Linnell (1996).[9] They used two jigsaw tasks, i.e. two-way required information exchange tasks. A house-sequence task required the description of attributes, states, and conditions. A storytelling task required attention to the sequence of events. Broadly speaking, then, these tasks generated the discourse modes of 'object description' and 'narrative' respectively. Because both tasks were two-way tasks, the researchers anticipated that both would provide plentiful opportunities for meaning negotiation. However, the results show that the story task elicited significantly more of the topic-incorporation devices associated with meaning negotiation than did the house task. For example, both native speakers and learners produced many more responses containing modified input in the story task than in the house task.

There are strong theoretical and empirical reasons for believing that the discourse mode associated with a task will affect the extent to which participants modify their input and output in negotiation exchanges and the type of communication strategies they employ. Halliday's (1986) functional grammar provides a theoretical rationale for expecting a strong correlation between language use and language form. Biber's (1989) study of linguistic variation in oral and written texts provides empirical evidence for such a correlation. It is no surprise, therefore, to find that discourse mode is an important dimension of tasks. It is somewhat surprising, however, that there has been relatively little attention to this dimension in task-based research to date.

Cognitive complexity

Cognitive complexity is clearly an umbrella term, covering many different factors that can influence the difficulty of a task. Here we will focus on studies that have investigated cognitive complexity in relation to meaning negotiation and, also, communication strategies.

There is a broad body of theory that identifies context-dependency as a major factor determining cognitive complexity. Cummins (1983) describes a model of language proficiency based on a two-way distinction concerning: (1) the extent to which a communicative activity is context-embedded, i.e. how closely it is tied to the situation in which the communication takes place; or context-reduced, i.e. not supported to any great extent by information available from the situation; and (2) the amount of information that must be processed simultaneously or in close succession. According to this model, a cognitively demanding task would be one that required language use that was context-free and that necessitated a large amount of detailed information to be communicated. It is reasonable to hypothesize that cognitively demanding tasks will promote more meaning negotiation than cognitively undemanding tasks as learners will need to engage discourse management and repair strategies more frequently to prevent or cope with non-understanding.

Shortreed (1993) operationalized task complexity in terms of two factors that resemble the factors in Cummins' model: (1) the amount of shared reference in a task, and (2) the level of production required to complete a task. He compared two one-way required information exchange tasks. The first task required one speaker to describe a set of photographs so that a second speaker could arrange them in the same order on a grid. The second task required one speaker to describe a set of objects drawn on a grid so the other speaker could draw them on an empty grid. Shortreed hypothesized that the second task was more complex than the first because there was less shared reference and it required more descriptive detail. He also hypothesized that the second task would elicit greater use of repair strategies. The subjects in this case were native speakers and L2 learners of Japanese. The results showed a significantly higher use of repair strategies on task two. There were more requests for clarification, more comprehension checks, and in particular, more confirmation checks used in this task.

Further support for the hypothesis that the level of detail in the information to be communicated affects the extent of meaning negotiation can be found in Samuda and Rounds (1993). They examined the interactions resulting from a 'spot-the-difference' task performed in pairs. Their analysis was based on the identification of 'critical episodes', defined as exchanges that centred on communication about specific differences in the pairs of pictures used in the task. Their analysis revealed three types of critical episode. Types 1 and 3 involved an absence of a feature, i.e. one picture contained a feature that was missing from the other picture. They were distinguished according to whether the learners possessed the vocabulary needed to describe the missing feature. Type 2 entailed a perceptual ambiguity, i.e. the absence of a feature caused one of the pictures to become ambiguous. Samuda and Rounds found that whereas the interactions in Types 1 and 3 were 'quite straightforward' those in the Type 2 episodes constituted a 'site for enhanced L2 performance'. Type 2 episodes contained both more turns and longer turns. They suggest that the pushed output that occurred in Type 2 episodes had greater 'acquisition potential'.

Poulisse (1990) considers the effects of task complexity on the use of communication strategies. She discusses three tasks: Task 1—a picture description task involving photographs of everyday objects, the names of which the Dutch learners of L2 English were unlikely to know; Task 2—a story retelling task, where the learners listened to a story in Dutch and retold it in English with the help of picture prompts; and Task 3—an oral interview on familiar and less familiar topics, where the interviewer frequently challenged the learners who were thereby 'talked into lexical problems' (ibid. 79). These tasks differ on a number of dimensions but the one Poulisse considers the most crucial concerns the degree of contextual support. In Task 1 the problems were not embedded within a context, as each photograph was presented in isolation, and thus the learners had to make sure that their strategies were 'intrinsically effective' (ibid. 147). This led to the use of elaborate and time-consuming analytic strategies (see Figure 3.4). In contrast, Tasks 2 and 3 allowed the learners to rely on context to assist listeners in interpreting their communication strategies. These tasks led to greater use of holistic and transfer strategies. In a later article, Poulisse (1997) discusses these task-related differences in strategy use in terms of the clarity principle and economy principle (Leech 1983). Undemanding tasks allow learners to satisfy both principles with minimal effort whereas demanding tasks (such as the picture description task) force learners to expend more effort to achieve clarity (at the expense of economy). More complex analytic compensatory strategies, then, arise when learners cannot rely on context or feedback to make themselves clear and when the goal of the task requires precise information.

It should be noted, however, that the task differences Poulisse found might also be accounted for in terms of discourse domain as Task 1 called for detailed description, whereas Task 2 called for conversation, and 3 for narrative. It is also conceivable that certain discourse domains are more cognitively demanding than others.

The studies by Shortreed (1993), Samuda, and Rounds (1993), and Poulisse (1990) indicate that tasks that are context-free and require detailed information to be communicated seem to induce more sustained interaction, more attempts to repair communication, more pushed output and greater use of communication strategies. From the perspective of interactionist theories, then, cognitively challenging tasks, so defined, may promote acquisition. There are, of course, important caveats to be acknowledged. The studies do not address what degree of cognitive complexity works best. Presumably, if a task is too challenging it may cause learners to simply give up! Also, no study has yet shown that tasks that are cognitively complex in these ways actually assist language acquisition. Finally, there are many other factors that are likely to contribute to the cognitive complexity of a task.

Summary

The research we have examined can be considered only *suggestive* of what features of task design might result in the kinds of interactions hypothesized to be important for acquisition. Table 3.1 below, which summarizes the main findings with regard to the quality of interaction, should be read in this light. The various features summarized in Table 3.1 are likely to interact in complex ways, not necessarily additively. Little is known about the nature of these interactions.

Task Features	More positive	Less positive
Information exchange	Required (information gap)	Optional (opinion gap)
Information gap	Two-way	One-way
Outcome	Closed	Open
Topic	Human–ethical Familiar	Objective–spatial Less familiar
Discourse domain	Narrative Collaborative	Description Expository
Cognitive complexity	Context-free Detailed information	Context-dependent Less detailed information

Table 3.1: Task dimensions hypothesized to impact positively on L2 acquisition according to the Interaction Hypothesis

Task implementation

The way in which a task is performed can also have an impact on the kind of interaction that occurs and thereby on comprehension and language acquisition. For example, we have already noted that the amount of negotiation arising out of a two-way information gap task can vary depending on whether it is performed in a whole-class environment or in small groups (Pica and Doughty 1985b). Here we will look at a number of task procedures that have been found to influence the negotiation of meaning, the use of communication strategies and communicative effectiveness. These are: (1) participant role, (2) task repetition, (3) interlocutor familiarity, and (4) type of feedback.

Participant role

One-way tasks can be performed in two different ways. The person holding the information can take entire responsibility for the information exchange, i.e. the one-way task is non-interactive, or the person holding the information can be assisted by the other participant(s) asking questions to obtain or clarify information, i.e. the one-way task is interactive. Obviously the effectiveness of a one-way task in promoting negotiation (and therefore comprehension and acquisition) can depend on whether learners are asked to perform it interactively or non-interactively.

Gass and Varonis (1994) and Polio and Gass (1998) investigated this using a describe-and-do task. The task provided one subject with a board with objects placed on it and another subject with a blank board and the objects placed to the side of it. The individual with the completed board was required to describe that board so the other person could accurately place the objects on his/her board. One of the conditions manipulated in the Gass and Varonis study was interactivity, i.e. some of the learners performed the one-way task interactively while others did not. The results showed that the learners were better able to understand the native-speaker interlocutors, who held the information to be exchanged, when they had the chance to interact with them. However, surprisingly, interaction did not help the native speakers to understand the learners when the latter were responsible for communicating the information. In the Polio and Gass study, however, interaction did result in better native-speaker comprehension in the interactive condition. Polio and Gass explain the difference in results between their study and the earlier Gass and Varonis study in terms of the 'strategic ability' of individual learners and who took the lead role in the performance of the task. They noted that some learners had a better feel for communicating the detail needed to accomplish the task than others. They also found that even though the learners held the information to be communicated some native speakers took charge of the interaction by requesting information. Native speakers comprehended learners better when the learners were adept at providing the right information and the learners were allowed to 'lead' the interaction. Thus, the effectiveness of a one-way task would seems to depend on (1) whether they are performed interactively or non-interactively and (2) the communicative skills and styles of the participants in the interactive condition.

Task repetition

Several researchers have found that asking learners to repeat a task has a marked interactive effect. Gass and Varonis (1985) asked learners to repeat a describe-and-draw task in pairs, reversing the roles on the second occasion. The number of indicators of non-understanding decreased in the second performance. Plough and Gass (1993) compared the performance of two groups of adult ESL learners on a spot-the-difference task and a survival task. One group was familiar with this kind of task, having been asked to do similar tasks before, while the other group was not. However, the results revealed no substantial differences in the two groups' performance. From these two studies it would appear that task repetition has an effect on interaction when it involves the same task but not when it involves a different task of the same type. Bygate (2001) reports similar results in a study that examined the effects of task and task-type repetition on aspects of learners' production (see Chapter 4).

Yule, Powers, and McDonald (1992) were able to demonstrate that repeating a task improves communicative efficiency. They asked pairs of high–low proficiency international teaching assistants to perform two similar map tasks containing referential problems, i.e. the maps the learners used were not identical. Using the typology of communicative outcomes shown in Figure 3.4, they found that whereas the participants favoured non-negotiated solutions in the first task they were more likely to opt for negotiated solutions in the second task. Yule *et al*. note that this confirms an earlier finding that 'speakers in the sender role can become more likely to negotiate solutions to referential conflicts simply through practice in performing a task' (ibid. 271).

Clearly more research is needed to investigate the effect of task repetition on interaction. This research should examine the relative effects of asking learners to perform the *same* task and a *similar* task, i.e. a task of the same kind with similar content. It should also examine whether the effects of task repetition transfer to entirely new tasks. In Chapter 4 we will examine further research that has examined the effects of task repetition, focusing on aspects of learner production.

Interlocutor familiarity

Learners can perform a task with other learners they know or with strangers. Plough and Gass (1993), in the same study referred to above, examined the effects of interlocutor familiarity. The results contrasted markedly for those obtained for task repetition. For example, familiar dyads used more clarification requests and confirmation checks than un-familiar dyads. This led Plough and Gass to suggest that 'the most fruitful areas for investigation are those which are relevant to the people involved as opposed to those which relate to task familiarity' (ibid. 52). Similarly Zuengler (1993: 193), in evaluating her own and others' research, con-cludes that it is not topic knowledge per se that is important but rather how 'topic knowledge is interactionally determined according to comparisons the interlocutors make of each other'.

There is ample evidence in sociolinguistic enquiry to show that speakers vary their use of language according to their addressee (see Bell 1984). It should come as no surprise, then, to find that the nature of the interaction varies according to whether the interlocutors are familiar with each other. It is, perhaps, somewhat surprising that this implementation factor has received so little attention from researchers investigating tasks.

Type of feedback

The task-implementation variable that has received the most attention is certainly the type of feedback. Feedback varies according to the indicator used to respond to the triggering move in a negotiation sequence (see Figure 3.1). This in turn has been found to affect the learner's response, in particular whether the output is modified or not. Pica (1988) found that when native speakers signalled a comprehension problem the learners modified their output by making it more grammatical in less than half of the cases and concluded that negotiation may work for acquisition because it supplies models of correct language, i.e. via comprehensible input, and not because of the opportunities to modify output that arise, i.e. via comprehensible output. However, Pica, Holliday, Lewis, and Morgenthaler (1989) showed that learners were more likely to modify their output by making it more grammatical following requests for clarification than following confirmation checks, suggesting that what is crucial is type of feedback.

This finding has led to a number of task-based studies designed to investigate the effects of feedback on (1) the output learners produce in their response move (referred to as *uptake*) and (2) subsequent acquisition. Many of these studies have involved focused tasks, i.e. tasks designed to permit a focus on some specific grammatical feature, and therefore will be considered in Chapter 5. Here we will consider one study that has examined the effects of feedback and pushed output arising in unfocused tasks.

Van den Branden (1997) investigated 10–11-year-old children performing a two-way task with native speaking peers and with a researcher. The type of feedback provided by these interlocutors differed, with the peers negotiating for meaning and content and the researcher negotiating more for form, i.e. alerting the learners to some of their morpho-syntactic errors and helping them to self-repair their errors. Van den Branden found that the children modified their output when confronted with negative feedback with both kinds of interlocutor. He also found that pushing learners to modify their output had beneficial effects when the learners performed a similar task as a post-test. Irrespective of the type of negotiation, it resulted in them producing a significantly greater amount of output, providing more essential information and displaying a greater range of vocabulary. However, neither type of feedback had any effect on syntactic complexity or grammatical correctness in the post-test. This study then suggests that negotiation involving pushed output aids communicative effectiveness but not grammatical accuracy. Somewhat surprisingly, it also suggests that the type of feedback (meaning-centred vs. form-centred) does not have a differential effect. One reason for this might be that the learners (children) treated all negotiation, whether of form or meaning, as message-oriented. Another reason might lie in the fact that the negotiation of form in Van den Branden's study was broadly targeted rather than focused on a specific linguistic feature. In Chapter 6 we will see that studies involving focused tasks have found that feedback has a positive effect on accuracy.

Summary

There have been fewer studies of task implementation variables than of task features to date. Conclusions, therefore, must necessarily be even more tentative. There is evidence to suggest that the participant role is an important factor—negotiation appears to be more effective if learners are active rather than passive participants in a task, for example, are required to contribute even when playing the listener role or are allowed to take the lead when playing the speaker in one-way tasks. Repeating a task results in increased interaction and greater communicative effectiveness. Doing a task with a familiar interlocutor can increase the amount of negotiation. Receiving feedback in the form of clarification requests rather than confirmation checks promotes modified output (uptake). However, there is no clear evidence as yet that any of these implementation variables impact on language acquisition.

Conclusion

This chapter has examined research that has investigated the role of task features and task implementation variables on interactions involving learners. The research has been informed primarily by the Interaction Hypothesis and, to a lesser extent, by work on communication strategies and communicative effectiveness. The goal of the research has been to identify the 'psycholinguistic properties' of tasks (Long 1989: 12).

We have been able to show that there are a number of design features and implementation features that impact systematically on interaction. For example, the extent to which negotiation of meaning occurs depends on such variables as whether the information exchange is required or optional and whether the outcome is closed or open. The extent to which learners prioritize clarity or economy is influenced by the extent to which the task provides contextual support. Communicative efficiency improves when the task is familiar to the learners. These are all important and useful insights. In general, however, the search for the psycholinguistic properties of tasks has proved somewhat disappointing. There are a number of reasons for this:

1 It is not clear to what extent the task variables that have been investigated are independent of each other or how they interact with each other. Also, the number of variables that influence interaction are potentially enormous.

2 There is an inherent problem in examining tasks without any consideration of other factors that are bound to impact on the kind of language use that occurs in a task performance, i.e. individual learner factors and situational factors. Such an approach views tasks deterministically and runs the risk of trivializing the contribution that learners make to the co-construction of the social reality of tasks.

3 The research to date has tended to focus generally on 'meaning negotiation'. However, the later version of the Interaction Hypothesis recognizes that interaction can foster acquisition through comprehensible
input, feedback, and modified output. What is needed is fine-grained
research directed at discovering the task features and implementation variables that result in interaction rich in these different aspects of meaning
negotiation. Pica *et al.*'s (1996) study is a move in this direction.
4 In general, the research examined in this chapter has focused on how
tasks affect interaction and has not attempted to show whether the interactive effects identified for different task features and implementation
variables have any impact on acquisition. We are really little further
forward in answering the question, 'What kind of tasks are needed to
promote L2 acquisition?'.

Despite these problems, the research can still be considered to be of value
if it is seen as contributing to an understanding of the potential factors
influencing interactional outcomes. Of course, the claim that we can only
identify the psycholinguistic potential of tasks is considerably weaker than
the claim that we can identify the psycholinguistic properties of tasks. The
question arises as to whether it is sufficiently powerful to be of use to teachers. Arguably, it is, as the very nature of language teaching makes it both
inevitable and even desirable that decisions are based on potentialities and
probabilities rather than on certainties. The construction of a task-based
syllabus (see Chapter 7) and the choice of methodological procedures in
task-based language teaching (see Chapter 8) can usefully draw on research
that points to the kinds of tasks and methods of implementation likely to
promote acquisition-rich interaction as long as it is remembered that what
actually transpires when the tasks are performed by specific learners in
particular classroom settings will not always match the results obtained by
researchers operating with different learners in a different setting.

Notes

1 Tarone (1983b: 65), however, adopts an interactive view of communicative
strategies, defining them as 'a mutual attempt of two interlocutors to agree
on a meaning in situations where requisite meaning structures do not seem
to be shared'. Such a definition encompasses the strategies involved in the
negotiation of meaning as well as those strategies that speakers use to overcome problems unassisted. For this reason, the less inclusive 'intra-
organism' perspective on communication strategies is adopted here.
2 Yule and McDonald (1990) suggest a way round this problem. They
designed a task in such a way that they could determine whether learners
had actually comprehended or not by examining whether specific
referential conflicts, in the form of discrepancies in the maps they were
working with, had been resolved.

3 It can also be argued, as a reader of an earlier draft of this chapter does, that the problems with the quantitative approach in research based on the Interaction Hypothesis have less to do with quantification per se than with what is counted; that is, the real problem is that researchers have chosen to count relatively uninteresting discourse phenomena.

4 Researchers have focused on the distinction between information gap tasks and opinion gap tasks. It should be noted, however, that Prabhu (1987) distinguishes a third kind of gap, which he calls a 'reasoning gap'. However, no research has examined interaction in relation to this type of task.

5 It is worthwhile noting that in one-way required information exchange tasks it is not always the person holding the information who does most of the talking. One strategy for completing such tasks is for the person without the information to interrogate his/her partner. When performed in this way the person with the information is required to do little more than respond 'yes' or 'no' (see Foster 1998: 11).

6 It is very likely that the degree of openness of a task will affect the nature of the interaction that takes place. Bitchener (1999) found that a free discussion task (where the topics were suggested but not stipulated) resulted in statistically more meaning negotiation than an open opinion gap task when performed by advanced learners of English.

7 The two closed Lego tasks in Berwick's study differed in the physical orientation of the learners. In one task they sat back to back and in the other they were facing each other. The results indicated that this influenced the type of negotiation that took place. For example, more comprehension checks occurred in the back to back Lego task but more confirmation checks occurred in the face to face condition.

8 Studies of tasks involving long turns are considered in Chapter 4, where, in particular, the effects of giving learners an opportunity to plan their output is considered.

9 This study was primarily concerned with comparing the quantity and quality of comprehensible input and output produced by and made available to learners when they interacted with other learners and when they interacted with native speakers.

4 Tasks, production, and language acquisition

Introduction

In the last chapter, we examined theories relating to the use of language in interaction and the task-oriented research they have spawned. Clearly, interaction involves learners speaking and writing, so in part, we have already considered how tasks can influence language production. However, the last chapter addressed how tasks are interactively accomplished, focusing on the negotiation of meaning, and did not consider the quantity and quality of learner output and how this contributes to acquisition. In this and the next chapter we will consider tasks in relation to learner output. This chapter examines how tasks affect such aspects as the overall fluency, accuracy, and complexity of the language that learners produce. It will be concerned with the production that results from *unfocused tasks* (see Chapter 1). The following chapter will consider output in terms of learners' use of specific linguistic features by examining *focused tasks*.

The general goal of language learning is the fluent, accurate, and pragmatically effective use of the target language. That is, learners generally aspire to speak without undue hesitation and fragmentation, without making (too many) linguistic errors, and without offending their interlocutors. How are learners to achieve this goal? To address this question we need to consider three more specific questions:

1 How is the learner's linguistic knowledge represented?
2 How is this knowledge processed in production?
3 How does using this knowledge in production contribute to language acquisition?

We will begin by examining the answers to these questions provided by a number of theories of L2 acquisition and then go on to consider how these theories have informed task-based investigations of learner production.

The representation of linguistic knowledge

The nature of linguistic knowledge is one of the most hotly disputed issues in linguistics and cognitive psychology. The controversy centres on three key issues: (1) whether linguistic knowledge is located in a specific linguistic or a more general cognitive faculty of the mind, (2) whether linguistic knowledge is implicit, explicit, or both, and (3) whether linguistic knowledge is rule- or exemplar-based. We will briefly consider each of these questions.

The nature of the faculty for language

Nativist theories of language (for example, Chomsky 1986) claim that human beings are unique in possessing a faculty for language and that this faculty constitutes a separate module of the human mind. Children are biologically endowed with knowledge of language in general, which equips them to acquire a particular language. According to Chomsky's theory of Universal Grammar (UG), this endowment takes the form of knowledge of certain abstract principles that govern the form of any single language, for example, the knowledge that sentences cannot be constructed by stringing together items in any order a speaker chooses (i.e. the structure-dependency principle). In addition, children have knowledge of the ways in which these principles can manifest themselves in particular languages and thus only need to discover which 'parameter' to select, for example whether a language has a subject-verb-object word order (as in English) or a subject-object-verb order (as in Japanese).[1] Equipped with this innate knowledge, children can acquire languages rapidly and effortlessly. According to UG, therefore, the linguistic knowledge (or 'competence') we draw on in 'performance' is highly specific. Hulstijn (2002) characterizes this view of language as 'symbolist'.

In contrast, a cognitive view stresses the essential similarity of linguistic knowledge and other forms of symbolic knowledge and disputes the existence of a separate mental module for language. Distributed processing models (Rumelhart, McClelland *et al.* 1986), for example, see linguistic knowledge as distributed widely over the neural network. It takes the form not of 'rules' or 'items' but of an elaborate system of weighted connections between non-representational nodes and, in this respect, is similar to any other kind of memory, for example perceptual memory. Linked to such a view of linguistic knowledge is the idea of 'chunking', the process of 'bringing together a set of already formed chunks in memory and welding them into a larger unit' (Newell 1990: 7) and, conversely, that of abstracting regularities from chunks. Learners learn languages both through repeated exposure to linguistic patterns in the input and through opportunities to repeat sequences in production. They also synthesize units forming larger wholes and analyze chunks into smaller components (N. Ellis 1996). This view of language is generally referred to as 'connectionist' or 'emergentist' (N. Ellis 1998; Hulstijn 2002).[2]

Thus, symbolist and connectionist theories assume very different views of how language is represented in the mind. Symbolist theories adopt an abstract view of linguistic representation. That is, linguistic knowledge is treated as consisting of a universal set of symbols, for example, phoneme, verb, noun phrase, morphological features, and rules for combining these symbols to construct the sentences of a language. As Gregg (1993) points out, symbolist theories make a clear distinction between 'property', i.e. the symbols and rules that constitute a linguistic system, and 'transition', i.e. the mechanisms responsible for making changes to the system. In contrast, connectionist theories view linguistic knowledge as a complex network of associations that allows for parallel processing. In such theories, no clear distinction is made between representation and learning mechanisms, as the networks are necessarily dynamic, constantly adjusting the associations in response to input frequencies. However, as Hulstijn (2002) has pointed out, it may be possible to reconcile these two accounts of representation. He suggests that as a result of constant activation, certain associations become relatively permanent mini-networks that can be viewed as symbol-like. According to this view of linguistic representation, then, associations can evolve into rules, allowing for hybrid models, i.e. models that incorporate both symbolist and connectionist representations (see Carpenter and Just 1999).

Implicit and explicit knowledge

Both generative and cognitive accounts of language acknowledge the distinction between implicit and explicit knowledge. Implicit knowledge refers to that knowledge of language that a speaker manifests in performance but has no awareness of. For example, native speakers of English know that the sentence,

* The teacher explained Koji the rule.

is ungrammatical and that the sentence,

The teacher showed Koji the rule.

is grammatical but are generally at a loss to explain how they are able to make the correct grammatical judgements. Explicit knowledge refers to knowledge about language that speakers are aware of and, if asked, can verbalize. For example, I know that there are some verbs, like 'explain', which are Latinate in origin and which do not permit dative alternation while there are other verbs, like 'show', that are Anglo-Saxon in origin and do. Whereas implicit knowledge is typically highly proceduralized, allowing rapid access, explicit knowledge is available only via controlled processing. It is true that, with practice, access to and use of explicit knowledge can be speeded up (Ellis 1993) but this results only in 'false automatization' (Hulstijn 2002) as it still does not allow for the easy and immediate access that characterizes the use of implicit knowledge.

The distinction between implicit and explicit knowledge is not controversial. What is disputed, however, is the relationship between them. According to Bialystok (1991), children begin by acquiring implicit knowledge and then 'analyse' it, thus making it explicit. Implicit knowledge, then, serves as a basis for the development of explicit knowledge. Such a model may also be applicable in some L2 learning situations, for example, when learners begin by picking up an L2 through natural exposure but it is less relevant to classroom situations where the teaching of explicit knowledge is emphasized. The question here is whether explicit knowledge can convert into implicit knowledge. Very different positions have been espoused on this point. Krashen (1981), Zobl (1995),[3] and Hulstijn (2002) adopt a non-interface position, i.e. explicit knowledge does not convert into implicit knowledge, Sharwood Smith (1981) and DeKeyser (1998) argue for a strong interface position and I have proposed a weak-interface position, according to which explicit knowledge facilitates the development of implicit knowledge rather than changes into it (see Ellis 1994). According to this view, explicit knowledge serves to prime attention to form in the input and thereby to activate the processes involved in the acquisition of implicit knowledge. My theory is explained more fully in Chapter 5.

Rule- and exemplar-based linguistic knowledge

A further issue relates to implicit knowledge. Does it consist of rules that enable speakers to construct sentences productively or does it consist of separate chunks that are stored and accessed as wholes? This question, then, addresses the extent to which our linguistic knowledge is analysed or unanalysed, grammatical or lexical. Consider the sentence:

Do you have any throat lozenges?

It is possible that this sentence is based on knowledge of the rules for constructing yes/no questions in English. But it is also possible that the production of this sentence drew on a fixed pattern, 'Do you have any ____?', functioning in memory as a lexical item and accessed as such.

There is now widespread recognition both by linguists, for example, Bolinger 1975, Pawley and Syder 1983, Nattinger and DeCarrico 1992, and by SLA researchers, Wong Fillmore 1976, Myles *et al.* 1999, that formulaic chunks constitute a substantial part of linguistic knowledge. Cognitive psychologists also acknowledge the existence of both modes of representation. Matthews *et al.* (1989), for example, conclude from a series of experiments investigating the acquisition of artificial grammars that their subjects constructed both a rule-based system, which is abstract in nature, and a memory-based system consisting of exemplars of possible grammatical strings. Similarly, Reber (1989: 226) has argued that implicit learning involves both abstract rules and 'a rather concrete, instantiated memorial system'. Thus, there appears to be plenty of evidence for what Skehan (1998a) calls 'a dual mode system'. Indeed, it is quite likely that speakers can produce sentences such as the one above directly by drawing on their memory-based system, or computationally by accessing their rule-based system. Hulstijn's (2002) claim that linguistic knowledge is both associative and rule-based in nature supports such a view.

The existence of a dual-mode system, then, is also not especially controversial but, again, disagreement occurs when the relationship between the two systems is at stake. One view is that the two systems are entirely independent and do not interact. Krashen and Scarcella (1978), for example, have argued that L2 learners do not analyse the formulaic chunks they have acquired but rather acquire rules independently by processing input. Wong Fillmore (1976), on the other hand, suggests that prefabricated patterns serve as a basis for subsequent rule development when learners come to recognize the separate units that comprise the patterns. The former view is generally held by grammarians who emphasize the generative nature of language, while the latter view is supported by cognitive psychologists who see word sequences as a database for the subsequent evolution of rules as patterns of connection that become fixed in memory, for example, N. Ellis 1996; Hulstijn 2002.

Final comment

From this brief discussion of how language is represented in the mind it is clear that a tension exists between generative accounts of language, which see language as a separate mental faculty and emphasize its rule-based nature, and cognitive psychological accounts, which view language as similar to other symbolic systems and emphasize the dual nature of linguistic knowledge. One of the major reasons for these differences lies in the relative importance that generative linguists and cognitive psychologists attach to performance. Generative linguists are primarily concerned with describing and explaining linguistic competence, which they treat as independent of performance (see, for example, Gregg 1989 for the supposed superiority of such an approach). Cognitive psychologists, however, work with information-processing models that try to account for how knowledge is used in performance; thus, for them, how knowledge is represented is a function of how it is used. Not surprisingly, perhaps, task-based researchers have been more attracted to cognitive models of linguistic representation (see, for example, the work of Swain 1995, Skehan 1998a, and Bygate 2001).

Language production

How then is spoken language produced? Information-processing models such as that proposed by Levelt (1989) see language production as a complex, multi-faceted phenomenon, involving a series of interlocking stages. Levelt's model contains three principal processing components, hierarchically organized. Processing begins in the Conceptualizer. The speaker establishes a communicative goal. Through macro-planning this is broken down into a series of sub-goals and the information needed for realizing these is retrieved. Then through micro-planning the propositional shape of each chunk of information to be communicated is assigned in accordance with the speaker's information perspective. In the next stage, Formulation, the speaker produces a phonetic plan for what is to be said. This involves selecting appropriate phonological, grammatical, and lexical features and mapping them on to the preverbal message. Finally, in the Articulation stage, the phonetic plan is converted into actual speech. Levelt recognizes that speech production does not proceed in a serial fashion but rather involves 'incremental processing', with the processes involved in conceptualizing, formulating, and articulating a message running in parallel.

Human beings possess a limited processing capacity. That is, they find it difficult to perform more than a single task at one time, especially if the knowledge and skills required to perform the tasks have not been automatized (Shriffin and Schneider 1978). A complex skill such as speaking requires the performance of a number of simultaneous mental operations, potentially causing speakers to experience considerable processing pressure. How then is speaking possible? How do speakers cope with the pressure?

According to Skehan (1998a) speaking is possible because of the way language is represented. Learners are able to draw on an exemplar-based system in the formulation stage, thus obtaining quick and easy access to the linguistic means needed to construct a phonetic plan. It is for this reason that speakers need to acquire a solid repertoire of formulaic chunks. Instance-based theories of fluency (for example, Logan 1988) suggest that fluent speech is not based on the rapid computation of rules but through the retrieval of ready-made exemplars, which require minimal processing capacity because they are accessed as wholes. According to this view, then, language must be represented as an exemplar-based system, in part at least, because if it was not, normal fluent speech would be impossible.

An assumption of this line of argument is that speakers can encode their propositional plans by recourse to ready-made chunks of stored language. However, it is not difficult to see that there will be times when this is not possible. Novel messages, for example, may not be expressible (or not effectively expressible) by means of canned language; they are likely to require careful formulation. In such cases, speakers can fall back on their rule-based system, constructing phonetic plans from their store of generative rules to achieve the precision and expressive force the message requires. It is likely, though, that the extra processing effort this demands will result in overload, reflected in speech marked by pauses and other disfluencies that signal that planning is effortful (Goldman-Eisler 1968). L2 learners are likely to experience special problems in formulating phonetic plans that require rule computation. In many cases the necessary connections will not have been firmly established in their implicit knowledge system, making access slow and effortful. In other cases, they may entirely lack implicit knowledge and be forced to fall back on explicit knowledge, which, as we have seen, is not amenable to rapid deployment. Further problems can arise if learners make efforts to articulate their messages in accordance with target language phonological norms—one reason, perhaps, why learners' L2 pronunciation typically manifests high levels of L1 transfer.

Two important points follow from this view of language production. The first is that there are likely to be trade-offs as L2 learners struggle to conceptualize, formulate, and articulate messages. Attention to one aspect of production is likely to be at the expense of others. For example, L2 learners concerned primarily with what they want to say, i.e. with conceptualizing, may not be able to give much attention to how they say it, i.e. with formulation, with the result that their speech is full of errors. This is especially likely if they are unable to draw on a rich exemplar-based system to ease the processing load. Conversely, L2 learners' attention to accuracy may interfere with their ability to conceptualize, leading to marked disfluency.

The need for L2 speakers to trade off accuracy and complexity as a result of limited processing capacity is not accepted by everyone, however. Robinson (1995), for example, adopts a multiple resources view of attention, according to which speakers have the capacity to handle different demands on their attention in parallel. According to this view, task demands affect accuracy and complexity in tandem. Skehan and Foster (2001) report the results of a factor-analytic study of the rival claims of the multiple resources and limited attentional capacity models. They report that measures of accuracy and complexity loaded on to different factors and conclude that 'the results do not sit well with the multiple resources view of attention'. The view adopted in this chapter is that accuracy and complexity can pose competing demands on learners, which can be manipulated by varying the kinds of tasks they are asked to perform.

The second point is that L2 learners' problems in production may be eased if they are given time to plan before they begin to speak. There are, in fact, several different kinds of planning, each serving a different function in the production process. First, there is what Wendel (1997) calls 'strategic planning'. This is the kind of planning referred to above—the planning that occurs before a speaker engages in communicative activity. It involves what Schmidt (2001) calls 'preparatory attention' and helps individuals to perform actions with greater accuracy and speed. Ochs distinguishes 'planned' and 'unplanned' discourse, defining the former as 'discourse that has been thought out and organized prior to its expression' (1979: 55). As might be expected, there are marked differences between these two types of discourse. Planned discourse, for example, manifests greater complexity in clause and sentence construction, and acquisitionally more advanced grammatical structures.

Second, there is the kind of online planning that Levelt discusses. This is the planning that occurs while a speaker is engaged in communicative activity. It involves both macro- and micro-planning, the former involving 'the long range semantic organization of a sizable chunk of speech' and the latter 'purely local functions, like marking clause boundaries and selecting words' (Butterworth 1980: 159). In contrast to strategic planning, which is necessarily conscious, online planning can take place with little or no awareness.

Thirdly, there is monitoring. This can be viewed as a kind of corrective planning, carried out when the speaker realizes that there is something wrong with an initial plan. Levelt's model affords a number of opportunities for monitoring. The speaker can monitor the preverbal message in the Conceptualizer, the phonetic plan in the Formulator or the actual articulation of the message as it is spoken. Monitoring, like online processing, takes place during the process of production. As Krashen (1985) has pointed out, L2 learners can monitor by feel, using their implicit knowledge, or they can monitor much more consciously, using their explicit knowledge.

One of the most obvious ways of manipulating learner output in the performance of a task is by creating conditions that favour one or more of these types of planning. For example, the researcher can allocate time for strategic planning (Mehnert 1998), can allow plenty of time for online planning (Hulstijn and Hulstijn 1984), or can encourage corrective monitoring by setting some post-task requirement (Skehan and Foster 1997). In this way researchers anticipate an effect on the kind of language learners produce and through this on their interlanguage development.

Production and language acquisition

From the perspective of the kind of computational model of language that informs this chapter, it is not so obvious that speaking plays a role in L2 acquisition. Krashen (1985) has claimed that 'speaking is a result of acquisition, not its cause'.[4] In one sense at least, it would seem he must be right—learners cannot learn items or rules that are completely new from their own production, they can only learn them from input. Of course, they may be able to learn new features from collaborative production, a point taken up in Chapter 6. Sometimes production may even get in the way of learning. Learners who are skilful in using communication strategies to overcome problems, for example, coining words like 'picture place' for 'art gallery', may become so strategically adept at maximizing their existing linguistic competence that they have no need to add to it by attending to new forms in the input. This may be what happens with learners like Wes

(Schmidt 1983), who over several years failed to increase the accuracy of his production, possibly because his personal goals for learning English and the type of communicative situations he found himself in required fluency rather than accuracy, leading him to concentrate on developing his strategic rather than his grammatical competence. Nevertheless, as we will now see, it is possible to develop a theoretical case for production playing a role in acquisition.

Skehan (1998a), drawing on and extending Swain (1995), suggests that production has six roles: (1) it serves to generate better input through the feedback that learners' efforts at production elicit; (2) it forces syntactic processing (i.e. it obliges learners to pay attention to grammar); (3) it allows learners to test out hypotheses about the target-language grammar; (4) it helps to automatize existing L2 knowledge; (5) it provides opportunities for learners to develop discourse skills, for example by producing 'long turns'; and (6) it is important for helping learners to develop a 'personal voice' by steering conversations on to topics they are interested in contributing to. To these, another role (7) might be added—production provides the learner with 'auto-input' (Schmidt and Frota 1986) in the sense that learners can attend to the 'input' provided by their own productions.

A close look at these seven roles, however, suggests that several of them do not contribute to acquisition directly but rather indirectly, through the input that learners secure for themselves by their efforts to speak. (1), (3), (6), and (7) would seem to fall into this category. In the case of (1) learners obtain feedback, i.e. negative input, from their interlocutors. Similarly in (3), while learners can venture the use of new structures in their output (which may be of some value), the validity of their hypotheses can only be established from the feedback they receive. (6) also implies that the input that learners receive can be enriched through production, in this case when the opportunity to talk on a topic of interest 'charges' the input, making it more powerful for acquisition (see Ellis 1998 for arguments in support of learner topicalization). These roles relate to the contribution that interaction can make to acquisition, for example, through recasts that reformulate a learner utterance (see Chapter 3). In the case of (7), output does play a more direct role in acquisition, making learners aware of what they do not yet know or cannot yet do in the L2. Swain (1985), following Schmidt and Frota (1986), refers to this function of output as 'noticing-the-gap'. This term is ambiguous, however. It can refer simply to the idea of learners becoming aware of a gap in their interlanguages, i.e. they recognize that there is something they cannot say or cannot say properly in the L2. In this sense, production clearly does have a role. But noticing-the-gap can also refer to learners both becoming aware of a gap and attempting to do something about it, i.e. by comparing what they actually said with what they would have been capable of saying if they had used their most advanced interlanguage knowledge. In this latter sense, noticing-the-gap can only be achieved when learners listen to themselves, thus making input out of their own output. I would argue that it is this latter sense of noticing-the-gap that is the more important. Thus, although these four roles are important for production, they do not constitute an argument to support the view that production is central for acquisition.

The other roles Skehan mentions, however, suggest that production can contribute more directly and centrally to acquisition. In effect, there would seem to be two basic arguments relating to the contribution of production. The first is that production enables learners to practise what they already know, thus helping them to automatize their discourse and linguistic knowledge. Roles (4) and (5) belong here. The second argument relates to (2), the idea that production engages syntactic processing in a way that comprehension does not.

The argument that production contributes to automaticity assumes that there is more to language acquisition than internalizing new forms and rules; there is also the need to achieve control over what has already been acquired. Bialystok (1982, 1990) distinguishes two dimensions of language acquisition: analysis and control. Analysis refers to the extent to which linguistic knowledge is differentiated, structured, and conscious, with knowledge gradually becoming more 'analysed' over time. This relates to the implicit/explicit distinction we discussed earlier. Bialystok initially used the term 'control' to refer to the ease and speed with which learners could access their knowledge. More recently, however, she has used it to refer to both the selection of items of knowledge and to their co-ordination in the performance of some task. In terms of this model, then, production can contribute to the control dimension of acquisition by practising the processes of selection and co-ordination of linguistic knowledge.

Skill-learning models of language acquisition also recognize the role of production in automatizing linguistic knowledge. For example, Anderson's Adaptive Control of Thought Model (see Anderson 2000) views language learning, like other kinds of skill, as involving a progression from an initial declarative knowledge stage to a final procedural stage where knowledge is automatic. According to Anderson, L2 learners achieve proceduralization through extensive practice in using the L2. Skill-building theories also view proceduralized knowledge as highly specific, with different sets of skills involved in comprehension and production (see Anderson 1993: 37–8). The implication here is that practice in processing input will only serve to develop learners' ability to comprehend the target language, not to produce it, and that production is necessary to develop automaticity in speaking.[5]

There is also the question of what kind of practice is required to achieve automatization of linguistic knowledge. The behaviourist view of learning (see, for example, Lado 1964) considered that control could be achieved, i.e. a 'habit' formed, if learners practised specific structures in highly mechanistic, form-focused exercises. However, cognitive theories of language acquisition emphasize the need for practice in the context of 'real operating conditions' (Johnson 1988). That is, learners need the opportunity to practise language in the same conditions that apply in real-life situations—in communication, where their primary focus is on message conveyance rather than linguistic accuracy. This provides a strong rationale for task-based teaching, given that the aim of tasks is to afford opportunities for learners to perform their competence in activities that emphasize using rather than learning language (see Chapter 1).

A theoretical case for the importance of production in task-based teaching, then, can be made solely on the grounds that it will promote greater control and automaticity. But can a theoretical case also be made for production assisting interlanguage development, either in the sense of extending it by adding new features or in the sense of complexifying it by inducing restructuring? Swain (1985, 1995) and Skehan (1996a, 1998a) have presented arguments that production does indeed perform these functions.

According to Swain's Output Hypothesis, production causes learners to engage in syntactic processing and in so doing promotes acquisition. Swain (1985) initially formulated the Output Hypothesis as a complement to Krashen's Input Hypothesis, arguing that evaluations of immersion programmes in Canada demonstrated that comprehensible input alone was insufficient to ensure that learners achieved high levels of grammatical and sociolinguistic competence. She pointed out that learners could employ 'semantic processing' to comprehend input without having to pay close attention to linguistic form—a point we discussed in Chapter 2. She argued that, in contrast, production necessitates syntactic processing, especially if learners are 'pushed' to produce messages that are concise and socially appropriate. As Swain (1995: 127) puts it, 'learners ... can fake it, so to speak, in comprehension, but they cannot do so in the same way in production'. Production requires learners to process syntactically; they have to pay some attention to form.[6]

Building on Swain's Output Hypothesis, Skehan suggests that production requires attention to form but only sometimes. He distinguishes three aspects of production: (1) fluency, the capacity of the learner to mobilize his/her system to communicate meaning in real time; (2) accuracy, the ability of the learner to handle whatever level of interlanguage complexity he/she has currently achieved; and (3) complexity, the utilization of interlanguage structures that are 'cutting edge', elaborate, and structured. Skehan suggests that language users vary in the extent to which they emphasize fluency, accuracy, or complexity, with some tasks predisposing them to focus on fluency, others on accuracy, and yet others on complexity. Furthermore, these different aspects of production draw on different systems of language. Fluency requires learners to draw on their memory-based system, accessing and deploying ready-made chunks of language, and, when problems arise, using communication strategies to get by. In this case, then, the kind of processing learners engage in is semantic rather than syntactic. In contrast, accuracy and, in particular, complexity are achieved by learners drawing on their rule-based system and thus require syntactic processing. Skehan (1995) describes the two types of processing in this way:

> When accessibility and time pressure are paramount, a lexical mode of communication will be relied on, which draws on a capacious, well-organized, and very rapid memory system. In contrast, when exactness or creativity matter, analysability, and a concern for form, for syntax, and for planning, will predominate.

In this way, Skehan explains why output has to be 'pushed' before it engages the learner's syntactical knowledge. It should be noted, though, that Skehan is careful to stress that both types of processing are important and that task-based instruction needs to cater to both.

On the face of it, Swain's and Skehan's arguments are persuasive—pushed output promotes acquisition. However, neither really provides a convincing explanation for how production leads to acquisition. Skehan avoids the issue entirely. Swain (1995) falls back on the metaphor of 'stretching interlanguage' but never explains what this means. She also suggests that learners' efforts at producing may make them aware of their linguistic limitations, which, as we have already seen, does constitute a limited role for production, but she then goes on to suggest that this cues learners 'to listen for a solution in the future input' (ibid. 127). In other words, she endorses Schmidt's 'noticing hypothesis' (Schmidt 1990), and thus, affirms the centrality of input rather than output in the acquisition process. In short, while the importance of production for acquisition has been clearly established, it would seem to play only a limited causal role, motivating learners to attend to input, but not contributing directly to the processing needed for acquisition to take place.

However, it may be possible to establish a stronger causal role for production. In accordance with Logan's (1988) Instance Theory (see Note 5), Skehan (1998a) suggests that lexicalized units may in part be acquired as a result of storing expressions that, in the first place, were generated by the rule-based system. In other words, learners construct strings consciously and then store them as wholes, thus avoiding the need to assemble them again later. In this way, then, production can serve as a conduit for material from the rule-based to the memory-based system. However, Skehan does not consider the other possibility, namely that learners break down formulaic chunks into their component parts and thereby bootstrap their way to syntactical rules. In this respect, he seems to silently concur with Krashen and Scarcella (1978), who explicitly reject any role for formulaic speech in interlanguage development. Clark (1974) in first language acquisition, Wong Fillmore (1976), Ellis (1984), Rescorla and Okuda (1987), and Myles *et al.*

(1999) in second language acquisition, show how learners work on their formulas systematically, gradually releasing elements for more creative use. This process of analysis occurs through production as learners experiment with combining chunks, replacing one item with another in a chunk, slotting in additional items, and modifying the form of one or more of the items. It constitutes what Widdowson (1989: 135) has called 'a packaging view of language use and acquisition'. It is difficult to imagine learners packaging and unpackaging their pre-assembled chunks without the opportunity to try them out in production. Production, then, may constitute the mechanism that connects the learner's dual systems, enabling movement to occur from the memory-based to the rule-based system and vice versa. If this interpretation is correct, learners may not be so reliant on input as has been generally assumed in SLA. They may be able to utilize their own internal resources, via using them in production, to both construct and complexify their interlanguages. Such an account affords an explanation of what Swain might have meant when she talked about output helping learners to stretch their interlanguages.

Task performance and production: a review of the research

In this section we will examine how SLA researchers have drawn on the various theoretical perspectives outlined above in order to investigate what effect task design and task implementation have on production. We will begin by considering the dependent variable of these studies, production, discussing how this has been operationalized for purposes of analysis. Then we will consider the independent variables in relation to both task design and task implementation.

Measuring language production

The measurement of language production, especially oral production, has long proved problematic for researchers. A major difficulty has been establishing a unit of analysis that can serve as a basis for assessing other, more specific features, for example, clausal complexity. The lack of an established unit makes it difficult to compare results across studies. This problem is exacerbated by the failure of many researchers to provide full and explicit definitions of their chosen unit of measure. To overcome this problem, Foster, Tonkyn, and Wigglesworth (2000) have proposed the 'analysis of speech unit' (AS-unit):

> An AS-unit is a single speaker's utterance consisting either of an independent clause, or sub-clausal unit, together with any subordinate clause(s) associated with either.

They go on to provide careful definitions of 'independent clause', 'sub-clausal unit', and 'subordinate clause'. Such a unit, if adopted by task-based researchers, will go a long way to overcoming the problem referred to above. However, the research to be reported in this section did not employ the AS-unit or any other standard unit of measurement.

Researchers have used a wide range of specific measures to quantify learner production. In an early study, for example, Tong-Fredericks (1984) measured the number of words learners produced per minute of speaking, the frequency of turns, and the amount of self-correcting. Berwick (1990, 1993), in addition to the measures of interaction we considered in Chapter 3, also examined a number of variables relating to language production, for example exophoric reference, for example, the use of context-bound referential pronouns such as 'this' and 'these', and anaphoric reference, for example, the use of pronouns to refer back to some previously mentioned referent. Brown (1991) measured task performance in terms of repetitions, prompts, rephrasings, repairs, instructional input, i.e. when one interlocutor explained something to another or gave an example, and hypothesizing. Newton and Kennedy (1996) investigated task-based production in terms of specific linguistic features, prepositions, and conjunctions. To a large extent, measures of production have been intuitively chosen or data driven, rather than theory-based.

An exception is Skehan. Skehan (1996a) distinguishes between *fluency*, *accuracy*, and *complexity*, drawing on his theoretical claims about a dual-competence system and trade-offs in learners' focus of attention. The following review of the research will discuss the results obtained by the different studies in relation to these three aspects of production. Inevitably this will involve a degree of interpretation of the results, as many of the original studies were not explicitly constructed with these three general categories in mind. Nevertheless, the danger that this approach entails is, hopefully, more than offset by its explanatory power. Table 4.1 classifies some of the specific measures used in the various studies in terms of fluency, accuracy, and complexity.

A key question is whether such measures as those shown in Table 4.1 do in fact distinguish fluency, accuracy, and complexity. Do they measure what they purport to measure? One way of demonstrating this is through a factor analysis of a range of measures purporting to measure the three aspects of language production. Skehan and Foster (1997) report the results of such an analysis. Measures of fluency, accuracy, and complexity obtained from learners' performance of three different tasks loaded consistently on to separate factors in accordance with predictions. This suggests that these dimensions of performance are indeed distinct and that they can be measured separately.

Dimension	Measures
1 Fluency	number of words per minute
	number of syllables per minute
	number of pauses of one/two second(s) or longer
	mean length of pauses
	number of repetitions
	number of false starts
	number of reformulations
	length of run, i.e. number of words per pausally defined unit
	number of words per turn
2 Accuracy	number of self-corrections
	percentage of error-free clauses
	target-like use of verb tenses
	target-like use of articles
	target-like use of vocabulary
	target-like use of plurals
	target-like use of negation
	ratio of indefinite to definite articles
3 Complexity	number of turns per minute
	anaphoric reference (as opposed to exophoric reference)
	lexical richness, e.g. number of word families used,
	percentage of lexical to structural words, type-token ratio
	proportion of lexical verbs to copula
	percentage of words functioning as lexical verbs
	percentage of occurrence of multi-propositional utterances
	amount of subordination, e.g. total number of clauses
	divided by total number of c-units
	frequency of use of conjunctions
	frequency of use of prepositions
	frequency of hypothesizing statements

Table 4.1: A classification of production variables used in task-based research

The effects of task design variables

Using the framework for describing tasks outlined in Chapter 1, we can see that task design variables involve: (1) the type of input the task supplies; (2) the task conditions; and (3) the task outcomes. Potentially each of these aspects of task design can impact on learner production. One of the major problems in investigating task factors, is that one factor, such as whether the task poses a single or double demand on the learner, may interact with other factors such as contextual support and discourse mode, making it unclear which factor is primarily responsible for the observed effect.

Input variables

Under this heading we will examine a number of specific design variables: contextual support, the number of elements to be manipulated, and topic.

1 Contextual support

Some of the most popular tasks in both research and teaching involve information transfer. That is, the input to the task takes the form of some non-verbal device, such as a picture, a map or a diagram, which must then be communicated verbally to the hearer. Such tasks can be designed so that the speakers can see the non-verbal device while they are communicating, a here-and-now condition, or so that they cannot see it, a there-and-then condition. This input distinction is potentially an important one as there is a wealth of research to show that reference to displaced activity is more cognitively demanding than reference to contiguous events. For example, the ability to refer linguistically to events displaced in time and place emerges later than the ability to refer to the here-and-now in L1 acquisition (Brown and Bellugi 1964). Also, reference to displaced activity requires access to tense and aspectual systems that are late acquired in L2 acquisition (Bardovi-Harlig 1994). It is reasonable to assume, therefore, that there will be differences in the output that results from tasks reflecting this design difference. Specifically, it can be hypothesized that here-and-now tasks will result in greater fluency and there-and-then tasks in greater complexity and, perhaps, accuracy.

A number of studies have investigated these hypotheses. Berwick (1990, 1993), in a study we considered in Chapter 3, found that what he calls 'experiential tasks' (where contextual support was available to the speaker) resulted in more exophoric reference than 'expository tasks' (where contextual support was not available). In contrast, the expository tasks favoured the use of anaphora. This can be taken as evidence that tasks without contextual support result in more complex language use. Robinson (1995) found that oral narratives produced while the speakers were able to look at a picture strip tended to be more fluent, i.e. they had longer length or runs, while narratives produced while the speakers could not see the picture strips tended to display greater accuracy, i.e. more target-like use of articles, and greater lexical complexity, i.e. a higher percentage of lexical words. However, this study failed to show that contextual support had a major impact on task performance as differences on most of the variables Robinson investigated were not statistically significant. Robinson, Ting, and Urwin (1995) report the results of two follow-up studies, which produced mixed results. One study, a replication of Robinson (1995), indicated that the there-and-then condition resulted in greater accuracy and lexical complexity but did not affect fluency. A second study, where structural support was operationalized in terms of whether the speaker's map had the route to be described drawn on it or not, found an effect for fluency but none for accuracy or complexity. Rahimpour (1997) found that narratives produced under a there-and-then condition were more accurate but less fluent than those produced under a here-and-now condition. Skehan and Foster (1999) examined the effects of contextual support by comparing learner production in a watch-and-tell condition, i.e. the learners had to simultaneously watch a Mr. Bean video and speak, and a watch-then-tell condition, i.e. they told the story after they had finished watching the video. Skehan and Foster found that the watch-then-tell condition led to more complex language use but that there was no statistically significant difference with regard to fluency and accuracy. In a study carried out in a testing situation, Iwashita, Elder, and McNamara (2001) found an effect for what they called 'immediacy' on accuracy (the there-and-then condition producing more accurate language use than the here-and-now) but no effect on fluency or complexity. Interestingly, the result for immediacy was replicated in an analysis of the ratings of learners' performances. The results of these studies are far from uniform but overall they suggest that when there is an absence of contextual support, production is more complex and accurate but less fluent, as claimed by Robinson (1995).

There is also the question of the medium through which the support is provided—pictorial (as in the studies referred to above), written, or aural. Brown *et al.* (1984) report that the language users they investigated, native-speaking high-school pupils, never gave up on tasks that provided pictorial support but did so when the task input was aural, suggesting that tasks involving pictures might be easier. Swain and Lapkin (2001) compared Grade 8 French immersion students' performance of an information gap task involving a picture-story and a dictogloss task where they first listened to the story and took notes before attempting to reconstruct it. In effect, then, it examined the relative effects of pictorial support and self-provided (and, therefore, variable) written support. Swain and Lapkin predicted that because the dictogloss task afforded the learners a linguistically-encoded content, they would have more time to attend to form (a corollary of accuracy) than in the information gap task where the information was supplied pictorially and thus had to be encoded linguistically by the learners. However, there were no statistically significant differences in the frequency of 'language-related episodes', i.e. occasions where the learners talked about the language they were producing, questioned their use of language or engaged in corrective moves, although the range of language-related episodes produced by the learners completing the dictogloss task was notably smaller, suggesting that the linguistic support this task provided constrained student responses to a greater extent than the information gap task.[7]

It is not really possible to come to any clear conclusions regarding the effects of contextual support on learner production. Obviously there are effects but precisely what these are remains uncertain. There is some evidence to suggest that a task that allows for a 'here-and-now' orientation promotes fluency. Equally, a 'there-and-then' orientation seems linked to greater complexity and, sometimes, to greater accuracy. However, such effects may not be evident in a situation where learners know they are being tested. The medium of the contextual support may also be important, with different effects evident for pictorial, written, and aural input.

2 Number of elements in a task

A second input factor concerns the number of features that need to be manipulated by the speakers. Brown *et al.* (1984) propose that the number of elements and relationships between these elements influences the difficulty of the task. For example, a story with four females interacting proved more difficult to narrate than a story with only one female and one male character. Similarly, a story with flashbacks and different locations was more difficult than a story that took place at a single time and in one location. Robinson (2001) compared learners' performance on two map tasks that differed in terms of the amount of information provided on the map. He reports that the learners produced more fluent language when working with the simple map and lexically more complex language with the detailed map. However, the tasks in this study also differed with regard to another variable (topic familiarity), making it impossible to determine the relative effects of the two task variables on learner production. Also, in calculating the type-token ratio (lexical complexity), Robinson did not correct for length of text, which has been shown to skew this measure.

3 Topic

An input variable that has received little attention is that of 'topic'. This is probably because of the difficulty of classifying topics in a rigorous manner. To a large extent the topic effects will be variable, depending on the individual learner's familiarity with a particular subject area. Selinker and Douglas (1985) argued that learners' representation of L2 knowledge is closely tied to particular 'discourse domains' and reported a study that showed that the extent to which learners conformed to target language norms depended on the domain in which they were operating. However, it is also possible that some topics are inherently more demanding or interesting than others.

In a study that set out to investigate the effects of different learner variables on task performance, Lange (2000) found that, contrary to expectations, the only variable to produce a statistically significant effect on the learners' performance was the task itself. She used two tasks. These had a similar design, both involving the exchange of information and opinions. Thus, the tasks differed only with regard to topic—one task centred around selecting a candidate for a heart transplant, while the other involved deciding who should be released from prison on probation. The Prison Task resulted in a significantly greater amount of talk, i.e. overall number of words produced, although there was no difference on speed of delivery or accuracy, i.e. accurate verb forms used. Lange also comments that the learners reported finding the Prison Task more interesting because the issues raised during discussion were more controversial and challenging.

In Chapter 3 we noted that topic familiarity has a dampening effect on the amount of meaning negotiation that occurs (Gass and Varonis 1984). In contrast, this variable has been found to have a positive effect on learner output. Chang (1999), for example, found that when learners had prior knowledge of a topic they performed a monologic task more fluently. However, no effect on accuracy was found in this study.

Task conditions

Somewhat surprisingly there has been little research into what effects different task conditions have on production, although, as we saw in Chapter 3, several studies have investigated their effects on meaning negotiation. Two factors will be considered—shared vs. split information and task demands.

1 Shared vs. split information

Newton and Kennedy (1996: 320) found greater use of conjunctions (a measure of complexity) in shared information tasks than in split information tasks. They explain this finding as follows:

> Shared information tasks involve interlocutors in having to argue a case on the basis of information they share rather than checking the accuracy of the information held by the interlocutors ... It is this reasoning or argumentation that requires conjunctions to mark the relationships between propositions.

This suggests the crucial factor may not be the task condition but the type of discourse that arises—shared tasks typically involve decision-making, for example, deciding on a new lay out for a zoo, and thus require argumentation, whereas split-information tasks result in description. Newton and Kennedy's finding is of interest, because it suggests that shared tasks involving decision-making are effective in 'pushing' learners' production. In this respect, shared-information tasks seem to be more effective than split-information tasks, although, as we have already seen, the latter work better in promoting meaning negotiation. Again, then, we see that different types of tasks can complement each other.

2 Task demands

Robinson (2001) suggests that production is influenced by whether learners are asked to carry out a single task demand or whether a secondary task demand is added. He gives as an example a task that requires learners to describe a route on a map where the route to be taken is marked on the map (single task demand) compared with a task involving a map where the route has not been marked. Robinson argues that the latter involves a dual task demand because the learners have to work out the route for themselves at the same time as giving directions. He cites an unpublished study (Robinson and Lim 1993) that found that learners were more fluent when performing with the map with the route marked on it. However, no effect on accuracy or complexity was found in this study.

Skehan and Foster's (1999) study can also be interpreted in terms of task demands. There were four conditions: (1) watch-and-tell simultaneously; (2) story-line given and then watch-and-tell simultaneously; (3) watch first and then watch-and-tell simultaneously; and (4) watch-then-tell. Conditions (1), (2), and (3) involved a dual task demand, i.e. learners had to follow the story on the video at the same time as telling it, whereas condition (4) involved a single task demand, as the learners had already had the chance to watch the video and work out the story. This study, as we noted above, found that the watch-then-tell condition resulted in more complex language but not more fluent or accurate language. However, as we noted above, this finding can also be explained in terms of the degree of contextual support the task conditions afforded learners and also by the different discourse modes they gave rise to (see below). This study is indicative of the problem mentioned at the beginning of this section, namely the difficulty of deciding which of several factors is responsible for a particular effect.

Task outcomes

The design of a task will, to some extent at least, determine the nature of the 'product outcome' (see Chapter 1). Here we will consider a number of factors related to this aspect of tasks—whether the outcome required of a task is open or closed, the degree of inherent structure in the required outcome, and the discourse mode the task is designed to elicit.

1 Closed versus open tasks

Two studies have investigated the effects of closed/open tasks on production. Tong-Fredericks (1984) compared three tasks, one of which, a problem-solving task, was closed and the other two, a role-play task and an 'authentic' interaction task where students had to find out from their partners what they had done the previous day, were open. Tong-Fredericks found that the problem-solving task elicited more spontaneous speech and a wider range of language functions, including the discourse management functions associated with meaning negotiation. In contrast, the two open tasks led to a rigid question-and-answer discourse structure but elicited greater attention to accuracy and more complex language. Brown (1991) also found that an 'interpretative task', which was open in nature, resulted in more complex language use, i.e. more 'hypothesizing', than closed decision-making tasks.

Another factor may also be important. As we saw in Chapter 3, open tasks vary depending on whether the speakers are required to 'converge' on a single outcome or allowed to 'diverge', i.e. maintain different viewpoints. Duff (1986) found that tasks with divergent goals, i.e. debates, led to longer turns and more complex language use than tasks with convergent goals, i.e. decision-making discussions. However, as noted below, Duff's results can also be explained in terms of differences in the discourse mode elicited by the two types of tasks.

To sum up, whereas closed tasks encourage meaning negotiation (see Chapter 3), open tasks, particularly if they are convergent, promote accuracy and complexity. Once again, then, we can see that tasks have complementary effects.

2 The inherent structure of the outcome

The term 'structure' here refers to whether the product the task elicits has to be 'creatively' constructed by the learners or whether it exists in some kind of pre-structured form. Compare, for example, these two 'personal tasks':

Task 1   Explain to your partner how to get to your house so that an oven that has been left on can be turned off. (Foster and Skehan 1996)

Task 2   Compare with one another the things that surprise you about British life, including positive and negative surprises. (Skehan and Foster 1997)

Both tasks require the speakers to draw on their own experiences but they differ with regard to how the relevant experiences are likely to be represented in memory. In the case of Task 1, the relevant information is likely to be clearly structured in memory because speakers will have a mental map of the route back to where they live and can draw on this to organize their directions. However, in Task 2, although they will have stored ideas relating to their responses to British life, it is unlikely that these will have been organized into a tightly-structured formal schema. It can be hypothesized, therefore, that Task 2 will require more macro- and micro-planning and thus afford less time for formulation.

Brown (1991) compared 'tight' and 'loose' tasks. The former structured the learners' performance by means of questions and a rigid set of subtasks. However, he found no difference in any of his measures of production, possibly because the tasks did not differ in terms of the inherent structure of the task content. Skehan and Foster (1997) report a study that investigated the effects of task structure in relation to opportunities learners had for strategic planning. They found that planning had a greater effect on accuracy in tasks with a clear inherent structure. They suggest that learners were able to devote attention to accuracy during planning because the clear structure of the tasks removed the need for planning content. The Skehan and Foster (1999) study referred to earlier also found an interaction between planning and task structure. This study compared learners' performance on two tasks that required them to relate Mr. Bean episodes presented on video. One episode, set in a restaurant, involved a series of clearly structured events while the other had a much less predictable structure. The learners in this study achieved only 40% accuracy in the unstructured task but 64% in the structured task where in both cases there was opportunity for planning. Skehan and Foster comment that 'pre-task preparation can have an effect in combination with task structure' (ibid. 112). This study also provided evidence to show that the structured task resulted in greater fluency, i.e. there were fewer repetitions, false starts, and replacements in the restaurant task. However, task structure did not appear to affect complexity.

It should be recognized, however, that it is not so much the inherent structure of the task itself that is important as the relationship between the task content and the speakers' background knowledge. When L2 speakers possess well-structured information, which can be encoded by their memory-based language system, they perform fluently and accurately. In contrast, when L2 speakers need to allocate attentional resources to macro-planning and to rule-based sentence construction, fluency and accuracy are likely to suffer. This effect derives not from the task itself but from an interaction between task content and the learners' personal knowledge. Also, Skehan and Foster's studies suggest that the effects of task structure arise though an interaction between this variable and others, such as the opportunity to plan.

3 Discourse mode
In Chapter 3 we saw that discourse mode affects the interactive properties of a task performance. There is also substantial evidence to suggest that it affects learner output. Results from the Skehan and Foster (1999) study can also be interpreted in terms of discourse mode, although they did not do so. The differences they found in the complexity scores for the watch-and-tell and the watch-then-tell conditions of the narrative tasks they investigated may reflect differences between the discourse modes these conditions elicit, with watch-and-tell leading to 'descriptive commentary' and watch-then-tell to 'narrative'. A narrative, we can reasonably surmise, will require greater

use of subordinating constructions than a descriptive commentary. Similarly, Swain and Lapkin's (2001b) study points to the influence of discourse mode. They note that whereas the dictogloss task resulted in the learners composing a story, the jigsaw task produced a list of numbered sentences.

A number of other studies testify to the effect discourse mode can have on production. Duff (1986) compared performance on 'problem-solving tasks' and 'debates' and helpfully provides examples of the productions that resulted from these tasks. These suggest that the problem-solving tasks called for the discourse mode of 'discussion' whereas the debates led to 'argument'. Most of Duff's measures related to the negotiation of meaning but she did include one measure of complexity—the ratio of clauses to c-units. Duff found that the discourse in the argument mode was almost twice as complex as that in the discussion mode. This is an interesting finding because the opposite was true for interactional modifications. Duff concluded that the two types of tasks are 'somehow complementary in pedagogic and psycholinguistic value' (ibid. 173).

Two other studies have examined effects of different discourse modes on adult L2 learners' use of specific grammatical features.[8] Newton and Kennedy (1996) analysed learners' use of prepositions and co-ordinators/subordinators in two different tasks. They found that a task requiring 'description' resulted in a significantly higher use of prepositions, although even in this task the frequency of prepositions was still less than half that found in corpora of native-speaker speech. No effect for discourse on the use of conjunctions was found. Bygate (1999b) compared learners' output on four tasks, two of which involved 'narrative' and the other two 'argumentation'. Results showed that the narrative tasks elicited a greater amount of production overall but that there was no difference in complexity. Interestingly, however, there was evidence that argumentation led to greater use of complex verb groups, i.e. a 'nominal' style of production involving the use of a greater number of noun phrases per finite verb, whereas the narrative involved greater use of individual verb forms (a 'verbal' style of production). In addition, argumentation resulted in more short turns involving echoic repetition and narrative in linguistically denser talk. Bygate concluded that 'the narrative tasks may be the ones that stretch the speakers more in terms of complexity of syntactic and lexical processing', whereas 'the argumentation tasks ... appear to push them towards less complex syntactic processing' (ibid. 204). Taken together, these studies suggest that tasks that involve different discourse modes can elicit very different kinds of language.

Summary

Table 4.2 summarizes the findings of research that has investigated the effects of task design variables on learner production. It shows that, to date, task design variables appear to have the greatest impact on complexity. Tasks that elicit more complex language use are those where the input: (1) does not provide contextual support, and (2) contains many elements, where (3) the information is shared rather than split, and where (4) the outcome is open, allowing for divergent solutions. In addition, complex language is much more likely in some types of discourse, for example, narrative, than in others, for example, description. There is also evidence that

Design Variable	Fluency	Accuracy	Complexity
A *Input variables*			
1 Contextual support	Tasks with contextual support	Tasks with no contextual support	Tasks with no contextual support
2 Number of elements in a task	Tasks with few elements		Tasks with many elements
3 Topic	Tasks that generate conflict, tasks that are familiar		
B *Task conditions*			
1 Shared vs. split information			Shared information tasks
2 Task demands	Tasks that pose a single demand		Tasks that pose a single demand
C *Task outcomes*			
1 Closed vs. open tasks	Closed task	Open tasks	Open tasks with divergent goals
2 Inherent structure of the outcome	A clear inherent structure	A clear inherent structure together with opportunity for planning	
3 Discourse mode			Narrative task > descriptive task Argument > discussion Narrative > argument

Key: > = greater than

Table 4.2: Task design features affecting learner production

task design variables influence fluency. Tasks that: (1) provide contextual support; (2) have familiar or involving topics; (3) pose a single demand; (4) are closed; and (5) have a clear inherent structure are likely to promote fluency. In contrast, design variables do not seem to impact so much on accuracy, although (1) tasks without contextual support, (2) open tasks, and (3) tasks with a clear inherent structure have been found to lead to more accurate language use, especially if there is an opportunity to plan strategically. Below we will see that implementation variables may be more important where accuracy is concerned.

The above review of the research has emphasized two key points. The first is that the factors that have been investigated obviously overlap and interact in complex ways, making it difficult to be sure which factors are responsible for the effects observed. The second point is that it is clear that the task design factors that impact on production are different from those that promote meaning negotiation (see Chapter 3). This suggests it may be impossible to claim that one task is better than another on psycholinguistic grounds. Rather, different kinds of task can potentially contribute in different ways to acquisition. Finally, as we saw in Chapter 3 with regard to the effects of task design on meaning negotiation, particular tasks may predispose learners to engage in certain types of production but they cannot guarantee them.

Task implementation factors

Any single task can be performed in a number of different ways, depending on how the speakers orient to it and the prior knowledge and skills they can bring to bear. As we will see in Chapter 6, it is ultimately the speakers themselves who decide what kind of 'activity' to engage in. However, it may also be possible to influence the activity that results from a task by manipulating the way the task is performed. In terms of the framework for describing tasks outlined in Chapter 1, this involves selecting from a range of procedural options. In this section we will consider a number of options that have figured in task-based research: planning, rehearsal, and post-task requirements.

Planning

We will examine the effects of planning on learners' production by distinguishing studies that have investigated online planning (allowing for monitoring) and strategic planning. The former examine how the planning that takes place during performance of a task affects production, while the latter examine how planning prior to performance influences production. As we will see, this distinction is potentially important for understanding how planning variables can impact on the three dimensions of language production—fluency, accuracy, and complexity.

1 The effects of online planning

Giving learners time to plan online and to monitor their output appears to have a clear impact on accuracy. Hulstijn and Hulstijn (1984) asked learners of L2 Dutch to perform short oral narratives under four conditions involving combinations of two variables: time, i.e. the learners were told to speak as quickly as they could or to take as much time as they wanted, and focal attention, i.e. learners were instructed to focus on form or on meaning. They found that time pressure by itself did not affect the accuracy of word order but that in combination with a focus on form it had a profound effect. This study, then, suggests that when learners use the time at their disposal to attend to formulation and to monitor the use of their grammatical resources their production becomes more accurate. However, if they use the time to plan content, no effect on accuracy is observed.

Ellis (1987) compared learners' performance on written and oral narrative tasks based on pictures. In the case of the written task (Task 1) the learners were given as much time as they wanted to write the narrative. In the first oral task (Task 2) they were asked to retell the same narrative but without recourse to their written versions. In the second oral task (Task 3) they were given a different set of pictures and instructed to tell the story with minimal opportunity for prior planning. Table 4.3 summarizes the kinds of planning opportunities afforded by these three tasks. Ellis found that the learners' use of the regular past tense forms (but not the irregular past tense or copular past tense forms) was most accurate in Task 1 and least accurate in Task 3, with Task 2 intermediate. The difference between Task 1 and 2 can be explained in terms of online planning; accuracy was greater when there was no time pressure. However, as Crookes (1989) and others have pointed out, Tasks 1 and 2 also differed with regard to medium.

Building on Ellis' study, Yuan and Ellis (2003) set out to compare the effects of pre-task and online planning on learner performance of a narrative task in a more systematic way. In the pre-task planning condition learners were given ten minutes to prepare the task and then performed it under time pressure. In the online planning condition, the learners were given no chance to prepare but were allowed to perform the task in their own time. There was also a control group that had no preparation time and was required to perform the task under time pressure. The results indicated

Task	Online planning–monitoring	Strategic planning
1	Yes	Yes (probably)
2	No	Yes
3	No	No

Table 4.3: Types of planning opportunities in Ellis (1987)

that opportunities for online planning assisted both accuracy and com-plexity but, as might be expected, inhibited fluency. The results for the strategic planning are considered below.

These three studies suggest that the time learners are given for online planning improves the accuracy of their production. However, the effects may only be evident when learners are drawing on their rule-based system. In both Hulstijn and Hulstijn (1984) and Ellis (1987), the effects of time pressure were only evident on grammatical structures that are clearly rule-based, i.e. Dutch word order rules and English regular past tense; they were not evident in structures that are more lexical in nature, i.e. irregular and copular past tense forms.

2 The effects of strategic planning

The role of strategic planning has attracted considerable attention from researchers. The effects of this kind of planning on all three dimensions of production—fluency, accuracy, and complexity—have been studied.

Several studies indicate that strategic planning helps to enhance fluency. Studies by Foster (1996), Foster and Skehan (1996), Skehan and Foster (1997), Wigglesworth (1997), Wendel (1997), Mehnert (1998), and Ortega (1999) all report that giving learners the opportunity to plan results in greater fluency. Foster (1996) and Foster and Skehan (1996) report that planners paused less frequently and spent less time in total silence than non-planners in all three tasks they investigated. However, the effect on fluency was stronger on the more difficult narrative and decision-making tasks than on the easier personal task. Skehan and Foster (1997), using similar tasks, replicated the result for total pauses. Wigglesworth (1997) found 'only tentative support' for the hypothesis that planners are more fluent in a testing situation but the planning time allowed in this study was only one minute. However, even this limited opportunity to plan helped high-proficiency learners to self-repair less on the most difficult task, which involved summarizing a conversation. Wendel (1997) found that the plan-ners in his study produced more syllables per minute and showed a lower mean length of pause in two narrative tasks. Ortega (1999) found a faster speech rate in learners of L2 Spanish on a story-telling task when they had an opportunity to plan strategically. Yuan and Ellis (2003) also report a clear effect for strategic planning on fluency. This result contrasts with that for online planning, which had a negative effect on fluency. Foster (2001) found that planning resulted in learners producing a greater amount of speech whereas it led to native speakers producing less. Interestingly, Foster reports that the percentage of learner talk accomplished by means of lexi-calized sequences did not change from the unplanned to planned condition, i.e. it remained steady at about 17%, whereas that of the native speakers did change, from 32% in the unplanned to 25% in the planned. This study suggests that planning opportunities may be used differently by learners and native speakers. The former lack the extensive store of lexicalized chunks available to the native speaker and thus are forced to rely more on rule-based procedures in both planned and unplanned talk. Planning enables them to operate their rule-based procedures more speedily. Only one study, Iwashita, Elder, and McNamara (2001), has failed to find that planning enhances fluency but this study, it will be recalled, investigated task performance in a testing context.

A question of obvious interest is what effect the amount of time allocated for planning has on fluency. A reasonable assumption is that the length of planning time is positively correlated with the degree of fluency. Mehnert (1998) set out to investigate this, allocating different groups of learners zero minutes, one minute, five minutes, and ten minutes of planning time. In general, she found that fluency did indeed improve in relation to the length of planning time. However, the main effect was that between the non-planners and the planners; the differences among the three planning groups were mostly non-significant.

In most of these studies, learners were simply given the task materials and told to plan what they wanted to say. However, a number of studies examined the effects of different kinds of strategic planning. Foster and Skehan (1996) investigated the effects of more guided planning. They compared the effects of 'undetailed' and 'detailed' planning, where the learners were given metacognitive advice about how to attend to syntax, lexis, content, and organization. The results showed that for the narrative task, the guided planners were notably more fluent than the unguided planners, but that there was no marked difference for the personal and decision-making tasks. Sangarun (2001) reports that both content-focused and form-focused planning promoted fluency in a task with low cognitive and linguistic demands but that only form-focused planning assisted fluency in a task with high cognitive and linguistic demands. These studies suggest that type of planning interacts with the type of task to influence fluency. Foster and Skehan (1999), however, found that asking learners to focus on form or meaning had no differential effect on fluency. In the same study, Skehan and Foster investigated the source of planning, comparing the effects of: (1) teacher-led planning; (2) individual learner planning; and (3) group-based planning on task performance. Where fluency was concerned, (2) proved most effective.

In contrast to fluency, the effects of strategic planning on accuracy appear to be quite mixed. Ellis (1987) found that planning that provided opportunities for both strategic and online planning resulted in more accurate use of the regular past tense (see above). Crookes (1989), however, found that planning had little effect on accuracy. Foster and Skehan (1996) report that both undetailed and detailed planners produced fewer errors than the non-planners on the decision-making task, that only the undetailed planners were more accurate than the non-planners on the personal task, while no effect for planning on accuracy was evident on the narrative task. Skehan and Foster (1997) found that planning (undetailed) led to greater accuracy on the personal and narrative tasks but not on the decision-making task. Wigglesworth (1997) reports that her high proficiency learners benefited from planning the most difficult task where verb morphology and articles were concerned but found no effect for plurals. Iwashita, Elder, and McNamara (2001), using a general measure of accuracy, found that three minutes of planning time had no effect on accuracy in a testing situation. Wendel (1997) concluded that strategic planning did not lead to greater accuracy on the narrative tasks he investigated. Ortega (1999) reports mixed findings—planning led to greater accuracy in the case of Spanish noun-modifier agreement but not in the case of articles. Yuan and Ellis (2003), using a general measure of accuracy, found that strategic planning had no effect, a result that contrasts with that which they report for online planning (see above). Mehnert (1998) reports a significant difference in the accuracy of one-minute planners over non-planners. However, the five-minute and ten-minute planners performed at the same overall level of accuracy as the one-minute planners. Foster and Skehan's (1999) study of the effects of the source of planning found that accuracy was greatest when the planning was teacher-led. However, rather surprisingly, directing learners' attention to form as opposed to content during planning had no effect on accuracy. In contrast, Sangarun (2001) found that all three planning conditions that she investigated—content-focused, form-focused and content/form-focused—assisted accuracy in the case of a task with a low cognitive and linguistic load but that only planning involving attention to content had any effect on accuracy in the task with a high cognitive and linguistic load.

It would appear from these results that whether or not strategic planning has any effect on accuracy depends on a variety of factors, which generally were not controlled for—the extent to which particular learners are oriented towards accuracy, the learners' level of proficiency, the type of task, and the particular grammatical feature. Also, with the exception of Yuan and Ellis (2003), these studies have made no attempt to control for online planning. Thus, it is possible that the different results reflect whether learners were able to or chose to engage in monitoring while they performed the task. Perhaps the only conclusion possible at the moment is that strategic planning will improve grammatical accuracy in task performance at least sometimes. Clearly, more research is needed to identify how planning interacts with task design variables, implementational procedures and learner factors.

The results are clearer for complexity. As for fluency, strategic planning has a definite, positive effect; planners produce more complex language than non-planners. Crookes (1989) reports that ten minutes of planning time led to learners producing more complex sentences and a wider range of lexis. Foster and Skehan (1996) found that detailed planners used significantly more subordination than undetailed planners who, in turn, produced significantly more subordination than the non-planners. This was broadly true for all three tasks. Skehan and Foster (1997), however, found that the planners' production was more complex on only two of the tasks. On the narrative task, where planning led to greater accuracy, no effect for complexity was evident. Wigglesworth (1997) reports that one-minute of planning time only led to more complex language use in the case of the high proficiency learners on the more difficult tasks. However, in accordance with their generally negative findings for planning in a testing situation, Iwashita, Elder, and McNamara (2001) failed to find any effect on complexity. Wendel (1997) found that his planners used more complex grammatical structures but not more lexically rich language. Mehnert (1998) also found a positive effect but only for the ten-minute planners, with the one-minute and five-minute planners performing at the same level as the non-planners. Ortega (1999) reports that mean number of words per utterance (a complexity measure) was significantly higher in the planning condition. Yuan and Ellis (2003) also found that strategic planning (like online planning) had a positive effect on complexity. With regard to the source of planning, Foster and Skehan (1999) found that individual learner planning worked best for complexity, as it did for fluency. Again, in this study, whether the learners focused their planning on form or content had no differential effect on complexity. Sangarun (2001), however, found that only planning involving attention to content led to increased complexity.

These studies indicate that giving learners the opportunity to plan can increase the complexity of their production. They also suggest that this effect can be enhanced if: (1) learners have a reasonable length of time to plan, say ten minutes; (2) they are given guidance in how and what to plan; and (3) they plan individually rather than in groups.

Three studies have investigated what learners actually do when they are given the opportunity to plan. Wendel (1997) interviewed his learners immediately on completion of the tasks. They varied somewhat in what they reported doing during the planning time but all of them said they had focused on sequencing the narrative events in chronological order. Only three reported attending to grammar but even these admitted it did not help them much when it came to telling the stories. As one learner put it, 'I feel like I'm pushing to tell you what's going on in the film. I focus on story, not grammar'. Wendel concluded that it is not useful for learners to try to plan the details of grammatical usage off-line. Ortega (1999) used retrospective interviews to investigate what learners did while they performed a narrative task. She found that they adopted an identifiable approach in their planning, for example, they worked on the main ideas and organization first and then the details, they attended to both content and linguistic form, and they made a conscious effort to plan at the utterance level. Ortega also reports that the learners varied considerably in the emphasis they gave to form and content. These two studies suggest that when planning strategically learners tend to prioritize content. However, Ortega's study suggests that they do also attend to form. Sangarun (2001) asked students to think aloud as they planned. She was interested in seeing if there was any relationship between what the learners did while they planned and how they performed the tasks. She found that whereas they were successful in making use of their content-focused planning in the task performance they were less so when it came to form-focused planning.

What general conclusions are possible from these studies? The first is that strategic planning has a stronger effect on fluency and complexity than accuracy. This suggests that when learners plan strategically they give more attention to drawing up a conceptual plan of what they want to say rather than to formulating detailed linguistic plans. Even when asked to engage in form-focused planning they may not do so, preferring to use the time given them to sequence ideas and to work out the semantic linkages among propositions. Only if they are given a very short time to plan, as in one of Mehnert's groups, do they spend this time thinking of the language they need to perform the task, with a resulting gain in accuracy. The second conclusion is that the trade-off effects we noted earlier are evident for planning. When learners plan they have to choose what aspect of production to focus on; focusing on fluency and complexity is at the expense of accuracy and vice versa. Finally, it would seem that strategic planning appears to have a greater effect on production when the task is cognitively demanding.

3 Conclusion

In this section, we have seen that the effects of online and strategic planning are somewhat different (see Table 4.4). Whereas opportunities for online planning result in more accurate and complex language use, probably because learners have the chance to monitor linguistic form, opportunities for strategic planning generally favour fluency and complexity, possibly because it leads to an emphasis on conceptualizing what has to

Aspect of performance	Strategic planning	Online planning
Fluency	Positive effect	Negative effect
Accuracy	Effects sometimes evident	Positive effect
Complexity	Positive effect	Positive effect

Table 4.4: The effects of strategic and online planning on L2 performance

be communicated rather than how it is said. An interesting possibility, then, is that learners' attention to fluency, accuracy, and complexity can be manipulated by means of the kind of planning they are required to undertake.

Rehearsal

Another procedural factor that has been found to influence task performance is rehearsal—giving learners the opportunity to repeat a task. The difference between Ellis' (1987) Task 1 and Task 2 (see Table 4.3) can be seen in this light. As we have already noted, the opportunity to rehearse led to more accurate use of the regular past tense. Bygate (1996) compared one learner's retelling of a Tom and Jerry cartoon on two separate occasions, three days apart. He found that rehearsal had a clear effect on complexity, with the learner using more lexical verbs (as opposed to copular), more regular past tense forms (as opposed to irregular), a wider range of vocabulary and cohesive devices, for example, words like 'then', 'so', and 'because', and fewer inappropriate lexical collocations on the second occasion. Interestingly, there were also more self-correcting repetitions on the second telling of the story. A possible explanation of these results is that rehearsal led to the learner drawing more extensively on her rule-based system, with a resulting gain in complexity but some loss in fluency because of a greater need to monitor rule-based output. Bygate (2001) reports a larger study that sought to investigate the effects of practising specific types of task (involving narrative and interview) on both a second performance of the same task and on performance of a new task of the same type. The study showed that the second performance manifested greater fluency and complexity, and also that the opportunity to practise that type of task helped. However, the practice did not appear to assist performance on a new task of the same type. In other words, disappointingly, there was no transfer of practice effect. Gass *et al.* (1999) report very similar findings in a study that compared learners' use of L2 Spanish in tasks with the same and different contents. In this study an effect for task repetition on ratings of overall proficiency, accuracy in the use of *estar* (= to be) to some extent, and on lexical complexity, measured by means of type-token ration, i.e. the number of different words used over the total number of actual words, was found. However, again there was no transfer of these effects to a new task.

A somewhat different kind of rehearsal was investigated by Yule, Power, and McDonald (1992). In this study, learners had the opportunity to listen to other learners performing a number of referential communication tasks before they tried them themselves. The hypothesis here was that such an experience would help the speakers to adapt their output to their listeners' needs. The results partially confirmed this.

Lynch and McLean (2000, 2001) made use of a unique task that involved rehearsal. In the context of an English for specific purposes course designed to prepare members of the medical profession to give presentations in English, they designed a 'poster carousel' task. This required students to read an academic article and prepare a poster presentation based on it. Students then stood by their posters while other members of the group visited and asked questions. Altogether, each 'host' had six 'visitors'. Given that visitors tended to ask the same questions, there was substantial opportunity for retrial. Lynch and McLean document how recycling output resulted in both greater accuracy and fluency. However, they noted that different learners appeared to benefit in different ways with level of proficiency the key factor. Thus, whereas a learner with low proficiency appeared to benefit most in terms of accuracy and pronunciation, a learner with higher proficiency used the opportunity for retrial to improve the clarity and economy of her explanations of a complex idea. Lynch and McLean also report considerable variation in the learners' awareness of the changes they were making in their production.

Finally, Nemeth and Kormos (2001) investigated the effects of task repetition on the quality of argumentation in opinion gap tasks by Hungarian learners of English. They found that repeating a task influenced the number of supports the participants provided for their claims but that it had no effect on the frequency with which lexical expressions of argumentation were used. In other words, when given the chance to repeat a task the learners attended to the content of their arguments rather than to the means of expression.

Task repetition, then, seems to have beneficial effects on learner performance. As Bygate (1999) suggests, learners are likely to initially focus on message content and subsequently, once message content and the basic language needed to encode it has been established, to switch their attention to the selection and monitoring of appropriate language. Bygate suggests that rehearsal may afford learners the extra processing space they need 'to integrate the competing demands of fluency, accuracy, and complexity'. Hulstijn and Hulstijn (1984) have proposed that when tasks are repeated learners can be instructed to pay attention to different features, for example, grammar, pronunciation, rate of speech, and completeness of information. Focusing learners' attention on form when they repeat a task may help them overcome what seems to be a natural tendency to prioritize content. However, before any strong claims can be made for rehearsal it will be necessary to show that the gains evident from repeating a task transfer to the performance of new, similar tasks.

A post-task requirement

Another possibility is that learners' performance of a task can be influenced by means of some post-task requirement, which they are made

aware of before they undertake the task. For example, informing learners that they will have to perform the task a second time before the whole
class might predispose them to pay more attention to accuracy when they
perform it privately initially. Skehan and Foster (1997) investigated this
possibility but found only limited support. The post-task condition did
result in greater accuracy on the decision-making task but not on the
personal and narrative tasks. The post-task condition also led to less
fluent production, contrary to the researchers' predictions. Skehan and
Foster concluded that the effect of the post-task requirement was
generally weak.

Summary

In this section, we have explored a number of procedural options relating
to task implementation. There is clear evidence that these affect learner
production. Providing learners with time for online planning appears to
encourage accuracy. In contrast, the opportunity for strategic planning
affects fluency and complexity more strongly. Strategic planning has a
profound effect on fluency—the more time available for planning (up to a
point, say, ten minutes), the more fluent the production. Where strategic
planning does have an effect on accuracy this may be limited to rule-
based grammatical features such as regular past tense. Strategic planning
has a strong effect on complexity, particularly if there is sufficient time
available (ten minutes) and guidance in how to plan is provided. There
is also some evidence to suggest that individual learner planning or
teacher-led planning is more effective than group-based planning.
However, there is less support in the research to date for the hypothesis
that directing students to attend to form or content in their strategic
planning will influence what aspect of language they attend to when they
perform a task.

Rehearsal, which can also be seen as a kind of strategic planning, also
improves the performance of a task, especially in terms of complexity. It
apparently encourages learners to provide more detailed content and to
draw more fully on their rule-based system. However, to date, including a
post-task requirement does not appear to affect production to any extent,
although this is clearly an option that requires further study.

The research reviewed in this section supports the earlier finding that
learners find it difficult to attend to all three aspects of production at the
same time, with the result that they need to trade off one aspect against
another. Thus, if task implementation variables induce attention to message
content, a process that may aid fluency and complexity, there may be few
attentional resources left for focusing on accuracy. Conversely, if they
attend to accuracy, fluency suffers.

Conclusion

The task-based research that has examined learner production is of both theoretical and practical relevance. It provides data that can be used to address such vital issues as the nature of learners' representation of language and of their language production mechanisms. Task-based research affords insights about implicit knowledge. Tasks typically call for real-time production and therefore elicit learners' use of implicit knowledge. This, as we noted earlier, has been hypothesized to consist of both exemplar-based and rule-based representations, which can convincingly explain the variation in learner production that results from manipulating tasks. For example, learners make full use of their exemplar-based system when the information to be communicated has a clear structure but they draw more extensively on their rule-based system when the information to be communicated is more complex and less structured. Tasks, when implemented in certain ways, can also shed light on the contribution that explicit knowledge can make to L2 performance. As we have seen, when there is opportunity for online planning, accuracy is enhanced, a finding that is perhaps best explained in terms of learners' use of explicit knowledge to monitor their performance. The results of the task-based research also lend support to hierarchical models of language production of the kind proposed by Levelt (1989). They indicate that the competing demands of conceptualization on the one hand and of formulation and articulation on the other are often severe, causing learners to prioritize one aspect of production.

However, although the research we have reviewed in this chapter tells us a lot about L2 use it says little about acquisition.[9] Indeed, cross-sectional studies of how learners perform on individual tasks cannot address what impact task performance has on their acquisition of language over time, especially when acquisition is operationalized in terms of general aspects of language, i.e. fluency, accuracy, and complexity. At this stage, it is only possible to hypothesize that the kind of production learners engage in will have long-term acquisitional effects—for example, that a solid diet of tasks that encourage fluency will result in the development of this aspect of proficiency at the expense of, say, accuracy. Skehan (1998b) is, of course, well aware of this limitation and has called for longitudinal studies of task-based learning in order to examine whether such hypotheses can be confirmed. However, it will be difficult to isolate the effect of performing a series of tasks on different aspects of development over a substantial period of time, given that in most language-learning situations learners will have been subject to numerous other learning opportunities during this period.

The research is, however, of obvious practical relevance to language teachers, as it sheds light on how teachers can manipulate the kinds of language that learners produce in a classroom. Language pedagogy is necessarily concerned with language *use*, not just with language *acquisition*.

Indeed, like Skehan, teachers are obliged to assume a relationship between use and acquisition. The research reviewed in this chapter provides important clues about what kinds of tasks and procedures teachers need to use to foster fluency, accuracy, and complexity in learner production. These clues can be used towards the goal that Robinson (2001: 27) sets for task-based research—'the development of a theoretically motivated, empirically substantiable, and pedagogically feasible sequencing criteria'. The clues will provide insights into how teachers can achieve a balance between the three aspects of learner production and thus, hopefully, contribute to the development of the kind of all-round proficiency most learners aim for. Chapter 8 discusses how the research findings can be utilized in the design of language courses.

It is important, though, to recognize the limitations of the research. The research is premised on the same assumption as that based on the Interaction Hypothesis and can be criticized on the same grounds, namely that it has largely ignored the contribution of individual learner factors and setting. This problem is exacerbated by the fact that in many of the studies the samples were extremely small (for example, Bygate 1996; Lynch and McLean 2000), thus making generalizations about the effect of specific task variables even more problematic. Also, it is not easy to disentangle the effects of different task variables as these interact in highly complex ways. These interactions are frequently accounted for post hoc as they were not experimentally manipulated, a point that Skehan (2001) readily admits. Finally, researchers have focused on analysing the 'text' that results from a task, giving little attention to how learners construct 'discourse' as they perform a task; with a few exceptions (for example, Sangarun, 2001) the research is product oriented and has neglected process. We need to know more about what learners do when they plan strategically and online and how they orientate while performing a task.

Notes

1 This account of UG is based on the Principles and Parameters model of grammar. However, the general claims of the theory also underpin the more recent Minimalist Program.
2 Not all cognitive models of language learning are connectionist. Later in this chapter and in Chapter 5, Anderson's ACT Theory, which is based on the distinction between declarative and procedural knowledge, is considered.
3 Zobl (1995) offers some very interesting evidence to support a non-interface position. He argues that implicit and explicit knowledge can be distinguished in a number of ways such as the degree of variance in scores obtained from measures of the two types of knowledge (the standard deviation is greater in the case of explicit knowledge) and the rate of forgetting (attrition of explicit knowledge is more rapid).

4 The computational model views 'acquisition' as something that occurs inside the mind of the learner as a result of processing input. This model contrasts with sociocultural theory, according to which acquisition takes place initially externally through social interaction (see Chapter 6 for an account of this theory).

5 Other cognitive theories of automatization also lend support to a role for production. Logan's (1988) Instance Theory proposes that skills acquisition is a process of moving from rule-based production, which is necessarily slow, to instance-based production, which requires less attention and is therefore automatic. 'Instances' are built up as a result of storing chunks derived from rule-based production. Thus, production practice in applying rules is needed in order to build up a repertoire of 'instances'.

6 This explanation of the role of output in promoting the acquisition of new L2 knowledge is based on a computational view of language acquisition. Swain's earlier work was informed by such a model. More recently, however, Swain has adopted sociocultural theory and has reformulated her views about the role of output accordingly (see Swain 2000). Swain's current theoretical position is considered in Chapter 6.

7 Swain and Lapkin (2000) in a study based on the same two tasks failed to find any statistically significant differences in the learners' use of their L1. The two tasks elicited the same amount of use of the L1 and for the same functions.

8 Although these studies analysed learner production in terms of specific linguistic features, the tasks used to elicit data were themselves 'unfocused', i.e. they were designed to elicit broad types of discourse, not specific linguistic features. For this reason, a discussion of these studies belongs in this chapter rather than Chapter 5, where 'focused tasks' are considered.

9 It is of course very difficult to demonstrate that acquisition arises out of the performance of unfocused tasks. It is easier with focused tasks and studies that show a clear relationship between production and acquisition in the context of this kind of task are discussed in the next chapter.

5   Focused tasks and SLA

Introduction

In the last two chapters, we examined unfocused production tasks, that is tasks that were designed to elicit general samples of learner language. We noted that these tasks may require specific modes of discourse, for example, narrative or description, and that this may result in learners using specific linguistic features, for example, past tense or prepositions. However, these tasks were not designed with the intention of eliciting these linguistic features; rather, researchers identified them a posteriori when they analysed the learner productions that resulted from the performance of the tasks. In this chapter, we will consider ways in which tasks can be employed to elicit use of specific linguistic features, either by design or by the use of methodological procedures that focus attention on form in the implementation of a task. Such tasks will be called *focused tasks*.

It is important to recognize that focused tasks, like unfocused tasks, must meet all the criteria of tasks in general (see Chapter 1). In particular, there must be a primary concern for message content (although this does not preclude attention to form), the participants must be able to choose the linguistic and non-linguistic resources needed, and there must be a clearly defined outcome. It is useful to distinguish between a focused task and a situational grammar exercise, i.e. an exercise that has been designed to provide contextualized practice of a specific linguistic feature. In the case of the former, the learners are not informed of the specific linguistic focus and therefore treat the task in the same way as they would an unfocused task, i.e. pay primary attention to message content. Of course, this does not mean that learners will not attend to the target form while they perform the task—indeed, a focused task is designed to elicit such attention. However, it will be incidental. In contrast, in a situational grammar exercise the learners are told what the linguistic focus is and thus, when they perform the task, are likely to make special attempts to attend to it. In this case, then, attention to form is intentional.

It should be clear, then, that the difference between focused tasks and situational grammar exercises rests in how they are implemented rather than how they are designed. To illustrate this important point, consider the task materials in Figure 5.1. These consist of information about four candidates for a job. The linguistic focus is the present perfect tense. The materials could be used in an unfocused task of the decision-making kind. In this case, the learners would be told to read the information provided and to discuss the different candidates in groups with a view to choosing one of them to take up the position of teacher in an English-language school. Such an activity meets all the criteria of a task. In the course of performing this task the learners may or may not attend to target structure in the input data and may or may not use it in their own production. The same materials could be used in a situational grammar exercise. In this case, the teacher might prepare the students for the task by pre-teaching the present perfect tense or alternatively they might specify the structural properties of the sentences the learners have to produce when they perform the task. For example, Ur (1988) suggests that students draw up criteria for evaluating the candidates using the structure 'The successful candidate must/should have ...'. Such an activity is not a task because (1) students are primarily concerned with practising a specific form and (2) they are not free to choose their own resources. It is clear that learners can orientate towards the same materials in very different ways and, as we will see below, these differences may be of psycholinguistic importance.

In this chapter we will be concerned mainly with focused tasks that involve production. It is also possible, of course, to have focused tasks that are receptive, i.e. that are designed to induce attention to specific forms in oral or written input. In fact, we considered such tasks in Chapter 2. The non-reciprocal tasks used in Ellis, Tanaka, and Yamazaki (1994) and Ellis and He (1999) were such tasks. They required learners to orientate to the message content but also induced noticing of specific, pre-determined lexis. As we will see later, it is, in fact, considerably easier to design tasks that focus incidental attention on form receptively than tasks that elicit incidental production of a targeted feature.

Focused communicative tasks involving both reception and production are of considerable value to both researchers and teachers. For researchers, they provide a means of measuring whether learners have acquired a specific feature. They are often preferred to tests because they provide evidence of what learners do when they are not consciously focused on using a form correctly and thus can be considered to elicit *implicit knowledge* rather than *explicit knowledge* (see Chapter 4). Many SLA researchers (for example, Pienemann 1985) would consider that only when learners demonstrate they are able to use a feature spontaneously in communicative activity can they be said to have acquired it. Focused tasks are of value to teachers because they provide a means of teaching specific linguistic features communicatively—under 'real operating conditions' (Johnson 1988).

We will begin this chapter by examining the psycholinguistic rationale for focused tasks. We will then examine how a focus can be introduced into a task through design. Finally, we will examine some of the ways in which procedures for implementing a task can afford a linguistic focus.

```
                Candidates for a job

JOCK, aged 30
B.A. in social studies.
Has spent a year working his way round the world.
Has spent six years teaching economics in state school.
Has written a highly successful novel about teachers.
Has lived in a back-to-nature commune for two years.
Has been married twice—now divorced. Two children.
Has been running local youth group for three years.

BETTY, aged 45
Has been married for 24 years, three children.
Has not worked most of that time.
Has done evening courses in youth guidance.
Has spent the last year teaching pupils privately for
  state exams with good results.
Has been constantly active in local government.
Has been elected to local council twice.

ROBERT, aged 27
Has never been married, no children.
Has served a term in prison—killed a man in a drunken
  fight; but has committed no further crimes since
  release two years ago.
Has recently become a Catholic, regularly goes to church.
Has been working in school for mentally retarded in
  poor area—has been recommended by principal of the
  school. Has followed no course of formal study.

CLAIRE, aged 60
Has been married, husband now dead, no children.
Has been a teacher for 35 years, mostly teaching English
  abroad.
Has lived many years in the Far East (husband was
  diplomat).
Has taught English in British Council school in
  Singapore and Hong Kong.
Has been Principal of British School for girls in
  Kuala Lumpur.
Husband died two years ago; since then has been in this
  country, doing voluntary youth work; has recently
  completed Diploma in Youth Counselling.
```

Figure 5.1: Materials for focused communication task

The psycholinguistic rationale for focused tasks

We will examine two psycholinguistic bases for focused communicative tasks. The first involves skill-building theories and the notion of automatic processing, as this figures in the skill-building theories found in cognitive psychology. The second rests on accounts of *implicit learning* and the claimed importance of noticing and noticing-the-gap in the context of what Long (1988, 1991) has called 'focus-on-form', i.e. the incidental attention to form in the context of communicative activity.

Skill-building theories and automatic processing

There are a number of different accounts of how skill-automatization takes place in cognitive psychology. Here we will focus on the accounts provided by McLaughlin (see McLaughlin 1987, 1990; McLaughlin and Heredia 1996), Anderson (1993, 2000) and Johnson (1988, 1996).

According to McLaughlin and Heredia (1996: 214),

> ... automatic processing involves the activation of certain nodes in memory each time the appropriate inputs are present. This activation is a learned response that has been built up through consistent mapping of the same input to the same pattern of activation over many trials.

Automatic processing contrasts with *controlled processing* (Shriffin and Schneider 1977), where activation of nodes involves attentional control. A key difference between automatic and controlled processing is that whereas the former occurs rapidly and in parallel form, the latter occurs more slowly and functions serially, i.e. only one process can be activated at any one time. Both types of processes have their advantages and disadvantages. Automatic processes are easy and rapid. They take up little processing capacity and thus make it possible for learners to focus attention on higher-order skills, i.e. attending to message content rather than to form. However, automatic processes can be suppressed or changed only with difficulty. In contrast, controlled processes are easily established and are flexible but they are very demanding on processing capacity. Thus learners who rely on the controlled processing of linguistic form have less capacity to attend to the content of their messages.

Automatization involves more than just a strengthening or speeding up of language processing. It also involves *restructuring* (McLaughlin 1990). In part, this involves the unpacking of formulaic speech, as learners move from exemplar-based representations to more rule-based representations. It also involves the reorganization of knowledge into new forms. For example, learners have been found to pass through stages in which knowledge of rules such as that for regular past tense in English are spontaneously overgeneralized, resulting sometimes in the abandonment of earlier learned correct forms, for example, 'fell' → 'falled'. Such restructuring explains why language acquisition follows a U-shaped pattern, i.e. learners initially manifest high levels of accuracy in the use of a given feature, then low levels, before eventually consolidating in correct use of the feature.

A not dissimilar view of automatization is found in the work of Anderson (1993, 2000). Anderson suggests that skill development involves the proceduralization of *declarative knowledge*. Declarative knowledge is factual. In the case of language it involves explicit knowledge of grammatical rules, for example, use the indefinite article 'an' before nouns that begin with a vowel sound. During the declarative stage of learning, learners apply general problem-solving procedures to the declarative knowledge they have stored. *Procedural knowledge* is declarative knowledge that has become fully automatized; it is evident when learners can use a particular feature (such as 'an') correctly without having to think about it. Proceduralization occurs in two stages. In the knowledge-compilation stage, learners construct procedures that enable them to access linguistic knowledge as part of a ready-made procedure. For example, learners construct a procedure that enables them to access the phrase 'an hour' or 'a horse' directly. In the procedural stage procedures are fine-tuned, i.e. procedures that realize target language forms are strengthened while those that realize deviant forms are weakened or abandoned. For example, learners drop procedures that result in deviant noun phrases like 'an hotel'.

Given that communicative language use requires rapid online processing there is an obvious need for learners to develop automatic processes/procedural knowledge. How then are these developed? According to McLaughlin and Heredia, automatic processes develop out of controlled processes. Learning involves the transfer of information from short-term to long-term memory and this transfer is regulated by controlled processes. Thus, the learning of any new skill involves an initial stage of controlled processing followed by a later stage of automatic processing. According to Anderson's theory, skill development begins with declarative knowledge (facts about language) and ends with procedural knowledge (target-like communicative behaviour), although, as DeKeyser (1998) points out, Anderson also allows for the possibility that not all knowledge is initially declarative. Also, Anderson acknowledges that the development of procedural knowledge does not necessarily entail the loss of declarative knowledge, i.e. learners may be able to produce a noun phrase such as 'an hour' both procedurally and by accessing declarative knowledge.

It would follow from Anderson's theory that learners can be assisted initially by being taught declarative knowledge. Johnson (1996), drawing on Anderson's theory, proposes that 'explanation' of a language point serves as an effective starting point. However, he points out that instruction involving 'hints' may be more effective in establishing the kind of declarative knowledge that can be proceduralized than 'elaborate, abstract and precise explanation' (108–9). Johnson also finds support in the skill-learning literature for 'demonstration', i.e. providing declarative information about linguistic features through examples.

In order for controlled processes/declarative knowledge to evolve into automatic processes/procedural knowledge, learners need to practise the skill. McLaughlin and Heredia comment:

> From a practical standpoint, the necessary component is overlearning. A skill must be practised again and again and again, until no attention is required for its performance. *Repetitio est mater studiorum*—practice, repetition, time on task—these seem to be the critical variables for successful acquisition of complex skills, including complex cognitive skills such as second language learning. (p. 216)

The need for practice in developing proceduralized linguistic knowledge is affirmed by Anderson. Practice is also seen as important for restructuring as it provides the means by which learners reorganize their internal representational framework.

However, 'practice' is a relatively crude concept, especially when applied to language learning. What exactly does it entail? The traditional view is that practice involves the process of repeatedly and deliberately attempting to produce some specific target feature. It was this view that led to the use of the mechanical drills found in the audiolingual and oral-situational methods of language teaching (see Richards and Rogers 1986). What was missing from this view, according to DeKeyser (1998), was recognition of the importance of practice directed at 'behaviour' rather than at 'structures'. Ellis (1988) has shown that practising linguistic structures is often not effective in enabling learners to use new structures autonomously—'practice does not make perfect' as Lightbown (1985) puts it. This is because practising a structure in a mechanical way reifies the structure by decontextualizing it and thus does not affect long-term memory or lead to any change in behaviour. To change behaviour (i.e. develop automatic processes) it is necessary to provide practice of the actual behaviour itself. In the case of language learning, 'behaviour' must entail attempts to communicate. Thus, for practice to work it must involve learners producing the target structure in the context of communicative activity.

According to this view, then, communicative practice serves as a device for proceduralizing knowledge of linguistic structures that have been first presented declaratively (see Figure 5.2). Instruction that incorporates such practice can be seen as an attempt to intervene directly in the process by which declarative knowledge is proceduralized. DeKeyser (1998: 49) draws on Anderson's skill-learning theory to argue for such an intervention:

> … proceduralization is achieved by engaging in the target behaviour—or procedure—while temporarily leaning on declarative crutches …

Presentation of declarative knowledge (controlled processing)	→	Communicative practice through focused tasks	→	Communicative language use (procedural knowledge/automatic processing)

Figure 5.2: Task-supported language teaching

Repeated behaviours of this kind allow the restructuring of declarative knowledge in ways that make it easier to proceduralize and allow the combination of co-occurring elements into larger chunks that reduce the working memory load.

Johnson (1988, 1996) also draws on skill-learning theory to justify practice. He emphasizes the importance of feedback in the learning process, suggesting that the instructional sequence is best seen as one of 'learn → perform → learn' rather than the traditional sequence of 'learn → perform'. During (or perhaps after) the 'perform' stage learners must have the opportunity to receive feedback. This feedback, Johnson suggests, should consist of mistake correction, i.e. negative evidence about the misuse of features that the learners already have knowledge of but cannot yet use automatically.[1] Johnson emphasizes that for feedback to be effective learners 'need to see for themselves what has gone wrong in the operating conditions under which they went wrong' (1988: 93). He suggests that this can probably be best achieved by means of extrinsic feedback, i.e. feedback from an outside source that shows the learner what is wrong by modelling the correct form while they are attempting to communicate.[2]

The role of tasks in such a theory of teaching is to provide opportunities for learners to practise forms that have been first presented declaratively and to receive feedback on their mistakes under real operating conditions. The tasks must necessarily be of the focused kind as they serve to practise pre-determined linguistic features. Thus, the kind of language teaching envisaged here is of the task-supported kind referred to in Chapter 1. The danger, of course, is that if learners are told what form they are required to practise, they give priority to producing the form accurately and thus the tasks turn into situational grammar exercises and end up practising 'structures' rather than 'behaviours'.

Theories of implicit learning

In Chapter 4 we considered the difference between implicit and explicit knowledge. We will now consider accounts of how implicit knowledge is acquired and will also consider the role of explicit knowledge in this process. It should be noted from the outset that the theoretical position discussed in this section conflicts with that of the previous section in a number of ways.

N. Ellis (1994: 1) provides the following definition of implicit learning:

> Implicit learning is acquisition of knowledge about the underlying structure of a complex stimulus environment by a process which takes place naturally, simply and without conscious operations.

From this definition, we can see that there are two principal aspects of implicit learning; it takes place unconsciously and it is automatic. Ellis goes on to specify more precisely what is involved. He argues that implicit learning is associative learning, that is, it involves not so much the implicit abstraction of rules from input but the development of highly complex networks of connections that over time might become so established as to lead to behaviour that appears rule-like. Thus, 'implicit learning is based on memory for particular instances' (ibid.: 15) and is driven by the human mind's ability to detect regularities in the input and to store recurrent patterns. It is responsive to the frequencies and salience of different forms in the input. According to this view, then, implicit learning entails a connectionist model of linguistic representation (see Chapter 4).

Whereas in the case of L1 acquisition there is general agreement that it is achieved primarily by means of implicit learning, there is less agreement regarding L2 acquisition, with some theorists (for example, Krashen 1981) arguing that L2 acquisition is essentially the same as L1 acquisition in involving implicit learning and others claiming that L2 learning necessarily involves explicit learning. Indeed, the theories of skill-building described above imply that the initial stage of learning is conscious, involving explicit attempts on the part of the learner to understand what is to be learned. As DeKeyser (1998: 57) acknowledges, 'the concept of proceduralization implies that rules are acquired in a learning process that starts out as explicit'. However, as we have seen, skill-building theories also recognize that the restructuring of knowledge can take place implicitly as well as explicitly. Therefore, they are best seen as incorporating both explicit and implicit learning.

The key difference between theories of implicit learning and theories of skill-building lies in the particular role that explicit knowledge is seen to play in language learning. As we have seen, skill-building theories see learning as primarily a process by which explicit knowledge is converted into implicit knowledge via communicative practice. In contrast, theories of implicit learning view the processes by which learners acquire implicit and explicit knowledge as inherently different and separate. Where implicit learning is unconscious and automatic, explicit learning involves a conscious search for structure and is highly selective. The different perspectives of skill-learning theories and theories of implicit learning are often referred to in terms of the *interface position* and the *non-interface position* (see Chapter 4). With regard to the latter, explicit knowledge can be seen to play no role whatsoever in the acquisition of implicit knowledge (the strong non-interface position) or a limited role of facilitating the process of implicit learning (the weak non-interface position).

Drawing on Schmidt's Noticing Hypothesis (see Chapter 2), Ellis (1993 and 1994) proposes a weak non-interface model where explicit knowledge is seen as facilitating implicit learning in two major ways. First, it aids the process of *noticing*. That is, if learners are armed with explicit knowledge of a linguistic feature, they are more likely to notice its occurrence in the communicative input they receive and thus to learn it implicitly. In other words explicit knowledge helps to make a feature salient. Second, explicit knowledge may assist *noticing-the-gap* (see Chapter 4). If learners know about a particular feature they are better equipped to detect the difference between what they themselves are saying and how the feature is used in the input they are exposed to. Explicit knowledge of the feature can make it easier for them to carry out 'cognitive comparisons', i.e. to compare their own norms with the target norms exemplified in the feedback. These two roles for explicit knowledge are shown in Figure 5.3 below. In this model, implicit learning is characterized as a process involving two stages: (1) intake, i.e. forms are taken into short-term memory, and (2) the acquisition of implicit knowledge, i.e. forms enter long-term memory. Explicit knowledge, acquired through self-study, conscious reflection on the nature of one's implicit knowledge or formal instruction, serves to prime the intake through noticing and to feed the internal monitoring that arises when learners notice the gap between their output and what they know consciously.

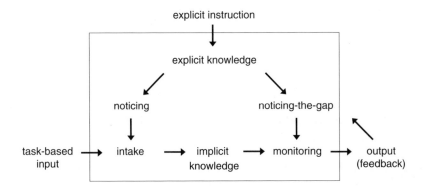

Figure 5.3: The role of explicit knowledge in implicit learning

N. Ellis provides a not dissimilar account of how explicit knowledge can assist implicit learning:

> Declarative rules can also have 'top-down' influences on perception. They can influence the 'Central Executive' of working memory ... to guide input to working memory in a variety of ways: (i) they can focus attention on the relevant modality, representation and level of processing, e.g. to concentrate on the phonology, or the morphology or the stress, etc.; (ii) they can make salient the relevant features, e.g. concentrating on the end of the word or the phrase boundaries; (iii) by making active particular units in working memory this in turn may reinforce corresponding output patterns of the input systems, thus allowing learning mechanisms to tune the operation of input modules ... (1994: 17).

As both R. and N. Ellis make clear, implicit learning is not dependent on explicit knowledge. Rather the processes involving explicit knowledge that they describe are secondary in nature, supplementing but not replacing the processes involved in implicit learning.

This theory of implicit learning supports the 'strong' version of communicative language teaching (Howatt 1984), according to which practice must engage learners in authentic communicative activity. It is in accordance with Prabhu's (1987: 1) view about teaching:

> ... the development of competence in a second language requires not systematization of language inputs or maximization of planned practice, but rather the creation of conditions in which learners engage in an effort to cope with communication.

According to this view, acquisition arises out of communicative activity and all that is required is the provision of opportunities to communicate naturally. The role for tasks here is obvious; they constitute the means by which learners can be provided with opportunities to communicate. This results in what was described as 'task-based language teaching' (see Chapter 1). It can be conducted entirely with unfocused tasks, as Prabhu proposes. However, there is also the possibility of utilizing focused tasks if the aim is to provide opportunities for the implicit learning of specific linguistic features. It can also be argued that such tasks may even be necessary to ensure the acquisition of certain grammatical features, for example, the distinction between *passé composé* and *imparfait* in French, which do not seem to be acquired as a result of unfocused tasks (see Swain 1985 and Harley 1989).

The model shown in Figure 5.3 also supports the direct teaching of explicit knowledge. However, because it does not claim that explicit knowledge is the antecedent of implicit knowledge or can be transformed into explicit knowledge, the teaching of explicit knowledge needs to be viewed as supplementary to task-based language teaching, not as a step in an instructional sequence. The kind of language curriculum this would suggest is one where there are separate components, one directed at developing implicit knowledge (through task-based instruction) and one directed at developing awareness of key aspects of the target language (see Ellis 2002). In a similar vein, Hulstijn (2002) suggests that a programme for adult, literate learners might consist of listening and reading activities designed to promote implicit learning and an 'awareness component' involving rules of thumb derived from pedagogical grammars. However, another possibility for developing explicit knowledge, examined later in this chapter, is making language the content of tasks, so that learners communicate together in order to discover for themselves how some feature of the language works.

Summary

We have examined two rather different cognitive accounts of learning. One views language learning in terms of skill-learning, i.e. a process by which controlled or declarative procedures are transformed into automatic procedures through practice. A theory of teaching based on such an account emphasizes:

1 The need for declarative knowledge of language to be taught.
2 The need for communicative practice, i.e. practice involving 'real operating conditions', to proceduralize declarative knowledge.
3 The need for feedback that shows learners where they are going wrong.

Focused tasks have a role to play in such a theory by providing communicative practice directed at specific linguistic forms.

The second cognitive account views learning as an implicit process that cannot be directly influenced through instruction but that can be facilitated by explicit knowledge. A theory of teaching based on such an account emphasizes:

1 The need for opportunities to learn implicitly through communication.
2 The importance of attending to form when communicating, i.e. 'noticing'.
3 The need to teach explicit knowledge separately as a means of facilitating attention to form.

Such a theory obviously lends support to the use of unfocused tasks. But focused tasks also have a role to play here as they provide a means by which learners can be given opportunities to communicate in such a way that they might be able to learn specific linguistic forms implicitly.

Designing focused tasks

In this section we will consider three principal ways in which researchers have set about designing focused tasks: (1) *structure-based production tasks*, (2) comprehension tasks, and (3) *consciousness-raising tasks*.

Structure-based production tasks

In a key article, Loschky and Bley-Vroman (1993) discuss what they call 'structure-based communication tasks'. They distinguish three ways in which a task can be designed to incorporate a specific target language feature. The first is 'task-naturalness'. In this case, the target structure may not be necessary for completion of the task but nevertheless can be expected to arise naturally and frequently in performing the task. The example Loschky and Bley-Vroman give is of a task that involves the exchange of information about a travel itinerary. They suggest that this will lead naturally to the use of the present simple tense, for example, 'You leave Honolulu at 7.10', but acknowledge that it could also be performed using other ways of expressing the future, for example, 'will' or 'going to'. They refer to research on inter-language variation, which has shown that different types of tasks result in different uses of grammatical features (for example, Tarone and Parrish 1988) found that a narrative task elicited frequent use of definite noun phrases whereas an interview task elicited many generic noun phrases.

The second way of incorporating a linguistic focus is in terms of 'task-utility'. By this Loschky and Bley-Vroman mean that even though a targeted feature is not essential for completing the task it is very 'useful'. They give as an example the kind of spot-the-difference task shown in Figure 1.2 in Chapter 1, pointing out that learners can perform such a task without recourse to prepositions but that using them will make it easier to perform the task and perhaps ensure that the outcome is more successful. Of course, as Loschky and Bley-Vroman acknowledge, the utility of a structure is relative to the learner's existing stage of acquisition. They point out that students who have already achieved full mastery of a specific structure, for example, prepositions will not benefit acquisitionally from producing the structure.

The third way of designing a focused task is to try to ensure the 'task-essentialness' of the targeted feature. This requires that learners *must* use the feature in order to complete the task successfully—if they fail to use it they will not be able to achieve a satisfactory outcome. In this respect, the targeted feature becomes the 'essence' of the task. However, the examples Loschky and Bley-Vroman give are all of comprehension rather than production tasks. They acknowledge that it may be impossible to design tasks that make the production of the target feature essential and that, in fact, task-essentialness can only be achieved by receptive tasks.

Loschky and Bley-Vroman also consider what aspect of acquisition structure-based tasks are likely to influence. They express doubts as to whether the kinds of production tasks they give as examples will trigger acquisition of new linguistic forms, noting that learners cannot be expected to use a targeted structure unless they have already internalized it. For this reason, they suggest that the role of such tasks in language pedagogy should be seen as that of automatizing existing knowledge.

The challenge facing researchers (and teachers) is that of designing structure-based communication tasks that make the target structure 'natural', 'useful', or 'essential'. To what extent can this be achieved in production tasks? As Loschky and Bley-Vroman are at pains to point out, it is not easy. Of course, learners can be directed or led to use the target feature, for example, by pre-teaching it, but, as we have already noted, this may result in the learners orienting to the activity more as an exercise that requires them to practise a 'structure' than as a task that leads to 'behaviour'. From the perspective of teaching based on theories of skill-learning this need not be a problem but it is a problem from the perspective of teaching based on a theory of implicit learning. What evidence is there that learners do produce the targeted structure as 'behaviour' when they perform a structure-based production task? Let us consider a number of studies and ask what we can learn from them.

The first study (Tuz 1993) involved the use of a task as part of an instructional sequence designed to practise the use of attributive adjectives referring to shape, size, etc., for example, 'two small round white buttons'. The sequence consisted of: (1) presentation involving demonstration and direct explanation of adjectival ordering; (2) a number of controlled practice activities; and (3) a structure based production task. This required students to sit in pairs back to back and describe a set of cards depicting clocks, which differed in terms of colour, size, and shape. Native speakers on whom the task was piloted were found to produce noun phrases containing multiple adjectives, although Tuz notes that the order of the adjectives was variable, i.e. it did not always confirm to the pedagogic rule she had taught. Tuz was interested in whether the students were able to transfer the adjectival order they had been practising to actual communication. She found that only one out of the six students who completed the task used adjectival ordering. This student ordered adjectives for shape and colour on seventeen occasions. However, interestingly the order this student followed was colour + shape, for example, 'a red square clock', whereas the order that had been taught was shape + colour, for example, 'a square red clock'.

Sterlacci (1996) carried out a study to investigate whether a task designed to elicit the productive use of modal verbs did in fact do so. The subjects were 19 adult Japanese intermediate learners of English. The task required them to: (1) read some information about a problem a person (Hiro) was facing; (2) write down the advice they would give Hiro using the prompt, 'I think Hiro ...'; and (3) discuss what advice to give in a group. At the end of the task the students were also asked to write down what they had learned from the task, as suggested by Allwright (1984). Sterlacci analysed the learners' written responses in part (2) of the task. Altogether there were 115 responses, 96 (83%) of which contained a modal verb. Only one of the learners failed to use at least one modal verb. The principal modals used were *should* (69), *has to* (10), and *had better* (9).

In response to the request to indicate what they had learned from the task none of the students indicated 'modals'. Their responses referred to what they saw as the aim of the task, i.e. to develop the ability to speak fluently, the difficulties they had in performing it, or to Hiro's problem. This study indicates that the task was successful in eliciting the targeted structure and that the learners did not intentionally set out to use modal verbs, i.e. they did not treat it as a situational grammar exercise.

The third study (Mackey 1999) we will consider made use of tasks designed to elicit various question forms. The tasks, together with the forms they targeted, are summarized in Table 5.1. Mackey comments that the tasks had been tested in a number of research projects, demonstrating that they led to learners producing a large number of questions of different types. The subjects in the study were 34 adult ESL learners in lower proficiency classes in a private language school in Sydney, Australia. Mackey notes that when the tasks were performed interactively with native speakers, the learners often had difficulty producing a particular question form. However, if they persisted they were able to reformulate the question making it more target-like or comprehensible to their interlocutor. She

Task	Description	Structures targeted
Story completion	Working out a story by asking questions	*wh*-questions, *do*/aux. questions, SVO questions, neg./*do* second questions
Picture sequencing	Discovering the order of a picture story	SVO questions, negatives (neg. and SVO and neg. and verb)
Picture differences	Identifying the differences between similar pictures	*wh*-questions, copula inversion questions, *yes/no* inversion questions, *wh-/do* fronting questions, negatives (neg. and SVO and neg. and verb), neg./*do* second questions
Picture drawing	Describing or drawing a picture	*wh*-questions, copula inversion questions, yes/no inversion questions, *wh-/do* fronting questions, negatives (neg. and SVO and neg. and verb)

Table 5.1: Tasks used to elicit question forms (Mackey 1999: 568)

also notes that many learners then used that question form on subsequent occasions in the task, resulting in a clustering of the form. She comments 'learners may have been coming to an understanding of which forms are most successful at eliciting the information they need for successful task completion' (p. 580–1).

What can we learn from these studies about the validity of structure-based production tasks? First, the studies by Sterlacci and Mackey suggest that it is possible to design tasks that successfully target the use of specific grammatical structures. Second, it seems to be easier to elicit some features than others. Eliciting the use of modals (as in Sterlacci) or the use of question forms (as in Mackey), for example, would seem to be much easier than eliciting noun phrases with multiple attributive adjectives (as in Tuz). It simply may not be possible to design tasks that make the use of some grammatical structures 'essential' or even 'natural'. Third, there is likely to be individual learner variation. Whereas some learners use the structure that has been targeted other learners do not. This lends support to Loshcky and Bley-Vroman's claim that whether a task is successful in eliciting use of the target structure will depend on the learner's stage of development. If the task is to assist acquisition it should be directed at a structure that learners are in the process of acquiring. The target structure in Tuz's study was probably beyond the capacity of the learners at their stage of development. Sterlazzi's learners, however, seemed to have already known how to use modal verbs and thus benefited only in terms of automatization. Only in Mackey's study was the target structure 'learnable' in the sense that it lay within their developmental capacity and yet also posed problems. It is, of course not easy to design tasks that take learners' stage of development into account. For one thing, learners may not all be at the same stage, while for another, ascertaining what stages learners have reached is a time-consuming business (Lightbown 1985). Fourth, there is evidence from all three studies that when performing structure-based communicative tasks learners treat them as opportunities for communicating rather than for learning. This was true even in Tuz's study where the task was preceded by direct instruction and controlled practice. Thus, any learning that does occur as a result of performing a structure-based task is likely to be incidental.

To date, there has been little research investigating whether learners actually learn the target structure as a result of performing a structure-based production task. Mackey's study found that learners who completed the tasks shown in Table 5.1 manifested clear developmental gains in the questions they produced, as measured by pre- and post-tests consisting of the same kinds of tasks. Of the learners who performed the tasks interactively, for example, 11 out of 14 made advances. Much may depend on whether learners 'notice' the target structure while they are performing the task. Mackey, Gass, and McDonough (2000) report a study that suggests that what learners notice may depend on the nature of the linguistic feature that has been targeted. In this study, learners reported noticing lexical, semantic and phonological features in the feedback they received on their efforts to communicate. However, they generally did not notice morphosyntactic features.[3] The learners in Mackey's (1999) study may have 'noticed' questions because they were pragmatically important for completing the task and because of the struggle they experienced in trying to produce them. More studies are needed to establish whether performing structure-based production tasks consistently leads to noticing and to acquisition.

Finally, we will consider a rather different kind of structure-based production task. Wajnryb (1990) describes a technique she calls *dictogloss*. This makes use of a short text that has been selected or devised to have a structural focus. The text is read at normal speed, sentence by sentence, while the learners note down key words and phrases, i.e. the content words. The learners then work in groups to try to reconstruct the text collaboratively. Wajnryb emphasizes that the aim is not to generate an exact replica of the original text but rather to reproduce its content. Dictogloss meets the essential requirements of a task—the primary focus of attention is on meaning, learners can choose their own linguistic resources when reproducing the text (although they can also 'borrow' from the notes they made as they listened) and there is a clear outcome (the reproduction of the text) the success of which is determined in terms of its propositional rather than linguistic content. The 'focus' comes from the 'seeding' of the original text.

How effective are dictogloss tasks in promoting noticing and production of the targeted form? Kowal and Swain (1997) found that Grade 8 French immersion students both noticed and produced exemplars of the present tense when working in pairs to reconstruct a text that had been devised to practise this structure. They discuss an episode in which a pair of students worked out that the subject of 'tracassent' in the string 'problèmes qui nous tracassent' is not 'nous' but rather 'problèmes' by attending to the '-ent' ending on the verb. However, Kowal and Swain note that the learners did not focus exclusively on the targeted structure but rather dealt with a wide range of linguistic features. They comment 'the dictogloss approach might be better suited to promoting syntactic processing skills in general than as a means for drawing attention to a particular grammatical point' (ibid. 300).

Dictogloss tasks by their very nature might be expected to focus learners' attention on form as learners are forced to consider the language they need to reconstruct the text carefully. Interestingly, however, Swain and Lapkin (2001) did not find any statistically significant difference in the number of *language-related episodes* observed in the dialogue resulting from a dictogloss task and a two-way information gap (jigsaw) task.[4] Nor was there any difference in the task outcomes (the stories the students wrote) or in post-test measurements of the target structures. They explain this somewhat surprising finding by pointing out that the all the learners received a mini-lesson on the target structures prior to completing the tasks and that this served to focus their attention equally on these forms. Thus this study bears out the point made above—namely, that when the task follows the presentation stage of a lesson (see Figure 5.2), it influences how learners perform the task.

Izumi and Bigelow (2000) investigated a task similar to dictogloss. Their *text-reconstruction tasks* required learners to read a short written passage that had been seeded with the target structure (English hypothetical/counterfactual conditionals) and to underline the parts they felt were especially important for subsequently reconstructing the passage. The passage was then collected and the learners were told to reconstruct it as accurately as possible. The learners were then asked to repeat this procedure, i.e. they reread and underlined the passage and reconstructed it a second time. These tasks were part of an extended treatment that also involved the learners in first completing an essay-writing task and reading a model essay containing exemplars of the target structure. The text-reconstruction tasks were successful in eliciting attempts to use the conditional structure. Also, the study showed a significant gain in the learners' accurate use of the target structure from the first to the second reconstruction in one of the two tasks used. However, the learners that completed the experimental procedure did not differ significantly from a comparison group (that had opportunity to comprehend but not to produce the target structure) in either noticing target-like use during the treatment or in post-test measures of the target structure.[5]

It is clear that dictogloss is an effective means of getting learners to talk about linguistic forms, although not necessarily the targeted form. Dictogloss tasks differ from the other structure-based production tasks we have considered in this section in another respect—they result in very explicit attention to form of the kind that is characteristic of consciousness-raising tasks (see below). The text-reconstruction task used by Izumi and Bigelow was more effective in eliciting use of the target structure, perhaps because the tasks were part of an extended treatment that encouraged noticing as well as use. However, there is, as yet, little evidence to support the claim that dictogloss/text-reconstruction tasks benefit acquisition if the measure of this is performance in post-tests.

Comprehension tasks

We have already noted that comprehension-based tasks may be more successful in eliciting attention to a targeted feature than production-based tasks because learners cannot avoid processing them. Here we will consider tasks that are designed to obligate learners to process a specific feature in oral or written input. These tasks go under various names—comprehension tasks (Loschky and Bley-Vroman 1993), *interpretation tasks* (Ellis 1995) and structured-input tasks (VanPatten 1996).

Comprehension tasks are based on the assumption that acquisition occurs as a result of input-processing. This is the assumption that underlies Figure 5.3, which posits that intake arises as a result of learners paying conscious attention to linguistic forms in the input ('noticing'). Noticing, as we have seen in Chapter 2, involves attention to form as learners attempt to understand the message content. In the case of unfocused comprehension tasks no attempt is made to structure the input to promote intake; thus learners can avoid processing syntactically by relying on semantic processing (see Swain 1985). In the case of focused comprehension, however, the input is contrived to induce noticing of predetermined forms; syntactic processing is required. We will consider two ways in which this has been attempted—*input enrichment* and input processing.

Input enrichment

Input enrichment involves designing tasks in such a way that the targeted feature is (1) frequent and/or (2) salient in the input provided. For example, the input in the task in Figure 5.1 contains numerous exemplars of the present perfect tense. Enriched input of this kind can take many forms. It can consist of oral/written texts that learners simply listen to or read (as in Figure 5.1), or written texts in which the target structure has been graphologically highlighted in some way (for example, through the use of underlining or bold print), or oral/written texts with follow-up activities designed to focus attention on the structure, for example, questions that can only be answered if the learners have successfully processed the target structure.

A number of research studies have investigated the effects of input enrichment on noticing and language acquisition. Jourdenais *et al.* (1995) found that English-speaking learners of L2 Spanish were more likely to make explicit reference to preterite and imperfect verb forms when thinking aloud during a narrative writing task if they had previously read texts where the forms were graphologically highlighted. They also found that learners exposed to the enhanced text were more likely to use past tense forms than learners who read the non-enhanced texts even though both texts had been enriched. This study suggests that highlighting a structure aids noticing and also that noticing may have an impact on learners' use of a structure.

Trahey and White (1993) examined whether enriched input was sufficient to enable francophone learners of L2 English to learn that English permits adverb placement between the subject (S) and the verb (V), for example, 'Simone stupidly forgot her book', but not between verb and direct object (O), for example, '* Simone forgot stupidly her book'.[6] The experimental treatment, i.e. the instruction, took the form of stories, games and exercises containing numerous sentences with adverbs in the three sentence positions permitted by English, i.e. ASVO, SAV, and SVOA. The adverbs were not highlighted in the input. Exposure occurred one hour a day for ten days. Tests administered one day and three weeks after the end of the instruction showed that the learners succeeded in learning the SAV position but failed to 'unlearn' the SVAO position. Interesting, a comparison with the results of an earlier study involving explicit instruction (White 1991) indicated that the input flood worked as well where SAV was concerned but was much less effective in helping learners discover the ungrammaticality of SVAO. This study, then, suggests that input enrichment may be effective in helping learners acquire completely new L2 features but is not very effective in enabling them to eliminate incorrect rules that have entered their interlanguage. This study involved the provision of an 'input-flood', i.e. massive amounts of input containing the targeted structure. Other input-enrichment studies (for example, Alanen 1996) that have provided a more limited quantity of enriched input have been less successful in demonstrating that it has any effect at all on acquisition.

These two studies suggest that enriched input where the target structure is highlighted and where it is not highlighted can assist acquisition. The question arises as to which type of enriched input works best. J. White (1998) investigated this in a study that compared the effects of three types of enriched input: (1) a typographically enhanced input flood plus extensive listening and reading, (2) a typographically enhanced input flood by itself, and (3) a typographically unenhanced input flood. White found no differences in the three groups' acquisition of the possessive determiners, 'his' and 'her', with all three groups improving equally. She concludes that the target structure was probably equally salient in all three types of input.

Input processing

'Input-processing instruction' is a term coined by VanPatten (1996). Its goal is 'to alter the processing strategies that learners take to the task of comprehension and to encourage them to make better form–meaning connections than they would if left to their own devices' (p. 60). There are three key components: (1) an explanation of a form–meaning relationship, for example, the use of the passive to topicalize the patient of a sentence by placing it in subject position); (2) information about *processing strategies*, for example, the need to attend to the form of the verb to determine whether the subject is the agent of the verb, as is most generally the case, or the patient, as is the case with passive verbs; and (3) *structured-input* activities where learners have the chance to process the targeted feature in a controlled manner. In some ways, input-processing instruction resembles traditional production-based instruction in that it involves a presentation stage followed by a practice stage. However, VanPatten is at pains to emphasize its differences; unlike traditional instruction, it provides explicit information about processing strategies that is designed to overcome the 'default strategies' that characterize the way learners naturally process input in accordance with their interlanguage; and also, of course, the practice stage is input- rather than output-based.

Our main concern here is with the 'structured input' stage of a lesson as this involves the use of focused tasks. In Ellis (1995: 98–9) I list some general principles for designing this kind of focused task, which I call 'interpretation tasks'. These include the following:

1 An interpretation task consists of a stimulus to which learners must make some kind of response.
2 The stimulus can take the form of spoken or written input.
3 The response can take various forms, for example, indicate true–false, check a box, select the correct picture, draw a diagram, perform an action, but in each case the response will be completely nonverbal or minimally verbal.
4 The activities in the task can be sequenced to require first attention to meaning, then noticing the form and function of the grammatical structure, and finally error identification.
5 Learners should have the opportunity to make some kind of personal response, i.e. relate the input to their own lives.

Figure 5.4 gives an example of part of an interpretation task that was designed to teach psychological predicate instructions and the kind of errors learners have been observed to make with this structure, for example, learners misunderstand a sentence like 'Mary worries her mother' as meaning 'Mary worries about her mother'.

A Answer the following questions.
  1 Do tall people frighten you?
  2 Do people who cook impress you?
  3 Do smartly dressed people attract you?
  4 Do argumentative people annoy you?
  5 Are you interested in physically attractive people?
  6 Are you bored by self-important people?
  7 Are you irritated by fat people?
  8 Are you confused by clever people?

B On the basis of your responses in A, make a list of the qualities of people whom
  1 you like.
  2 you dislike.

Figure 5.4: An example of an interpretation task
(based on Ellis 1995)

Input-processing instruction has attracted considerable attention from researchers. Most of the studies (see Ellis 1999 for a review) have sought to compare the learning outcomes of traditional production-based instruction and input-processing instruction. The study that set this research activity in motion was VanPatten and Cadierno (1993). The focus of this study was the positioning of object clitic pronouns in Spanish. The subjects were university level learners in the US, with one group receiving input-processing instruction, another traditional production-based instruction and a third (the control group) no instruction on clitic pronouns. Learning gains were measured by means of both a listening comprehension test and a discrete-item written production test. The results showed that the input-processing group outperformed the production-based group and the control group on the listening test. This group also did just as well as the production group on the production test. These results were confirmed by follow-up tests administered one month later. This study, then, suggests that input-processing instruction involving interpretation tasks is more effective than production-based instruction that involves both controlled and situational grammar exercises.

It is, of course, not possible from this study to determine whether the advantage found for the input-processing instruction derived from performing the interpretation tasks or the explicit explanation of processing strategies. To address this, VanPatten and Oikennon (1996) carried out a study that investigated the comparative effects on learning of three instructional conditions: (1) explicit instruction plus structured input; (2) explicit instruction only; and (3) structured input only. The target structure was again Spanish clitic pronouns and the subjects were high school students in the US. On the comprehension test, groups (1) and (3) did better than group (2). There was no difference between (1) and (3). On the production test only (1) did better than (2), i.e. there was no difference between groups (2) and (3). VanPatten and Oikennon conclude 'significant improvement on the interpretation tests is due to the presence of structured input activities' and that even on the production test 'the effects of explicit instruction are negligible' (p. 508). This study, then, suggests that it is the structured input provided in the interpretation task that contributed most to the positive effect of input-processing instruction on learning.

There are, however, a number of reasons to be cautious about the acquisitional benefits of interpretation tasks. First, the tests used to measure learning were of the discrete-item kind. There is to date no clear evidence that interpretation tasks result in the ability to use the targeted structure in communication. Indeed a study by VanPatten and Sanz (1995) which set out to examine this failed to demonstrate that input-processing instruction enhanced communicative production of the targeted structure (Spanish clitic pronouns again), although this was in part because the structure-based communicative task they used to measure acquisition elicited very few examples of this structure—a problem in the design of such tasks we have already noted. Second, a number of more recent studies (for example, DeKeyser and Sokalski 1996; Salaberry 1997; Allen 2000; Erlam 2001; Kim 2001) have failed to show that instruction involving interpretation tasks is more effective than production-based instruction. These studies either find no difference in learning outcomes between groups that received the different types of instruction or alternatively some advantage for production-based instruction. However, it is important to note that all these studies did find that interpretation tasks were effective in the sense that learners who received it showed statistically significant greater gains than students who received no instruction in the targeted structure. One conclusion that does seem to be robust, therefore, is that input-processing instruction involving interpretation tasks does result in measurable gains in learning as measured by discrete-item tests.

There is a final problem with these studies that needs consideration. It is not always clear whether the structured input activities were 'tasks' in the sense this term is being used in this book (see Chapter 1). Consider, for example, the structured-input activities used in Allen (2000: 83). To induce processing of the French causative structure, Allen used the following kind of activity:

> In this exercise, you will decide who is doing a particular activity. Circle who is doing the activity.
> (Students hear, 'Nous faisons balayer la chambre.'/ 'We sweep the bedroom.') a. nous b. someone else

Such an activity does not meet two of the essential criteria of a task. First, it does not really involve a primary focus on meaning in the sense that it incorporates some kind of 'gap' that needs to be filled. This is because the activity only requires attention to the semantic meaning of the sentence, not to its pragmatic meaning. Second, it does not really involve real-world processes of language use, i.e. we do not go around saying who is doing the activity in a sentence. Third, there is no clearly defined non-linguistic outcome by which to measure whether the activity has been accomplished successfully. Thus, this activity is more exercise-like than task-like. It is probably true to say that the input-processing research to date speaks more to the effectiveness of structured input *exercises* than structured input *tasks*.

Consciousness-raising tasks

Consciousness-raising (C-R) tasks differ from the kinds of focused tasks we have considered above in two essential ways. First, whereas structure-based production tasks, enriched input tasks, and interpretation tasks are intended to cater primarily to implicit learning, C-R tasks are designed to cater primarily to explicit learning—that is, they are intended to develop awareness at the level of 'understanding' rather than awareness at the level of 'noticing' (see Schmidt 1994). Thus, the desired outcome of a C-R task is awareness of how some linguistic feature works. Second, whereas the previous types of task were built around content of a general nature, for example, stories, pictures of objects, opinions about the kind of person you like, C-R tasks make language itself the content. In this respect, it can be asked whether C-R tasks are indeed tasks. They are in the sense that learners are required to talk meaningfully about a language point using their own linguistic resources. That is, although there is some linguistic feature that is the focus of the task learners are not required to use this feature, only think about it and discuss it. The 'taskness' of a C-R task lies not in the linguistic point that is the focus of the task but rather in the talk learners must engage in in order to achieve an outcome to the task.

The rationale for the use of C-R tasks draws partly on the hypothesized role for explicit knowledge as a facilitator for the acquisition of implicit knowledge (see Figure 5.3) and partly on the claims in the psychological literature that learning is more significant if it involves greater depth of processing (for example, Craik and Lockhart 1972). C-R tasks cater for discovery learning through problem solving (Bourke 1996), in accordance with the general principle that what learners can find out for themselves is better remembered than what they are simply told.

From Ellis (1991: 234), we can identify the main characteristics of C-R tasks:

1 There is an attempt to *isolate* a specific linguistic feature for focused attention.
2 The learners are provided with *data* that illustrate the targeted feature and they may also be provided with an *explicit rule* describing or explaining the feature.
3 The learners are expected to utilize *intellectual effort* to understand the targeted feature.
4 Learners may be optionally required to verbalize a rule describing the grammatical structure.

A C-R task consists of (1) data containing exemplars of the targeted feature and (2) instructions requiring the learners to operate on the data in some way. In Ellis (1997) I list the different data options and types of operations that are possible. Data options include authentic vs. contrived, oral vs. written and gap vs. non-gap. Types of operations include identification, for example,. learners underline the target structure in the data, judgement, i.e. they respond to the correctness or appropriateness of the data, and sorting, i.e. they classify the data by sorting it into defined categories. By permuting data options and types of operations, a considerable variety of C-R tasks can be designed. A C-R task constitutes a kind of puzzle which when solved enables learners to discover for themselves how a linguistic feature works.

An example of a C-R task is given in Activity 2 of Figure 1.3 on page 18. The linguistic focus here is English prepositions of time. The data options utilized in this task are: (1) contrived; (2) written; (3) continuous text (as opposed to discrete sentences); (4) well-formed (as opposed to deviant); and (5) non-gap. The operations involved in this task are (1) sorting and (2) verbalizing a rule. A further example is provided in Figure 5.6 below.[7] This task addresses dative alternation. The data options here are: (1) contrived; (2) written; (3) discrete sentences; (4) deviant; and (5) non-gap. The operations are (1) judgement and (2) verbalizing a rule. These tasks could be easily redesigned to incorporate other data options and operation types. For example, in the first task an information gap could be created by giving one learner a text from which the times and dates of the appointments had been omitted and another learner a schedule of the attempted appointments. The talk this task would generate would centre around checking that the various time expressions had been correctly identified and classified and formulating a rule to explain their use. Fotos and Ellis (1991) provide an information gap version of the task in Figure 5.5.

A What is the difference between verbs like 'give' and 'explain'?

She gave a book to her father. (= grammatical)
She gave her father a book. (=grammatical)

The policeman explained the law to Mary. (= grammatical)
The policeman explained Mary the law. (= ungrammatical)

B Indicate whether the following sentences are grammatical or ungrammatical.

1 They saved Mark a seat.
2 His father read Kim a story.
3 She donated the hospital some money.
4 They suggested Mary a trip on the river.
5 They reported the police the accident.
6 They threw Mary a party.
7 The bank lent Mr. Thatcher some money.
8 He indicated Mary the right turning.
9 The festival generated the college a lot of money.
10 He cooked his girlfriend a cake.

C Work out a rule for verbs like 'give' and 'explain'.

1 List the verbs in B that are like 'give' (i.e. permit both sentence patterns) and those that are like 'explain' (i.e. allow only one sentence pattern).
2 What is the difference between the verbs in your two lists?

Figure 5.5: An example of a C-R task

A number of studies have investigated whether C-R tasks are effective in developing explicit knowledge of the L2. Fotos and Ellis (1991) compared the effects of direct consciousness-raising by means of grammar explanations and of indirect consciousness-raising by means of a C-R task on Japanese learners' ability to judge the grammaticality of sentences involving dative alternation such as those in the task in Figure 5.6. They found that both methods of consciousness-raising resulted in significant gains in understanding of the target structure, although the direct method seemed to produce the more durable gains. However, Fotos (1994) found no statistically significant difference between these two methods in a follow-up study that investigated three different grammatical structures (adverb placement, dative alternation, and relative clauses). Sheen (1992) compared direct and indirect consciousness-raising in a six-week beginners' French course for Japanese students, reporting that students in the two groups did equally well in a written post-test of the structures taught. However, the group taught by the direct method did better in an oral test, a result he explains by the extra oral practice this group received.[8] Mohamed (2001) found that indirect consciousness-raising was more effective than direct consciousness-raising with groups of high intermediate ESL learners from mixed L1 backgrounds but not with a group of low-intermediate learners. This study suggests that the effectiveness of C-R tasks may depend on the proficiency of learners. Clearly, learners need sufficient proficiency to talk metalingually about the target feature and, if they lack this, they may not be able to benefit to the same degree from a C-R task.

Obviously much depends on how learners perform the C-R task, in particular what level of awareness of the target form they achieve. To investigate this it is necessary to investigate what learners are attending to as they perform the task. Leow (1997) used a crossword puzzle task to investigate the extent to which learners of L2 Spanish noticed and demonstrated explicit understanding of the forms targeted in this task (irregular third person singular and plural *pretérito* forms of stem-changing *-ir* verbs such as *repetir*).[9] The learners were asked to think aloud as they completed the puzzle. Leow eliminated learners who provided no evidence of having noticed the forms in the think-aloud protocols and then analysed the extent to which different learners demonstrated meta-awareness. He was able to show that increased levels of meta-awareness correlated with greater 'conceptually-driven processing' such as hypothesis testing and morphological rule formation. Furthermore discrete-item post-tests showed that those learners who demonstrated high levels of meta-awareness were better able to both recognize and produce the correct target forms.

It is, of course, one thing to show that C-R tasks result in increased understanding of the targeted feature, i.e. in explicit knowledge, and entirely another to demonstrate that this aids the process by which learners acquire the ability to use the feature in their communicative behaviour. If explicit knowledge does not convert directly into implicit knowledge (as claimed by the non-interface position), then an *immediate* effect on communicative behaviour cannot be expected. There are, however, obvious difficulties in designing a study to investigate whether explicit knowledge has a *subsequent* effect on the acquisition of implicit knowledge. One way of overcoming this difficulty might be to show that explicit knowledge acquired from completing C-R tasks aids subsequent noticing of the targeted features. Fotos (1993) provides evidence that this is what happens. Several weeks after the completion of the C-R tasks, the learners in her study completed a number of dictations that included a few exemplars of the target structures. They were then asked to underline any particular bit of language they had paid special attention to as they did the dictation. Fotos found that they frequently underlined the structures that had been targeted in the C-R tasks.

The value of C-R tasks lies not just in whether they are effective in developing explicit knowledge and subsequently promoting noticing but also in the opportunities they provide for learners to communicate. A key question, then, is the extent to which C-R tasks do promote communicative behaviour and also its quality. One way of answering this question is by examining whether C-R tasks lead to the negotiation of meaning (see Chapter 3). Fotos and Ellis (1991) found that the information-gap C-R task they used did result in quite extensive negotiation but that much of this was very mechanical in nature, a point that has also been made of the negotiation that arises in unfocused tasks (see Seedhouse 1999). Fotos (1994) compared the amount and quality of negotiation in unfocused tasks and C-R tasks that shared the same design features and found no significant differences. She also notes that the negotiations were not as mechanical as those observed in Fotos and Ellis and suggests that this was because in the later study the students were more familiar with performing tasks in groups.

C-R tasks seem to be an effective means of achieving a focus on form while at the same time affording opportunities to communicate. They appear to be as effective (and in some cases more effective) in developing explicit knowledge than direct consciousness-raising. They have been shown to promote subsequent noticing of the targeted features. They can be as effective as unfocused tasks in generating modified input through the negotiation of meaning. However, as Ellis (1991) and Sheen (1992) have pointed out, they also have their limitations. They may not be well-suited to young learners, who view language as a tool for 'doing' rather than as an object for 'studying'. Beginner learners will need to use their L1 to talk about language although the product of their discussion could still be L2 encoded. Learners lacking in metalanguage may also find it difficult to talk about language problems (Storch 1999), although Swain's research (for example, Swain 1998) suggests that learners can talk metalinguistically without using metalinguistic terms. Because C-R tasks are problem-solving in nature they are 'essentially intelligence-related' (Sheen 1992) and thus may not appeal to learners who are less skilled at forming and testing conscious hypotheses about language. It should be emphasized, however, that I have always stressed that 'consciousness-raising is not an alternative to communication activities, but a supplement' (Ellis 1991: 241).

Implementing focused tasks

So far we have considered how the design of various kinds of focused tasks (structure-based production tasks, interpretation tasks and C-R tasks) can cause learners to produce, notice and understand targeted structures. We have seen, however, that this is not unproblematic. We will now consider whether some of the difficulties in achieving a language focus can be overcome methodologically, i.e. by the way in which the task is implemented. We will examine both implicit and explicit ways of drawing attention to form.

Implicit methodological techniques

Implicit methodological techniques involve providing feedback on learners' use of the targeted feature in a manner that maintains the meaning-centredness of the task. In effect, this involves the strategic use of the negotiation of meaning. Thus, from the learner's perspective the feedback is directed at solving a communication problem created by something the learner has said while performing the task. From the perspective of the learner's interlocutor, however, the feedback is targeted very specifically in response to errors the learner makes in using the structure that has been targeted. Researchers have examined two ways of providing this feedback—*clarification requests* and *recasts* (see Chapter 3) .

Nobuyoshi and Ellis (1993) devised a treatment in which a teacher responded to any error a student made in the use of the past tense in an oral narrative task with a request for clarification, as in this example:

Learner	He pass his house.
Teacher	Uh?
Learner	He passed, he passed, ah his sign.

They suggest that such a technique provides a way of teaching grammar communicatively because the opportunities to reformulate deviant utterances occur in the context of trying to communicate and because the learners are not aware that the teacher is intentionally focusing on form. The results of this small-scale study were interesting. Out of the three learners Nobuyoshi and Ellis investigated, two regularly reformulated when pushed to do so through requests for clarification while one did not. The two learners who reformulated demonstrated higher levels of accurate use of the past tense in a subsequent oral narrative task one week later while the learner who did not reformulate showed no gain in accuracy. Ellis and Takashima (1999) also provide evidence to suggest that *focused feedback* consisting of requests for clarification led to more accurate use of past tense forms in subsequent tasks. However, in this study, learners who just listened to other students performing the tasks and reformulating did better than those learners who actually took part. They suggest that it was the 'modified input' the listeners received rather than the 'modified output' the speakers produced that was important for learning. Obviously, learners can only benefit from the opportunity to modify their own output if they possess the necessary linguistic knowledge to do so. It would seem, therefore, that feedback in the form of requests for clarification is more likely to contribute to the automatization of existing knowledge than to the internalization of new knowledge.

Where the acquisition of new linguistic knowledge is concerned recasts may be a more promising technique. Recasts, which were considered in Chapter 3, involve rephrasing an utterance 'by changing one or more of its sentence components (subject, verb, or object) while still referring to its central meanings' (Long 1996: 436). An example is:

Learner   I go to cinema at weekend.
Teacher   Oh, you went to the cinema at the weekend.
Learner   Yeah, I went to the cinema.

Recasts occur quite frequently in naturally-occurring meaning-focused communication where they will be directed at a broad range of linguistic features that have caused some kind of communicative problem or uncertainty. Recasts can be used to give a 'focus' to a task if they are directed at some pre-determined feature whenever this is used incorrectly by a learner. They provide opportunities for a learner to uptake the correction, which may or may not be seized on. The example above illustrates *uptake*.

There are strong theoretical grounds for believing that recasts aid acquisition. In the context of first language acquisition, for example, Farrar (1992) has pointed to a number of facilitative features of recasts: (1) they reformulate a syntactic element; (2) they expand a syntactic element or semantic content or both; (3) the utterance providing the recast is semantically contingent; and (4) a recast immediately follows the learner's utterance. Ayoun (2001) notes an additional characteristic that may be important—(5) learners' emotional involvement in communicating may predispose them to attend to any recasts they receive.

Studies that have investigated the effects of recasts on acquisition have produced mixed results to date. Long, Inagaki, and Ortega (1998) sought to compare the relative effect of 'models' and recasts on the acquisition of L2 Japanese and Spanish grammatical features in the context of a task. Models consisted of sentences that the learners listened to and then repeated.

Recasts provided negative feedback on the learners' own utterances. No significant gains in the accurate use of the Japanese structure were found for either group of learners. However, in the case of the Spanish structure both models and recasts proved effective with recasts producing higher post-test scores than models. Long *et al.* acknowledge that the results of their study are somewhat disappointing but claim that they provide some support for the use of recasts as a way of promoting L2 acquisition. More convincing evidence comes from Mackey and Philp (1998). This study investigated the effects of two kinds of interaction—one with intensive recasts and one without—on the acquisition of question forms by 35 adult ESL learners in Australia. One group of learners received intensive recasts in response to any ill-formed questions they produced while the other group performed the same tasks (those shown in Figure 5.4) without recasts. In the case of the more advanced students (those who were developmentally 'ready'), the interaction with recasts proved more effective than the interaction without recasts in enabling them to produce advanced questions forms. However, in the case of learners who were less advanced developmentally, no difference in the two treatments was found. Mackey and Philp also investigated the effects of learner uptake on acquisition but found that whether learners modified their output or not in response to a recast did not affect development. Doughty and Varela (1998) report a study of the effects of implicit feedback that consisted of repetitions and recasts of the utterances students produced in a series of tasks involving oral and written science reports. This treatment was provided in the classroom as part of their normal curriculum. The grammatical focus here was the English simple past tense. It resulted in clear gains in accuracy in the use of this structure and also in greater use of more advanced interlanguage forms (for example, 'toke' as opposed to 'take'). In comparison, a control group showed little improvement. Finally, Ayoun (2001) investigated the relative effects of written explicit grammar instruction, recasts and models on the acquisition of French *imparfait* and *passé composé* in an experimental study involving a computerized reading task. Ayoun found that all three treatments produced gains in acquisition and that recasts proved more effective than direct grammar instruction. However, the gains of the group receiving the recasts were not statistically different from those of the group receiving models.

These studies are instructive. First, they demonstrate that it is possible to achieve a specific linguistic focus when learners perform a task by negotiating utterances that contain errors in the targeted feature. Both requests for clarification and recasts seem to work in this respect. A methodologically contrived focus by means of requests for clarification and recasts may be one way of overcoming the difficulty of designing tasks to make the targeted structure essential, natural or useful. Second, this focus is achieved 'communicatively', i.e. it results in 'behaviour', not 'structural practice'.

Third, there is growing evidence to suggest that an implicit focus on form in the context of negotiating for meaning aids acquisition.

Explicit methodological techniques

A focus can also be given to a task if learners are provided with explicit information relating to the targeted structure during the performance of the task. An explicit focus can be provided either pre-emptively or responsively. In the case of a *pre-emptive focus* the teacher draws attention to the targeted feature by asking a question or by making a metalingual comment. A *responsive focus* occurs through negative feedback involving explicit attention to the targeted feature. This can be achieved in various ways, for example, by means of an explicit correction ('You should say …') or a meta-linguistic comment/question.

Explicit feedback may play a crucial role in enabling learners to make new form/meaning connections. In a review of the research on recasts, Nicholas, Lightbown, and Spada (2001) conclude 'in general, recasts appear to be most effective in contexts where it is clear to the learner that the recast is a reaction to the accuracy of the form, not the content, of the original utterance', i.e. recasts work best when they function as explicit corrections of learner utterances.

Samuda (2001) reports an interesting study illustrating this point. It shows how in some circumstances implicit feedback, for example, using recasts, may not be sufficient to ensure that learners attend to targeted features and that explicit feedback may be needed. Samuda's starting point was to design a task that targeted a specific area of meaning and to then identify formal exponents; that is, her approach was one of meaning to form rather than form to meaning. She designed a task that created a 'semantic space' for using modal verbs to express degrees of possibility/certainty, i.e. epistemic modality. The task required the learners to work in groups to speculate on the identity of a person based on the contents of their pockets. They were asked to record hypotheses about the person's name, sex, age, and marital status on a chart. During the group discussion, the learners used a number of devices for expressing possibility, deriving these both from the input of the task itself, for example, 'possible' and 'certain', and from their existing interlanguage resources, for example, 'maybe' and 'sure'. However, conspicuously missing from their speech were instances of the target feature, i.e. modal verbs such as 'may' and 'must'. During this stage the teacher did not attempt to intervene by focusing on these forms. During the next stage of the lesson, when the groups made oral presentations of their hypotheses to the whole class, the teacher did intervene—first implicitly and then explicitly. In the implicit language focus the teacher mined formulaic chunks from the input data to highlight novel form/meaning relationships in the context of assisting the learners' communicative efforts. However,

Samuda found that not one of these 'interweaves' was taken up by the learners. She suggests that this was not surprising given the learners' 'intense focus on meaning'. The teacher then switched to providing a much more explicit focus on form. This involved the teacher introducing a modal verb and offering a direct metalingual comment about its meaning or form, as in this example:

> 100%? 100% Then you can say IS a businessman (writes on board). When you when you're NOT 100% certain, you can use 'must'. OK? Not he is a business man, but he must be a businessman. So 'be' here (pointing to *must be* on the board) is from this verb (pointing to *is*).

The learners participated actively in this explicit focus by asking questions about the forms the teacher raised to attention. In the final stage of this task, in which the learners had to prepare a poster, the teacher resumed her 'communicative' role. Interestingly, the learners now spontaneously employed the modal verbs the teacher had earlier drawn explicit attention to, interweaving these into the language they mined from the input data. This study, then, suggests that explicit attention to form may be helpful (and even necessary) to ensure that a task achieves its intended linguistic focus.

A key question is the extent to which explicit attention to form detracts from the communicative flow of the task performance. Evidence from studies of immersion classrooms (Lyster and Ranta 1997) and from communicative ESL lessons (Ellis, Basturkmen, and Loewen 2001) suggests that the use of explicit methodological techniques need not unduly disturb the primary focus on meaning. Also, Seedhouse (1997) discusses how what he calls a dual focus, i.e. on meaning and form, can be achieved through 'camouflaged' repair, i.e. repair work by the teacher that does not interrupt the flow of the interaction. He provides the following example from Mathers (1990):

Learner 1	And what did you do last weekend?
Learner 2	... I tried to find a pub where you don't see—where you don't see many tourists. And I find one
Teacher	Found.
Learner 2	I found one where I spoke with two English women and we spoke about life in Canterbury or things and after I came back
Teacher	Afterwards ...

A feature of this kind of unobtrusive repair work is that is brief and does not involve metalingual comment. Also, as Seedhouse notes, it may work best with 'mistakes' which do not interfere with communication rather than 'errors'. Obviously, though, continuous and lengthy explicit treatment is likely to threaten the primary focus on meaning and thus destroy the 'taskness' of a task.

Conclusion

In this chapter, we have examined cognitive theories of language acquisition that suggest the need for conscious attention to specific linguistic forms *while* learners are attempting to communicate. Focused tasks constitute a device for inducing such attention. They can be seen to serve three major purposes. They can be (1) 'language activating/fluency stretching' or (2) 'knowledge-constructing' (Samuda 2001). That is, focused tasks can be directed at providing opportunities for learners to use targeted features that are already part of their repertoire or they can be aimed at enabling learners to acquire new forms or to restructure their interlanguage. (3) Focused tasks can also contribute to the development of explicit linguistic knowledge. We have examined a number of studies that suggest that focused tasks 'work', both in the sense that they force processing (or understanding) of the targeted features and contribute to language acquisition.

We have examined various ways of designing focused tasks—structure-based production tasks, comprehension tasks and C-R tasks. A number of problems with these tasks have been considered, for example, the difficulty of designing a structure-based production task to make use of the targeted feature 'essential'. However, we have also seen that a focus can be provided methodologically by means of implicit and explicit techniques that draw attention to form as a task is being performed. In order to ensure that learners do indeed process the feature that has been targeted a combination of careful design and planned implementation involving both implicit and explicit techniques, as in Samuda (2001), would seem ideal.

Notes

1 Corder (1981) distinguishes between 'errors' and 'mistakes', arguing that the latter are of little significance in the process of language learning. Johnson (1988) rightly points out that from the perspective of skill-learning theories, 'mistakes' are important phenomena because they show what learners have learned but not proceduralized.

2 One way in which such modelling can occur is by means of a 'recast', i.e. a reformulation of parts or all of a learner utterance in such a way that a deviant linguistic form is replaced with a target language form. Long (1996) stakes out the acquisitional case for using recasts. These are discussed later in this chapter.

3 Mackey, Gass, and McDonough (2000) used an unfocused task. They examined the feedback that learners received on a variety of forms, using a stimulated recall procedure, i.e. they played back extracts from the recording of the interactions and asked learners to comment on them, to ascertain whether they noticed these forms or not. In the case of a structure-based communicative task, learners are perhaps more likely

to notice the target structure given its salience and frequency in the task performance.

4   Swain and Lapkin (2001) do report qualitative differences between the dictogloss and jigsaw tasks however. These suggested that the dictogloss was more likely to generate a conscious focus on form in general.

5   Izumi and Bigelow (2000) point out that the failure to find a group advantage for their output-based treatment does not mean that it was not effective for individual learners. They suggest that the marked variance in individual learners' results reflected whether they became conscious of a problem when they were trying to produce the target structure and therefore paid subsequent attention to it in the input.

6   The acquisition of adverbial placement rules is difficult for francophone learners of English because the rules for French are the exact opposite, i.e. French allows an adverbial between verb and direct object but not between subject and verb.

7   I have used the dative alternation many times with teachers, both native speakers of English and non-native speakers. The task addresses a grammar point that few teachers know and, as a result, arouses considerable curiosity. Interestingly, there is always someone who can solve the problem and provide an explanation; verbs like 'give' are monosyllabic and Anglo-Saxon in origin whereas verbs like 'explain' are polysyllabic and Latin in origin.

8   Sheen argues that direct consciousness-raising is to be preferred because it takes less time than problem-solving tasks thus allowing more time for practice activities. This seems a rather fatuous argument as it all depends on how long a teacher chooses to spend on consciousness-raising work, whether this is of the direct or indirect kind. Sheen's study was designed to find in favour of direct consciousness-raising. Thus the fact that he did not do so on the writing test is itself noteworthy!

9   The crossword puzzle task included clues that related specifically to the target structure— for example, 'La forma de la tercera persona singular ('el') del pretérito del verbo *dormirse*. Por ejemplo, "Ayer por la noche, mi novia (fell asleep) _____ en el sofá"' (Leow 1997: 502).

.

6   Sociocultural SLA and tasks

Introduction

So far the task-based research we have examined has been informed by mainstream SLA and the computational metaphor on which this is based— i.e. the idea of the human mind as a black box, which 'contains' the know- ledge that results from processing linguistic input and that is then accessed for output. Lantolf (1996: 725) argues that this metaphor has become so pervasive 'that many people find it difficult to conceive of neural computa- tion as a theory, it must surely be a fact'. Certainly this metaphor underlies the various SLA theories we considered in Chapters 2, 3, 4, and 5. For example, in Chapter 3, 'interaction' was viewed simply as the means by which input is made available to the black box or as an opportunity for producing output. In Chapter 4, the role of output was also examined in relation to how it contributes to the development of L2 knowledge inside the 'black box'. In Chapter 5, the importance of a 'focus on form' was dis- cussed in terms of its importance for knowledge construction through input and output processing.

A **sociocultural theory of mind** (SCT) based on the work of Vygotsky (1987), Leontiev (1981), and Wertsch (1985), among others, offers a way of viewing learning which is based on a very different set of metaphors and which is slowly establishing itself as an alternative paradigm in SLA. Lantolf (2000a) provides a label for this new paradigm—'sociocultural SLA'. Here we will provide a brief outline of the theory, paying special attention to how it can inform task-based research. We will then review the task-based research that draws on this theory.

Mediated learning

As Lantolf (2000a) points out 'the central and distinguishing concept of sociocultural theory is that higher forms of mental activity are *mediated*'. The theory seeks to explain how mediated minds (Lantolf and Pavlenko 1996) are developed out of social activity. Through social activity gen- etically endowed capacities are modified and reorganized into higher order forms, which allow individuals to exercise conscious control over such mental activities as attention, planning and problem-solving. *Mediation* according to Vygotsky (1978) can occur in three ways: through the use of some material tool such as tying a knot in one's handkerchief in order to remember something, through interaction with another person, or through the use of symbols. The most powerful of these symbolic means or 'signs', as Vygotsky called them, is language. For example, alphabetic writing systems, once developed, had a profound effect on the way we view language in terms of sentences, words, and phonemes. Language comes to serve as an autonomous tool for organizing and controlling thought. In Vygotskian theory, then, language is viewed as both a means of accomplishing social interaction and of managing mental activity. In sociocultural SLA, language learning involves both developing the means for mediating learning, i.e. the tools, and the language itself, i.e. the object. As Swain (2000) puts it, it involves learning how to use language to mediate language learning.

Lantolf (2000a) suggests that mediation in second language learning involves: (1) mediation by others in social interaction; (2) mediation by self through private speech; and (3) mediation by artifacts, for example, tasks and technology. Mediation can occur externally, as when a novice is given assistance in the performance of some function by an expert or by some artifact (such as a calculator or computer) or internally, as when an individual uses his or her own resources to achieve control over a function. The essence of a sociocultural theory of mind is that external mediation serves as the means by which internal mediation is achieved. Thus, according to Lantolf (2000a), development is 'about the appropriation by individuals (and groups) of the mediational means made available by others (past or present) in their environment in order to improve control over their own mental activity'.

Sociocultural theorists prefer to talk of 'participation' rather than 'acquisition' (Sfard 1998) to emphasize the point that development is not so much a matter of the taking in and the possession of knowledge but rather of the taking part in social activity.[1] In this view of learning, then, the distinction between 'use' of the L2 and 'knowledge' of the L2 becomes blurred because knowledge is use and use creates knowledge. For this reason, research based on SCT has typically eschewed the use of pre- and post-tests in favour of detailed 'micro-genetic' analyses of 'tool-mediated goal-directed action' (Zinchenko 1985, as cited in Lantolf 2000b). In the case of task-based research, this would involve detailed analyses of the way new linguistic forms and meanings arise out of the social or intrapersonal linguistic activity that learners engage in while they are performing a task. However, recent research by Swain and her co-researchers (for example, Swain 2001) has employed pre- and post-tests to examine the changes that result from performing collaborative tasks.

Verbal interaction and learning

A primary means of mediation is verbal interaction. Thus, SCT sees learning, including language learning, as dialogically based. Artigal (1992) goes so far as to suggest that the 'language acquisition device' is located in the interaction that takes place between speakers rather than inside their heads. That is, acquisition occurs *in* rather than *as a result of* interaction. From this perspective, then, L2 acquisition is not a purely individual-based process but shared between the individual and other persons.

Verbal interaction can be monologic or dialogic. Whereas both can serve to mediate learning, dialogic interaction is seen as central. Dialogic interaction enables an expert (such as a teacher) to create a context in which novices can participate actively in their own learning and in which the expert can fine-tune the support that the novices are given (Anton 1999). In particular, dialogic discourse is better equipped to identify what a learner can and cannot do without assistance. It serves to create the *intersubjectivity* that enables verbal interaction to mediate learning.

In theory, then, there is a close relationship between interpersonal activity and intramental activity, the former serving as the precursor of the latter. As Vygotsky (1981) puts it, new, elaborate psychological processes become available as a result of the initial production of these processes in social interaction. Vygotsky provides this explanation of how children develop mental skills:

> Any function in the child's development appears twice or on two planes, first it appears on the social plane, and then on the psychological plane, first it appears between people as an interpsychological category, and then within the child as an intrapsychological category. (ibid. 163)

Children progress from object-regulation, where their actions are determined by the objects they encounter in the environment, to other-regulation, where they learn to exert control over an object but only with the assistance of another, usually more expert person, and finally to self-regulation, where they become capable of independent strategic functioning. Verbal interaction, especially dialogic, serves as the principal means by which children progress from other- to self-regulation. Foley (1991) suggests, for example, that the topic-incorporation devices, in which the Interaction Hypothesis invests so much, can be viewed as devices for achieving self-regulation. As we noted in Chapter 2, young children need to learn how to use these devices to manage a conversation.

Applied to language learning, this means that learners first manifest new linguistic forms and functions in interactions with others and subsequently internalize them so they can use them independently. Furthermore, they are likely to experience problems in using new forms when placed in communicatively demanding situations with the result that they fall back on earlier acquired and more stable skills (see, for example, Appel and Lantolf 1994)—a phenomenon known as 'back-sliding' in mainstream SLA. Social talk is also the means by which they achieve self-regulation with new forms. This suggests that tasks can cater for learning by providing opportunities for learners: (1) to use new language structures and items through collaboration with others; (2) to subsequently engage in more independent use of the structures they have internalized in relatively undemanding tasks; and (3) to finally use the structures in cognitively more complex tasks. In theory, learning takes place when learners actually use a new skill in the accomplishment of some goal. It requires not just understanding input containing unknown language forms but actually producing them. Central to this process are the collaborative acts learners participate in. Tasks, then, can be seen as tools for constructing collaborative acts, although, as we will see shortly, these tools cannot be considered independently of the agents who employ them.

Private speech

While interpersonal interaction holds a privileged place in SCT, it is not the only way in which language activity can mediate language learning. Self-mediation through *private speech* is also possible. Ohta (2001b: 16) defines private speech as 'audible speech not adapted to an addressee'. She suggests that it can take a number of forms including imitation, vicarious response, i.e. responses that a classroom learner produces to questions the teacher has addressed to another learner, and mental rehearsal.

Young children frequently resort to talking to themselves, even when they are in the company of others. This self-directed speech can take the form of questions that they ask themselves, instructions regarding what to do or not to do, and evaluations of their performance. It is similar to the language used by conversationalists who are very familiar to one another—that is, it is paratactic and consists largely of comments (new information) on unstated topics (Lantolf 1999). Such talk seems to function as a proxy for social talk and serves the same basic purpose of enabling the child to obtain control over the mental functioning needed to perform an activity.

Adults as well as children employ private speech. According to the principle of continuous access (Frawley and Lantolf 1985), adults continue to have access to the knowing strategies they have used previously. In difficult situations adults are able to reactivate developmentally primitive strategies as a way of achieving self-regulation. When faced with performing a new function, the adult learner is able to revert back to private speech in order to achieve self-regulation. As Foley (1991: 63) puts it, 'when an individual finds himself faced with a difficult task, he externalizes the inner order so that he may regulate himself'. Ohta (2001) sees private talk by adult learners as the means by which new linguistic forms are manipulated and practised and thus come to move from the inter-psychological to the intrapsychological plane. It lies between social and inner speech.

Lantolf (2000a) notes that self-directed speech is well-attested in the psycholinguistic literature. In Lantolf (2000b), for example, he refers to a study by Wertsch (1985) of how children learned to carry out cognitive tasks such as using a model to reconstruct a wooden puzzle. Wertsch found that the children were initially dependent on verbal assistance from their parents but that subsequently they began to instruct themselves in what pieces of the puzzle to select and where to place them and to evaluate their actions. This occurred in the company of their parents. This study illustrates the important point that private speech can occur in social situations as well as when the individual is alone. Lantolf (2000a) also cites a number of L2 studies that provide evidence of the use of private speech by adult learners (for example, DiCamilla and Anton 1997). In another paper Lantolf (1999) points out that private speech provides crucial evidence of the linguistic forms that learners have internalized from their environment.

Because private speech is intended for the speaker, not the listener, it is not constrained by the same norms that affect social speech. In L2 learners this is evident in two ways. First, they may resort to the use of their L1 in self-directed speech. Second, if they use the L2, they may not employ target language forms even if they have internalized these. Thus what are apparent 'errors' may simply be the private forms that learners use in their struggle to maintain control over a task. The notion of 'deviance' cannot be easily applied to private speech. Such a perspective suggests that to evaluate the accuracy of learners' productions (as in the kind of research discussed in Chapter 4), it is important to distinguish whether the talk that arises in the performance of a task is 'social' or 'private'.

The zone of proximal development

It is clear, then, that the development of new skills has both a social and a psychological dimension. The psychological dimension entails the extent to which an individual is ready to perform the new skill. Vygotsky (1978) evokes the metaphor of the *zone of proximal development* (ZPD) to explain the difference between an individual's actual and potential levels of development. The skills that the individual has already mastered constitute his or her actual level. The skills that the individual can perform when assisted by another person (or some other means of mediation) constitute the potential level. Thus, learnt skills provide a basis for the performance of new skills. When these skills in turn become autonomous and stable a new zone can be created to make possible the acquisition of still further skills. The implication for effective task-based learning is that tasks must be structured in such a way that they pose an appropriate challenge by requiring learners to perform functions and use language that enable them to dynamically construct ZPDs. One of the goals of task-based research within a SCT framework must be to determine how this can be achieved.

On the face of it the ZPD is analogous to Krashen's i+1, i.e. the notion that what learners can acquire is governed by their current interlanguage and what structure comes next in the 'natural order' of development. Such is the position adopted by some SCT researchers (for example, Schinke-Llano 1993). However, Dunn and Lantolf (1998) have disputed such a comparison, arguing that whereas Krashen's i+1 relates to features of language, the ZPD applies to individuals involved in the learning. Indeed, SCT's insistence that learning originates in social interaction constitutes a challenge to the claimed universality of the order and sequence of acquisition, as individuals' experiences will necessarily vary. Lantolf (personal correspondence) argues that acquisition sequences are subject to individual variation. He claims that universal sequences are derived from statistically based analyses and that there is little work on individual learners to lend support to the existence of a universal route of development.[2] Currently, the ZPD is conceptualized not as an attribute of the learner with 'relatively fixed dimensions' but rather as 'task-specific, reciprocal, and open-ended' and therefore 'emergent' (Wells 1998: 345).

The ZPD is a key construct in SCT. It explains a number of important phenomena about learning. First, it explains why there are some structures that learners fail to perform no matter what the external mediation; learners are unable to construct the ZPDs that make the performance of such structures possible. Second, it explains why learners are able to perform some structures with social assistance but not independently; they are able to construct ZPDs for performing these even though they have not internalized them. Third, it explains how learners come to internalize new structures; they appropriate the structures for which, with the help of external mediation, they have created the necessary ZPDs.

What are the implications for task-based learning? Perhaps the most obvious is that it is not tasks themselves that create the context for learning but rather the way the participants carry out the task, i.e. the activity. The task is simply a tool that can be used by the participants to identify where assistance can be profitably provided in order to enable appropriate ZPDs to be created. Such a view has important implications for the grading of tasks (see Chapter 7). This point is elaborated in the section on activity theory below.

Scaffolding, collaborative dialogue, and instructional conversations

The social dimension of the development of a new skill is handled in SCT through the notion of *scaffolding*. This part of the theory is of particular relevance to the study of task-based learning. Scaffolding is the dialogic process by which one speaker assists another in performing a function that he or she cannot perform alone. Wood, Bruner, and Ross (1976) identify the following features of scaffolding:

1 recruiting interest in the task
2 simplifying the task
3 maintaining pursuit of the goal
4 marking critical features and discrepancies between what has been produced and the ideal solution
5 controlling frustration during problem solving
6 demonstrating an idealized version of the act to be performed.

Scaffolding, then, involves attending to both the cognitive demands of a task and the affective states of the person attempting the task. In this respect, SCT is much more encompassing than the Interactional Hypothesis, which addresses only the cognitive aspects of language learning.

The following extract from Ellis (1985) illustrates a number of these features of scaffolding. A teacher is showing a beginner learner a picture of a bicycle with no pedals. The teacher wants the learner to explain what is wrong with the bicycle, but clearly the learner is unable to construct a ZPD to enable him to perform this function. The learner responds by performing a skill he has already developed (naming colours), perhaps in accordance with the goal of 'saying something about the picture'. The teacher finally accepts the learner's response (see turn 7) and encourages him to extend it. The learner then produces 'black /taes/', which, in a longitudinal study, was the first two-word utterance he was observed to make. This interaction shows the teacher simplifying the original task and controlling frustration by accepting the learner's contributions. It also shows the teacher providing idealized versions of the learner's one-word utterances, for example, 'Red'—'It's red.' Finally, the extract shows how the learner's final utterance, which, simple though it is, lies at the cutting edge of his development, is constructed with assistance from the teacher. The teacher's question, 'Black what?', provides the learner with a frame that he uses to form his own utterance. In this way, the learner's final utterance can be said to be 'co-constructed'.

1	*Teacher*	I want you to tell me what you can see in the picture or what's wrong with the picture.
2	*Learner*	A /paik/ (=bike)
3	*Teacher*	A cycle, yes. But what's wrong?
4	*Learner*	/ret/ (=red)
5	*Teacher*	It's red yes. What's wrong with it?
6	*Learner*	Black.
7	*Teacher*	Black. Good. Black what?
8	*Learner*	Black /taes/ (= tyres)

In this example, then, the learner interacts with an expert—his teacher. The teacher is able to draw on his experience of communicating with low-level proficiency learners to adjust the demands of the task and to scaffold the interaction so that a successful outcome is achieved. Clearly, when learners have the opportunity to perform tasks with skilled teachers their opportunities for learning are maximized. However, dialogic activity between peers can also provide the right level of scaffolding for skill development. As we will see later, there is clear evidence that L2 learners can collaboratively succeed in performing a task which none of them could perform alone.

Scaffolding can be seen as one feature of a more general characteristic of dialogic discourse—what van Lier (1992) has called 'contingency'. This refers to the way in which one utterance is connected to another to produce coherence in discourse. Coherence, according to van Lier, is achieved when the motivation for the utterance is apparent to the interlocutors and when the expectations that it sets up are subsequently met in one way or another. Drawing on Vygotskian theory, he argues that 'contingency can be seen as the essential ingredient making the transformation of social processing into cognitive processing possible' (ibid. 15). In the extract above, there is initially an absence of contingency until the teacher accepts the learner's topic and adjusts the goal of the task. Contingency, then, constitutes an important condition for learning through social interaction to take place and scaffolding serves as one of the chief means of achieving it with low-proficiency learners. It follows that the effectiveness of tasks can be examined by studying the extent to which the interactions that derive from them manifest contingency. As we noted above, SCT considers that this is best achieved by means of the micro-analysis of specific interactions.

In more recent publications, 'scaffolding' has fallen out of favour, the preferred term now being *collaborative dialogue* or *instructional conversation*. Lantolf (personal correspondence) suggests this is because the term has become reified tautology. He argues that dialogic mediation needs to be viewed as an 'activity' that is jointly constructed by the participants involved and not as some kind of apparatus that one of the participants applies to conversation. Swain (2000: 102) uses the term 'collaborative dialogue', defined as 'dialogue in which speakers are engaged in problem solving and knowledge building'. Knowledge building arises both as a result of the learners 'saying', i.e. using the L2 to jointly address a problem, and responding to 'what is said', i.e. consciously attending to the language forms that arise in the utterances they produce. Another frequently used term, 'instructional conversation', (Tharp and Gallimore 1988, as cited in Donato 2000) refers to pedagogic interaction that is teacher-led and directed towards a curricular goal, for example, enabling students to perform a structure that they have not yet internalized, but is conversational in nature, for example, it manifests equal turn-taking rights and is unpredictable.

These constructs are of obvious importance for exploring how tasks can assist language acquisition. Where tasks result in scaffolding, collaborative dialogue, and instructional conversations, opportunities for learners to extend their knowledge of the L2 can be expected to arise. Again, though, it is clear that these opportunities are not created by the tasks themselves but rather by the way in which the tasks are performed by the participants. This crucial point is addressed directly in the following account of *activity theory*.

Activity theory

Lantolf (2000b: 8) describes activity theory as 'a unified account of Vygotsky's original proposals on the nature and development of human behavior'. According to Leontiev (1978), people possess motives that determine how they respond to a particular task.[3] Motives can be biologically determined, for example, the need to satisfy hunger, or, more importantly from our perspective here, socially constructed, for example, the need to learn an L2. The learners' motives determine how they construe a given situation. Thus people with different motives will perform the same task in different ways. For example, Wertsch, Minick, and Arns (1984) found that middle-class and rural uneducated mothers in Brazil responded differently in the kind of guidance they provided their children in a puzzle-copying task. The middle-class mothers' activity reflected their desire to teach their children the skills they needed to perform the task so they could perform other, similar tasks later, i.e. their motive was pedagogic. Thus, they consistently employed strategic statements like 'now look to see what comes next' and only when these failed did they resort to referential statements like 'try the red piece here'. In contrast, the rural mothers viewed the task as a labour activity of the kind they were familiar with in their daily work. In such activity, mistakes are costly, and, therefore, the mothers strove to prevent their children making errors by directing their actions through referential statements. Thus, the different motives that the two groups of mothers brought to the task led to different activities, reflected in different patterns of language use. This example also shows how motives are socioculturally determined.

Activity theory distinguishes three dimensions or levels of cognition—motives, goals, and operations. Lantolf and Appel (1994a: 21–2) distinguish these as follows:

> ... the level of motive answers why something is done, the level of goal answers what is done, and the level of operations answers how it is done. The link between socioculturally defined motives and concrete operations is provided by semiotic systems, of which language is the most powerful and pervasive.

Therefore, we can expect a task to result in different kinds of activity (as in the case of Wertsch's puzzle-copying task) because different people will approach the task differently depending on their underlying motives. As Lantolf (2000b) emphasizes, activities are differentiated in terms of motives. Thus, we can expect that a learner who views a task (such as the same-or-different task on p. 11) as a 'game' will engage in a different kind of activity to a learner who views the same task as 'work' warranting serious attention. These different activities, however, may or may not result in different operations.[4] Furthermore, activity theory recognizes that changing social conditions can result in individuals realigning their motives and, perhaps, the operations they employ to achieve them. Thus, we can anticipate that learners might view a task as a 'game' on one occasion and as 'work' on another, depending on how they approach the task at different times. One of the implications of this is that researchers need to ascertain what motives learners bring to a task if they are to understand the interactions that occur when the task is performed. In this respect, much of the task-based research that has taken place to date is seriously at fault.

Summary and final comment

A sociocultural theory of mind, then, provides a number of important insights for task-based research. It suggests that the study of dialogic interactions can provide a window for viewing the cognitive processes the learner is internalizing. It suggests what it is in these interactions that the researcher should be on the lookout for—for example, how scaffolding creates the contingency that makes it possible for learners to perform beyond their existing developmental level. Crucially, it warns the researcher to treat tasks not as blueprints for interaction but as tools that learners interpret and use to construct an activity in accordance with their own particular motives and goals. It also suggests the kind of methodology that researchers will need to explore the worlds of tasks—the qualitative micro-analysis of interactions directed at understanding how learning takes place.

However, SCT does not provide a set of operational constructs for investigating tasks. As Schinke-Llano (1993: 25) notes 'grappling by Vygotskian theory can sometimes be frustrating, much like dealing with a video camera that slips in and out of focus'. How exactly do learners come to internalize for subsequent independent language use the new linguistic forms that they accomplish through collaborative activity? Are all such forms internalized or only some and, if the latter, what determines which forms are remembered and which ones are not? Why is contingency so important for this transformation? How can we actually demonstrate that the transformation has taken place? How does the zone of proximal development work where language acquisition is concerned? It is perhaps fair to say that, to date, a sociocultural theory of mind provides somewhat incomplete and uncertain answers to these questions. Despite these limitations, SCT is important because it helps to redress the current psycholinguistic imbalance in SLA by emphasizing the social and cultural nature of task performance.

Task-based research based on a sociocultural theory of the mind

From a Vygotskian perspective, both dialogic and monologic talk can mediate learning. For this reason, this chapter will include references to studies involving both non-reciprocal tasks, for example, oral recall tasks, and reciprocal tasks. The review of the research will address two key issues. The first concerns how the participants in an activity construct the activity they engage in. SCT researchers aim to show how 'performance depends crucially on the interaction of individual and task' (Appel and Lantolf 1994b) rather than on the inherent properties of the task itself. The second issue deals with how tasks—or rather the activities that comprise participants' task performances—serve as a form of mediation that can bring about learning. To this end, we will examine what the research has shown about the role of collaborative activity, metatalk, and private speech in learning.

Constructing an activity out of a task

As we have seen, SCT claims that the same task can result in very different kinds of activity when performed by different learners and, also, that it can result in different activities when performed by the same learners at different times. This is because whenever individuals perform a task they 'construct' the activity in terms of their motives and goals, which can vary. How is this accomplished?

Task vs. activity

This distinction between 'task' and 'activity' is examined in a study by Coughlan and Duff (1994). They compared the performances of five different learners (one Cambodian and four Hungarians) on a picture description task performed face to face with a researcher. In the case of the Cambodian learner, the task was performed as part of regular hour-long meetings at the researcher's home. In the case of the Hungarian learners, the picture description task was one of a series of tasks that were performed by the learners at their school during one-off meetings of 20 minutes' duration. The activities resulting from this task varied considerably. With the Cambodian learner, the intended monologue became more like a dialogue as he constantly engaged the researcher in talk by means of comprehension checks and requests for assistance with vocabulary. Coughlan and Duff conclude that it is not really possible to describe the

characteristics of the discourse of the learner and the researcher independently of each other 'since both were doing the task, not just the subject' (ibid. 180). In contrast, the activity resulting from the Hungarian
learners' performance of the task resulted in very little 'off-task' talk as the
researcher was concerned to complete the task in the allotted amount of
time. In this context, the learners varied in the goals they established for the
task. One subject treated the task as requiring her to simply name the
objects in the picture. Another sought to relate the picture to her personal
experience. A third listed the people in the pictures and the activities they
were performing. Coughlan and Duff conclude that despite the relatively
controlled nature of the task 'a range of discourse types may result from
learners' multiple interpretations of that task' (ibid. 185). They then go on
to show that the same task was interpreted very differently by the
Cambodian learner when he was asked to repeat it on a later occasion.

   Coughlan and Duff conclude that the interviewer-researcher plays a
large role in shaping task-based activity. They also note that the picture-
description task does not constitute a 'natural communicative activity'—a
point that could be made about nearly all the tasks in the research reviewed
in the previous chapters—and that the primary activity is, therefore,
'speaking for the sake of speaking' (ibid. 189). Not surprisingly, different
learners react very differently to such a task, some endeavouring to make
it more genuinely communicative by seeking out appropriate interactional
roles, others treating it more mechanically as a language elicitation device.
Coughlan and Duff warn against treating 'task' as a constant in research,
as 'the activity it generates will be unique' (ibid. 191).

   Further support for this claim comes from a number of other studies.
Platt and Brooks (1994), for example, show how a role-play task is interpreted variably by different groups of students. One group simply carried
out the instructions in a mechanical fashion. Another group reconstructed the task in accordance with their own goals. The kind of talk
produced by these two groups differed greatly, with far more metatalk
evident in the second. Foster (1998) reports a study which, although not
conducted within the framework of SCT, testifies to the importance of the
participants' motives and goals in determining the kind of activity tasks
give rise to. Noting that most of the modified input/output studies have
been carried out in laboratory-like settings, Foster investigated tasks that
students performed as part of a timetabled lesson in their normal classroom. The tasks were: (1) a grammar-based task that required students
to collaborate in composing questions for given answers; (2) a spot-the-
difference task; (3) a convergent opinion-gap task involving solving a
problem; and (4) a map task involving split information. She found that
none of the tasks led to much negotiated input or output. She suggests
that the students were motivated to make the tasks fun and to this end
minimized negotiation in order to keep the interaction moving. In short,

the students performed the task in a way that was compatible with their own motives and goals. Wang (1996, cited in Donato 2000) also shows how different groups of learners interpreted the same task very differently and notes that this frustrated the teacher. In this case, the task required students to rank in order a list of seven effects of excessive TV viewing 'from the most immediate to the most remote'. Wang reports that one group did not perform the task as instructed because they did not agree with most of the effects listed in the task materials. Another group did rank the effects, but from 'more remote to more immediate'. This caused the teacher to change the activity to that of simply 'finding things that go naturally together'. Roebuck (2000) shows that the way in which L2 learners of Spanish position themselves in written recall tasks has a profound effect on the actual writing they produce. Not only did the learners orient to the task in different ways but also some of them re-oriented themselves in the course of completing the task. For example, one learner began the task by trying to reproduce the text she had read only to switch halfway through to just listing points she could remember. Learners who experienced difficulty in completing the task did not comply with the role they had been assigned ('subject in an experiment') but repositioned themselves in various ways, for example, by criticizing the task they had been set. These studies support Donato's (2000: 44) conclusion that tasks are not 'generalizable' and also that 'tasks do not manipulate learners to act in certain ways'.

Thus tasks of the kind commonly used in SLA research are not just performed but rather are interpreted, resulting in activity that is 'constructed' by the participants in accordance with their particular motives and goals. Much of the task-based research in the Vygotskian tradition has focused on identifying how this process of construction takes place. Key concepts in this research are orientation to a task and *intersubjectivity*; these explain how learners build a shared reality through talk.

Orientation

Orientation refers to how learners view a task, the nature of the goals they form in order to perform it and the operations they use to carry it out. The particular orientation learners adopt determines the kind of activity that results. In part, how they orient to a task will reflect their previous experiences not just with similar tasks but with the kind of activity they associate with the particular setting in which they are communicating. In this way, how learners orientate to a task is socio-historically determined. Hall (1993, 1995a) describes how the linguistic resources participants bring to an interaction and the way they use them both reflect their experiences of communicating in the same setting previously and also serve as the means by which they make sense of the talk.

Brooks (1990) gives an example of how this can affect the way learners perform a task. At one stage during an elementary level university Spanish class the teacher asked the students to perform a communicative task that required students to use the information provided on cue cards to talk about a number of fictitious people. However, the learners orientated to this task as an opportunity to practise the correct form of adjectives in Spanish rather than to communicate (i.e. they treated it as an exercise). Brooks suggests that in doing so they simply reflected the general form-focused tenor of their class. Brooks also shows how the students adopted the roles and behaviours of the teacher in their correction strategies. This study shows how the classroom setting contextualizes the way learners respond to a task.[5]

But how do learners actually set about orienting themselves to a task? One way is through metatalk, which serves to help them externalize the goal or end result of the task. Platt and Brooks (1994) describe how university level learners of L2 Spanish spent a considerable amount of time talking about the jigsaw task they had been asked to perform, its goals, and their own language production, using their L1 (English). Brooks and Donato (1994) describe how third-year high school learners of L2 Spanish used language to mediate their goals in a two-way information-gap task that required them to describe where to draw shapes on a matrix sheet consisting of unnumbered small squares. They found that even though the teacher carefully explained the task goals, the learners often felt the need to discuss these between themselves in metatalk about the task. Typically this talk was conducted in the L1, as in this example:

S1   You go ahead Jamar.
S2   Din-wait yo tengo dinero en abajo izquierda.Wait wait.
      Am I supposed to tell you and you write stuff on your paper?
S1   Yeah, that's what he said to do. We make a picture.
S2   Okay.

Brooks and Donato also provide examples of the learners' use of metatalk to orient themselves to how they might accomplish the task. For example, one pair of students hit on the highly effective metacognitive strategy of numbering the small squares in the matrix sheet to facilitate easy reference to where each shape needed to be drawn. They spent considerable effort in jointly establishing this strategy, on this occasion using the L2. It was by orienting themselves to the task in these ways that the students were able to regulate and make sense of their behaviour.

However, there is also evidence that the nature of the task itself influences the way in which learners orientate themselves. Appel and Lantolf (1994) examine how a group of native speakers and very advanced learners of English as a foreign language managed two text-recall tasks—one involving an expository passage about coffee growing in Brazil and the other a conventional folk-tale. They examine the participants' orientations in terms of their externalization of the 'macro-structures' of the two texts, which they defined as the gist of a text for a reader. In the case of the narrative text, both native speakers and learners showed little need to make explicit the macrostructure of the story, the majority electing to move straight into 'telling' it. However, in the case of the expository text, speakers often needed to externalize the macrostructure and displayed greater variance in how they set about this, reflecting the difficulty they experienced in achieving control over this text.

As we have already noted, participants' orientation can change during the performance of a task. Appel and Lantolf (1994) document how the participants reoriented themselves when faced with problems of reference in the narrative task. They point out that if the task was conceived as that of 'recalling' the story there was no need for the speakers to be concerned with giving away the true identity of the beggar character in the story (he was in fact a prince) and they could refer to him throughout as 'the beggar'. However, if their goal was 'retelling' the story it was necessary to hide the prince's true identity until the denouement. Appel and Lantolf show how some of the speakers chose to reorient from 'recalling' to 'retelling' the story and how they coped with the problems of reference this caused them.

Intersubjectivity

In most cases, the participants in a dialogic task seek to establish intersubjectivity. This is generally, although not necessarily (see Matusov 1996), achieved when they can agree on the nature of the activity they are engaged in by sharing a common motive and goals for performing the task. In this way they form a kind of joint ownership of the activity as they work through the task. Let us take another look at the interaction between the teacher and the beginning language learner on p. 181. Here we can see that initially the discourse is discontinuous because of their failure to establish intersubjectivity. They begin with different goals—the teacher wants the learner to say what is wrong with the picture while the learner just wants to be able to say something about the picture and thus resorts to a routinized naming of objects and colours. In this case, perhaps because of the learner's low level of English proficiency, intersubjectivity is achieved only when the teacher accepts the learner's goals and they engage in the same activity.

Intersubjectivity, then, facilitates contingency and, thereby, learning. DiCamilla and Anton (1997) describe one of the ways subjectivity can be achieved. They examined five dyads discussing how to write a common composition. They illustrate the learners' use of repetition to establish joint ownership of the task as they worked through it. They repeated phrases, words, and sometimes syllables as a means of accepting and extending each other's contributions. Repetition, DiCamilla and Anton suggest, serves to give the members of a dyad a single voice by ensuring that they work with a shared perspective. They emphasize that repetition does far more than increase the frequency of input, or make the input comprehensible; it serves as a socio-cognitive tool for accomplishing the task.

Goal-directedness and L2 acquisition

We have seen how the activity that learners construct out of a task by the way in which they orientate to it and attempt to establish intersubjectivity has a profound effect on how the task is performed. As yet, there have been no studies demonstrating what effect the goal-directedness of an activity has on language learning. The results of the study by Ellis and He (1999), which was considered in Chapter 3, are suggestive however. In this study, learners who were given the opportunity to negotiate and produce the target items in pairs outperformed those that received just premodified input or opportunities to negotiate input from the teacher. This study was designed to test the claims of the updated Interaction Hypothesis (Long 1996) but Ellis and He suggest that its findings might best be explained in terms of SCT. They point out that although the task used in the study was intended to be identical in all three conditions, the activity differed in ways that had not been predicted. In the premodified and interactionally modified conditions the teacher treated the task as a kind of test, the goal of which was to measure if the learners could understand the directions and learn the new words. The resulting discourse was constrained and mechanical. In contrast, the learners in the output condition treated the task as a collaborative problem-solving activity and sought to arrive at a joint, negotiated solution to the task. The resulting discourse was much more elaborate and, Ellis and He argue, supportive of learning. This study, then, indicates that the nature of activity that arises from a task can have a marked effect on what is learned.

However, although we can expect the learners' motives and goals to have an impact on what is learned, it is clearly wrong to presume that all learning is *directly* tied to them. As Lantolf (2000a) notes, 'the goal of an activity, which is usually intentional, may well have consequences which are not'. The most obvious example of this is language play (Cook 1997). Sullivan (2000) suggests that, in the EFL classrooms she studied in Vietnam, playfulness while performing role-play tasks served to mediate the learning process. Sullivan's point is that the 'fun' generated by ludic activity can help to create the 'receptivity' to language learning that Allwright and Bailey (1991) consider an essential element of the acquisition-rich classroom. It can also create incidental opportunities for learning, for example by stimulating creativity in the use of language. Tarone and Liu (1995) report a study that shows that one young Chinese learner of

English appeared to benefit acquisitionally most when engaged in play sessions with the researcher. Thus the motives and goals learners have for performing a task are best seen as *indirectly* related to learning, their effect mediated by the nature of the operations used to accomplish an activity. We will now turn to consider these operations.

Tasks as instruments of cognitive change

It follows from the preceding discussion that tasks are instruments of cognitive change only in the sense that interactants co-construct an activity that promotes development. How then does task-derived activity promote development? A sociocultural theory of mind posits that development entails a movement from object- to other- and finally to self-regulation. It suggests that development in this sense arises out of talk where: (1) there is scaffolding for the learner's efforts to use a new linguistic feature; (2) metatalk heightens consciousness about linguistic form; and (3) the learner reverts to private speech to regulate thinking.

Scaffolding and collaborative dialogue

A number of studies have examined the role of scaffolding and collaborative dialogue in assisting learners to acquire new language. Swain *et al.* forthcoming provide a comprehensive review of the research to date. Here we will focus on some illustrative studies.

Aljaafreh and Lantolf (1994) examined the one-on-one interactions arising between three L2 learners and a tutor who provided corrective feedback on essays they had written. They developed a 'regulatory scale' to reflect the extent to which the help provided by the tutor was implicit or explicit. For example, asking learners to find and correct their own errors is considered an implicit strategy while providing examples of the correct pattern is highly explicit. An intermediate level occurs when the tutor indicates the nature of an error without identifying it for the learner. In detailed analyses of selected protocols, they show how the degree of scaffolding provided by the tutor for a particular learner diminished, i.e. the help provided became more implicit over time. This was possible because the learners assumed increased control over the L2 and, therefore, needed less assistance. Aljaafreh and Lantolf's study was not task-based.[6] However, the idea of a 'regulatory scale' is an interesting one that might usefully be applied to the analysis of task-based interactions.

In a follow-up study, using the same regulatory scale as in Aljaafreh and Lantolf (1994), Nassaji and Swain (2000) examined a tutor's oral feedback on the written compositions of two Korean learners of English. This study sought to compare the effectiveness of feedback on the two learners' acquisition of articles. The assistance to one learner was provided within her ZPD, i.e. the tutor systematically worked through Aljaafreh and Lantolf's scale to negotiate the feedback she supplied, while the assistance to the other learner was random, i.e. the tutor was supplied with a random list of correcting strategies drawn from the scale. The results showed that providing feedback within the learner's ZPD was effective in: (1) helping the learner to arrive at the correct form during the feedback session; (2) enabling the learner to arrive at the correct form with much less explicit assistance in subsequent sessions; and (3) enabling the learner to use the correct form unassisted in a post-test consisting of a cloze version of the compositions she had written previously. In contrast, random feedback did not always succeed in enabling the learner to identify the correct article form in the feedback sessions and was much less effective in promoting unassisted use of the correct forms in the post-test. Also, interestingly, the tutor who provided the random feedback reported that he found it very difficult and unnatural. This study provides clear evidence that when scaffolding works to construct a ZPD for a learner, learning results.

Clearly, however, the expert needs considerable skill to determine the appropriate level of scaffolding needed. In a subsequent paper, Lantolf and Aljaafreh (1995) note that the tutor was not always successful in tuning his assistance to the learner's level of development. Sometimes he provided more scaffolding than was required, thereby failing to push the learner towards greater autonomy. In other studies, however, the expert sometimes fails to provide the support the learners needed to accomplish the task. Schulte (1998), for example, asked a group of high school ESL learners to perform a task that required them to choose one of four words to fill the gap in a short poem. She shows that the expert (the teacher) was unable to scaffold the task effectively for the learners with the result that they remained object-regulated for much of the time, i.e. they were unable to locate clues to help them decide which word to choose and thus responded by guessing mindlessly.[7]

The notion of scaffolding the learner's ZPD can also be applied to interactions that take place through the medium of writing. Nassaji and Cumming (2000: 103) report a study of the written interactions between one six-year-old ESL student (named Ali) and his teacher in the context of dialogic journal writing over a ten-month period. A key characteristic of these interactions was 'complementary, asymmetric scaffolding'. The asymmetry was reflected in the different distribution of language functions in the two participants' writing. The learner engaged mainly in 'reporting'. The teacher also did 'reporting' but also performed other functions—'requesting', 'evaluating', predicting', and 'giving directions'. Nassaji and Cumming suggest that the teacher's functions reflected her 'striving to scaffold their written interactions to prompt Ali's potential for learning English' (ibid. 104). The nature of this scaffolding changed over the ten-month period, reflecting the learner's growing proficiency in English.

For example, initially the teacher asked predominantly yes/no questions but later switched to using more demanding 'why' and 'how do you' questions. The learner gradually picked up these questioning patterns and, as this occurred, the teacher decreased the proportion of 'questioning' overall, i.e. from 39% initially to 27% finally. In this way, the teacher and learner constructed and reconstructed a ZPD for the writing task through reciprocal activity.

Scaffolding is not dependent on the presence of an expert, however; it can also arise in interactions between learners. DiCamilla and Anton (1997), in the study we have already referred to, show how learners make use of repetition to provide scaffolded help for each other. For example, they demonstrate how it serves as a kind of platform on which the learners can rest while they struggle to find the next word and how it is used to finalize a collaborative solution. Lantolf (1995) sees repetition as a form of language play that is important for language acquisition. His learners repeated items and structures that lay within their zone of proximal development. Ohta (1995: 109) illustrates how learners scaffold each other's contributions in a role-playing task, making the point that even a less proficient learner can assist a more proficient learner. She also notes that in learner-learner interactions the notions of novice and expert are 'fluid conceptions'; the same learner can function as both expert and novice at different times in a conversation.

Donato (1994) describes the collective scaffolding employed by groups of university students of French performing an oral activity based on a scenario from Di Pietro (1987).[8] In a detailed analysis of an exchange involving the negotiation of the form 'tu t'es souvenu', Donato shows how they jointly manage components of the problem, distinguish between what they have produced and what they perceive as the ideal solution, and use their collective resources to minimize frustration and risk. The scaffolding enables the learners to construct the correct form of the verb even though no single learner knew this prior to the task. Thus this study goes further than most in demonstrating the essential claim of a sociocultural theory of mind, namely that 'higher mental functioning is situated in the dialectal processes embedded in the social context' (ibid. 46). Donato also provides evidence to suggest that internalization was taking place. The joint performance of new structures on one occasion was frequently followed by independent use of them by individual learners on a later occasion.

In a series of studies, Swain and her co-researchers have examined the contribution of collaborative dialoguing to language learning. Kowal and Swain (1994) used a dictogloss task (see Chapter 5), which required learners to first listen to take notes as their teacher read a short text containing specific grammatical features and then to work in pairs to reconstruct the text from their joint notes. In this study, too, the learners talked about language form and were often able to decide collectively what forms to use to reconstruct a text. However, Kowal and Swain report that hetero-geneous dyads worked less effectively together, possibly because 'neither student's needs were within the zone of proximal development of the other' (ibid. 86) and because they failed to respect each other's perspective. Swain (1995, 1998) also reports a study by Lapierre (1994), which used tailor-made tests to establish whether learners actually retained the forms they jointly negotiated in the 'critical language-related episodes' (LREs) that arose in the course of reconstructing a text. Lapierre found that the test results closely matched the negotiated solutions; correct and incorrect solu-tions led respectively to correct and incorrect test answers. Swain (1998: 79) comments 'these results suggest rather forcibly that these LREs, during which students reflect consciously on the language they are producing, may be a source of language learning'. Further evidence of the role that collab-orative dialogue can play in language learning comes from Swain and Lapkin (1998). They provide a detailed analysis of two Grade 8 French immersion students performing a jigsaw task, showing how their joint solu-tions to linguistic problems led to learning as measured in post-tests. Again, though, they note that on a few occasions their solutions were incorrect.

Swain (2000a) reports an interesting study by Holunga (1995) that investigated the effects of metacognitive strategy training on the accurate use of verb forms by advanced learners of English. This experimental study involved three instructional conditions: (1) metacognitive strategy training plus communicative practice; (2) metacognitive strategy training plus a requirement to verbalize the strategies plus communicative practice; and (3) communicative practice only. During the instructional period the learn-ers performed a focused task. A detailed analysis of the three groups' per-formance of this task showed marked differences. Whereas groups (1) and (3) attended predominantly to message content, producing interaction that was typical of a 'negotiation of meaning' task, group (2) focused on both message content and the conditional verb form that the task required. In a detailed discussion of an interaction involving a pair of learners in group (2), Swain comments 'through their collaborative effort, they produce the appropriate verb form accurately, and propose a concrete plan to monitor its accuracy in future use' (ibid. 108). This study is of particular interest because immediate and delayed post-tests of both a closed and open-ended nature demonstrated significantly greater gains in the ability to use com-plex verb forms accurately in group (2). It points to two major conclusions. First, the collaborative activity that learners engage in when they perform a task can assist both the performance of new structures and their inter-nalization. Second, this process is assisted if learners pay explicit attention to the language they are using by together discussing their linguistic prod-ucts as they perform the task.

Finally, in an interesting longitudinal classroom study of learners of L2 Japanese, Ohta (2001) showed how students were able to produce utterances collaboratively that were beyond them individually and describes the various techniques that learners used to scaffold each other's L2 speech. These included the use of prompts, co-constructions and recasts. One of the strengths of Ohta's research in comparison to work based on the Interaction Hypothesis (see Chapters 2 and 3) is that it acknowledges that interaction does not have to break down to assist the processes of internalizing new L2 forms. Ohta also reports that although the students did not always produce error-free utterances they only infrequently incorporated incorrect utterances.

Swain *et al.* (forthcoming) conclude their review of peer-peer dialogue research by commenting that 'few adverse effects of working collaboratively were noted'. However, as Lapierre (1994) and Swain and Lapkin (1998) have shown, peer mediation is not always effective; occasions can arise when 'expert' mediation is required. Lantolf (2000a), for example, refers to a study by Platt and Troudi (1997) which showed how a teacher's belief that peer rather than expert mediation was more effective in promoting learning had a negative effect when it came to certain content areas, for example, maths. Lantolf goes on to comment that 'while peer assistance is effective for learning everyday functional language, it may not be as effective for development of academic language'. There will obviously be situations in which the mediation provided by an 'expert' language user is required to negotiate a learner's ZPD. Thus, Swain and Lapkin (1998) argue that teacher feedback on the recorded oral dialogue generated by a task or the written product of the task is needed to resolve learner uncertainty and to point out incorrect solutions to linguistic problems.

Metatalk

We have already seen that participants use metatalk to establish what kind of 'activity' to make of a task and also what operations to employ in performing it. Here we will consider the metatalk that arises when learners focus explicitly on language in the course of performing a task.

A central claim of the collaborative dialogue investigated by Swain and her fellow researchers is that it involves language-related episodes where the participants talk about linguistic form as an object. This is made possible because, as Wells (2000) puts it, an utterance can be viewed in terms of process, i.e. as 'saying', and as product, i.e. as 'what was said'. By scrutinizing and reflecting on specific forms, learners treat language products as cognitive tools and learn from them. As Swain and Lapkin (2001b: 3) put it:

> To make their meaning as clear, coherent and precise as possible, learners will debate language form (morphosyntax through to discourse and pragmatics) and lexical choice. This talk about language (metatalk)

mediates second language learning. Talk supports the process of internalization—the 'moving inwards' of joint (intermental) activity to psychological (intramental) activity.

In Chapter 5 we considered the case for 'consciousness-raising' from the perspective of an information-processing model, arguing that talking about form resulted in explicit knowledge that could subsequently be used in the processes responsible for the acquisition of implicit knowledge—*noticing* and *noticing-the-gap*. In sociocultural theory, however, metatalk is seen as serving a somewhat different function. It does not just prime acquisition but rather serves to regulate thinking and through this enable learners to arrive at new knowledge.

Clear evidence for the role that metatalk can play in helping learners internalize new linguistic forms is evident in several of the studies referred to above. Here we will consider one further study—Swain and Lapkin (2001b). This made use of a reformulation task (Cohen 1982) that involves asking students to write a composition, to compare their composition with a reformulated version, and finally to rewrite the composition. The full procedure that Swain and Lapkin followed is shown in Table 6.1. The discussions from stages 1, 2, and 3 were transcribed and all the language-related episodes identified. These episodes constitute occasions when metatalk occurred. Swain and Lapkin compared the changes that the students made to their initial compositions when they rewrote them in stage 4. They found that 78% of both students' changes were correct. Interestingly, however, the changes did not always correspond to the reformulated version. One third of the time, the students found an alternative

Stage	Description
1 Writing	The students completed a jigsaw writing task. They were each given three pictures from a picture story, described them to each other and then wrote the story.
2 Comparing	The students were asked to compare their compositions with the reformulated version and to notice the differences. Their discussion was videotaped.
3 Simulated recall	The students were shown the videotape of their discussion and asked to comment on each difference between their own compositions and the reformulated version they had noticed in stage 2.
4 Rewriting	Each student was given a copy of her original story and asked to rewrite it independently.

Table 6.1: Reformulation writing task (from Swain and Lapkin 2001b)

of their own, and out of these three quarters were correct. Swain and Lapkin suggest that the process of 'talking it through' enabled their students to find their own correct solutions by encouraging them to reflect on differences between their own compositions and the reformulated version.

Private speech

Private speech serves as the third principal means of development. As we noted earlier, SCT predicts that private speech occurs when learners are required to perform tasks that cause them cognitive stress, making total self-regulation impossible. In other words, private speech functions strategically to enable learners to gain control over language forms, the use of which are problematic in the context of a challenging task. Frawley and Lantolf (1986) propose that private speech can be object-regulated, where it reflects strategic use of the task itself, other-regulated, where it takes the form of questions directed to the researcher and to the self, and self-regulated, where the subject indicates having understood a problem or source of difficulty. Researchers working in the sociocultural tradition emphasize that when low-proficiency learners perform a task they may spend a substantial portion of the time self-regulating through the use of private speech. However, as learners become more proficient, they rely less on private speech.

The bulk of the research that has investigated L2 learners' private speech has made use of oral narrative tasks (see McCafferty 1994a for a survey). These tasks vary in a number of ways. In most of them, the participants are presented with a series of pictures depicting a story one at a time. However, in some studies the participants are shown all the pictures together while in others they read a story and subsequently try to recall it. Oral narrative tasks that learners perform by themselves are obviously biased in favour of the use of private speech. Nor is it always easy in such tasks to determine which utterances constitute private speech and which communicative. For example, Frawley and Lantolf (1986) suggest that both native speakers and intermediate level learners use the past tense in their narratives as a form of object regulation but McCafferty (1994b) takes the more obvious line that the past tense is used communicatively to signal temporal relationships cohesively. However, Frawley and Lantolf's main point—that what appears to be non-target use by L2 learners may represent private speech and in this respect resemble native-speaker use—is well-taken.

The nature of the task is one of several factors that have been found to impact on learners' use of private speech. Narrative tasks, where the participants are shown the pictures one at a time, are more cognitively stressful than tasks where they see all the pictures together and result in greater use of private speech. In Appel and Lantolf (1994), the expository text led to more private speech than the narrative text, again because of the difficulty the participants (both native speakers and learners) experienced in achieving control in the former. Other factors that impact on the use of private speech according to McCafferty (1994a) are the proficiency of the learners, their cultural background and how they relate to the task and to each other.

Private speech by adult learners is also evident in interactive situations. Donato (1994), for example, finds examples in his study. He suggests that the scaffolded help his learners provided each other with triggered the use of private talk as a means of organizing, rehearsing and gaining control over new verbal behaviour. McCafferty (1994a) refers to research by Ahmed (1988), which found differential levels and types of private speech in two kinds of communicative tasks. Both tasks were simulation games but one type involved imaginary situations and the other a real situation, i.e. the participants sought solutions to maths problems for an upcoming examination which they all had to take. The first type produced relatively little private speech. Also, the native speakers tended to dominate, with the L2 learners showing little real interest in the outcome. In contrast, the second type led to greater and more varied use of private talk and a genuine commitment to finding solutions, with the L2 learners as likely to take on the role of 'expert' as the native speakers. Children, however, may be less likely to resort to private speech in social situations. Saville-Troike's (1988) study of child L2 learners in a US classroom shows that they frequently repeated words to themselves, often manipulating the form playfully but not when they were interacting with the teacher or another child.

There is little clear evidence as yet that private speech contributes to language acquisition. Lantolf (1997) attempted to investigate this issue by means of a questionnaire that asked Spanish FL and ESL students to report on their use of private speech. He found that the reported frequency of private speech correlated with language proficiency and learners' goals for studying the language. Beginning level Spanish learners reported a low use of private language play but more advanced learners reported a higher level of use. The ESL learners reported less use than the Spanish FL learners, possibly because they had a much higher level of proficiency in the L2 and thus little need to use private speech for self-regulation. Learners who were learning the L2 for personal interest or for a clear instrumental purpose reported greater use of private speech than those who were taking a language class to fulfill a degree requirement. Self-report studies of this kind, however, do not demonstrate that private speech assists language learning, only that there may be a relationship between attained proficiency and reported use of private speech. Ohta's (2001b; cited in Lantolf 2001a) study is more promising in this respect. She provides evidence to show that classroom learners often repeat sotto voce the reformulations of incorrect utterances that teachers and other learners make. In terms of the computational model of acquisition, these repetitions can be viewed as 'uptake', which, as we have seen in Chapters 3 and 5, may contribute to acquisition. In terms of SCT, however, they serve a broader function, helping the learner to construct a ZPD by participating in the activity.

Investigating the contribution of private speech to L2 development in the context of task-based research is obviously problematic. A major problem is deciding what constitutes private speech in a corpus of language use. At the moment the lack of a tight operational definition is an obvious threat to the reliability of studies of private speech. For example, Lantolf (2000a) notes that it is difficult to be sure that the sotto voce repetitions of Ohta's learners are instances of private speech as they might also be 'reduced volume attempts at complying with the group nature of the exercise'. When (if) this problem is solved there is the further problem of demonstrating that private speech actually contributes to L2 development.

Summary and conclusion

To date, there have been relatively few studies investigating tasks from a sociocultural perspective. The following are the main findings to date:

1 Tasks cannot be externally defined and classified because the 'activity' that results from a 'task' will vary from learner to learner and also within a single learner on different occasions.
2 For this reason, it is impossible to ignore the setting in which learners perform a task. Also, in tasks where learners interact with a researcher, the researcher should be seen as a participant who helps shape the resulting activity.
3 How learners orientate to a task and the extent to which they achieve intersubjectivity with regard to goals and operations will influence the activity that results and thus need to be carefully studied. Furthermore, learners may re-orientate to a task as the activity proceeds.
4 Learners may view communicative activities as simply requiring 'speaking for the sake of speaking' and as a result make little effort to achieve self-regulation by negotiating or using private speech.
5 Scaffolding, whether arising between experts (teachers/researchers) and novices (L2 learners) or in the collaborative dialogue of learners, creates conditions in which learners can develop awareness of new L2 forms and/or actually produce them. There is also some evidence that it aids acquisition (see, for example, Nassaji and Swain 2000).
6 Metatalk can also mediate language learning by enabling learners to achieve a deeper understanding of a linguistic feature and thus helping the process of internalization.
7 The private speech that occurs when learners perform a task sheds light on how learners achieve self-regulation when faced with a difficult task.

It can be seen as evidence that learners have 'noticed' an L2 feature. It may also explain why learners sometimes appear to 'regress', i.e. resort to developmentally earlier strategies and L2 forms, as private speech makes natural use of forms that in social speech would be considered non-standard.

8　Learners often use their L1 to achieve control of a task, for example, to set and revise goals and to engage in private speech. In this respect, the use of the L1 should be viewed positively.

9　Some tasks pose a greater cognitive burden on learners than other tasks. The extent to which learners need to struggle to achieve self-regulation in the performance of a task will influence their mental functioning and behaviour, for example, the degree of scaffolding or the kind of private speech used.

It is clear that these are important findings that cannot be ignored by researchers concerned with investigating how tasks shape interaction conducive to L2 acquisition.

Not surprisingly, however, given the relative infancy of sociocultural SLA, there are some obvious limitations in the research. In general, researchers have concentrated on describing task-based interactions and have documented what learners learn in terms of 'participation'; they have made little attempt to investigate internalization. Researchers have given theoretical grounds for claiming that if learners are led to use a specific structure through scaffolded help they are acquiring it (see, for example, Ohta 1995) but it is obviously important to examine how participation leads to internalization. This requires showing how learners progress from assisted to independent use of a language feature. The research by Swain and her co-researchers (for example, Nassaji and Swain 2000; Swain and Lapkin 2001b) has gone some way to addressing this issue but further work along these lines is needed. Sociocultural SLA could also benefit from tighter ways of identifying the ZPD in learners. To claim that a cognitive operation lies within a learner's ZPD, two things must be demonstrated: (1) that the learner *cannot* perform the operation independently, and (2) that he/she *can* perform it with scaffolded assistance. Quite often the demonstration of (2) by itself seems to be taken as evidence of the ZPD. The need for a tighter operationalization of the ZPD is being addressed, however, as the studies by Nassaji and Swain (2000) and Nassaji and Cummins (2000) indicate. Definitional problems also exist with other key constructs. We have noted that there are no clear operational guidelines for distinguishing private and communicative speech, while the classification of private speech into object-, other-, and self-regulated is clearly problematic (see McCafferty 1994a). Also, in some studies the idea of 'scaffolding' seems synonymous with that of 'interacting' and therefore loses definitional precision.

Another limitation in the research is the lack of longitudinal studies. This is surprising given that an essential element of the microgenetic method that researchers claim to be following actually requires that cognitive functioning be studied over time (Hall 1997). Too many of the studies involve 'rich' and unsupported interpretations of data collected at a single point in time. Again, though, this limitation is being addressed and a number of longitudinal studies are beginning to appear (for example, Ohta 2001b; Storch 2000). Also, researchers have typically eschewed quantification, although, as McCafferty (1994a) rightly points out there is nothing wrong with counting observables.

There is also a danger in the claim of some researchers that what counts is the 'activity' that arises from a task rather than the 'task' itself. While acknowledging that task performances are necessarily always constructed rather than determined, recognition needs to be given to the propensity of certain tasks to lead to particular types of language behaviour. There is sufficient research (see especially Chapter 4) to demonstrate that such variables as the inherent structure of a task, the availability of planning time and the opportunity to repeat a task have certain probabilistic process outcomes. It is, therefore, not appropriate to reject 'task' as a legitimate target for study and to insist on the overriding importance of learner agency in determining 'activity'. Tasks are best seen as devices for enabling learners to learn through participating in 'communities of practice' (Foley 1991). To some extent at least the device chosen will influence the nature of this participation.

Quite frequently proponents of sociocultural SLA present their theoretical position in opposition to the prevailing computational view of L2 acquisition. For example, just about all the articles in the special issue of *Modern Language Journal* devoted to the study of sociocultural SLA attack 'encodingism', 'input/output models', 'computationalism', etc. as a prelude to claiming validity for their own preferred metaphors. Doubtlessly, this reflects the felt need of researchers in this tradition to claim a more central position in SLA. Many of the criticisms they level at research based on the Interaction Hypothesis are not justified, however. It is inaccurate, for example, to claim that mainstream SLA researchers have failed to acknowledge the effects that social context can have on task performance (see, for example, Pica 1987) or of the importance of learner factors (see, for example, Plough and Gass 1993).

There are two possibilities for reconciling the computational and sociocultural perspectives on tasks. One is to develop a general theory that incorporates both approaches. However, given the very considerable differences that exist between the two traditions it is difficult to see how they can be linked into a single theory. Even if it is possible it is beyond the scope of this book. The other way is to accept the inevitability of theoretical pluralism by recognizing that both perspectives offer valid insights into how tasks create the conditions that promote language acquisition. From the standpoint of both research and language pedagogy, the need for a pluralistic approach is clear.

In Ellis (2000), I attempted to formulate such an approach, drawing on van Lier's (1991, 1996) distinction between two dimensions of teaching—'planning' and 'improvisation', i.e. the actual behaviours that arise during the process of a lesson and that have not been planned for. Any lesson needs to achieve a balance between these two dimensions. 'Balanced' teaching involves teachers moving back and forwards between planned and improvised decision-making in the course of a lesson. Van Lier, of course, is talking about teaching in general but the distinction is of obvious relevance to task-based language pedagogy and research. Research in the positivistic tradition of the kind we examined in Chapters 2, 3, 4, and 5 has an obvious role to play in the 'planning' dimension of language teaching. It provides information that can be used to select and grade tasks to suit the needs of particular groups of learners. In other words, it can assist in the design of task-based courses. It can also help guide general methodological decisions, such as when and when not to provide learners with opportunities to plan before performing a task, what kind of planning to require of them or whether to repeat a task. In contrast, research in the sociocultural tradition can make teachers aware that the activity that arises from a task may not be exactly what was planned and that this is not a consequence of poor planning or bad teaching but of the participants adapting the task to their own purposes. It can also help to illuminate how teachers can improvise in order to construct activity from tasks in ways that promote the development of linguistic abilities and skills. From a pedagogic perspective, then, the two research traditions need not be seen as incompatible. Rather, they mutually inform task-based instruction.

Notes

1 In addition to 'participation', sociocultural theorists talk of 'appropriation' to refer to the notion that what is internalized is taken from (or appropriated) from social interaction.
2 This claim is of doubtful validity. There are, for example, numerous longitudinal case studies of the acquisition of L2 negation that point to a very robust sequence of acquisition (see Ellis 1994 Chapter 3 for a summary).
3 According to Lantolf and Appel (1994a), activity theory was developed by a group of Russian psychologists called the Kharkovites, of which the best known is A. N. Leontiev. This theory was a development of Vygotskian theory. It aimed to provide a more orthodox Marxian account of mental functioning by emphasizing that mediation arises as a result of people's practical experience with the world of objects, a

position much closer to that advanced by Piaget. In this respect it down-played the role of socioculturally determined activity.

4 Lantolf's point is that different activities must necessarily have different motives but that the same operations can occur in different activities and, conversely, different operations can be used to undertake the same activity. For example, learners who treat a task as an opportunity to develop oral fluency will be involved in a different activity to learners who treat the same task as an opportunity to learn new language. However, the 'operations' they engage in to perform the task may or may not differ and, also, there may be differences in the way learners with the same motive perform the task. What activity theory emphasizes is the primary importance of the learner's motive for performing the task.

5 Donato and McCormack (1994) make a very similar point in their dis-cussion of learners' use of learning strategies. They criticize the trad-itional taxonomic approach to learning strategies, as reflected in the work of Oxford (1990), and argue instead for an approach that looks at strategy use *in situ*. They note 'language learning strategies are generat-ed from the primary social practice of the classroom culture' (1994: 454). They show how the strategies of the learners they investigated changed over time as the need to keep a portfolio providing concrete evi-dence of their ability to recognize and use the language functions they were being taught led to a changed orientation towards learning, with different goals.

6 Samuda's (2001) study discussed in Chapter 5 can also be interpreted in terms of the teacher's attempt to scaffold a ZPD to enable learners to use modal verbs like 'must'. This study is clearly task-based.

7 In fact, one of the learners in this study did eventually hit on the right word. However, it is not clear that he was able to explain the reasons that motivated his choice to the others.

8 The students were asked to plan a conclusion to a scenario in which a man was discovered by his wife to have bought a fur coat for another woman.

7 Designing task-based language courses

Introduction

Course design is concerned with the selection and sequencing of content—the 'what' of teaching. As such, it contrasts with 'methodology', which addresses the 'how' of teaching, i.e. the participatory structure of the classroom and the actual teaching procedures. Together, 'design' and 'methodology' comprise the language curriculum. This chapter is concerned with design of task-based syllabuses and the following chapter with the methodology of task-based teaching.[1]

The separation of 'design' and 'methodology' is not uncontroversial. This is because the choice of teaching content may have implications for the kinds of methodological procedures to be employed. For example, a structural syllabus, i.e. a syllabus that specifies the content in terms of the linguistic structures to be taught, is closely associated with a methodology involving present–practise–produce (PPP). However, such an association, while traditional, is not a necessary one. As I have argued elsewhere (Ellis 1993), a structural syllabus can serve as a basis for an entirely different methodology, i.e. one based on consciousness-raising tasks. Design and methodology, while often linked, are always potentially separable. As Widdowson (1990: 129) puts it, 'methodology can always find some room to manoeuvre'.

It has also been suggested that the distinction between 'design' and 'methodology' is not relevant in task-based teaching. Nunan (1989) argues that in this kind of teaching the focus shifts from 'the outcomes of instruction', i.e. the linguistic knowledge or skills to be mastered, towards the 'processes of learning', i.e. what learners need to do in order to learn. Thus, Nunan claims, the 'what' and the 'how' of teaching are merged. Similarly, Kumaravadivelu (1993: 73) argues that 'methodology becomes the central tenet of task-based pedagogy', since the goal is to allow learners to navigate their own paths and routes to learning. However, these arguments ignore the fact that a task-based curriculum still involves making decisions about content, i.e. what tasks to include in the syllabus, and methodology, i.e. how the tasks will be used in the classroom. Skehan (1996) acknowledges this by distinguishing between 'syllabus considerations' and 'implementing tasks' and I shall do likewise.

A framework for task-based course design

Figure 7.1 identifies the key elements in the construction of a task-based course. The figure shows that the construction of a task-based syllabus requires a specification of the tasks to be included in the syllabus. To achieve this it is helpful to classify tasks in terms of their type, to determine their thematic content and then to sequence them using appropriate criteria for grading their level of difficulty for the learner. This will suffice in the preparation of a task-based syllabus consisting entirely of linguistically unfocused tasks. However, an optional element in the framework is a specification of the features of language, i.e. the forms and functions of language, to be incorporated into the design of the syllabus. If this option is chosen the result is a syllabus consisting entirely of linguistically focused tasks or possibly of a mixture of focused and unfocused tasks. Such a syllabus introduces a focus on form into a meaning-centred curriculum; that is, the syllabus consists of 'tasks' as these have been defined in Chapter 1 but also allows for the systematic treatment of linguistic form. In such a case, consideration needs to be given to both the sequencing of the tasks and of the linguistic content. Finally, Figure 7.1 shows that the syllabus serves as a basis for the preparation of teaching materials in the form of task workplans.

This chapter begins with a review of the rationale for task-based courses. It will then explore the elements shown in Figure 7.1. The focus of the chapter is a priori task-based syllabuses, i.e. syllabuses where the teaching content is specified before teaching begins. No consideration will be given to task-based 'process syllabuses' (Breen 1984; Breen and Littlejohn 2000), where a syllabus is arrived at through 'procedural negotiation' aimed at

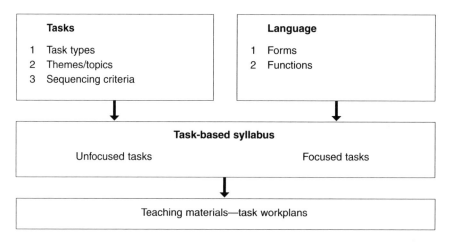

Figure 7.1: Designing a task-based course

achieving agreement between the classroom participants as to the content, methodology and evaluation of the teaching. Such syllabuses can only be described a posteriori and inevitably conflate syllabus and methodology.[2]

The rationale for task-based courses

The theoretical bases of task-based teaching and learning have been discussed in some detail in the previous chapters. Here, therefore, we will focus on the specific reasons that researchers/educationalists have given for advocating task-based instruction and the critical response these have received.

Traditionally, the content of a language course has been specified in terms of the linguistic items to be taught. The type of syllabus that results from this approach to course design has been variously labelled, for example, as 'synthetic' (Wilkins 1976) and 'Type A' (White 1988). For the sake of transparency, I will use the term 'linguistic'. A *linguistic syllabus* focuses on 'what is to be learned'; it is 'interventionist' and 'external to the learner'. Traditionally, it consists of a graded list of grammatical structures. An alternative approach, based on theories of communicative competence (for example, Hymes 1971; Widdowson 1978) and functional grammar (for example, Halliday 1986), involves identifying the linguistic exponents for performing notions (such as 'definiteness' or 'possibility') and functions (such as 'apologizing' or 'requesting information').[3] However, the 'notional/functional approach' is still essentially a linguistic syllabus as it still involves specifying the linguistic content to be taught and it is still essentially interventionist and external to the learner. Thus, the shift from structural to notional/functional syllabuses did not involve any radical rethinking about the basic type of syllabus, although it did make it easier to design courses based on learners' needs, as these could be specified much more clearly in terms of notions/functions than linguistic structures.

The reappraisal of linguistic syllabuses arose in part from the continuing sense of the failure of existing approaches; learners were seen as achieving little in the way of ability to communicate in an L2 despite years of instruction based on such syllabuses (Stern 1983). Reappraisal was also motivated by research that demonstrated that, irrespective of what they were taught, learners followed their own 'built-in syllabus' (Corder 1967) when acquiring the grammatical properties of a language. Thus Long and Crookes (1992: 30–1) argued that linguistic syllabuses are 'flawed because they assume a model of language acquisition unsupported by research findings on language learning in or out of classrooms'. They saw such syllabuses as incompatible with what is known about L2 acquisition because they 'present linguistic forms separately' and because they 'attempt to elicit immediate target-like mastery of these forms' (ibid. 31). Nor, according to Long and Crookes, do notional/functional syllabuses overcome this problem as a linguistic exponent of a notion or function, for example, 'I really like your X' for complimenting, is no more plausible as an 'acquisition unit' than a grammatical structure.[4] Linguistic syllabuses, then, are seen as inadequate because they result in fruitless attempts to interrupt the cognitive processes involved in interlanguage development, which involve the progressive mapping of forms and functions and the attendant restructuring of existing L2 knowledge. In addition, Long and Crookes claimed that linguistic syllabuses result in 'stilted samples of the target language' (ibid. 30).

Proposals for task-based syllabuses, then, arose out of the recognition that it was not possible to specify what a learner would learn in linguistic terms. Thus, as Prabhu (1987) argued, it was necessary to abandon the pre-selection of linguistic items in any form and instead specify the content of teaching in terms of holistic units of communication, i.e. tasks. In this way, he claimed, it would be possible to teach 'through communication' rather than 'for communication'. Prabhu's *procedural syllabus* was a first attempt to develop a syllabus on such grounds. The syllabus consisted of a set of tasks, sequenced according to difficulty. Interestingly, it was developed for use in secondary schools in southern India, a challenging context for what was then an innovatory approach to language teaching. As we will see later, Prabhu's tasks were problem-oriented and designed to be intellectually challenging in order to engage learners and sustain their interest.

A somewhat different approach to task-based teaching has been advanced by Long (see Long 1985; Long and Crookes 1992). Like Prabhu, Long explicitly grounds his proposal on a theory of L2 acquisition but the theory differs in one key respect. Whereas Prabhu views language acquisition as an implicit process that takes place when learners are grappling with the effort to communicate, Long emphasizes the need for learners to attend to form consciously while they are communicating—what he calls 'focus on form' (see Chapter 5). Tasks, then, have to be designed in ways that will ensure a primary focus on meaning but also allow for incidental attention to form. Building on Long's claim about the importance of focusing on form *while* learners are engaged in processing for meaning, Doughty (2001) examines the psycholinguistic mechanisms for achieving this. She argues that speech processing provides windows of opportunity for drawing attention to form while learners are planning utterances. However, such pedagogical interventions, which Doughty refers to as 'cognitive intrusions', must facilitate rather than interrupt natural language processing to be effective. This is the case, she suggests, with recasts that focus contingently and intensively on the specific learner errors that arise in the course of attempts to communicate.

Long also advances proposals for using tasks in courses for specific purposes. He distinguishes what he calls *target tasks* and *pedagogic tasks* and argues that to ensure the relevancy of a task-based syllabus the starting point is a needs analysis to establish the target tasks that a specific group of learners need to be able to perform. For Long, 'task' is the ideal unit for specifying the content of specific purpose courses because it most closely reflects what learners need to do with the language.

It can be seen, then, that the rationale for task-based syllabuses that have been advanced by SLA researchers and educationalists draws on a variety of arguments. First and foremost it is premised on the theoretical view that the instruction needs to be compatible with the cognitive processes involved in L2 acquisition. Second, as in the case of Prabhu, the importance of learner 'engagement' is emphasized; tasks, as long as they provide a 'reasonable challenge', will be cognitively involving and motivating. Third, tasks serve as a suitable unit for specifying learners' needs and thus for designing specific purpose courses.

However, this rationale for task-based teaching can be challenged on a number of fronts. First, the dismissal of linguistic syllabuses on the grounds that learners do not learn the grammatical structures that they are taught may be unwarranted. Early studies of the effects of form-focused instruction (for example, Ellis 1983; Lightbown 1983; Pica 1983), whose findings achieved axiomatic status, did point to this conclusion. However, a number of recent studies suggest learners can achieve clear gains in accuracy as a result of being taught a structure, especially if the type of form-focused instruction is planned in accordance with what is known about acquisitional processes (for example, Harley 1989; White 1991; VanPatten and Cadierno 1993). There is now clear evidence that instruction of the focus-on-form kind can influence the accuracy with which learners use the targeted features, even in unplanned language use (see Ellis 2002). The noted failure of linguistic syllabuses may have had more to do with how the syllabuses were implemented, i.e. with their methodology, than with their design.

Second, the claims regarding the effectiveness of task-based learning have been challenged. Sheen (1994) observes that if immersion programmes have failed to achieve high levels of grammatical and sociolinguistic competence despite the thousands of hours of instruction they afford, one can only be sceptical of what might be achieved by the far fewer hours available in a second or foreign language course based on tasks. However, this criticism takes no account of Long's argument that task-based teaching needs to incorporate attention to form. Sheen also notes that there is actually no empirical evidence that task-based teaching works and that Long and Crooke's advocacy of it is based entirely on theoretical arguments. However, while it is true that no study has demonstrated that task-based teaching results in higher levels of language proficiency than teaching based on traditional linguistic syllabuses, there is some evidence that a meaning-centred approach is effective in developing proficiency (for example, Lightbown 1992) and there is growing experimental evidence that the attention to form that arises from the negotiation of meaning in task-based activity promotes acquisition (for example, Mackey 1999). Sheen's criticisms are salutary but overstated.

To sum up, task-based syllabuses have been promoted by SLA researchers and educationalists as an alternative to linguistic syllabuses on the grounds that (1) linguistic syllabuses are not effective in promoting acquisition, and (2) task-based syllabuses conform to what is known about acquisitional processes. It should be noted that the rationale for task-based syllabuses is largely theoretical in nature, there being little empirical evidence to demonstrate that they are superior to linguistic syllabuses. However, as will be suggested later in this chapter, the argument over whether a task-based syllabus should replace a linguistic syllabus is an unnecessary one, as it is possible to design modular syllabuses containing both types.

We will now turn to a consideration of the design of task-based syllabuses. To this end we will consider: (1) how to classify tasks; (2) what the thematic content of the tasks should be; and (3) how to sequence tasks in accordance with explicit grading criteria. We will conclude with a general procedure for constructing a task-based syllabus. Following this, we will address how a linguistic focus might be incorporated into the design of a task-based syllabus. My purpose throughout is *not* to produce a blueprint for the development of task-based syllabuses. Instead, I have attempted to synthesize the information that will need to be considered in arriving at a set of working procedures. Thus, I do not seek to direct pedagogic action but rather to outline the issues that both researchers and language teaching methodologists have identified as important for designing task-based courses. The specifications that follow are, therefore, 'provisional' both in the sense that they inform rather than guide and in the sense that they will need to be interpreted and acted on by course designers working in their specific instructional contexts. This approach accords with my belief that the primary role of the applied linguist should be to contribute to teachers' understanding of what can be done rather than to tell them what to do (see Ellis 1987a).

Classifying tasks

The survey of the research literature on tasks in the previous chapters has revealed a bewildering array of types of tasks, variously labelled. There are various 'gap' tasks, for example, information-gap and opinion-gap tasks, which are also sometimes referred to in terms of how the information has been organized in the task, i.e. split versus shared information tasks. There are also reciprocal and non-reciprocal tasks, i.e. tasks that require or do not require interaction to achieve the outcome (see Chapter 2). Tasks can be labelled according to the kind of activity they require of the learner, for example, role-play tasks and decision-making tasks, or according to the language skill they focus on, for example, listening tasks or writing tasks. They can be named according to the type of discourse they are intended to elicit, for example, a narrative or descriptive task, or according to the input materials they involve, for example, a map task. Tasks can also have their own individual names, for example, 'spot-the-difference' and 'dictogloss'. Such diversity in nomenclature points to the richness of the task construct. It is, however, potentially problematic for the design of task-based courses.

Task classification is important for a number of reasons. First, it provides a basis for ensuring variety; syllabus designers can refer to the classification to ensure that they incorporate a range of task types into the course. Second, it can be used to identify the task types that match the specific needs or preferences of particular groups of learners. Third, it affords teachers a framework for experimenting with tasks in their classrooms; they can systematically try out the different types of tasks to discover which tasks work for their students. The aim of this section is to develop a check-list of task-types as an aid to task selection. To this end, we will examine four approaches to classifying tasks: (1) pedagogic; (2) rhetorical; (3) cognitive; and (4) psycholinguistic. Then, drawing on these approaches, I will propose a general framework for classifying tasks.

A pedagogic classification

An example of a pedagogic classification of tasks is to be found in Gardner and Miller (1996). This offers a number of 'recipes' for tasks directed at learner training, the traditional four language skills (reading, writing, listening, speaking), two areas of linguistic knowledge (vocabulary and grammar), and paralinguistics. Such a system for classifying tasks has the obvious advantage of being readily applicable to both the design of course books which are traditionally structured around these categories and to supplementary textbooks focusing on specific aspects of language skill or knowledge. However, such a classification runs against the primary rationale for tasks, namely that they provide opportunities for holistic and experiential learning. The kind of pedagogic classification of tasks found in Gardner and Miller serves as a basis for incorporating the task construct into a traditional language course. The danger is that the tasks will lose their 'taskness', i.e. will become more like exercises focusing on discrete aspects of language. Indeed, many of the so-called tasks in Gardner and Miller would not satisfy the definition of a task provided in Chapter 1.

Willis (1996) offers a somewhat different pedagogic classification of tasks based on an analysis of the kinds of tasks commonly found in textbook materials. The types reflect the kind of operations learners are required to carry out in performing tasks:

1 Listing, i.e. where the completed outcome is a list.
2 Ordering and sorting, i.e. tasks that involve sequencing, ranking, categorizing or classifying items.

3 Comparing, i.e. tasks that involve finding differences or similarities in information.
4 Problem-solving, i.e. tasks that demand intellectual activity as in puzzles or logic problems.
5 Sharing personal experiences, i.e. tasks that allow learners to talk freely about themselves and share experiences.
6 Creative tasks, i.e. projects, often involving several stages that can incorporate the various types of tasks above and can include the need to carry out some research.

Willis acknowledges that this classification is not exhaustive but argues that it will help to generate a variety of actual tasks. To assist in this she provides a detailed specification of the operations involved in each task type (see Appendix A on p. 149–54 in Willis 1996), suggesting starting points, sample tasks and follow-up tasks for each operation.

A rhetorical classification

A rhetorical classification of tasks draws on theories of rhetoric that distinguish different discourse domains in terms of their structure and linguistic properties—narrative, instructions, description, reports, etc. Such a classification often underlies language courses for academic purposes (for example, Arnaudet 1984) and is often linked to the specific language functions that figure in academic written discourse, for example, definitions, classifications, giving examples. Such courses often follow a linguistic (often functional) syllabus, employing tasks to provide opportunities for the free production of language that has been previously presented and practised, i.e. they constitute examples of 'task-supported' teaching. However, it would be possible to design a task-based syllabus drawing on a rhetorical classification of tasks, although it would still be necessary to draw on some other system of classification to determine which type of task within each rhetorical category should be included. One advantage of adopting a rhetorical classification is that discourse domain has been shown to be a factor that influences both the negotiation of meaning (see Chapter 3) and the quality of learner production (see Chapter 4). Another advantage is that it lends itself to the design of specific purpose courses, as learners' needs can often be readily specified in terms of the specific domains they need to master.

An alternative, more theoretically satisfying approach to classifying tasks rhetorically is to utilize the concept of *genre*, defined by Swales (1990: 58) as 'a class of communicative events, the members of which share some set of communicative purposes'. Exemplars of a given genre share not just a given structure and style but a communicative purpose. However, they can be more or less prototypical of the genre. Examples of genres are recipes, political speeches, job application letters, good/bad news letters, medical consultations and radio-telephonic flight control messages. Swales shows how genre analysis can be used effectively to describe the types of discourse found in academic settings and provides an extended account of one such genre—the research article. He suggests that the ideal pedagogic vehicle for teaching genres is 'task', as defined in this book. For Swales, however, a task must incorporate an authentic communicative purpose in order to qualify as a genre-based task. This requires establishing the 'socio-cultural situation' of a task by identifying the discourse community to which the genre under consideration belongs. Swales provides an example of a pedagogic task designed to raise students' awareness of the role that 'request letters for papers' play in the academic community and how these are organized discoursally.

A cognitive classification

A cognitive approach to classifying tasks is based on the kind of cognitive operations different types of tasks involve. Prabhu (1987) distinguishes three general types of tasks based on the kind of cognitive activity involved:

1 *Information gap activity* involves 'a transfer of given information from one person to another—or from one form to another, or from one place to another—generally calling for the encoding or decoding of information from or into language' (ibid. 46). Prabhu gives two examples. One involves a standard information-gap activity while the other involves what Widdowson (1978) has called information transfer, for example, using information in a text to complete a chart or table.
2 *Reasoning-gap activity* involves 'deriving some new information from given information through processes of inference, deduction, practical reasoning, or a perception of relationships or patterns' (Prabhu: 1987: 46). Prabhu points out this activity also involves sharing information but requires going beyond the information provided. An example is a task that requires students to work out a teacher's timetable from a set of class timetables.
3 *Opinion-gap activity* involves 'identifying and articulating a personal preference, feeling, or attitude in response to a given situation' (ibid. 47). Examples are story completion and taking part in a discussion. Such tasks are open in the sense that they afford many possible solutions.

Underlying Prabhu's evaluation of these three kinds of activity is his conviction that for tasks to be successful they need to instigate 'negotiation' which he defines somewhat differently from the sense of this term discussed in Chapter 3. For Prabhu, negotiation is 'moving up and down a given line of thought or logic'. He argues that when learners engage in this ideal conditions for language learning are created. According to Prabhu, reasoning-gap tasks were most effective in promoting negotiation. They required learners to express their own meanings but within a context that offered some support. They were also well-suited to the teacher providing support by leading learners though the steps in a reasoning process needed to achieve an outcome. Information-gap tasks resulted in less negotiation because they did not require students to formulate their own meanings. However, they did involve learners in other cognitive operations of value, i.e. determining criteria of success and relevancy, and were often needed to provide the students with the body of information needed to carry out the reasoning task. Opinion-gap tasks proved the least successful in promoting negotiation. They did require students to express their own meanings but they were open-ended, thus depriving the learners of the sense of security that arises when they know that there is a definite answer to a task.

Prabhu's classification of tasks is interesting because it rests on an account of the kinds of cognitive operations that underlie the actual performance of different kinds of tasks. It is based on the premise that using language for reasoning fosters acquisition, a premise that is certainly intuitively appealing. But it is untested. There is no empirical research to show that reasoning-gap activities work better for acquisition than information-gap or opinion-gap activities. Indeed, much of the research that has demonstrated a relation between performance on a task and acquisition (for example, Ellis, Yamazaki, and Tanaka 1984; Mackey 1999) has examined information-gap tasks. However, a strength of Prabhu's classification is that it was derived from an actual attempt to construct a task-based syllabus for a specific teaching context. One lesson we might draw from Prabhu's account of the Communicational Teaching Project is that the type of task that works best may depend on the contingencies of individual teaching contexts. In the context of high schools in southern India, Prabhu and the teachers involved in the project found reasoning-gap tasks suited their needs best.

A psycholinguistic classification

A psycholinguistic classification of tasks sets out to establish a typology of tasks in relation to their potential for language learning. In the previous chapters we have examined various features of tasks that resulted in language use hypothesized to be supportive of language acquisition (see Figure 3.5 in Chapter 3 and Figure 4.2 in Chapter 4). However, given the range of psycholinguistic theories that have informed task-based research, it is not surprising that no all-encompassing psycholinguistic classification of tasks exists. Indeed, one of the points that has been emphasized in the preceding chapters is that different tasks can complement each other when different aspects of language use serve as the criterion. Here we will examine the classificatory system proposed by Pica, Kanagy, and Falodun (1993), which was informed by the Interaction Hypothesis (see Chapter 3).

The system is 'psycholinguistic' in the sense that it is based on inter-actional categories that have been shown to affect the opportunities learners have to comprehend input, obtain feedback, and to modify their own output. The categories are:

1 Interactant relationship: this concerns who holds the information to be exchanged and who requests it and supplies it in order to achieve the task goals. It relates to the distinction between one-way and two-way tasks. This category is derived from research that indicates that when there is a mutual relationship of request and suppliance, negotiation of meaning is more likely to occur.

2 Interaction requirement: this concerns whether the task requires participants to request and supply information or whether this is optional. Again, research has shown that the negotiation of meaning is enhanced if the interactional activity is required of all participants in a task.

3 Goal orientation: this concerns whether the task requires the participants to agree on a single outcome or allows them to disagree. In Chapter 3 we saw that tasks that require collaboration (convergence) result in more meaning negotiation than tasks that allow for independence (divergence).

4 Outcome options: this refers to the scope of the task outcomes available to the participants in meeting the task goals. In the case of 'closed' tasks a single outcome is required whereas 'open' tasks permit several possible outcomes. Again, research suggests that closed tasks are more effective in promoting negotiation of meaning.

Table 7.1 below shows how these four categories can be used to distinguish a number of different types of tasks. Jigsaw tasks (Geddes and Sturtridge 1979) share information among the participants, who are then required to pool their information in order to reach an outcome to the task. Thus the interactant relationship is two-way, interaction involving all the participants is necessary, the participants have to collaborate, and the outcome is closed. An information-gap task differs from a jigsaw task in one key

Task type	Interactant relationship	Interaction requirement	Goal orientation	Outcome options
jigsaw	two-way	required	convergent	closed
information gap	one-way or two-way	required	convergent	closed
problem solving	one-way or two-way	optional	convergent	closed
decision making	one-way or two-way	optional	convergent	open
opinion exchange	one-way or two-way	optional	divergent	open

Table 7.1: A psycholinguistic typology of tasks (based on Pica, Kanagy, and Falodun 1993: 19)

respect—the interactant relationship is primarily one-way because only one participant holds information to be exchanged. However, as Pica, Kanagy, and Falodun point out, if the participants reverse roles from one task to another, i.e. participant A holds the information in the first task and participant B in the second, the overall effect is the same as for jigsaw tasks. Problem-solving tasks, decision-making tasks and opinion-exchange tasks differ from jigsaw and information-gap tasks in that the participants can choose whether they wish to take part in the interaction or remain silent. These types of tasks can be designed so that the interactant relationship is either one-way or two-way. A problem-solving task (Ur 1981) has a single outcome whereas decision-making and opinion-exchange tasks permit a number of possible outcomes. A decision-making task requires participants to reach an agreed solution whereas an opinion-exchange task does not.

According to this taxonomy of tasks, then, a jigsaw task has the greatest psycholinguistic validity and an opinion-exchange task the least. The difficulty with such a classification is that it is only as good as the theory of language learning on which it is based. The theoretical premise underlying Pica, Kanagy, and Falodun's taxonomy is that two-way interaction involving plentiful negotiation of meaning creates the conditions needed for acquisition. While there is certainly research to support this premise (see Chapter 3), there are alternative theoretical premises that emphasize other aspects of language use, for example, learner output. Thus, it is likely that we will need different psycholinguistic taxonomies to account for the different aspects of language use hypothesized to be important for acquisition. Skehan (1998a: 116–7), for example, offers a very different taxonomy based on the characteristics of tasks that promote fluency, complexity and accuracy in language production. Thus, while psycholinguistic frameworks are theoretically derived and have a basis in empirical findings, it is doubtful whether they can do much more than illuminate task selection at this stage. For example, we might choose to include jigsaw tasks on the grounds that they promote plentiful meaning negotiation but we might also decide to include opinion-exchange tasks on the grounds that they result in greater complexity of language in learner production (see Duff 1986). At the moment there is no basis, other than common sense, for balancing the different task types that different psycholinguistic theories give support to.

A general framework

From the above account of task classification, it is clear that there is currently no accepted single typology of tasks nor is there any consensus regarding the choice of organizing principle for constructing such a typology. At best then, task classification can be informed by a general framework based on a number of key dimensions of tasks. Table 7.2 (an expansion of Table 1.1 in Chapter 1) is an attempt at such a general framework. It draws on the rhetorical, cognitive, and psycholinguistic typologies described above. If the starting point is a pedagogic task type of the kind proposed by Willis (1996), it can be narrowly delineated in terms of the dimensions shown in Table 7.2. Table 7.3 provides an example of a task specification.

Design feature	Key dimensions

Input, i.e. the nature of the input provided in the task	**1** Medium
	    a pictorial
	    b oral
	    c written
	2 Organization
	    a tight structure
	    b loose structure

Conditions, i.e. way in which the information is presented to the learners and the way in which it is to be used	**1** Information configuration
	    a split
	    b shared
	2 Interactant relationship
	    a one-way
	    b two-way
	3 Interaction requirement
	    a required
	    b optional
	4 Orientation
	    a convergent
	    b divergent

Processes, i.e. the nature of the cognitive operations and the discourse the task requires	**1** Cognitive
	    a exchanging information
	    b exchanging opinions
	    c explaining/reasoning
	2 Discourse mode
	    a monologic
	    b dialogic

Outcomes, i.e. the nature of the product that results from performing the task.	**1** Medium
	    a pictorial
	    b oral
	    c written
	2 Discourse domain/genre, e.g. description, argument; recipes, political speeches
	3 Scope
	    a closed
	    b open

Table 7.2: A general task framework

Pedagogical task type	Comparing	
Input	1	Medium: pictorial
	2	Organisation: tight structure
Conditions	1	Information configuration: split
	2	Interactant relationship: two-way
	3	Interaction requirement: required
	4	Orientation: convergent
Processes	1	Cognitive: exchanging information
	2	Discourse mode: dialogic
Outcomes	1	Medium: oral
	2	Discourse mode: description
	3	Scope: closed

Table 7.3: Specification of a spot-the-difference task

The thematic content of tasks

In addition to deciding what type of task to include in a syllabus, the course designer also needs to make decisions about what the students will be asked to communicate about. Thus, a key element in the design of tasks must be the choice of thematic content. The academic literature on task-based teaching has paid scant attention to choice of thematic content, although some research relating to this factor was considered in Chapters 3 and 4.[5] In contrast, practical guides attach much more importance to this aspect of task selection. In Estaire and Zanon's (1994) framework for developing a task-based unit of work, for example, 'select theme or interest area' is the starting point. Similarly, a key element in the preparation of the 'final task' of a unit is determining the 'thematic aspects' of the task.

The choice of theme will depend to a considerable extent on whether the pedagogic purpose of the task-based course is general proficiency or some specific use of the L2. In the case of the former, the guiding principles in the selection of content for tasks will be (1) topic familiarity and (2) intrinsic interest. Some appeal may also be made to (3) topic relevancy by predicting the general situations that learners may later find themselves in. Estaire and Zanon (1994) provide a 'theme generator' (reproduced as Figure 7.2 below). This is organised in terms of thematic areas that are close or remote to the learner. Thus topics relating to the students themselves are obviously close while topics relating to a theme like 'fantasy' are remote. Estaire and Zanon offer a number of specific topics for each thematic area based on suggestions made by teachers they have worked with. For example, topics relating to 'students' include 'birthdays', 'eating habits', and 'how the body works'. Of course, the themes/topics chosen for a particular group of learners will depend on both the students' level of proficiency, i.e. close topics being more suitable for beginner learners and remote topics for more advanced learners, and also on local cultural values and interests.

In the syllabus developed for the Communicational Teaching Project (Prabhu 1987) many of the tasks are built around themes that relate fairly directly to the school curriculum or aspects of school organisation, for example, the letters of the alphabet, calendars, maps and school timetables. Other topics reflect aspects of social life with which the students might be expected to be familiar, for example, family structures, the postal system, buses and trains, libraries. There are also themes that relate to social artifacts that the students will need to deal with in the future, for example, bills, curriculum vitae, telegrams. Finally, perhaps to offset the instrumental nature of many of these topics, there are tasks that draw on stories. These tasks show a clear relationship to the thematic areas shown in Figure 7.2.

In the case of a specific-purpose course design, topic selection may be motivated primarily by an analysis of the target tasks the learners will

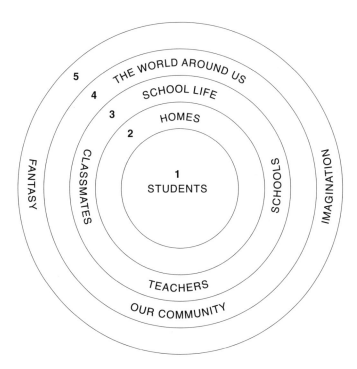

Figure 7.2: The theme generator (Estaire and Zanón 1994: 21)

need to perform. Long (1985) notes that there are ready-made job descriptions in task format (for example, *The Dictionary of Occupational Titles*, U.S. Department of Labor, 1977). These provide accounts of not only what people in particular occupations do but also the kinds of topics they deal with. Together these constitute what Long calls the *target tasks*, i.e. the real-world activities they engage in. For example, a shipping and receiving clerk has to keep records on incoming and outgoing shipments and to verify bills of lading. Long suggests that target tasks need to be generalized into 'task types' to ensure more cost-effective teaching and to allow for the principled selection of pedagogical tasks. This is achieved largely by generalizing the topic of a number of related target tasks. For example, the target tasks of 'serving breakfast', 'serving lunch', and 'serving dinner' performed by a flight attendant can be generalized into the task type of 'serving meals'. In effect, then, task types in Long's proposal are determined primarily by thematic content and choice of task types is driven by learners' communicative needs.

Sequencing tasks

We have now considered how tasks can be classified into types and the factors that need to be considered in determining their thematic content. This provides a basis for specifying which tasks to include in a syllabus. However, the design of a syllabus also requires that the content be sequenced so as to facilitate maximum learning. In effect, this requires determining the complexity of individual tasks so that tasks can be matched to learners' level of development.

Widdowson (1990) notes that sequencing tasks faces several problems, in particular the grading criteria to be used. He points out that we do not possess a sufficiently well-defined model of cognitive complexity to establish such criteria and concludes that task-based syllabuses thus face exactly the same problem as linguistic syllabuses—they cannot be modelled on the sequence of language acquisition. Widdowson is clearly right in drawing attention to the difficulty of formulating grading criteria. However, his conclusion that tasks cannot be graded in ways that take account of how learners acquire L2s is unwarranted. It is arguably difficult if not impossible to determine what linguistic content learners will learn at specific points in their development, but it is much more feasible to determine what tasks are suited to learners' developmental level given that tasks allow learners to choose the linguistic (and non-linguistic) resources they will use to arrive at an outcome. Tasks do not need to be graded with the same level of precision as linguistic content.

The ease with which learners are able to perform different tasks depends on three sets of factors. First, there are the inherent characteristics of the task itself. These relate to the nature of the input, the task conditions, the processing operations involved in completing the task and the outcome that is required. Robinson (2001: 29) refers to these factors under the heading of *task complexity*. He comments:

> Task complexity is the result of the attentional memory, reasoning, and other information processing demands imposed by the structure of the task on the language learner. These differences in information processing demands, resulting from design characteristics, are relatively fixed and invariant.

Task complexity can account for intra-learner variability, i.e. the variability evident when the same learner performs different tasks. Second, Robinson identifies factors relating to learners as individuals, which can influence how easy or difficult a particular task is for different participants. These factors include, obviously, the learner's level of proficiency and also various factors such as the learner's intelligence, language aptitude, learning style, memory capacity, and motivation. Robinson sees these factors as relating to *task difficulty*, which is dependent on 'the resources the learner brings to the task' (ibid. 31). Task difficulty accounts for inter-learner variability. The third set of factors involves the methodological procedures used to teach a task. These procedures can increase or ease the processing burden placed on the learner. They include the use of a pre-task activity, for example, pre-teaching the vocabulary needed to perform the task or carrying out a task similar to the main task with the assistance of the teacher, and planning time, i.e. giving students the opportunity to plan before they undertake the task. In accordance with Figure 1.4 in Chapter 1, we will refer to this group of factors as **task procedures**.[6] Like task complexity factors, they result in intra-learner variability. In this chapter, where we are concerned with course planning, we will focus solely on factors that influence task complexity. The following chapter will consider the role of task procedures.

A number of criteria for grading tasks have been proposed (see Brindley 1989; Candlin 1987; Nunan 1989; Skehan 1998; and Robinson 2001 for reviews). We will not examine these different proposals in detail but instead attempt a synthesis by identifying the various criteria that account for task complexity in terms of: (1) input, (2) conditions (3) processes, and (4) outcomes. We will draw on the research in the previous chapters but concentrate on the factors identified by those who have directly addressed grading criteria for tasks. The various factors will be presented taxonomically as currently little is known about how they interrelate to determine complexity. However, we will conclude this section by suggesting how the criteria might be applied in designing courses.

Factors relating to input

Tasks frequently supply learners with information and this can vary in complexity in several ways. We will consider the following factors: (1) medium; (2) code complexity; (3) cognitive complexity; (4) context dependency; and (5) familiarity of information.

Input medium

With regard to input medium, information that is presented in written or pictorial form, which can be decoded in the learner's own time, is likely to be easier to process than information that is provided orally, which requires online decoding. However, the validity of this claim will depend on the learners' level of literacy in the L2. Prabhu (1987) notes that the students in the Communicational Teaching Project (beginner learners in Indian secondary schools) found tasks with an oral input easier than tasks presented in writing. It can also be surmised that pictorial input will be easier than verbal input as it makes no demands on the learners' linguistic resources. An exception, of course, would be pictorial input that was culturally marked so as to be unfamiliar to the learners. Tasks involving pictures and diagrams frequently figure in courses designed for learners of limited proficiency (for example, Prabhu 1987).

Code complexity

The code complexity of the input, i.e. its lexical and syntactical complexity, is also likely to influence the learner's ability to comprehend. Input texts with high frequency vocabulary and a low level of subordination are easier to understand than texts with low frequency vocabulary and complex sentence structure. Studies of the effects of linguistic modifications on the comprehension of texts (for example, see Chaudron 1988 for a review) lend support to this claim. However, 'there is no absolute reason whereby a complexifying of the code inevitably involves a corresponding increase in the interpretative density of the text' (Candlin 1987: 20). It should also be noted that there is growing evidence that elaborative input, i.e. input that employs devices such as paraphrases and glosses rather than simplification, is more comprehensible than simplified input (Oh 2001).

Cognitive complexity

Cognitive complexity is as important as, if not more important than, code complexity. This concerns the cognitive demands of processing the informational content of the input material. Brown *et al.* (1984) suggest that it involves two dimensions. First, there is the information type. This can be 'static', i.e. the information remains the same throughout the performance of the task, 'dynamic', i.e. the information contains changing events and activities as in a video story, or 'abstract', i.e. tasks that present information that has to be used to form an opinion or justify a position. Brown *et al.* claim that static tasks are easiest and abstract tasks the most difficult, with dynamic tasks intermediate. Prabhu (1987) also notes that tasks that require learners to work with 'concepts' proved more difficult than tasks involving the names of objects and actions.

The second dimension of cognitive complexity referred to by Brown *et al.* concerns the amount of information to be processed—the number of different elements or relationships involved. For example, a static task involving describing a diagram is easier when the input contains few elements of a similar size presented in a regular array than when it involves many elements of varying sizes in an uneven display. Similarly, in a dynamic task, a storyline that contains few characters and objects is easier to tell than one that contains many.

Skehan (2001) suggests that another factor that can potentially affect the cognitive complexity of the input is degree of structure, which concerns whether the information has a clear macrostructure, as in a story where the time sequence is readily identifiable (see Chapter 4). Tasks where the input is clearly structured may be easier to perform than those where it is more loosely structured because learners can call on ready-made schemata to help them organize their productions.

Context dependency

The context dependency of the input may have an impact on complexity. Textual input that is supported by visual information in some form is generally easier to process than information with no such support (see Chapter 4). Robinson (1995) bases his claim that context-free input is more complex on the results of L1 and L2 studies that show 'there-and-then' reference to be developmentally later. Nunan (1989) also notes that texts supported by photographs, drawings, tables, and graphs are easier to understand. However, as we saw in Chapter 4, the research to date has failed to show conclusively that tasks involving displaced reference are more complex than those involving contextually supported reference.

Familiarity of information

Arguably, 'familiarity of information' relates to 'task difficulty' as much as to 'task complexity', as it concerns the relationship between the theme of the task and the individual learner's world knowledge. Prabhu (1987: 88), for example, comments that 'learners' knowledge of the world can make tasks more or less difficult for them, depending on whether they are more or less familiar with purposes and constraints of the kind involved in the tasks'. However, I have included this factor here because it is perhaps best seen as a task factor rather than an individual difference factor and because it clearly relates to the choice of thematic content, which we considered earlier.

A number of task designers also refer to familiarity of information as an important criterion influencing task complexity. Prabhu (1987) reports that high school children in India found tasks based on money earned and spent easier than those based on a bank account, as they had no personal experience of the latter. Candlin (1987) and Skehan (1998a) point out that asking learners to communicate about a topic they are unfamiliar with is inherently stressful. They discuss this factor under the general heading of 'communicative stress'.

Factors relating to task conditions

In comparison to input factors, the relative complexity of task conditions has received little attention by task-designers—an obvious omission. We will consider three factors that have been discussed in the literature: (1) conditions relating to the negotiation of meaning; (2) task demands; and (3) the discourse mode required by the task.

Conditions influencing the negotiation of meaning

Markee (1997: 98) notes that 'some tasks are psycholinguistically more difficult to complete than others'. He bases this claim on research that indicates that one-way tasks promote less negotiation of meaning than two-way tasks (see Chapter 3), which he sees as affecting the complexity of the task. There is some research that suggests that providing learners with the opportunity to negotiate leads to more successful task outcomes (for example, Gass and Varonis 1994; Ellis, Tanaka, and Yamazaki 1994). One possible explanation is that negotiation increases the amount of time learners spend on a task. If this is correct, then, the other factors known to influence the amount of negotiation, i.e. information configuration, interaction requirement, and orientation (see Table 7.1) may also play a role in task complexity.

Task demands

One condition that has received some attention is task demands, specifically whether the task imposes a single or a dual demand. Robinson (2001) notes that this has been investigated extensively in educational research by studying the effect on performance of adding a second task to the main task. As we noted in Chapter 4, Robinson operationalized this factor in a map task in which the route to be described was either marked on the map (single task) or not marked, thus requiring the learner to identify the route to be followed as well as describe it (dual task). Brown *et al.* (1984) and Yule and McDonald (1990) operationalized dual task demands somewhat differently. They designed tasks that required one participant to describe the route marked on his/her map to another participant. The conditions differed in terms of whether the maps given to the participant contained referential conflicts. That is, they used maps that were the same for the participants (single task) and maps that differed in one or more features (dual task).

Discourse mode

As we saw in Chapter 4, Skehan's research used a variety of tasks that differed in terms of whether they called for a monologue on the part of the participants or dialogue. Skehan (2001) proposes that dialogic tasks promote greater accuracy and complexity and monologic tasks greater fluency. This proposal would seem more relevant to the selection than the grading of tasks, however.[7] Intuitively, dialogic tasks would seem to be easier than monologic tasks as they offer opportunities for the participants to scaffold each other's performance. Skehan (1996) suggests that the extent to which the participants are able to influence how the task is performed is a key factor in communicative stress; clearly, the opportunity to negotiate for meaning by means of requests for clarification in dialogic tasks is one way in which learners can exert control.

Factors relating to the process of performing a task

The nature of the cognitive operations required to complete the task has a major influence on task complexity. Here we will consider the role of the reasoning needed to complete a task.

Reasoning needed

Of the three types of tasks that Prabhu (1987) describes (see above), information-gap tasks proved the easiest and opinion-gap tasks the most difficult, with reasoning-gap tasks intermediate. In the case of reasoning-gap tasks, Prabhu identifies the reasoning needed as a key factor determining complexity:

> The 'distance' between the information provided and the information arrived at as outcome, i.e. the number of steps involved in the deduction, inference, or calculation, is a measure of the relative difficulty of tasks.

He gives as an example two tasks based on class timetables. In one task the students were asked to use the information in the timetables to work out a teacher's personal timetable. In the other task they were asked to use the same information to identify when the teachers were not teaching. This latter task involved an additional step and thus was considered more complex.

Factors relating to task outcomes

Finally, we consider a number of factors that relate to the task outcomes: (1) the medium; (2) the scope; (3) the discourse domain; and (4) the complexity of the outcome.

Medium of the outcome

As with input, the medium of the outcome is a potential factor influencing task complexity. Again, pictorial and written products may prove easier than oral products, especially if the latter involve a public presentation of some kind. However, this will again depend on the difficulty individual learners experience with the different media. Possibly the least complex outcome is one that involves some simple visual product such as a map, a drawing, or a diagram, as this poses no linguistic demands at the level of outcome. In effect tasks with such outcomes function as comprehension rather than production tasks. It would seem sensible to make use of simple comprehension tasks with beginner learners, who cannot be expected to speak or write in the L2 until they have developed some L2 competence. In Prabhu's procedural syllabus, the initial tasks did not require learner production; they consisted of instructions that students were required to act out to demonstrate their understanding, as in Total Physical Response (Asher 1977).

The scope of the outcome

There is no literature on the relative complexity of tasks with closed and open outcomes. Intuitively, tasks with closed outcomes will be easier in that the participants know there is a 'right' answer and thus can direct their efforts more purposefully and, perhaps, more economically.

The discourse domain of the outcome

Similarly, there is no basis in research for determining which discourse domain poses the greatest cognitive demands. Intuitively, lists and descriptions are less of a challenge than instructions or arguments, with classification and narration intermediate. In general, however, the degree of complexity of these discourse domains will depend on the level of detail required in the product. Instructions, for example, can be more or less complex depending on the number and content of the specific directives.

Complexity of the outcome

Skehan (2001: 173) identifies complexity of outcome as an important factor in decision-making tasks. He comments:

> Some tasks require only straightforward outcomes, in which a simple decision has to be made. Others require multi-faceted judgements, in which the case or position a learner argues during a task can only be effective if it anticipates other possible outcomes, and other learners' contributions.

Thus, the nature of the outcome impacts on the task performance, affecting the complexity of the arguments that need to be made. Prabhu (1987: 88) makes a similar point, noting that 'outcomes may need to be expressed in more or less precise terms' and claims that the greater the precision, the more complex the task. Like Skehan, he sees the degree of precision as dependent on the number of plausible options that have to be addressed. Prabhu also points out that outcomes that involve a high level of precision also require greater lexical and syntactical accuracy.

Summary

Table 7.4 below summarizes the various criteria discussed above. Some of the criteria have a clear warrant in empirical research, for example, the information type of the input and single/dual task demands. Other criteria, however, are obviously more speculative, the product of common sense rather than hard evidence. Ideally the various criteria should be weighted but it is not possible to do so with the present state of knowledge. We do not know with any certainty, for example, whether a task involving static but unfamiliar information is more or less difficult than a task involving abstract but familiar information. Nor do we know very much how the various criteria combine to determine task complexity. Also, as Prabhu (1987: 89) points out, 'no syllabus of generalized tasks can identify or anticipate all the sources of challenge to particular learners'. Thus grading tasks cannot follow a precise algorithmic procedure but rather must proceed more intuitively in accordance with a general assessment of task complexity, informed by the criteria considered above and by the designer's experience of how particular groups of learners respond to different tasks. The question arises as to whether the inability to sequence tasks in accordance with explicitly defined criteria constitutes a damaging limitation of task-based syllabuses. Widdowson (1990) thinks it is. I would argue that,

Criterion	Easy	Difficult
A Input		
1 Medium	pictorial → written	→ oral
2 Code complexity	high frequency vocabulary; short and simple sentences	low frequency vocabulary; complex sentence structure
3 Cognitive complexity		
a information type	static → dynamic	→ abstract
b amount of information	few elements/ relationships	many elements/ relationships
c degree of structure	well-defined structure	little structure
d context dependency	here-and-now orientation	there-and-then orientation
4 Familiarity of information	familiar	unfamiliar
B Conditions		
1 Interactant relationship (negotiation of meaning)	two-way	one-way
2 Task demands	single task	dual task
3 Discourse mode required to perform the task	dialogic	monologic
C Processes		
1 Cognitive operations:		
a type	exchanging information → reasoning	→ exchanging opinions
b reasoning need	few steps involved	many steps involved
D Outcomes		
1 Medium	pictorial	→ written → oral
2 Scope	closed?	open?
3 Discourse mode of task outcome	lists, descriptions, narratives, classifications	→ instructions, arguments

Table 7.4: Criteria for grading tasks

although problematic, it does not seriously threaten the case for task-based teaching. For one thing, as we have already seen, interventionist syllabuses are no better in this respect; we cannot grade linguistic structures to ensure their learnability. But, more importantly, in a non-interventionist syllabus, i.e. a syllabus that does not seek to dictate what linguistic forms a learner will learn at any time, the need to ensure a precise match between the teaching and the learner's syllabus no longer arises. I would propose, therefore, that course designers first assess the complexity of tasks informally and then use the criteria summarized in Table 7.4 to evaluate the reliability of their assessment.

Constructing a task-based syllabus

The above discussion of task types, choice of thematic content, and criteria for grading provides a checklist of factors that need to be considered in planning a task-based syllabus. The planning itself will involve the following procedures:

1 The starting point is the determination of the goal(s) of the course in terms of its pedagogic focus (general or specific purpose), skill focus (listening, speaking, reading, writing, learner training) and language focus (unfocused or focused).
2 The designer then needs to make a broad choice of task types and to specify the particular themes the tasks will deal with. The result of this stage is a list of tasks organized by theme and specified in terms of the general activity that the learners will be required to undertake, as shown in columns 1 and 2 of Table 7.5.
3 The third step would be to specify the nature of the tasks to be used in detail by selecting options relating to input, conditions, processes, and outcomes, as shown in the third column of Table 7.5. The selection would need to be motivated both by a consideration of the psycholinguistic value of the different options and by practical considerations relating to the specific teaching context.

Topic	General activity	Task options
School timetables	1 Listing: constructing timetables from instructions/ descriptions	Input: pictorial/written tight structure
	2 Comparing: examining timetables to identify the frequencies of lessons in different subjects	Conditions: shared information two-way optional information requirement convergent
	3 Problem solving: constructing timetables for teachers of particular subjects from given class timetables	Processes: explaining/reasoning dialogic Outcomes: pictorial/written closed

Table 7.5: An example of part of a task-based syllabus for general proficiency (based on Prabhu 1987).

4 Finally, the tasks need to be sequenced. As pointed out above, this might
   be best achieved by using the criteria summarized in Table 7.4 as a
   means of evaluating an intuitive assessment of task complexity.

This procedure is adequate for a syllabus based on linguistically unfocused
tasks. However, if in (1) a decision is taken to include a language focus,
consideration will need to be given to ways of incorporating a focus on
form into the syllabus. How this can be achieved is considered in the next
section.

Incorporating a focus on form into a task-based syllabus

There are two principal ways of attempting to include a specific focus on
form into task-based teaching:

1 By means of tasks that have been designed to focus attention on
   specific properties of the code. I have referred to these as 'focused
   tasks' (see Chapter 5). Such tasks represent a proactive approach
   towards integration at the level of the syllabus.
2 By incorporating a focus on form methodologically into the performance of linguistically unfocused tasks. This entails incidental attention to
   form and can be accomplished pre-emptively, i.e. the teacher or student
   can elect to address a form that arises in the communication, or
   reactively though feedback, which can be instant, i.e. can occur as an
   immediate response to a learner error, or delayed, i.e. take place after the
   communicative task has been completed.

In this chapter we will be concerned only with (1). Methodological ways of
achieving a focus on form will be addressed in Chapter 8.
   As we saw in Chapter 5, there are problems in designing focused tasks
involving production of the targeted feature. Learners are adept are side-
stepping the grammatical focus while performing a task, unless of course
they are told what the focus is, in which case, it can be argued that the task
ceases to be a task and becomes an exercise. However, there are solutions
to this problem. What I have called 'interpretation tasks' are well suited to
a task-based syllabus that seeks to incorporate a focus on form. Such tasks
involve 'seeding' the input in such a way that learners are obligated to
attend to the target structure in order to understand the information.
Another solution to the problem is to make use of consciousness-raising
tasks where the content of the task becomes a grammatical feature. Both of
these types of focused task were considered in Chapter 5.
   In this section we will first consider the thorny problem of how to select
and sequence the linguistic content for a syllabus of focused tasks. We will
then examine two proposals for incorporating form into a communicative
syllabus.

Selecting and sequencing linguistic content

The incorporation of a linguistic focus into a task-based syllabus raises once more the key issues of selection and sequencing. Which forms should be included and in what order? These questions raise in turn the problem facing linguistic syllabuses in general, namely how the teaching syllabus can be made to match the learner's built-in syllabus. A focus-on-forms approach will flounder if the forms taught do not correspond to those the learner is capable of acquiring. A syllabus of focused tasks will fail for the same reason. For a task-based syllabus that incorporates a specific focus on form to be successful it must be compatible with interlanguage development. N. Ellis (2002) has characterized this as a gradual process of computing and analysing sequences in the input, a process that takes place largely implicitly and results in complex mental networks that produce fuzzy rather than monothetic categories. In other words, the 'forms' that appear in a teaching syllabus bear no direct relationship to the 'forms' that are actually internalized. Thus, our descriptions of linguistic forms, on which the selection of linguistic context must necessarily be based, have no direct psychological correlates.

We can address this problem by distinguishing two possible goals for incorporating a focus on form into a task-based syllabus—the development of *implicit* and *explicit L2 knowledge* (see Chapter 4 for a discussion of these two types of knowledge). The difficulties of designing a syllabus of focused tasks arise when the goal is implicit knowledge. I will argue the problems are different and more manageable when the goal becomes explicit knowledge.

Specifying the linguistic content for developing implicit knowledge

A graded list of structural features is of little use where the development of implicit knowledge is concerned, for the reason outlined above. This suggests, therefore, that designing a syllabus of focused tasks with the goal of enabling learners to develop implicit knowledge of the targeted features is pointless. However, this need not be the case.

One possibility, mooted by Skehan (1998a: 130), is that tasks should not target specific features but rather clusters of features. Skehan argues that it is futile to fix on a particular structure because the 'power of internal processing factors is simply too strong' making it impossible to determine externally what learners should acquire. However, Skehan acknowledges that teachers need some method for keeping track of interlanguage development and suggests this can be accomplished by identifying a range of structures for individual tasks. However, he does not explain how this can be accomplished. The identification of a range of structures as the acquisitional target for a task runs up against the same learnability problem, albeit to a lesser extent, as the identification of a specific structure.

However, while it is probably useless to attempt to draw up a graded list of items to be systematically treated either individually or in clusters, it may be feasible to work with a checklist of items. Teachers can use such a checklist to help them establish which forms their students have and have not mastered and, crucially, which forms they are in the process of currently mastering. Features that learners show signs of acquiring, i.e. features learners have attempted to use but cannot yet use correctly, constitute the ideal targets for incorporation into focused tasks. This is precisely the approach that focus-on-form researchers have adopted. Williams and Evans (1998: 140), for example, state that they selected present and past participle adjectives, for example, 'interesting' and 'interested', for treatment because 'the forms were actively used in the speech and writing of the learners but were often used incorrectly'.[8] In other words, the linguistic syllabus, as a checklist, becomes a basis for the *remedial* teaching of form.

But how exactly should the content of such a checklist be determined? One possibility is to base it on the commonly observed errors that learners (or particular groups of learners) have been observed to make. Error analyses, once fashionable but now less so, have a role to play here. So too do books like Swan and Smith's (1991) *Learner English*, which describe the typical errors made by learners with different L1s. Another possibility is to include items that have a propensity to cause learners problems. Harley (1994) suggests that forms are likely to be problematic to learners if they:

1 differ from the learner's first language in ways that are difficult to perceive
2 lack saliency because they are irregular or occur infrequently in the input[9]
3 are communicatively redundant
4 are likely to be misinterpreted or misanalysed by learners.

These constitute useful criteria for selecting the linguistic content of a checklist. However, it is still necessary to determine whether the selected features constitute actual learning problems for learners. Also, it would be pointless to attempt to sequence the items as the items in the checklist may or may not need to be dealt with and the order in which they are treated will depend on when they are found to be problematic.

In summary, where implicit knowledge is concerned course designers can only identify linguistic content with the potential to be incorporated into tasks. They cannot determine in advance exactly which forms, or range of forms, should be addressed nor can they stipulate when they should be addressed. All that is possible is a checklist of items and procedures for deciding when a particular item can usefully be addressed.

Specifying the linguistic content for developing explicit knowledge

The kinds of tasks needed to develop implicit knowledge will be either structure-based production tasks or interpretation tasks; in the case of explicit knowledge, consciousness-raising (CR) tasks are needed. Here we will be concerned with the linguistic content of such tasks. The selection of linguistic content for CR tasks will be informed by the same considerations as that for developing implicit knowledge—an analysis of the kinds of linguistic problems learners face in acquiring the L2. However, where explicit knowledge is concerned, it may be feasible to draw up a graded syllabus, not just a checklist.

What is difficult to acquire as implicit knowledge may be quite easy to understand declaratively. For example, it is notoriously difficult for learners to acquire third person -s as implicit knowledge but easy for learners to cognize the rule ('add -s to the simple form of the verb'). The learnability problem, which precludes sequencing for implicit knowledge, does not apply to explicit knowledge. Just as one can develop general criteria to determine the order in which to teach mathematical theorems, so one can establish criteria for grading grammatical rules as declarative knowledge— some rules will be easier to *understand* than others. The question that needs to be addressed, then, is what factors influence the level of difficulty learners are likely to experience in acquiring explicit knowledge of features? I would like to suggest that, by and large, these are exactly the kind of criteria that have been traditionally used in grading items for a structural syllabus. Table 7.6 lists and illustrates some of these criteria.

Using such criteria, then, it ought to be possible to draw up a graded list of grammatical items for teaching explicit knowledge. For example, third person -s would be classified as an easy rule on the grounds that it is formally and functionally simple, is very reliable, is narrow in scope and can be explained using minimal metalanguage. In contrast, verb complementation constitutes a difficult rule because it is formally complex (there are different ways in which a verb can be complemented), is functionally opaque, is difficult to construct a reliable 'rule' for, is broad in scope and requires the use of terms like 'infinitive' and 'participle' to explain it. A feature such as negation in English can be considered of intermediate difficulty on the grounds that the rule is functionally simple, reliable, and broad in scope, but is formally quite complex and necessitates distinguishing 'auxiliary' and 'main verb' metalingually.

Linguistic features constitute the 'topics' of consciousness-raising tasks. The design of a syllabus based on such tasks is initiated by the linguistic content. The tasks themselves, however, must conform to the definition of a task in general and thus designers will still need to make principled decisions regarding the types of task they wish to use and the sequencing of these tasks. Thus, the various factors considered earlier in this chapter relating to the classification and sequencing of tasks (see Table 7.2 and 7.4) will still need to be considered.

Criteria	Definition	Example
1 Formal complexity	The extent to which the structure involves just a single or many elements	Plural -*s* is formally simple; relative pronouns are complex.
2 Functional complexity	The extent to which meanings realized by a feature are transparent or opaque.	Plural -*s* is transparent; articles are opaque.
3 Reliability	The extent to which the rule has exceptions.	Third person -*s* is very reliable; the rule for periphrastic genitives has many exceptions.
4 Scope	The extent to which the rule has a broad or narrow coverage.	The present simple tense has broad scope; the future perfect tense has narrow scope.
5 Metalanguage	The extent to which the rule can be explained simply with minimum metalanguage.	Plural -*s* is simple; reflexive pronouns are more difficult to explain; subject–verb inversion is very difficult.
6 L1/L2 contrast	A feature that has a correlate in the L1 is easy. A feature that has no correlate is more difficult.	Japanese 'wa' and 'ga' are difficult for English learners because English has no such particles.

Table 7.6: Criteria for determining the difficulty of grammatical structures as explicit knowledge (from Ellis 2002).

It would be possible for a task-based course to consist entirely of consciousness-raising tasks but this is not recommended for a number of reasons (see Chapter 5 for a discussion of the limitations of this type of task). A better approach might be to thread consciousness-raising tasks into a syllabus comprised primarily of linguistically unfocused tasks. How this might be achieved is considered in the following section.

Two approaches for incorporating a focus on form

We will turn now to examine two different proposals for incorporating a focus on form into a task-based course. The first proposal originates in work on content-based instruction (a kind of task-based approach) in school contexts with ESL learners, although it is arguably relevant to other teaching contexts. The second proposal involves a modular syllabus and is broadly applicable to all teaching situations.

An integrated approach

Content-based courses are premised on the assumption that learners will best learn language while they are engaged in learning subject content. However, as we have noted earlier, such courses do not result in learners achieving high levels of grammatical and sociolinguistic accuracy. This has led content-based instructors to consider how a focus on form can be embedded into content-based teaching.

Snow, Met, and Genesee (1989) outline a conceptual framework for integrating language and content instruction. This gives priority to content. As Genesee (1994: 49) puts it, 'from the learners' point of view, activities in some integrated second language classrooms are about content and not about language per se'. Thus the starting point in course design is the selection of activities that are important and interesting to the learners, familiar to them but also contain some new elements and are suited to the learners' level of intellectual development. However, in designing such activities attention also needs to be paid to linguistic form. Met (1994: 163) explains how this can be achieved:

> By selecting content from the school's curriculum that is compatible with ESL objectives teachers can use the content as a communicative and cognitively engaging means of developing language and also help to promote mastery of content material.

Thus, course designers need to refer to both a linguistic syllabus that specifies the forms a student needs to master and a content syllabus (based on the school curriculum).

How then can course designers select content that is 'compatible with ESL objectives'? Snow, Met, and Genesee suggest that this can be achieved by analysing the linguistic forms that arise in specific content domains. To this end they distinguish between *content-obligatory language*, i.e. the language that is required to learn a particular content, and *content-compatible language*, i.e. the language that can be usefully taught within the context of a particular content domain but which is not required for successful mastery of the content. For example, if the topic is 'gravity', content-obligatory language might include the lexical items 'to pull' and 'to force' and the use of apostrophe -s, for example, 'the earth's gravity'. Content-compatible language might include such items as 'mass' and 'when' clauses, for example, 'When we throw a ball up into the air ...'. Snow, Met, and Genesee propose that content-obligatory items for a given content domain be identified first. Secondly, content-compatible linguistic items can be drawn from three sources: (1) the second/foreign language curriculum, which provides a checklist of such items, (2) an assessment of learners' ongoing language needs, and (3) the anticipated linguistic demands of the content curriculum. These items can then be incorporated into the content-based instruction. Snow, Met, and Genesee illustrate how this approach can be used in mainstream classrooms with L2 learners, in pull-out ESL classes, in immersion classes, and in foreign language classrooms.

Of course, attempts to integrate form and content in this way face the same learnability problem we discussed above and will require the same solutions. We will now consider an alternative approach that in some ways is more practicable because it sidesteps the learnability problem.

A modular approach

In the kind of modular approach I have proposed (see Ellis 2002), no attempt is made to integrate content and form. Instead, the syllabus is conceived of as two entirely separate modules—a communicative module and a code-based module. The communicative module constitutes the main component of such a syllabus. It consists of linguistically unfocused tasks, selected and graded with reference to the criteria outlined earlier in this chapter. Students work their way systematically through this module, which provides opportunities to develop fluency, accuracy and complexity through message-centred activity. Of course, this does not mean that learners will not attend to form when they perform tasks in this module. As we have seen in the previous chapters, learners quite naturally focus on form while they are performing unfocused tasks. It simply means that no attempt is made to predetermine through the design of a task which forms learners will attend to.

The code-based module constitutes the secondary component of the syllabus. It consists of a checklist of linguistic features that are potentially difficult for learners to learn and serves a 'remedial' purpose by helping learners to acquire features that prove resistant to learning 'naturally'. The features in the code-based module could be taught in accordance with a focus-on-forms methodology, for example, using present-practise-produce. However, they could also be taught by means of focused tasks—structure-based production tasks, interpretation tasks, and consciousness-raising tasks. There would be no need to create any design links between the two components of the syllabus. Teachers would make their own decisions about when to call on the tasks in the code-based module.[10]

In such a modular syllabus consideration needs to be given to the staging of the two components. Figure 7.3 below outlines one possible way. The beginning stages of the course would be devoted entirely to the communicative module. The code-based module would be introduced from the intermediate stage onwards, gradually assuming more of the total teaching

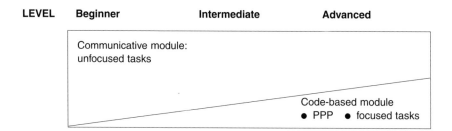

Figure 7.3: A modular approach to designing a task-based syllabus

time. The result is a version of the proportional curriculum model proposed by Yalden (1983). The rationale for such a model lies in the claim that early L2 acquisition is lexical in nature (for example, Johnston 1986; Lewis 1993) and largely looks after itself as long as learners have access to input and opportunities to use the L2. At this stage errors abound in learner language and there is little point in trying to address them as many of them will be eliminated fairly rapidly in natural ways. The need for a focus on form arises later, when learners have acquired some communicative ability and when they run the risk of fossilizing. The code-based module kicks in at this time with the goal of drawing attention to form in order to destabilize learners' interlanguage. In effect, this reverses the sequence found in traditional language curricula, where form is taught first and opportunities to communicate introduced later.

Summary and final comment

In this section we have examined ways in which attention to form can be incorporated into a task-based syllabus. We have seen that this is problematic if the goal is to develop learners' implicit knowledge but that a remedial approach informed by a checklist of potentially problematic features may be possible. In contrast, a syllabus of linguistic properties can be more easily constructed if the goal is explicit knowledge. Such a syllabus delineates the content of consciousness-raising tasks, which serve the dual purpose of focusing attention on specific forms and providing opportunities to communicate.

Two types of design incorporating attention to form have been considered. In the integrated syllabus recommended by Snow, Met, and Genesee (1989) content and form are closely interwoven by identifying the content-obligatory and content-compatible language of each topic area in the curriculum. Such an approach reflects mainstream thinking about the importance of teaching form and meaning conjointly (see, for example, Doughty 2001). However, it is demanding on the skills of the syllabus designer and there can be no guarantee that the links the designer establishes between form and meaning will be valid for the learner. A modular approach consisting of unrelated components of linguistically unfocused and focused tasks is arguably easier to design while remaining compatible with the process of L2 acquisition. Such an approach gives primacy to the kind of task-based syllabus proposed by Prabhu but also provides opportunities for form-focused work as learners develop and reach a stage where attention to form is likely to be of benefit to them.

Designing tasks

A syllabus provides a blueprint for the development of task workplans, i.e. the actual tasks to be used in the classroom. But what exactly do these workplans consist of and how do designers go about constructing them? We conclude this chapter by examining the final step in the preparation of task-based courses, as shown in Figure 7.1.

One source of information that can be used to answer these questions is practical guides. Estaire and Zanón (1994) offer such a guide, drawing on their experience of teacher development courses for secondary school teachers. They propose 'a framework for planning units of work' involving two general phases, each with a number of steps. Phase 1 involves a 'general statement' and is concerned with stipulating what the unit of work is intended to achieve. The general statement is arrived at in three steps to be carried out in this order: (1) determining the theme or interest area for the unit; (2) planning the final task to be done at the end of the unit; and (3) determining the unit objectives. Phase 2 consists of 'details' and stipulates how the unit of work is to be carried out. There are three further sequential steps: (4) specifying the contents (thematic and linguistic) needed to carry out the final task; (5) planning and sequencing the 'enabling tasks' that will prepare learners to perform the final task; and (6) planning the procedures for evaluating the unit. Lee (2000), while recognizing that there is no one way to construct tasks, suggests four criteria to guide the process: (1) identify a desired informational outcome; (2) break down the topic into sub-topics; (3) create and sequence concrete tasks, for example, filling in a chart or making a list; and (4) build in linguistic support, either lexical or grammatical or both. Guides such as this serve an obviously useful teacher education purpose. They provide a schematic and idealized set of procedures for developing task-based materials.

But what procedures do materials writers actually follow when they are preparing task-based materials? This question was addressed in a project entitled 'Capturing expertise in task design for instruction and assessment' (Johnson 2000). This asked a group of experienced and less experienced designers to think out loud as they designed a task. Transcripts of the think-aloud protocols were then analysed to identify the control procedures, i.e. 'global decisions regarding selection and implementation of resources and strategies' (Schoenfeld 1985), designer schemata, i.e. 'the knowledge and belief systems the designer brings to the design activity', and heuristics, i.e. the local strategies and techniques used in the design process. Johnson identified three general ways in which the designers viewed tasks—in terms of task function, for example, 'describing a person', task genre, for example, information gap, or task frame, i.e. giving consideration to a cluster of factors such as the participatory organization, skills to be practised, timing, and teacher roles. In an analysis of the designers' control procedures, Johnson found that the less experienced designers utilized task frames as a starting point for design whereas the experienced designers opted predominantly for task genre and to a lesser extent for task function. There were also differences in the designers' schemata. Within each group some designers manifested a 'language-oriented' approach and others a 'task-oriented' approach. These differences were evident in the amount of attention the designers paid to language or activity when designing the tasks.[11] Heuristics used by the experienced task designers included searching their repertoire of tasks for one that would fit the design specifications, simulating the language output of a putative task, and trading off authenticity in one aspect of the task, for example, authenticity of situation, for another, for example, interactional authenticity. Johnson's study illuminates the procedures that experienced task-designers were found to follow. Interestingly, these do not entirely correspond to those found in Estaire and Zanon's or Lee's general guides. For example, whereas these authors propose 'thematic content' as the starting point, Johnson's experienced designers generally preferred to begin by selecting a 'task genre'. Samuda, Johnson, and Ridgeway (2000) offer a manual for designing tasks based on the research that Johnson (2000) reported. This addresses what tasks are, what designers do, what they can draw on and, in an appendix, offers a useful list of terms for talking about task design.

Conclusion

The purpose of this chapter has not been to provide a blueprint for designing task-based courses but rather to explore a number of key issues that need to be considered in the preparation of such courses. These issues were:

1 What rationale have applied linguists and educationalists offered for task-based courses?
2 What types of task are available for inclusion in such a course and what factors should be considered in the selection of task-types?
3 How should the thematic content for a task-based course be chosen?
4 How can tasks be sequenced?
5 How can a focus on form(s) be incorporated into the design of a task-based course?

6 How do experienced teachers go about developing task-based teaching materials?

These are all complex issues and it must be acknowledged that clear and non-controversial answers to the above questions are not available. Widdowson (1990) is rightly sceptical of the ability of research to provide definitive answers. However, this situation is not new, as similar issues relating to the design of more traditional syllabuses remain unresolved. Also, as I have pointed out elsewhere, the function of research is not to provide definitive answers but to identify options that can be experimented with pedagogically. In this respect, the research does have something to offer course designers.

'Task' is a powerful construct for designing courses, as it constitutes the primary means for implementing the 'experiential strategy' in teaching (Stern 1990). This chapter has sought to identify some of the factors that need to be considered in the construction of task-based courses and a number of options that can be experimented with.

Notes

1 Elsewhere (i.e. Chapter 1 and Chapter 5) a distinction was made between the use of tasks in 'task-based language teaching' and 'task-supported language teaching'. In the case of task-supported language teaching, tasks do not serve as the unit for designing courses but only as the means for implementing a methodological procedure, i.e. 'free production'. In such teaching some other unit, e.g. 'structures', is used to design the course. This chapter is concerned only with task-based language teaching, where teaching content is specified in terms of tasks.

2 Another reason for not considering process syllabuses is that these are based on a very broad definition of 'task' (see Breen's definition in Figure 1.1 of Chapter 1) and not the much narrower definition that has informed this book.

3 Wilkins (1976) used the term 'analytic' to refer to a notional/functional syllabus. This term has also been used to refer to task-based syllabuses but misleadingly so, given that Wilkins' proposal for an 'analytic' syllabus still involved a specification of linguistic exponents of the language uses and thus was essentially still a linguistic syllabus.

4 The claim that the linguistic exponents of functions do not qualify as tenable 'acquisition units' is challengeable, however. These exponents take the form of chunks—formulaic expressions. There is ample evidence in SLA to show that language acquisition involves chunk-learning of the kind that a notional/functional syllabus fosters.

5 None of the older (for example, Nunan 1989) or more recent books on tasks, for example, Bygate, Skehan, and Swain (2001) address thematic content.

6 Robinson (2001) also has a third category of factors—'task conditions'. These include such factors as the direction of the information flow (one-way vs. two-way) and the communicative goals (one of many solutions). As such, they clearly relate to the *design* of tasks and thus are best seen as a subcategory of 'task complexity'. Robinson does not have a separate category for task procedures.

7 Robinson (2001), however, makes the opposite prediction, suggesting that monologic tasks will promote more accurate and complex but less fluent production (see Chapter 4). This illustrates the uncertainty regarding many of the proposed criteria of task complexity.

8 Williams and Evans (1998: 141) also chose another structure for attention—the passive. This form, however, 'was rarely found in the learners' oral or written production'. Interesting, the linguistically focused tasks used in this study were effective in the case of present/past participles but much less effective for the passive. Williams and Evans note that the learners who made the greatest acquisitional gains for both structures were those who had demonstrated partial mastery of them before the treatment.

9 It should be noted, however, that not all irregular forms are infrequent. For example, irregular forms of the English past tense, for example, 'ate', are frequent in the input and are typically acquired early and without difficulty—although they may be subsequently replaced with overgeneralized regular verb forms, for example, 'eated'.

10 This proposal for a modular syllabus is similar to Brumfit's (1979) spiral syllabus. In Brumfit's proposal, however, the 'core' was code-based, with notions/functions introduced at relevant points. In my proposal the core is task-based.

11 Many task designers might feel the need for a balanced orientation. Thomson (1992: 530) draws the following lesson from her experience of designing and implementing a task with beginner level students of Japanese at the National University of Singapore: 'give equal importance to language skill objectives and to language learning skill objectives in creating tasks'.

8 The methodology of task-based teaching

Introduction

In addition to selecting and sequencing a set of tasks and preparing appropriate workplans for each task, decisions have to be taken regarding the methodological procedures for executing the workplans in the classroom. The purpose of this chapter is to consider these procedures. They are two basic kinds. Firstly, there are those procedures that specify how the activities mentioned in the syllabus can be converted into actual lessons. Secondly, there are procedures relating to how the teacher and learners are to participate in the lessons. These two types of procedures will be considered under the headings of *lesson design* and *participatory structure*. They figure in teaching in general and thus apply to all classroom activities. The purpose of this chapter is to describe the main procedures available to teachers in task-based teaching.

Lesson design

The design of a task-based lesson involves consideration of the stages or components of a lesson that has a task as its principal component. Various designs have been proposed (for example, Prabhu 1987; Estaire and Zanon 1994; Skehan 1996; Willis 1996; Lee 2000). However they all have in common three principal phases, which are shown in Table 8.1. These phases reflect the chronology of a task-based lesson. Thus, the first phase is 'pre-task' and concerns the various activities that teachers and students can undertake before they start the task, such as whether students are given time to plan the performance of the task. The second phase, the 'during task' phase, centres around the task itself and affords various instructional options, including whether students are required to operate under time pressure or not. The final phase is 'post-task' and involves procedures for following up on the task performance. Only the 'during task' phase is obligatory in task-based teaching. Thus, minimally, a task-based lesson consists of the students just performing a task. Options selected from the 'pre-task' or 'post-task' phases are non-obligatory but, as we will see, can serve a crucial role in ensuring that the task performance is maximally effective for language development.

Phase	Examples of options
A Pre-task	framing the activity, e.g. establishing the outcome of the task planning time doing a similar task
B During task	time pressure number of participants
C Post-task	learner report consciousness raising repeat task

Table 8.1: A framework for designing task-based lessons

Access to a clear framework for a task-based lesson is of obvious advantage to both teachers and learners. Richards (1996) shows how many experienced teachers adhere to a maxim of planning ('Plan your teaching and try to follow your plan') while Numrich (1996) reports on how novice teachers feel the 'need to be creative and varied in teaching'. A framework such as the one outlined in Table 8.1 caters to both needs. It provides a clear structure for a lesson and it also allows for creativity and variety in the choice of options in each phase.

The pre-task phase

The purpose of the pre-task phase is to prepare students to perform the task in ways that will promote acquisition. Lee (2000) describes the importance of 'framing' the task to be performed and suggests that one way of doing this is to provide an advance organizer of what the students will be required to do and the nature of the outcome they will arrive at. Dörnyei (2001) emphasizes the importance of presenting a task in a way that motivates learners. Like Lee, he sees value in explaining the purpose and utility of the task. This may be especially important for learners from traditional 'studial' classrooms; they may need to be convinced of the values of a more 'experiential' approach. Dörnyei also suggests that task preparation should involve strategies for whetting students' appetites to perform the task, for example, by asking them to guess what the task will involve, and for helping them to perform the task. Strategies in this latter category are discussed below.

Skehan (1996: 25) refers to two broad alternatives available to the teacher during the pre-task phase:

> an emphasis on the general cognitive demands of the task, and/or an
> emphasis on linguistic factors. Attentional capacity is limited, and it is

needed to respond to both linguistic and cognitive demands ... then engaging in activities which reduce cognitive load will release attentional capacity for the learner to concentrate more on linguistic factors.

These alternatives can be tackled procedurally in one of four ways: (1) supporting learners in performing a task similar to the task they will perform in the during-task phase of the lesson; (2) asking students to observe a model of how to perform the task; (3) engaging learners in non-task activities designed to prepare them to perform the task; and (4) strategic planning of the main task performance. We will consider each in some detail.

Performing a similar task

The use of a 'pre-task' was a key feature of the Communicational Teaching Project (Prabhu 1987). It was carried out as a whole-class activity with the teacher and involved the learners in completing a task of the same kind as and with similar content to the main task. Thus, it served as a preparation for performing the main task individually. For example, if the main task involved working out a class timetable from the timetables of individual teachers, then the pre-task would be the same but with different information in the teachers' timetables.

Prabhu explains that the pre-task was conducted through interaction of the question-and-answer type. The teacher was expected to lead the class step by step to the expected outcome, to break down a step into smaller steps if the learners encountered difficulty and to offer one of more parallels to a step in the reasoning process to ensure that mixed-ability learners could understand what was required. The teacher was provided with a lesson plan that included (1) the pre-task and (2) a set of graded questions or instructions together with parallel questions to be used as needed. When implemented in the classroom, the plan results in a 'pedagogic dialogue'. Prabhu emphasizes that the pre-task was not a 'demonstration' but 'a task in its own right'. It is clear from this account that the 'pre-task' serves as a mediational tool for the kind of 'instructional conversation' that socio-cultural theorists advocate (see Chapter 6). The teacher, as an expert, uses the pre-task to scaffold learners' performance of the task with the expectancy that this 'other-regulation' facilitates the 'self-regulation' learners will need to perform the main task on their own.

Providing a model

An alternative is to ask the students to observe a model of how the task can be performed without requiring them to undertake a trial performance of the task (see Aston 1982 for an early example of such an approach).

Minimally this involves presenting them with a text (oral or written) to demonstrate an 'ideal' performance of the task. Both Skehan (1996) and Willis (1996) suggest that simply 'observing' others perform a task can help reduce the cognitive load on the learner. However, the model can also be accompanied by activities designed to raise learners' consciousness about specific features of the task performance—for example, the strategies that can be employed to overcome communication problems, the conversational gambits for holding the floor during a discussion or the *pragmalinguistic devices* for performing key language functions. Such activities might require the learners to identify and analyse these features in the model texts. Alternatively, they might involve pre-training in the use of specific strategies. Nunan (1989: 81) lists a number of learning strategies, for example, 'Learning to live with uncertainty' and 'Learning to make intelligent guesses', that students can be taught to help them become 'adaptable, creative, inventive and above all independent' and thus more effective performers of a task.

However, the effectiveness of such training cannot be taken for granted. Lam and Wong (2000) report a study that investigated the effects of teaching students to seek and provide clarification when communication difficulties arose in class discussions. However, although this resulted in greater use of these strategies in a post-training discussion, the strategies were often not employed effectively, for example, the students were unable to clarify something they had said, suggesting that pre-task training in the use of communication strategies may not be effective unless students also learn how to scaffold each other co-operatively when performing the task. There is also a danger in directing pre-task training based on a model at specific aspects of language or language use; learners may respond by treating the task they are subsequently asked to perform as an 'exercise' for practising the strategies/features that have been targeted. A key question, then, is the extent to which students are to be primed to attend to specific aspects of the model. Clearly, there is a need to evaluate carefully the effects of any such priming on task performance.

Non-task preparation activities

There are a variety of non-task preparation activities that teachers can choose from. These can centre on reducing the cognitive or the linguistic demands placed on the learner. Activating learners' content schemata or providing them with background information serves as a means of defining the topic area of a task. Willis (1996) provides a list of activities for achieving this, for example, brainstorming and mind maps. When learners know what they are going to talk or write about they have more processing space available for formulating the language needed to express their ideas with the result that the quantity of the output will be enhanced and also fluency and complexity (see Chapter 4). Recommended activities for addressing the linguistic demands of a task often focus on vocabulary rather than grammar, perhaps because vocabulary is seen as more helpful for the successful performance of a task than grammar. Newton (2001) suggests three ways in which teachers can target unfamiliar vocabulary in the pre-task phase: (1) predicting, i.e. asking learners to brainstorm a list of words related to the task title or topic; (2) cooperative dictionary search, i.e. allocating different learners words to look up in their dictionary; and (3) words and definitions, i.e. learners match a list of words to their definitions. Newton argues that such activities will 'prevent the struggle with new words overtaking other important goals such as fluency or content-learning' when learners perform the task. However, there is always the danger that pre-teaching vocabulary will result in learners treating the task as an opportunity to practise pre-selected words. In the case of task-supported teaching this can be seen as desirable but in the case of task-based teaching it can threaten the integrity of the task.

Strategic planning

Finally, learners can be given time to plan how they will perform the task. This involves what I termed 'strategic planning' in Chapter 4 and contrasts with the 'online planning' that can occur during the performance of the task. It can be distinguished from other pre-task options in that it does not involve students in a trial performance of the task or in observing a model. However, it may involve the provision of linguistic forms/strategies for performing the task depending on the amount of guidance the teacher wishes to provide. A distinction can still be drawn between the non-task preparation procedures described above and strategic planning, however, as the former occur without the students having access to the task they will be asked to perform while strategic planning involves the students considering the forms they will need to execute the task workplan they have been given.

There are a number of methodological options available to teachers who opt for strategic planning. The first concerns whether the students are simply given the task workplan and left to decide for themselves what to plan, which as we saw in Chapter 4 typically results in priority being given to content over form, or whether they are given guidance in what to plan. In the case of the latter option, the guidance may focus learners' attention on form or content or, as in Sangarun's (2001) study, form and content together. Skehan (1996) suggests that learners need to be made explicitly aware of where they are focusing their attention—whether on fluency, complexity, or accuracy. These planning options are illustrated in Table 8.2. Here the context is a task involving a balloon debate (i.e. deciding who should be ejected from a balloon to keep it afloat). The guidance can also be 'detailed' or 'undetailed' (Foster and Skehan 1996).

Strategic planning options	Description
1 No planning	The students were introduced to the idea of a balloon debate, assigned roles and then asked to debate who should be sacrificed.
2 Guided planning—language focus	The students were introduced to the idea of a balloon debate and then shown how to use modal verbs and conditionals in the reasons a doctor might give for not being thrown out of the balloon, e.g. 'I take care of many sick people—if you throw me out, many people might die.'
3 Guided planning—content focus	The students were introduced to the idea of a balloon debate. The teacher presented ideas that each character might use to defend his or her right to stay in the balloon and students were encouraged to add ideas of their own.

Table 8.2: Options for strategic planning (based on Foster and Skehan 1999).

The examples in Table 8.2 are of the undetailed kind. Skehan (1998a) gives an example of detailed planning for a personal task involving asking someone to go to your house to turn off the oven that you have left on. This involved instructions relating to planning content, for example, 'think about what problems your listener could have and how you might help her', and language, for example, 'think what grammar you need to do the task'. These options do not just provide for variety in planning activities; they also enable the teacher to channel the learners' attention on to different aspects of language use, as we saw in Chapter 4. For example, Foster and Skehan (1996) found that when students were given detailed guidance they tended to prioritize content with resulting gains in complexity when they performed the task.

Another option concerns the amount of time students are given to carry out the pre-task planning. Most of the research studies discussed in Chapter 4 gave between one and ten minutes. An effect on fluency was evident with very short periods of planning in some studies but longer was needed for an effect on complexity. Skehan (1998a) suggests ten minutes is optimal. Finally, planning can be carried out individually, in groups, or with the teacher (see section on participatory structure later in this chapter).

Summary and final comment

In these four ways, teachers can help to create conditions that will make tasks work for acquisition. As Skehan (1998a) points out, they serve to introduce new language that the learners can use while performing the task, to mobilize existing linguistic resources, to ease processing load and to push learners to interpret tasks in more demanding ways. However, it is not yet possible to 'fine-tune' learners' performance of a task through selecting specific pre-task options. At best, all that the research to date has demonstrated is the likely effects of some of the procedures referred to above. Important questions remain unanswered. For example, we do not know whether task preparation that involves an actual performance of the task is more or less effective than preparation that involves just observation. Nor is it clear to what extent linguistic priming subverts the 'natural-ness' of a task resulting in teaching of the present–practise–produce (PPP) kind (see Chapter 5). Only in the case of strategic planning do we have some idea of how the different options affect task performance.

The during-task phase

The methodological options available to the teacher in the during-task phase are of two basic kinds. First, there are various options relating to how the task is to be undertaken that can be taken prior to the actual per-formance of the task and thus planned for by the teacher. These will be called 'task performance options'. Second, there are a number of 'process options' that involve the teacher and students in online decision making about how to perform the task as it is being completed.

Task performance options

We will consider three task performance options that have figured in the research examined in the earlier chapters. The first of these options con-cerns whether to require the students to perform the task under time pres-sure. The teacher can elect to allow students to complete the task in their own time or can set a time limit. Lee (2000) strongly recommends that teachers set strict time limits. As we saw in Chapter 4, this option is im-portant because it can influence the nature of the language students pro-duce. Yuan and Ellis (2003) found that giving students an unlimited time to perform a narrative task resulted in language that was both more com-plex and more accurate in comparison to a control group that was asked to perform the same task under time pressure. The students used the time at their disposal to monitor and reformulate their utterances. Interestingly, the opportunity to plan online produced a different effect from the oppor-tunity to engage in strategic planning, which led to greater fluency and complexity of language. It seems, then, that if teachers want to emphasize accuracy in a task performance, they need to ensure that the students can complete the task in their own time. However, if they want to encourage fluency they need to set a time limit.

The second task performance option involves deciding whether to allow the students access to the input data while they perform a task. In some tasks access to the input data is built into the design of a task, for example, in spot-the-difference, describe-and-draw, or many information-gap tasks. However, in other tasks it is optional. For example, in a story retelling/recall task the students can be permitted to keep the pictures/ text or asked to put them on one side as they narrate the story. We noted in the preceding chapter that this can influence the complexity of the task, as tasks that are supported by pictures and texts are easier than tasks that are not. Joe (1998) reports a study that compared learners' acquisition of a set of target words (which they did not know prior to performing the task) in a narrative recall task under two conditions—with and without access to the text. She found that the learners who could see the text used the target words more frequently, although the difference was evident only in verbatim use of the words, not generated use, i.e. they did not use the target words in original sentences. Joe's study raises an important question. Does borrowing from the input data assist acquisition? The term 'borrowing' in this context comes from Prabhu (1987: 60). He defines it as 'taking over an available verbal formulation in order to express some self-initiated meaning content, instead of generating the formulation from one's own competence'. Prabhu distinguishes borrowing from 'reproduction' where the decision to 'take over' a sample of a language is not made by the learner but by some external authority, i.e. the teacher of the textbook. Borrowing is compatible with task-based teaching but reproduction is not. Prabhu sees definite value in borrowing for maintaining a task-based activity and also probable value in promoting acquisition. Certainly, from the perspective of sociocultural theory (see Chapter 6), where learning occurs through 'participation', borrowing can be seen as contributing directly to acquisition.

The third task performance option consists of introducing some surprise element into the task. Foster and Skehan (1997) illustrate this option. They asked students to complete a decision-making task that required them to decide what punishment should be given to four criminals who had committed different crimes. At the beginning of the task they were given information about each criminal and the crime he/she had committed. Halfway through the task the students were given further information of a surprising nature about each criminal. For example, the initial information provided about one of the criminals was as follows:

> The accused is a doctor. He gave an overdose (a very high quantity of a painkilling drug) to an 85-year-old woman because she was dying

painfully of cancer. The doctor says that the woman had asked for an overdose. The woman's family accuse the doctor of murder.

After talking for five minutes, the students were given the following additional information:

> Later, it was discovered that seven other old people in the same hospital had died in a similar way, through overdoses. The doctor refuses to say if he was involved.

However, this study failed to find that introducing such a surprise had any effect on the fluency, complexity, or accuracy of the learners' language. This does not mean that this option is of no pedagogic value, as requiring learners to cope with a surprise serves as an obvious way of extending the time learners spend on a task and thus increases the amount of talk. It may also help to enhance students' intrinsic interest in a task.

Process options

Process options differ from task-performance options in that they concern the way in which the discourse arising from the task is enacted rather than pedagogical decisions about the way the task is to be handled. Whereas performance options can be selected in advance of the actual performance of the task, process options must be taken in flight while the task is being performed.

The teacher's online decision about how to conduct the discourse of a task reflect his/her 'theory-in-use' (Schön 1983) and 'practical knowledge' (Eraut 1994). On the learners' part, they reflect the language-learning beliefs (Horwitz 1987) they bring to the classroom and, more particularly, to a specific task. How teachers and learners conduct a task will be influenced, to a large extent, by their prior experiences of teaching and learning and their personal definitions of the particular teaching-learning situation. Thus, the options described below are primarily descriptive, reflecting an internal rather than external perspective (Ellis 1998) on the methodology of task-based teaching.

A common assumption of task-based teaching is that the texts, the discursive practices, and the social practices of the classroom (Breen 1998) that are constructed by and through a task resemble those found in non-pedagogic discourse. To achieve this, however, is no mean feat, especially if the teacher is directly involved in the performance of the task. As Breen points out, the 'texts' of lessons, i.e. the actual language produced by the participants, are typically teacher-centred with learners 'not actually required to do much overt or explicit discursive work' (ibid. 123), while the 'discursive practices', i.e. the means by which the texts are produced, 'construct learners as primarily responsive and seemingly fairly passive participants in the discourse' (ibid. 124) and the 'social practices', i.e. the organizational and institutional circumstances that shape the texts and discursive practices, are directed at the avoidance of 'social trouble'. Task-based teaching, however, seeks the converse—texts that are learner-centred, discursive practices that encourage the learner to actively engage in shaping and controlling the discourse, and social practices that are centred on allowing and resolving social trouble. This poses a problem which teachers need to address.

Table 8.3 contrasts two sets of classroom processes. The first set corresponds to the classroom behaviours that are typical of a traditional form-focused pedagogy where language is treated as an object and the students are required to act as 'learners'. The second set reflects the behaviours that characterize a task-based pedagogy, where language is treated as a tool for communicating and the teacher and students function primarily as 'language users' (Ellis 2001). Thus, which set of behaviours arise is crucially dependent on the participants' orientation to the classroom and to their motives for performing an activity.

Two questions arise. The first concerns what the participants in a task need to do to ensure that the interactions they engage in manifest the processes described in column B in Table 8.3. Implicit in this question is an acknowledgement of the importance of these processes for task-based instruction. The second question, however, challenges this assumption by asking whether in fact these processes are criterial of task-based pedagogy and whether, minimally, they need to be complemented by processes from column A.

It has often been pointed out (see, for example, Gremmo *et al.* 1978; Kasper 1986; Nunan 1987) that the processes described in column B are a rarity even in classrooms where the teacher claims to be teaching communicatively. The main reason for this lies in the difficulty teachers and students have in achieving the required orientation. As Goffman (1981) has pointed out, classrooms are governed by an 'educational imperative' which dictates the kind of discourse that arises. It is for this reason that teachers and students find it difficult to consistently orient to language as a tool and to adopt the role of language users when they both know that the *raison d'être* for their being together is to teach and learn the language. In effect, task-based teaching calls for the classroom participants to forget where they are and why they are there and to act in the belief that they can learn the language indirectly through communicating in it rather than directly through studying it. This is asking a lot of them, especially if the social practices the participants bring to the classroom belong to a pedagogy of transmission rather than of interpretation (Barnes 1976). It is probably easier to achieve when students are interacting among themselves, without the teacher being present, as the greater symmetry of social roles this affords leads naturally to the kinds of risk-taking behaviour required of a

A Traditional form-focused pedagogy	B Task-based pedagogy
Rigid discourse structure consisting of IRF (initiate-respond-feedback) exchanges	Loose discourse structure consisting of adjacency pairs
Teacher controls topic development	Students able to control topic development
Turn-taking is regulated by the teacher	Turn-taking is regulated by the same rules that govern everyday conversation, i.e. speakers can self-select
Display questions, i.e. questions that the questioner already knows the answer to	Use of referential questions, i.e. questions that the questioner does not know the answer to
Students are placed in a responding role and consequently perform a limited range of language functions	Students function in both initiating and responding roles and thus perform a wide range of language functions, e.g. asking for and giving information, agreeing and disagreeing, instructing
Little need or opportunity to negotiate meaning	Opportunities to negotiate meaning when communication problems arise
Scaffolding directed primarily at enabling students to produce correct sentences.	Scaffolding directed primarily at enabling students to say what they want to say
Form-focused feedback, i.e. the teacher responds implicitly or explicitly to the correctness of students' utterances	Content-focused feedback, i.e. the teacher responds to the message content of the students' utterances
Echoing, i.e. the teacher repeats what a student has said for the benefit of the whole class	Repetition, i.e. a student elects to repeat something another student or the teacher has said as private speech or to establish intersubjectivity

Table 8.3: Stereotypical classroom processes in traditional form-focused pedagogy and task-based pedagogy

task-based pedagogy (Pica 1987). This is one reason why pair and group work are seen as central to task-based teaching (see section on participatory structure).

However, even when the participants in a task are oriented to treat language as a tool and to function as language users, the text of the task may disappoint, manifesting few of the characteristics facilitative of acquisition (as discussed in earlier chapters). Seedhouse (1999) has pointed out that the characteristics of task-based interaction do not always match those described in Table 8.3. He illustrates how in some tasks where the turn-taking system is conspicuously constrained, there is a tendency for students to rely on topic-comment constructions where verbal elements are omitted (a feature also noted in pidgins) and to produce highly indexicalized utterances. An even greater limitation in task-based interaction, according to Seedhouse, is the minimalization that characterizes some task-based interactions. This is illustrated in the extract below where the students were required to complete and label a geometric figure:

L1   What?
L2   Stop.
L3   Dot?
L4   Dot?
L5   Point?
L6   Dot?
LL   Point, point, yeh.
L1   Point?
L5   Small point.
L3   Dot.
(From Lynch 1989:124, cited in Seedhouse 1999).

Here all the utterances but one consist of a single word. Clearly, such interactions do not help to 'stretch' learners' interlanguages, one of the stated goals of task-based pedagogy (Nunan 1989). Seedhouse suggests that such limited interactions arise because 'learners appear to be so concentrated on completing the task that linguistic forms are treated as a vehicle of minor importance' (ibid. 154). In other words, the very nature of a task, i.e. the fact it is directed at accomplishing a specified outcome, may result in a restricted variety of communication.

It seems to me, though, that Seedhouse overstates this limitation of tasks. First, it is possible to argue that the restricted nature of the talk shown in the extract above is well suited to the students' purpose (see further discussion of the extract later in this chapter). Second, as shown in Chapters 3 and 4, the nature of the interaction depends crucially on the design characteristics of tasks and procedures for implementing them. Thus, richer varieties of communication characterized by more complex language use, are achievable if, for example, students are asked to perform open tasks with divergent goals and are given the opportunity to plan their performance beforehand (see Chapter 4). Nevertheless, Seedhouse's critique needs to be addressed. Clearly, teachers need to monitor their students' performance of a task carefully, examining to what extent the processes described in Table 8.3 arise and, crucially, whether the interactions manifest the minimalized and pidgin-like uses of language Seedhouse sees as endemic. The information obtained from such monitoring can be used to inform decisions about what tasks and procedures to use in subsequent tasks. In this way, teachers can build up a fund of experience of the task characteristics and methods of implementation that will ensure the kinds of interactions hypothesized to promote acquisition. Thus, the solution to the problem Seedhouse identifies lies not in attempting to manipulate process options directly, which may well be impossible without imperilling the 'taskness' of the task, but through careful selection from the pre-task options and the performance options described above.

Where Seedhouse questions whether the kinds of behaviours shown in Table 8.3 are achievable in task-based teaching, others have challenged whether they constitute appropriate goals for interaction in a classroom. Cullen (1998), drawing on Breen and Candlin (1980), has pointed out that the classroom context constitutes a communicative environment in its own right that is distinct from the communicative contexts of the world outside and on these grounds has challenged the basis for assessing the communicativeness of classroom discourse. In effect, then, Cullen disputes the assumption that underlies task-based pedagogy—that classrooms need to replicate the kind of communicative behaviour found outside the classroom. He illustrates how 'what appears to be non-communicative teacher talk is not necessarily so in the classroom context' (Cullen 1998: 183) with an extract from an English lesson in Egypt. This interaction is teacher-led, is full of display questions, includes feedback that is form-focused and contains a lot of echoing—all processes associated with a traditional form-focused pedagogy. However, Cullen argues that in the context of the classroom, the interaction can be considered 'communicative' in that the entire sequence manifests a focus on message content, the teacher's questions are carefully structured, the feedback is clear and the use of echoing serves to ensure that the students' attention is not lost. He claims that the discourse is pedagogically effective because the teacher has successfully combined the role of 'instructor' and 'interlocutor'. Arguably, this is what a task-based pedagogy needs to strive for. How might it be achieved?

One way is by incorporating a focus on form into the performance of the task. Ellis, Basturkmen, and Loewen (2001) report this can be achieved in either responding focus-on-form episodes, where one of the participants, usually the teacher, responds to a student utterance containing an error, or in initiating episodes, where either the teacher or a student elects to take time out from the exchange of message content to attend briefly to form, usually by means of a direct query about a specific form. Such attention to form differs from that arising in lessons of the traditional, focus-on-forms kind because, as Wilberg (1987: 27) notes, 'the content is dictated by the student, the form only by the teacher'. It also differs in another way. As Prabhu (1987: 63) points out, correction during a task is 'incidental' rather than 'systematic' in nature. In incidental correction, only 'tokens' are addressed, i.e. there is no attempt to generalize the type of error, it is seen by the participants as 'a part of getting on with the activity in hand, not as a separate objective' and, crucially, it is transitory. Prabhu excludes preventive or pre-emptive attention to form but, as Ellis, Basturkmen, and Loewen's study shows this too can be 'incidental'.

In Chapter 5, we saw that teachers can employ both implicit and explicit techniques to achieve this focus on form. These techniques can be used when some kind of communication problem arises (as occurs in the negotiation of meaning) or they can be used when the teacher chooses to abandon his/her role as a language user momentarily in order to function as an instructor, i.e. to negotiate form rather than meaning. Teachers can play a very direct role by initiating this negotiation but, as Lynch (1997) illustrates, they can also intervene to support a process that students have started for themselves, a technique that he describes as 'nudging' the learners towards a solution. Teachers can also allow or even encourage students to use the same techniques themselves— for example, by accepting and responding to students' queries about form.

Table 8.4 describes some of the techniques that can be used by the task participants. Evidence from research (Lyster and Ranta 1997; Ellis, Basturkmen, and Loewen 2001) indicates that the use of these techniques, even when quite frequent, need not detract from the primary focus on message, which is the defining characteristic of a task. Thus, they serve as important process options for reconciling the roles of 'instructor/learner' on the one hand and 'interlocutor/language user' on the other. Furthermore, as suggested in Chapter 5, they potentially enhance the acquisitional value of a task by inducing noticing of linguistic forms that lie outside or at the edges of students' current interlanguages.

Finally, we can turn to sociocultural theory (see Chapter 6) for insights as to the kinds of processes that characterize a successful task-performance. This theory stresses the need for participants to construct an 'activity' that is meaningful to them out of the 'task'. It emphasizes the importance of the participants achieving intersubjectivity. In this respect, the L1 can play a useful role as it enables participants to establish the goals for the activity and the procedures for accomplishing it. Thus sociocultural theory contradicts the advice often given to teachers, namely that students should strive to complete the task entirely in the L2. Most importantly, sociocultural theory shows how the 'scaffolding' that an expert can afford a novice or that novices construct jointly among themselves can result in the production of new linguistic features. This points to the importance of the task participants working collaboratively, showing sensitivity to the needs of their interlocutors, and being prepared to adapt their contributions to these

Type of technique	Interactional device	Description
Implicit	1 Request for clarification	A task participant seeks clarification of something another participant has said, thus providing an opportunity for the first participant to reformulate.
	2 Recast	A task participant rephrases part or the whole of another participant's utterance.
Explicit	1 Explicit correction	A task participant draws explicit attention to another participant's deviant use of a linguistic form, e.g. 'Not x but y.'
	2 Metalingual comment/question	A task participant uses metalanguage to draw attention to another participant's deviant use of a linguistic form, e.g. 'Past tonoc not present tense.'
	3 Query	A task participant asks a question about a specific linguistic form that has arisen in performing the task, e.g. 'Why is "can" used here?'
	4 Advice	A task participant (usually the teacher) advises or warns about the use of a specific linguistic form, e.g. 'Remember you need to use past tense.'

Table 8.4: Implicit and explicit techniques for focusing on form during a task

needs. The six features of scaffolding described by Wood, Bruner, and Ross (1976) (see Chapter 6) offer task participants guidelines for constructing the kind of discourse through which learning can take place. Through 'instructional conversations' teachers can help students to construct zones of proximal development that will enable them to perform new linguistic features. In such conversations, teachers communicate with students as partners but shape the discourse towards a pedagogical goal; in Cullen's terms they combine the roles of 'instructor' and interlocutor'. I will comment further on the importance and nature of these instructional conversations when considering the participatory structure of task-based lessons.

To sum up, it is clear that process options cannot be prescribed. Nevertheless, it is possible to identify, in broad terms, the kinds of processes that the participants in a task performance need to strive for. These are:

1 Discourse that is essentially 'conversational' in nature, i.e. as described in column B of Table 8.3. Such discourse can include 'instructional conversations'.
2 Discourse that encourages the explicit formulation of messages.
3 Opportunities for students to take linguistic risks.
4 Occasions where the task participants focus implicitly and/or explicitly on specific linguistic forms.
5 Shared goals for the task (including the use of the L1 to establish these).
6 Effective scaffolding of the participants' efforts to communicate in the L2.

Achieving these processes is challenging. It depends on how the participants orientate to a task and on their personal skills in navigating the roles of interlocutor/language user and instructor/learner as the task is performed. As Skehan (1998b: 25) notes 'fine-tuning tasks while they are running is not easy'.

The post-task phase

The post-task phase affords a number of options. These have three major pedagogic goals: (1) to provide an opportunity for a repeat performance of the task; (2) to encourage reflection on how the task was performed; and (3) to encourage attention to form, in particular to those forms that proved problematic to the learners when they performed the task.

Repeat performance

As we saw in Chapter 4, there is a case for asking students to repeat a task. Several studies reviewed in Chapter 4 (for example, Bygate 1996 and 1998; Lynch and McLean 2000 and 2001) indicate that when learners repeat a task their production improves in a number of ways, for example, complexity increases, propositions are expressed more clearly, and they become more fluent. A repeat performance can be carried out under the same conditions as the first performance, i.e. in small groups or individually, or the conditions can be changed. One interesting possibility examined by Skehan and Foster (1997) is that of requiring students to carry out the second performance publicly. As their study examined the 'threat' of such a requirement on learners' initial performance of the task, it technically constituted a during-task option. However, if students are not told to repeat the task publicly until after they have completed the first performance, it becomes a post-task option. There has been no research comparing the learner production that results from a second performance carried out under 'private' conditions, as in the initial performance, and publicly. Clearly, performing a task in front of the class increases the communicative stress (Candlin 1987) placed on the learner and thus can be predicted to lead to a reduction in fluency and complexity. However, it is not without value if students need experience in using English in front of an audience, as, for example, might be the case with foreign academics training to give oral presentations in the L2. Public performance is likely to encourage the use of a more formal style and thus may push learners to use the grammaticalized resources associated with this style (Givón 1979).

Reflecting on the task

Willis (1996) recommends asking students to present a report on how they did the task and on what they decided or discovered. She considers this 'the natural conclusion of the task cycle' (ibid.: 58). The teacher's role is to act as a chairperson and to encourage the students. The reports can be oral or written. Willis' examples make it clear that the reports should primarily focus on summarizing the outcome of the task. However, it would also be possible to ask students to reflect on and evaluate their own performance of the task. For example, they could be invited to comment on which aspect of language use (fluency, complexity, or accuracy) they gave primacy to and why, how they dealt with communication problems, both their own and others, and even what language they learned from the task, i.e. to report what Allwright (1984) has called 'uptake'.[1] Students could also be invited to consider how they might improve their performance of the task. Encouraging students to reflect on their performance in these ways may contribute to the development of the metacognitive strategies of planning, monitoring, and evaluating, which are seen as important for language learning (O'Malley and Chamot 1990). Holunga's (1995) study, discussed in Chapter 6, testifies to the value of asking learners to verbalize the strategies they use.

There is also a case for asking students to evaluate the task itself. Such information will help the teacher to decide whether to use similar tasks in the future or look for a different type. I have suggested that student-based evaluations of tasks can be carried out quickly and effectively using simple questionnaires (see Ellis 1997c for an example). The evaluation of tasks is considered further in Chapter 10.

Focusing on forms

Once the task is completed, students can be invited to focus on forms, with no danger that in so doing they will subvert the 'taskness' of the task. It is for this reason that some methodologists recommend reserving attention to form for the post-task phase of the lesson. Willis (1996), for example, sees the primary goal of the 'task component' as that of developing fluency and promoting the use of communication strategies. The post-task stage is needed to counter the danger that students will develop fluency at the expense of accuracy. In part, this is met by asking students to report on their performance of the task, as discussed above, but it can also be achieved by a direct focus on forms. It should be noted, however, that this is the not the position taken in this chapter. I have emphasized that a focus on form constitutes a valuable during-task option and that it is quite compatible with a primary focus on message content, which is the hallmark of a task. Furthermore, in some tasks, for example, consciousness-raising tasks, a linguistic feature is made the topic of the task. Attention to form, in one way or another, can occur in any (or indeed all) of the phases of a task-based lesson. In the pre-task and post-task phases the focus will be on *forms* while in the during-task phase it will be on *form*, to invoke Long's (1991) distinction (see Chapter 5).

Two obvious methodological questions arise regarding attention to form in the post-task phase. The first concerns which forms should be attended to. The answer is fairly obvious; teachers should select forms that the students used incorrectly while performing the task or 'useful' or 'natural' forms (Loschky and Bley-Vroman 1993) that they failed to use at all. In other words, teachers should seek to address errors or gaps in the students' L2 knowledge. Consideration also needs to be given to how many such forms a teacher should seek to address. Should the focus be placed on a single form that is treated intensively or a number of forms that are treated extensively? Both approaches are warranted and are reflected in the various options described below.

The second question concerns how the target forms should be dealt with. There is a whole range of options available to the teacher. It should be noted however that in many cases the effectiveness of these options has not been investigated.

1 *Review of learner errors*

While the students are performing a task in groups, teachers can move from group to group to listen in and note down some of the conspicuous errors the students make, together with actual examples. In the post-task phase, the teacher can address these errors with the whole class. A sentence illustrating the error can be written on the board, students can be invited to correct it, the corrected version is written up, and a brief explanation provided. Lynch (2001) offers an interesting way of conducting a post-task analysis, which he calls 'proof-listening'. This involves three cycles based on repeated playing of a recording of the task. First, the students who did the task review and edit their own performance. Second, the recording is replayed and other students are invited to comment, correct, or ask questions. Finally, the teacher comments on any points that have been missed.

2 Consciousness-raising tasks

CR tasks constitute tasks in their own right and therefore can be used as the main task in a lesson. But they can also be used as follow-up tasks to direct students to attend explicitly to a specific form that they used incorrectly or failed to use at all in the main task. Willis and Willis (1996) and Ellis (1997b) offer descriptions of the various options that are available for the design and implementation of CR tasks (see also Chapter 5). When used as follow-up tasks, CR tasks can profitably take their data from recordings of the students' performance of the task. For example, students might be presented with a number of their own utterances, all illustrating the same error, and asked to identify the error, correct the sentences, and work out an explanation.

3 Production-practice activities

An alternative or addition to CR tasks is to provide more traditional practice of selected forms. Traditional exercise types include repetition, substitution, gapped sentences, jumbled sentences, transformation drills, and dialogues. Willis (1996:110) offers a number of more novel ideas. The value of such production-practice activities has been called into question (see, for example, Ellis 1988 and VanPatten 1996) on the grounds that they have no direct effect on learners' interlanguage systems. However, they may help learners to automatize forms that they have begun to use on their own accord but have not yet gained full control over.

4 Noticing activities

A number of suggestions have been made for developing noticing activities as a follow-up to a task performance. Fotos (1994) used dictation exercises that had been enriched with the target structures that students had tackled initially in CR tasks to examine whether the subjects in her study subsequently attended to the structures. She found that they did so quite consistently. Lynch (2001) recommends getting students to make transcripts of an extract (90–120 seconds) from their task performance as a method for inducing noticing. After transcribing, they are required to make any editing changes they wish. The teacher then takes away the word-processed transcripts and reformulates them. The next day the students are asked to compare their own edited transcript with the teacher's reformulated version. In a study that investigated this procedure, Lynch found that students co-operated effectively in transcribing, made a number of changes (most of which resulted in accurate corrections of linguistic forms), and engaged in both self- and other-correction. Lynch also analysed the types of changes the students made, noting that the majority involved grammatical corrections, 'editing' slips, i.e. removal of redundancies, literal repetitions and dysfluencies, and 'reformulation', i.e. changes directed at more precise expressions. Finally, Lynch comments that there was plenty left for the teacher to do after the students had made their changes. This post-task activity seems to result in the same kind of 'language-related episodes' that Swain and her co-researchers have observed in collaborative dialogue between learners (see Chapter 6).

Using the framework for designing a lesson

It should be noted that what constitutes the main activity of a lesson is largely a matter of perception and therefore, to some extent at least, arbitrary. For example, Prabhu (1987) talks of a 'pre-task' and a 'task'. The former is carried out between the teacher and the whole class. The latter is performed by the students working individually. But, such a sequence of activities could easily be described in terms of 'task' and 'post-task'. Indeed, Prabhu's 'pre-task' involves the type of activity that most task-based methodologists would consider to belong to the during-task phase of a lesson. Similarly, a sequence of activities consisting of 'task' and 'post-task' where the latter involves the kind of transcribing activity advocated by Lynch could also be described in terms of 'pre-task' and 'task', if the transcribing activity is viewed as the main activity.

However, this caveat does not detract from the usefulness of the design framework described above as a basis for planning task-based lessons. Teachers need to decide first on the basic format of the lesson. Minimally, it will consist of the during-task phase but it can also include either a pre-task phase or a post-task phase, or both of these. Once the basic structure of the lesson has been decided, the specific option(s) to be included in each phase of the lesson can be considered. The description of the process options for implementing the during-task phase of the lesson also provides a guide for the navigation of the actual task and for the teacher's ongoing monitoring of the task performance.

The planning and process decisions teachers make need to be guided by clear principles. However, before we consider these, we will turn to the second major aspect of task-based methodology—the participatory structure of lessons.

Participatory structure

The participatory structure of a lesson refers to the procedures that govern how the teacher's and students' contributions to the performance of the task are organized. A basic distinction can be made according to whether the type of participation is individual, i.e. each student works by him- or herself, or social, i.e. interaction occurs between the participants. In the case of social organization various options are possible; the teacher can conduct an activity in lockstep with the whole class, a student can take on the role of 'teacher' and perform the task with the rest of the class or the students can be asked to interact among themselves in small groups or pairs. The choice of participatory structure will influence to what extent there is interaction in the classroom and also its nature, as suggested in Table 8.5. Thus, given the importance attached to interaction in task-based learning (see Chapters 2, 3, and 6), this aspect of classroom methodology is clearly highly significant.

These options are available in each phase of a lesson, including the main task phase. However, discussions of task-based teaching are often based on the assumption that the main task will be performed in pairs or small groups. For example, Pica (1987) calls for tasks that require information exchange and emphasize collaboration and 'equal participant structure'. Willis (1996: 52) states that 'students do the task in pairs or small groups' in her overview of the 'task cycle'. Similarly, Skehan's (1998b) account of how to implement a task-based syllabus simply takes for granted that tasks involve student-student interaction. Task-based research has reinforced this view, as the vast bulk of the studies referred to in the preceding chapters have involved the study of small-group interactions. However, this assumption is not justified. First, as we saw in Chapter 2 not all tasks are interactive; non-reciprocal tasks by definition do not require interaction between the task participants. Many reading and writing tasks, for example, need to be performed by the students working individually. Second, reciprocal tasks, which by definition are social, can also be performed in whole-class interaction.

Participatory structure	Prototypical form of interaction
A Individual	Intrapersonal, e.g. by means of private speech
B Social	Interpersonal
1 Teacher-class	Teacher ↔ students
2 Student-class	Student ↔ teacher and other students
3 Small group or pair work	Student ↔ student (teacher)

Table 8.5: Types of classroom participatory structure

An example will help to illustrate how the same task can be performed using different participatory structures. The task is a standard jigsaw task. It consists of a set of five pictures depicting a story. The pictures are cut up and jumbled. The outcome required of the students is to tell the story. When the task is performed individually by the students, each student will need to be in possession of all five pictures, which they sequence before telling the story (either orally or in writing). The task can also be performed in groups by giving each student in a group of five one of the pictures. The students take it in turn to describe their pictures without showing them to each other and then work out the story collaboratively. Finally, the task can be performed in a whole-class context, using the procedure described in Table 8.6. Note that the teacher's role here is as a manager/organizer of the activities and not as a participant. However, it is also possible for the teacher to function as a task participant in a whole-class context. For example, in a spot-the-difference task the teacher might hold all the A pictures and the students the B pictures. In this case, the teacher interacts with individual class members to establish whether each pair of pictures is the same or different, with the rest of the class listening in. Tasks, then, allow for a variety of participatory structures, obliging the teacher to make a principled decision regarding which structure to use for a particular task. We will now examine the pros and cons of each participatory structure.

Step	Description
1	Teacher asks five students to come to the front of the class. Randomly, each student is given one of the pictures. The students are not allowed to look at the other pictures.
2	Each student takes it in turn to describe his/her picture. The pictures are not described in sequence.
3	Students in the rest of the class are allowed to ask questions about the pictures. The students at the front of the class answer their questions.
4	The teacher invites a student from the rest of the class to try and tell the story.
5	The teacher informs the class that part of the student's story is not quite correct. The teacher allows the class to ask the students more questions about their pictures. At this stage, the students at the front can look at each other's pictures.
6	Steps 4 and 5 are repeated until a student from the class is able to tell the story accurately.

Table 8.6: Performing a split-picture task in a whole-class context

Individual student work with tasks

In the Communicational Teaching Project, students complete the main task on their own. This, according to Prabhu (1987: 58) results in 'sustained self-dependent effort by learners'. However, Prabhu does not seek to preclude collaborative effort, only to make it optional. The students in this project could consult with each other or with the teacher if they wished. One obvious advantage of such an approach is that it caters to individual differences in students, allowing them to opt for an independent or social approach to the task in accordance with their personalities and learning styles.

There are other advantages of allowing students to work on tasks individually. It can help to foster independence and autonomy. Nunan (1989) draws on Dickinson's (1987) list of reasons for encouraging self-directedness in students in his account of the learner 'roles' that task-based instruction needs to foster. Among these are practical reasons, i.e. for some learners self-instruction is a necessity; educational reasons, i.e. self-direction learning is a characteristic of the 'good language learner'; and motivational reasons, i.e. working on one's own can be intrinsically motivating. We should also note that it is much easier to manipulate the time that students spend on task (and, thereby, influence the extent to which they engage in monitoring output) when they are working individually than when they are in groups. Finally, in accordance with socio-cultural theory, we need not characterize an individual participant structure as non-interactive, if we view private speech as a form of inter-action-with-self. Students can be encouraged to use private speech to mediate their way through a task. As socio-cultural theory makes clear, such mediation can assist language learning in much the same way as social talk. Working independently on tasks also enables learners to engage in the 'private manipulation and experimentation with ... language' (Lantolf 2000c), which many theorists (for example, Skehan 1998a) see as essential for interlanguage development. Such experimentation is fostered because when students work privately on tasks the cost of making errors is minimized.

Individual student work is not just an option for the during-task phase; it is also an option for the pre-task and post-task phases. Strategic planning, for example, is typically performed by the students working on their own. It is interesting to note that Foster and Skehan (1999) found that individual planning was effective in promoting more complex and more fluent language whereas group-based planning resulted in the least fluent, complex, and accurate language (see Chapter 4).

There are disadvantages of asking students to work on tasks individually, however. As we saw in Chapter 6, collaborative work on tasks enables learners to perform beyond the capacities of any individual learner. When working independently, students are entirely reliant on their own resources. It is for this reason, as Nation (1990) points out, that it is important to ensure that the tasks learners perform by themselves are pitched at an appropriate level of difficulty. Alternatively, a pre-task activity can help to make a difficult task more accessible to individual work. A second problem is that students may lack the strategic competence to perform successfully on their own. For this reason pre-task strategy training may be especially helpful when selecting this type of participatory structure.

Working on tasks in pairs and groups

The advantages of working in pairs and groups

The case for a social participatory structure that allows for students to interact with each other was succinctly stated by Dewey (1916: 302) many years ago: 'certain capacities of an individual are not brought out except under the stimulus of associating with others'. Building on Long and Porter's account (1985) of the advantages of group/pair work for language pedagogy, Jacobs (1998) provides a comprehensive list of ten potential advantages (see Table 8.7), comparing the typical characteristics of group work with those of teacher-centred instruction.

Some disadvantages

However, while Dewey's axiom is widely accepted in education, including language pedagogy, it has not gone unchallenged. Not all learners are positively disposed towards working together on tasks. Willing (1987), for example, reports that the ESL learners in Australia that he surveyed included 'pair work and language games' among the activities they liked the least. Nunan (1989) suggests that learners often tend to favour 'traditional' over 'communicative' activities, showing a preference for teacher-centred over learner-centred participatory structures. Group/pair work has also been challenged on the grounds that it does not ensure the conditions needed to achieve satisfactory task outcomes or language learning. Wells (1999) points out that the ephemeral nature of spoken discourse makes it difficult for the group participants to pursue a line of reasoning so that they can be sure progress has been made and can understand the nature of that progress. He comments 'memory for the exact words spoken is extremely short and, without recourse to a definitive text of what is said, it is difficult to work systematically to improve it and the understanding that it embodies' (ibid. 115). This, together with the limitations in learners' oral proficiency, may be one reason why many tasks in L2 pedagogy are cognitively undemanding.

Advantage	Comment
1 The quantity of learner speech can increase	In teacher-fronted classrooms, the teacher typically speaks 80% of the time; in group work more students talk for more of the time.
2 The variety of speech acts can increase	In teacher-fronted classrooms, students are cast in a responsive role, but in group work they can perform a wide range of roles, including those involved in the negotiation of meaning.
3 There can be more individualization of instruction	In teacher-fronted lessons, teachers shape their instruction to the needs of the average student but in group work the needs of individual students can be attended to.
4 Anxiety can be reduced	Students feel less nervous speaking in an L2 in front of their peers than in front of the whole class.
5 Motivation can increase	Students will be less competitive when working in groups and are more likely to encourage each other.
6 Enjoyment can increase	Students are 'social animals' and thus enjoy interacting with others in groups; in teacher-fronted classrooms student-student interaction is often proscribed.
7 Independence can increase	Group activities help students to become independent learners.
8 Social integration can increase	Group activities enable students to get to know each other.
9 Students can learn how to work together with others	In typical teacher-fronted classrooms, students are discouraged from helping each other; group work helps students to learn collaborative skills.
10 Learning can increase	Learning is enhanced by group work because students are willing to take risks and can scaffold each other's efforts.

Table 8.7: Ten potential advantages of group activities in language instruction (based on Jacobs 1998)

Prabhu (1987: 81) did not incorporate group work into the methodology of the Communicational Language Project on the grounds that it was less likely that students would be exposed to the 'good models' of English needed to promote interlanguage development than if the pre-tasks were performed with the teacher:

> Since differences between the internal systems of different learners are much smaller than those between the internal systems of the learners as a group and that of the teacher, sustained interaction between learners is likely to provide much less opportunity for system revision.[2]

According to this view, then, student-student interaction may result in pidginized use of the L2 and concomitant interlanguage fossilization. Prabhu also advances an affective argument against group work. Contrary to Jacob's view that group work can help to reduce anxiety, Prabhu suggests that some students find it more humiliating to make mistakes in front of their peers than in front of the teacher. Perhaps this is an area where there are marked cultural differences.

There is another reason why group/pair work may be less effective for language learning than is often claimed. Earlier in this chapter (and in Chapter 5) the importance of students attending to form during the performance of a task was noted. Such activity has been found to occur regularly when the teacher performs a task with the students. Does 'noticing' arise in student-student interaction? There is very little research that has addressed this issue. However, a study by Williams (2000) suggests that group work may not be conducive to students paying attention to form. Williams found that beginner and intermediate proficiency learners rarely focused on form while performing communicative tasks and when they did so it was only when the teacher was in attendance. Advanced level learners addressed form more frequently. The actual forms attended to by learners, irrespective of their proficiency, were lexical; there were very few occasions when they addressed grammatical or phonological problems. However, the tasks in Willams' study were entirely oral in nature. Group work produces greater attention to form when a pre-task activity directs learners' attention to form and the outcome is a written product, as in Swain and Lapkin (2001b).

Finally, there are various problems associated with the conduct of group/pair work that can have a negative effect on the performance of a task (see Jacobs 1998: 176–7). The physical characteristics of the classroom, in particular the layout of the furniture, can impede effective interaction. Group discussions can become very noisy and disruptive. Students may contribute very unequally to the completion of the task, with some learners trying to dominate and others freeloading by getting their peers to do the work for them. There is also the risk that students will overuse their L1 or engage in off-task talk.

Cooperative learning

How can we reconcile the potential advantages of group work for task-based pedagogy with the possible problems? The answer lies in the extent to which group work results in cooperative learning through collaborative dialogue. Social interaction between students does not by itself guarantee either a successful outcome for the task or the conditions that promote language learning. It is not enough to simply put students into groups to complete a task. What counts is the quality of the interaction, and whether this enables students to engage effectively with the task and to support each other's language learning. A key to using group/pair work in task-based language pedagogy, then, lies in ensuring that students are able to work together effectively. As we have already seen in the discussion of process options, sociocultural theory affords important clues as to how this can be achieved.

A study by Storch (2001) bears witness to the importance of collaborative activity in group work for achieving results. Storch investigated student-student interactions in a group task that required the learners to produce a written text in pairs. This study showed that the students did not always work collaboratively but that when they did so it had a beneficial effect on task performance. Storch identified the following characteristics of collaborative interaction:

1 Predominance of first person plural pronouns
2 Few, or absence directives thereof
3 Text co-constructed, i.e. each student adding to or extending his/her partner's contributions
4 Language-related episodes initiated by means of a request
5 Interactive responses that are often incorporated.
6 Evidence of scaffolding.

Storch concludes by suggesting that it is the students' attitude to working together that may be crucial.

Wells (1999) draws on and extends Bereiter's (1994) notion of 'progressive discourse' to describe what is required for collaborative knowledge building to occur. He outlines the commitments the participants need to make to achieve such discourse:

1 to work toward a common understanding satisfactory to all
2 to frame questions and propositions in ways that allow evidence to be brought to bear on them
3 to expand the body of collectively valid propositions
4 to allow any belief to be subjected to criticism if it will advance the discourse
5 to work collaboratively to improve a knowledge artifact. (Wells 1999: 112–3).

From this perspective, the interaction from the task performance discussed earlier in this chapter (p. 254), which Seedhouse (1999) dismissed as 'unimpressive' can be seen in a different light. It is clear that the participants are working towards a 'common understanding', i.e. the meaning of 'dot', and that they do frame questions in ways that help to expand the knowledge base of the students, i.e. by proposing synonyms for 'dot'. This results in a collectively valid proposition, i.e. a definition of 'dot' as a 'small point', and there is a clear 'knowledge artifact' that results from this interaction, i.e. the meaning of 'dot'. The fact that the students' language is 'minimal' (Seedhouse's criticism) can be seen as irrelevant. Indeed, the fact that the students have conducted a progressive discourse so economically is a sign of the efficiency of their collaboration. Ideally, task participants need to conduct the 'activity of knowing' parsimoniously. Minimal interactions of the kind illustrated in this extract are only a problem if they constitute the only or the predominant mode of talk. As I have argued above, this depends to a considerable extent on the nature of the 'problem' a task poses the students, i.e. it is a matter of task design.

The fifth of Well's list of commitments is also crucial in this respect. The activity of 'coming to know' through conversation depends crucially on the participants being able to utilize each other's utterances as objects that can be extended, questioned or rejected (see section on metatalk in Chapter 6). As we have seen, this can be accomplished much more easily if the 'knowledge artifact' that the task requires students to construct is written rather than oral.[3] When constructing a written text, students are able to focus on an 'improvable object' and, importantly, have the time and space to treat language itself as an object, thus achieving the focus on form considered crucial for acquisition. In tasks that afford such 'improvable objects' (Bereiter and Scardamalia 1996), the quality of the interaction is enhanced, with longer and more grammaticalized utterances apparent, as illustrated in the task performances in Swain's research (see, for example, Swain 2000, and Swain and Lapkin 2001b).[4] Thus again we can see that the extent to which students achieve effective collaboration depends on the nature of the task, as much as on their own efforts.

There are, however, a number of more practical matters that teachers can attend to in order to foster student cooperation in group/pair work. It should be noted, however, that there is little L2 research available that has directly addressed these issues. They include:

1 Students' orientation to the task
   For group work to be effective students need to be convinced that the task is worthwhile and not simply an opportunity for some 'fun' (as Foster (1998) suggests was the case in the learners she investigated; see Chapter 6). Students, then, need to be serious and committed towards obtaining the best outcome possible for the task.

2 Individual accountability
   Each student needs to be made accountable for his/her own contribution
   to the completion of the task. One way in which this can be achieved is
   by giving each group member a specific role to perform (Jacobs 1998).
   Another is by asking each student to make an explicit comment on their
   personal contribution in the post-task report.

3 Group composition
   The key questions here concern size and membership. Jacobs points out
   that many books on cooperative learning recommend groups of four,
   which can be subsequently divided into pairs. Mixed groups (in terms of
   ethnicity and proficiency) are considered to work better than homoge-
   neous groups, although Lange's (2000) study failed to demonstrate this.

4 Distribution of information
   In one-way information-gap tasks involving students of differing
   proficiency levels, collaborativeness is enhanced if the student with the
   lower proficiency is put in charge of the information to be exchanged
   (see reference to Yule *et al.* 1992 in Chapter 3).

5 Physical arrangement of students
   Jacobs (1998) proposes that students need to be seated in a way that
   they can easily talk together and maintain eye contact, share resources,
   talk quietly, and take up less space.

6 Collaborative skills
   Teachers can provide training in the strategies needed to engage in effective collaboration, for example, how to disagree and how to negotiate
   meaning. The extent to which students are able to use these strategies in
   group work needs to be constantly monitored.

7 Group permanence and cohesion
   Co-operative learning requires that students have time to consider how
   their group is functioning and find ways of working together effectively.
   If groups are constantly changing students will not have the opportunity to develop the 'positive interdependence' (Johnson, Johnson, and
   Holubec 1993) considered essential for group cohesion. The ability to
   work effectively with others is a process that requires time.

8 Teacher's role
   Jacobs (1998) mentions a number of possible roles for the teacher; modelling collaboration, observing and monitoring the students' performance, and intervening when a group is experiencing obvious difficulty.
   Also a teacher can function as a task participant, sitting with students to
   do the task. The problem with this latter role, however, is that many students find it difficult to react to the teacher as a group member rather
   than as an instructor.

To sum up this section, group work, while important to task-based instruction, is not an essential feature, and carries with it some notable disadvantages, not least the danger of fossilization. However, asking students to perform a task in pairs or small groups affords a number of advantages for both achieving successful outcomes and for language acquisition, although group work in and of itself does not guarantee these advantages. Students need to engage in the 'progressive discourse' that arises out of cooperative endeavour. To achieve such discourse is a challenge, depending in part on the choice of task and in part on ensuring that the conditions that make co-operation possible have been met.

Working on tasks in a whole-class context

We have now examined the advantages and disadvantages of individual student work and group work as ways of performing tasks. In this section we turn to a consideration of how tasks can be conducted in a whole-class context. Again, I would like to emphasize that this participatory option has often been ignored both by language-teaching methodologists (Prabhu excepted) and by researchers despite the fact that it affords a number of advantages.

In a whole-class context, the teacher's participation in the task becomes crucial. This contribution takes two forms depending on the task. In non-reciprocal tasks, the teacher typically becomes the main participant providing the input for the task, as in the listening tasks discussed in Chapter 2. Here, the nature and quality of the 'teacher talk' is crucial. In reciprocal tasks, the teacher functions as a more equal participant, but given his status and expertise has a special role to play in conducting 'instructional conversations' that guide students through the task. An alternative is to use peer teaching, i.e. to make a student responsible for conducting the task with the rest of the class.

Teacher talk

The importance of teacher talk for language acquisition has been widely acknowledged in L2 classroom research (see Ellis 1994 Chapter 8, and Chaudron 1988). Teacher talk is talk that is adapted to the student's L2 proficiency to ensure that the input is comprehensible. It involves modifications at all levels of language—phonological, lexical, grammatical, and discoursal. It is largely performed as a skill below the level of consciousness—that is, teachers are not usually aware that they are adapting how they speak. Like all skills, it is subject to considerable individual variation, with some teachers highly skilled at pitching their talk at the students' level and others much less so.

Teacher talk was of central importance to the pre-task phase of the Communicational Teaching project. Prabhu (1987: 57) describes it as follows:

> ... in the classroom, the teacher controlled the complexity of his or her language in more or less the same way as an adult does in speaking to a child—avoiding or paraphrasing what he or she felt might be too difficult, repeating statements, and speaking slowly when there seemed to be difficulties of understanding.

Teacher talk of this kind cannot be pre-planned; the process of simplification is necessarily ad hoc. Prabhu suggests it worked because it met a 'criterion of adequacy'—it enabled the teacher and the students to get on with the task. However, evidence of variability in the teachers' ability to implement teacher talk can be found in Beretta's (1990) evaluation of the project. Beretta noted that teachers differed in the extent to which they attempted to solve communication problems using the students' L1, depending on their awareness of the principles of the project. Also, teachers with limited proficiency in English tended to stick to the prepared script in the workplan of a task. For some non-native-speaking teachers, then, the accomplishment of skilled teacher talk may be problematic.

Nor is it necessarily any easier for native speakers. We noted in Chapter 2 when discussing the non-reciprocal tasks used in my own research that the native-speaking teachers used in this research sometimes manifested a tendency to over-elaborate their definitions of key words with a deleterious effect on learners' acquisition of those words. Apparently, teachers sometimes talk too much in the effort to ensure learners' understanding and in so doing impede learning.

Given the importance of teacher talk to task-based instruction it is surprising that so little attention has been paid to it in both research and pedagogy. While we have some idea of what constitutes effective (and ineffective) teacher talk, little is know about how teachers can be helped to become skilled practitioners. Is teacher talk trainable and, if so, how? These are key questions for the methodology of task-based teaching, which are currently without answers.

Instructional conversations

In Chapter 6 we defined instructional conversations as dialogic activity where the teacher guides the learner to perform a function that the learner is unable to perform by him or herself. Tasks which are meaning-focused and thus encourage conversation but which are also instructional in the sense that they are designed with a view to facilitate language learning are ideal vehicles for instigating instructional conversations. According to Donato (2000), such conversations require teachers to abandon the 'triadic dialogue' (Lemke 1990) of traditional teacher-centred classrooms. Such dialogue is associated with the pedagogy of transmission (Barnes 1976) but, as Wells (1999) and Nassaji and Wells (2000) illustrate, this need not be the case. Teacher-questions that 'introduce issues as for negotiation' (Nassaji and Wells 2000: 400) elicit richer contributions from students than closed information questions. Also much depends on the final move in the three-part IRF (initiate-respond-follow-up) exchange. Where this performs the function of evaluating the student's response against some predetermined notion of a correct answer the discourse is essentially pedagogic but where it serves to extend the student's response and to make connections with what has gone before and what will follow it becomes conversational. Wells also demonstrates that even within a triadic dialogue opportunities can arise for students' contributions to be taken up and developed into a topic for talking about. Ohta (2001b) reports that the Japanese learners she investigated appropriated the language they were exposed to in IRF exchanges for use in subsequent group work. Thus, it is clearly a mistake to dismiss 'communication = question and answer' interaction as readily as some proponents of task-based teaching, such as Lee (2000).

What then are the key characteristics of a teacher-led instructional conversation in the context of performing a task? They involve both conversational features and instructional goals (Tharp and Gallimore 1988). The conversational features include:

1 shared responsibility for directing the conversation
2 opportunities for students to make comments that are not elicited by the teacher
3 a clear thematic focus
4 the use of extending utterances to build on students' responses to the teacher's questions

The instructional goals relate to:

1 achieving an outcome to the task, i.e. by scaffolding solutions to problems
2 effective language use, i.e. by requiring that contributions are comprehensible
3 language learning, i.e. by focusing on form

Donato (2000) illustrates how in traditional foreign-language classrooms instructional conversations occur as interludes in more traditional discourse and are not sustained. However, Johnston (1986) provides several examples of lengthier exchanges in high school ESL classes in the US. Instructional conversations, then, constitute the principal means of ensuring the goals of a task-based curriculum when this is implemented through whole-class interactions.

Peer teaching

In peer teaching a student is chosen to act as the teacher to manage the performance of the task with the rest of the class. This has several advantages. First, the peer-teacher has all the opportunities for talk that accrue to the regular teacher. He/she will have to take responsibility for managing turn taking and for guiding the rest of the class to an outcome. This will result in the need to perform a wide range of language functions including those associated with the negotiation of meaning. Second, other students in the class are likely to find it easier to behave 'conversationally', for example, by initiating their own topics, when the teacher is a fellow student. Third, the amount of student talk generated by the task is likely to increase. To the best of my knowledge, there has been no research into peer teaching in task-based lessons, but Benson (2000) reports several studies, some involving foreign-language learners, that lend credence to these claims. One of these (Carpenter 1996), however, reported a number of problems, including lack of participation by some students, and concluded that peer teaching may be more effective with advanced-level students.

Summary and concluding comment

Planning a task-based lesson requires that careful consideration be given to the participatory structure of the different phases of the lesson. Whereas task-based teaching has typically based itself on group/pair work, other structures, i.e. students working independently and teacher-centred activities, including peer teaching, are also available. I have not attempted to argue the superiority of any one of these structures. Rather I have attempted to show that each structure has a number of potential advantages and disadvantages. It follows, therefore, that teachers should vary their choice of participatory structure, bearing in mind the aims of the phase of the lesson and the nature of the task itself.

Conclusion

Teachers need to ensure that the decisions they make with regard to the design and participatory structure of a task-based lesson are principled ones. Thus it seems appropriate to conclude this chapter with a list of general principles that can inform the planning and teaching of task-based lessons. Table 8.8 summarizes the principles proposed by Willis (1996) and Skehan (1998a). These include principles relating to the design of a task-based course and to methodological issues. My own list of principles, based on the preceding sections of this chapter, focuses on methodology, in accordance with the purpose of this chapter.

Willis (1996)		Skehan (1998)	
1	There should be exposure to worthwhile and authentic language.	1	Choose a range of target structures, i.e. ensure systematicity in language development without adhering rigidly to a structural syllabus.
2	There should be use of language.	2	Choose tasks which meet the utility criterion, i.e. make it 'useful' for students to perform the target structures.
3	Tasks should motivate learners to engage in language use.	3	Sequence tasks to achieve balanced goal development, i.e. prioritize fluency, accuracy, and complexity at different times.
4	There should be a focus on language at some points in a task cycle.	4	Maximize the chances of a focus on form through attentional manipulation.
5	The focus on language should be more or less prominent at different times.	5	Use cycles of accountability, i.e. mobilize students, metacognitive resources to keep track of what has been learned.

*Table 8.8: Principles of task-based teaching from Willis (1996)
and Skehan (1998)*

The overall purpose of task-based methodology is to create opportunities for language learning and skill development through collaborative knowledge building. The following principles can be used to guide the selection of implementational options and participatory structures that can help to achieve this:

Principle 1: Ensure an appropriate level of task difficulty.
Ensuring that a task is pitched at an appropriate level of difficulty is not just a matter of course design. Teachers can adjust the difficulty of a task methodologically, for example, by incorporating a pre-task phase into the lesson, by appropriate use of teacher-talk, or by choosing to perform the task with the students in the form of an instructional conversation. Teachers can also ensure that students possess the necessary strategies to engage in task-based interaction.

Principle 2: Establish clear goals for each task-based lesson.
As Skehan (1998a) has made clear, it is not sufficient to engage learners with tasks on the basis that they will develop their interlanguages simply as

a result of using the L2. Methodological options, for example, strategic and online planning, can be selected to help prioritize different aspects of language use, for example, fluency vs. accuracy.

Principle 3: Develop an appropriate orientation to performing the task in the students.
Students need to be made aware of why they are being asked to perform tasks. They need to treat them seriously, not just as 'fun'. In this respect, post-task options may play a crucial role as they demonstrate to the students that tasks have a clear role to play in developing their L2 proficiency and their ability to monitor their own progress.

Principle 4: Ensure that students adopt an active role in task-based lessons.
One of the major goals of task-based teaching is to provide learners with an opportunity to participate fully by playing an initiating as well as a responding role in classroom discourse. A key element of being 'active' is negotiating meaning when communicative problems arise. One of the principal ways of ensuring this is through group/pair work, although, as we have seen, it is also possible to achieve it in whole-class participatory structures.

Principle 5: Encourage students to take risks.
When students perform tasks they need to 'stretch' their interlanguage resources. This requires students to be prepared to experiment with language. Methodological choices that encourage the use of private speech when performing a task, that create opportunities for 'pushed output', and that help to create an appropriate level of challenge in an affective climate that is supporting of risk-taking will assist this.

Principle 6: Ensure that students are primarily focused on meaning when they perform a task.
The main purpose of a task is to provide a context for processing language communicatively, i.e. by treating language as a tool not as an object. Thus, when students perform a task they must be primarily concerned with achieving an outcome, not with displaying language. This can only be achieved if learners are motivated to do the task. One way in which this can be achieved is by varying task-based lessons in terms of design options and participatory structure.

Principle 7: Provide opportunities for focusing on form.
Both Willis and Skehan emphasize the need to attend to form in a task-based lesson. In this chapter, various options at the pre-task, during-task, and post-task phases of a lesson have been proposed for achieving such a focus. In particular, it has been emphasized that attention to form is both possible and beneficial in the during-task phase and need not conflict with Principle 6.

Principle 8: Require students to evaluate their performance and progress.
As Skehan points out, students need to be made accountable for how they perform a task and for their overall progress. A task-based lesson needs to engage and help to foster metacognitive awareness in the students.

These principles are intended as a general guide to the teaching of task-based lessons, not as a set of commandments. The approach throughout this chapter has been descriptive; that is, I have sought to codify and describe the various methodological possibilities relating to the design and participatory structure of lessons, drawing on a wide range of sources, but especially sociocultural theory. I do not believe it is possible to prescribe methodological choices, given the lack of knowledge about which options are the most effective. Teachers must make their own methodological decisions based on their understanding of what will work best with their own students (see Ellis 1997a).

Notes

1 Allwright's (1984) use of 'uptake' differs from that of researchers who have investigated corrective sequences in classroom discourse (see Chapter 5). Allwright uses the term to refer to what learners are able to explicitly report having learned as a result of participating in a lesson.
2 Not all the teachers involved in the Communicational Teaching Project viewed group/pair work so negatively however. Beretta (1990a: 332) reports that 'some of the teachers considered that more group work might improve the CTP' on the grounds that without it the demands placed on the students' 'productive abilities' were inadequate.
3 Wells (1999: 123) argues that 'the object that provides the focus should be the artefacts that are made and improved through the students' and teacher's participation in the activity'. He gives examples of such objects—a building constructed out of physical materials, a class newspaper, models of vehicles, a scripted play. In each case the object is tangible and has a degree of permanence. It is these qualities that appear to be crucial for fostering the kind of rich collaborative dialogue deemed important for learning in SCT.
4 The fact that there were relatively few differences between the two tasks Swain and Lapkin (2001a) investigated (see Chapter 6) may be because both tasks required students to interact to produce a written product.

9   Task-based assessment

Introduction

In this chapter we will consider how tasks are employed to assess learners' communicative ability in a second language (L2). It should be noted that language testers use the term 'task' as variably as language teaching methodologists. Traditionally, the term is used generically to refer to any device for carrying out an assessment (Chalhoub-Deville 2001). In this sense, a multiple choice grammar item or a cloze passage is just as much a 'task' as a role-play or an opinion-gap activity. This corresponds to Breen's (1987) broad definition of tasks in language pedagogy (Figure 1 in Chapter 1). More recently, in the context of performance-referenced testing, 'task' has assumed the narrower meaning adhered to in the previous chapters of this book (see Chapter 1 for a definition). In this sense, then, assessment tasks are viewed as devices for eliciting and evaluating communicative performances from learners in the context of language use that is meaning-focused and directed towards some specific goal. It is in this sense that the term is used in this chapter.

Just as language-teaching methodologists have argued that tasks constitute the prima facie means for promoting acquisition of an L2, so language testers have increasingly recognized the value of tasks for assessing learners' capacity to communicate in an L2. McNamara (1996) notes that *performance tests* based on tasks have arisen both because of the need to develop selection procedures for specific groups of L2 learners, for example, foreign students studying in English-medium universities, and the need to bring testing in line with developments in language teaching of the kind discussed in Chapters 7 and 8. Brindley (1994) identifies a number of specific advantages of what he calls 'task-centred assessment': it results in both teachers and learners focusing on language as a tool, i.e. it has favourable a *washback effect*; it enables assessment to be more easily integrated into the learning process; it provides learners with useful diagnostic feedback on progress and achievement; and it enables the results of an assessment to be reported in a way that is intelligible to non-specialists. More generally, task-based testing is seen as a way of achieving a close correlation between the test performance, i.e. what the testee does during the test, and the criterion performance, i.e. what the testee has to do in the real world, and thus of ensuring the validity of the assessment.

We will begin this chapter with a brief consideration of different paradigms of language assessment as a way of differentiating *task-based assessment* (TBA) from other types of language testing. We will then move on to a detailed account of the design of task-based tests and outline a procedure for developing them. This is followed by a discussion of the main problems of TBA. Finally, as a way of establishing closer links with the preceding chapters, where the focus has been on learning and teaching, we will consider the role that tasks can play in the formative assessment of learners.

Language assessment paradigms

Here we will consider three main language assessment paradigms: (1) the *psychometric* tradition in testing, (2) *integrative* language testing, and (3) *communicative language testing*. Following Baker (1989), we will then propose that these paradigms can be subsumed into a general framework based on a dual distinction between system-referenced/performance-referenced tests and direct/indirect tests.

The psychometric tradition

The psychometric tradition in language testing draws on the methods used in psychological testing in the first half of the twentieth century and on structural linguistics. Psychological tests were characterized by questions of the closed type, for example, multiple choice, and for this reason were considered 'objective' in nature. Test scores were then subjected to various statistical procedures, i.e. item and factor analysis, to establish reliability and validity. Structural linguistics provided a means for identifying the content of the tests. Language was broken down into levels, i.e. phonology/graphology, lexis and grammar, and each level into discrete elements, i.e. phonemes, vocabulary items, grammatical patterns, and morphemes. Knowledge of these different elements was tested in relation to the four language skills—listening, speaking, reading, and writing (Lado 1961). The Test of English as a Foreign Language (TOEFL) is a good example of a test belonging to this tradition.

The psychometric tradition has been attacked on a number of fronts. These are neatly summarized by Gipps (1994: 14):

> The impact of psychometrics goes beyond the specifics of item design and test construction to a broader range of implications: the emphasis on relative ranking rather than actual accomplishment; the privileging of easily quantifiable displays of skills and knowledge; the assumption that individual performances, rather than collaborative forms of cognition, are the most powerful indicators of educational progress; the notion that evaluating educational progress is a matter of scientific measurement.

According to this view, psychometric language tests emphasized *reliability*, i.e. objectivity and consistency, and generalizability, i.e. the applicability of the results to a wide range of contexts of language use, over construct *validity*, i.e. the demonstration of a clear relationship between performance in a test and some theory of language proficiency. However, such a view is not entirely justified, as test designers such as Carroll (1990) attended closely to the construct validity of their psychometric tests. It is also important not to lose sight of the strengths of this tradition.

Integrative language tests

Like psychometric tests, integrative language tests prioritize objectivity and reliability and employ the same battery of statistical procedures to ensure these. They differ from psychometric tests in that a unitary rather than multidimensional view of language informs their content. Oller (1979), for example, proposed that language proficiency was not composed of discrete elements but was unitary in nature. This claim was supported by the statistical analysis of discrete-point tests, which showed that the scores from separate tests, for example, of grammar and vocabulary, were highly correlated, indicating that they were measuring the same factor. Oller labelled this factor 'pragmatic expectancy grammar', which can be glossed as the ability to process language elements using linguistic and extra-linguistic context. Oller argued that to target this factor it was necessary to devise tests that tapped the learner's unitary language faculty in holistic, real-time language activities. He suggested that two such activities were cloze tests (although such tests can hardly claim to examine real-time processing) and dictations, scores from which he showed to be correlated strongly with each other and with the scores from discrete-point tests.

If language competence is unitary, as Oller claims, it is a simple matter to extrapolate from performance on an integrative test to performance in the real world. In this respect, then, integrative tests can be viewed as performance tests. However, Oller's view of language proficiency has been challenged on both conceptual and empirical grounds. The nature of the correspondence between the learner's language system (the 'expectancy grammar') and its use in context (the 'pragmatic') is not clearly specified, leaving the whole construct ('pragmatic expectancy grammar') somewhat vacuous. The construct has been challenged empirically on the grounds that the factor analyses that Oller used to find support for his claim were inconclusive and even plain wrong (see Hughes and Porter 1983). Also, it was noted that the absence of any oral test in Oller's research precluded a multi-factor solution. Nevertheless, integrative language testing constituted an important development, spawning a large body of research into the design and use of cloze tests. In its emphasis on holistic testing methods, integrative testing foreshadowed later developments in performance testing.

Communicative language testing

Early work in communicative language testing in the United Kingdom, as reflected in Morrow (1979), rejected the role that reliability and validity and the statistical procedures used to determine these had come to assume in language testing circles in the United States. It represented an attempt to assert the centrality of the human subject of the test. Morrow dismissed the psychometrician's concern for reliability, arguing that it was necessarily subordinate to face validity, i.e. the extent to which the test is perceived as acceptable by stakeholders, including the testee. An example of the kind of communicative test that resulted from this thinking is The Communicative use of English as a Foreign Language test (CUEFL) developed for the Royal Society of Arts (RSA) in the United Kingdom. This test provides scores for overall task fulfillment rather than for linguistic knowledge or language skills. A feature of this test, like other communicative tests, is that it included a component assessing speaking. In this respect, it differed from prototypical tests in the psychometric and integrative paradigms.

The early communicative language testing movement in the United Kingdom was negligent in failing to address reliability and also in eschewing systematic research relating to rating scale design and construction. It also failed to consider the construct validity of tests, claiming that it was sufficient to demonstrate face and content validity. Subsequently, however, these lacunae were addressed. Weir (1988), for example, in his account of communicative language testing stressed the need to attend to both the 'construct, content, face and washback validities of tests' and their 'statistical attributes and prognostic value' (p. 96) and demonstrated how this could be achieved in the development of his test of English for Educational Purposes. In the work of Bachman (1990) and Bachman and Palmer (1996), the concern for face validity that Morrow championed was matched with an equal concern for construct validity. Bachman (1990) based his proposals for testing on a modular model of language knowledge, which he saw as comprising two broad categories, organizational knowledge and pragmatic knowledge. The former was subdivided into grammatical knowledge and textual knowledge, while the latter was seen as consisting of functional and sociolinguistic knowledge. To explain how these knowledge sources were integrated into actual performance, Bachman's model also included strategic competence, which he defined as 'higher order executive processes that provide a cognitive management function in language use' (ibid. 70). Bachman also recognized the importance of reliability, pointing to a number of different sources of error in the measurements provided by a communicative test and how these could be reduced by the use of psychometric procedures, in particular those that allowed for test developers to examine several sources of variance simultaneously. Bachman's work in language testing has proved highly influential in task-based testing, as will become apparent later in this chapter.

What then is a communicative test? According to Fulcher (2000) there are three primary aspects. First, communicative tests involve *performance*. That is, the method of assessment should ensure that that the test perform- ance and the criterion performance were as far as possible the same. Inevitably, this meant the use of 'tasks' as defined in the Introduction to this chapter. It also meant that, as far as possible, the test tasks and tar- get-language use tasks should be closely matched. Second, communi- cative tests are *authentic* in the sense that the testee must be able to rec- ognize the communicative purpose of a task in order to respond appropri- ately, the input used in the task should not be simplified, and the testee must be tested on the ability to cope with a real situational context. Third, communicative tests are scored on *real-life outcomes*. That is, the real criterion of success in a language test should be whether the testee performs the task successfully by achieving a satisfactory outcome.

It is clear from this description that communicative language testing constitutes a form of TBA. It prioritizes 'real-world tasks' on the grounds that these ensure authenticity and face validity. However, the three aspects taken to be definitional of communicative tests (see above) have all proven problematic. It is doubtful, for example, whether a task in a test can ever correspond exactly to a real-world task, i.e. whether content validity is achievable; as Davies (1978) long ago pointed out, 'the search for authen- ticity is chimerical'. This is a point that will be examined more fully later.

A general framework

We will conclude this section by describing a general framework for clas- sifying the types of language tests described above. The framework also enables us to pinpoint the essential characteristics of TBA and to distin- guish two methods for accomplishing it.

Following Baker (1989), a general distinction can be made between *system-referenced tests* and *performance-referenced tests*. System- referenced tests assess knowledge of language as a system. As Baker puts it:

> Their aim is to provide information about language proficiency in a general sense without reference to any particular use or situation. (ibid. 10)

Thus, tests belonging to the psychometric and integrative paradigms dis- cussed above are system-referenced. Performance-referenced tests, in con- trast, seek to provide information about the ability to use the language in specific contexts; they are directed at assessing a particular performance, for example, the ability of a trainee pilot to understand and respond to messages from the control tower when landing an aircraft. Thus, whereas system-referenced tests are more construct-oriented, drawing on some explicit theory of language proficiency, performance-referenced tests are more content-oriented, drawing on a work-sample approach to test design. A communicative language test can be system-referenced, as in the case of Bachman's (1990) proposals, or performance-referenced, as in the case of many specific purpose tests. Arguably, communicative tests need to be both (MacNamara 1996).

System-referenced and performance-referenced tests can both be more or less direct/indirect. This second distinction concerns the relationship between the test performance and the criterion performance. Direct tests are based on a direct sampling of the criterion performance. Such tests are holistic in nature and aim to obtain a contextualized sample of the testee's use of language. The measure of proficiency obtained from such tests is not an integral part of the testee's performance but has to be derived from it, for example, by obtaining an external rating. Indirect tests are less contextualized and, arguably, therefore more artificial. Such tests are based on an analysis of the criterion performance in order to obtain measures of the specific features or components that comprise it. They seek to assess proficiency by means of specific linguistic measures, which are obtained from the test itself, for example, a cloze test provides a score based on the number of blanks the testee has been able to fill in correctly. It should be noted, however, that all tests are indirect to some degree. No test (except, possibly, one based on an observation of testees performing some real-world task) corresponds exactly to the criterion it seeks to measure.

Juxtaposing these two distinctions, four basic types of assessment can be identified, as shown in Table 9.1. Examples of each type are provided. From this we can see that traditional language tests such as free written compositions and tests based on communicative tasks involving the transfer of information are both examples of the direct system-referenced kind. They are based on a particular view of language proficiency and they are task-based. Tests belonging to the psychometric and integrative traditions are of the indirect system-referenced type. They are multi-itemed tests. Like direct system-referenced tests, direct performance tests are task-based and, therefore, holistic in nature but they differ from direct system-referenced tests in the kinds of task they utilize. They attempt to assess either actual communicative behaviour, for example, by observing the testee perform the task in the real world, or employ simulations of real-world tasks. Tests of this type are often aimed at assessing specific-purpose language ability, for example, the ability of a doctor to use the L2 effectively in a doctor-patient interview. Finally, there are indirect performance-referenced tests. These are analytic in design and thus they sample performances of specific skills, such as academic listening, or the ability to perform specific functions or strategies related to some real-world activity, for example, identifying examples used to illustrate a point in a reading text. Tests of academic language ability such as IELTS include assessments of this type.[1]

	Direct (holistic)	**Indirect (analytic)**
System-referenced	Traditional tests of general language ability: — free composition — oral interview Information-transfer tests: — information-gap — opinion-gap — reasoning-gap	Discrete-item tests of linguistic knowledge: — multiple-choice grammar or vocabulary tests — elicited imitation of specific linguistic features — error-identification tests Integrative tests: — cloze — dictation[2]
Performance-referenced	Specific purpose tests: — tests based on observing real-world tasks — simulations of real-world tasks	Tests that seek to measure specific aspects of communicative proficiency discretely: — tests of specific academic sub-skills, e.g. the ability to cite from a published work — tests of the ability to perform specific functions or strategies, e.g. the ability to write a definition of a technical term

Table 9.1: Types of language assessment (based on Baker 1989: 11)

Defining 'task-based assessment'

We are now in a better position to define TBA more precisely. Clearly, direct performance-referenced tests constitute a form of TBA. Clearly, too, indirect system-referenced tests can be excluded. However, direct system-referenced tests also employ tasks in the sense that this term has been used in this book. An oral interview and an information-gap task, for example, both satisfy the criteria of 'taskness' described in Chapter 1. Arguably, therefore, such methods of assessment should also be considered task-based. The status of indirect performance-referenced tests is less clear, however. Such tests seek to measure the specific abilities required to perform a task but their claim to be task-based is less obvious as they do not incorporate actual tasks in their design. TBA, then, will be taken to refer to assessment that utilizes holistic tasks involving either real-world behaviour (or as close as it is possible to get to this) or the kinds of language processing found in real-world activities.[3] Its defining characteristic, then, is that it is direct in nature, not that it is performance-referenced.

However, a caveat is in order. Baker is careful to emphasize that the distinctions between system-referenced and performance-referenced and between direct and indirect methods of assessment represent continua rather than dichotomies. Thus, it will not always be easy to determine whether a particular test is task-based. Take for example, a listening-comprehension test where testees are asked to listen to a contrived mini-lecture and then answer a number of multiple-choice questions to demonstrate their comprehension. Such a test is obviously performance-referenced but is it of the direct or indirect kind? It probably lies somewhere in between. Clearly it involves language processing of the real-world kind, i.e. listening to a lecture, and in this respect is direct. However, the testee's performance is measured indirectly by scoring the answers to the questions. In this respect it differs from direct tests where the measure of the testee's performance is not incorporated into the task itself but must be derived by an assessor separately through observation or analysis of the performance itself. It is this aspect of TBA that ultimately determines whether a test can be considered task-based or not.

The components of a task-based test

A task-based test consists of: (1) a task; (2) an implementation procedure; and (3) a performance measure, i.e. a means of assessing the testee's performance. In this section, we will consider first task design, then implementation procedures and finally how a task performance can be measured.

Task design

Two general approaches to task selection can be identified (cf. Messick 1994): (1) a construct-centred approach, and (2) a work-sample approach. The former entails the identification of a theory of language use as a basis for designing tasks, while the latter involves a careful analysis of the target language situation to determine what tasks the testee will need to perform in the real world. Broadly speaking these approaches correspond to the two kinds of TBA we have identified. That is, TBA based on direct system-referenced tests will need to adopt a construct-centred approach while that based on direct performance-referenced tests can follow a work-sample approach. That is, if we want to use tasks to establish the general nature of the testees' language proficiency, we will need to specify what we mean by 'language proficiency', while if we want to find out what a learner can do in a particular situation we will need to establish what tasks are typical of that domain. However, as we will see, such a correspondence is over-simplistic as both types of TBA ideally require both approaches.

Task design in direct system-referenced tests

What kind of 'construct' underlies the design of tasks in direct system-referenced tests? There are in fact several constructs that such tests might draw on. Two will be considered here: the view of language proficiency that underlies communicative oral tests, and the dual-mode theory of linguistic competence that underlies Skehan's work on tasks (see Chapter 4).

According to Chalhoub-Deville (2001) oral tests are based on the same view of language use and language acquisition as underlies task-based instruction. She identifies three key characteristics of tasks to be used in such tests. First, they must reflect learner-centred properties; that is, the tasks must not be 'conformity-oriented' or 'practice-oriented' but must encourage individual expression. Second, tasks must be contextualized, which can only be achieved by using 'meaningful situations' and requiring 'extended discourse'. Third, the tasks should be authentic in the 'real-life' use of this term, i.e. they should mirror as closely as possible target language use tasks. Chalhoub-Delville argues that tasks that have these three properties will 'produce rich language samples from test-takers' (ibid. 217). She claims that three oral interview tests (the Oral Proficiency Interview (OPI), the Simulated Oral Proficiency Interview, and the Contextualized Speaking Assessment) all, to a greater or lesser extent, manifest these properties. For example, she argues that the OPI, which involves a structured live conversation between a trained interlocutor/rater and a test-taker on a series of different topics affords a high level of personalization,[4] provides a high degree of situational embeddedness as well as the opportunity to produce extended discourse and, by seeking to replicate a genuine conversation, caters to authenticity. However, as we will see later, these claims are challengeable.

Skehan (1998: 164) argues that tests need to make 'functional statements about the nature of performance and the way it is grounded in competence'. To achieve this it is necessary to formulate a psycholinguistic theory of linguistic competence. He suggests that, following Widdowson (1989), this can best be achieved by a model that distinguishes 'analysability' and 'accessibility', as these concepts relate to how linguistic knowledge is stored and how it is used in real-time performance. Skehan's theory was outlined in some detail in Chapter 4. Briefly, it states that linguistic competence is comprised of lexical chunks that allow for easy and rapid access in performance and also rules that cater for greater precision and creativity, albeit at a cost in terms of processing effort. The extent to which language users call on their lexical knowledge, their rule-based system, or a combination of the two is influenced by a number of task design features, for example, the familiarity of the information, and implementational conditions, for example, planning time, and in turn influences what aspect of performance, i.e. fluency, complexity, and accuracy is prioritized. It follows that if task-based tests are to be used to infer the abilities of test-takers to predict performance and to generalize from context to context, it will be necessary to understand how the choice of task influences the way the testee performs.

Drawing on his earlier research, Skehan (2001) identifies five characteristics that affect the scores assigned to performances. These characteristics have been described earlier in Chapter 4. Their effects on accuracy, complexity, and fluency are summarized in Table 9.2.[5] The conclusion to be drawn from such a meta-analysis is that 'the task is hardly a constant'. Thus, if testees' performances are elicited by means of different tasks it will not be possible to determine if the source of difference is the testees' abilities (which the test seeks to measure) or the tasks. Three implications follow for the use of tasks in direct system-referenced tests. First, in tests that exist in different versions (as is the norm in many institutional tests such as IELTS) it is essential to ensure that the design features of the tasks are the same in all the versions. Second, great care must be taken in generalizing from context to context, as performance on one particular kind of task will not necessarily be matched by performance on a different kind. Third, if the aim of a test is to establish the testees' overall 'ability to use language' it will be helpful to include tasks that prioritize different aspects of performance (accuracy, complexity, and fluency).

It should be noted, however, that Skehan is extrapolating from studies carried out in classrooms or laboratories. Recent studies designed to investigate the effect of a number of task characteristics in testing situations have failed to find any substantial effect. Wigglesworth (1997a), for example, reports no difference in overall scores for gap vs. non-gap tasks. In a further study, Wigglesworth (2001) found no effect for task familiarity, although

Task characteristic	Accuracy	Complexity	Fluency
1 Familiarity of information	No effect	No effect	Slightly greater
2 Dialogic vs. monologic tasks	Greater	Slightly greater	Lower
3 Degree of structure	No effect	No effect	Greater
4 Complexity of outcome	No effect	Greater	No effect
5 Transformations	No effect	Planned condition generates greater complexity	No effect

Table 9.2: Summary of the effect of task characteristics on complexity, accuracy, and fluency (Skehan 2001: 181)

she did find that tightly structured tasks were easier. Iwashita, Elder, and McNamara (2001) investigated three design variables in narrative tasks, i.e. immediacy (here-and-now vs. there-and-then tasks); adequacy (telling vs. inventing a story); perspective (narrating in the first or third person). The test-takers' performances were subjected to external rating and to discourse analysis in order to provide measures of fluency, accuracy, and complexity. However, no significant effect was found for any of the measures with the exception of the here-and-now task, which produced more accurate language use. Further evidence of the difficulty of predicting task difficulty in a testing context can be found in a study by Norris, Brown, and Hudson (2000), to be discussed later. Clearly, it cannot be concluded that the task variables found to be significant in a teaching or laboratory context have the same effect in a testing situation.

Task design in direct performance-referenced tests

Tasks serve a very different purpose in direct performance-referenced tests. Instead of eliciting performances which can be used to assess the testees' *general* language proficiency, they are used to evaluate whether the testee can successfully perform some *specific* real-world activity. This allows for a different, needs-driven method for selecting tasks, i.e. a work-sample approach. Douglas (2000), drawing on proposals advanced by Bachman and Palmer (1996: 41), describes this method as follows:

> ... in specific purpose language testing, we want to make inferences about individuals' abilities to use language in specific academic, professional, or vocational fields on the basis of their performance on a language test in which the characteristics of tasks in the target language use (TLU) situation, or context, are incorporated into test tasks.

However, as Bachman and Palmer (1996) and Douglas (2000) make clear, a TLU context is not be understood simply as a bundle of features that pre-dispose the participants to use language in specific ways but also as a com-municative event that is dynamically constructed by the participants turn by turn through negotiation. Thus, a work-sample approach needs to specify not just the external features of the context in which a task is enact-ed but also its interactional properties.

Douglas uses the framework developed by Bachman and Palmer (1996) to analyse TLU situations and test task characteristics. The aim of this framework is to ensure a high level of equivalence between the TLU task and the test task, i.e. the authenticity of the test task. The framework identifies the following characteristics:

1   *Rubric*

Rubric refers to the objective of the task, the procedures for responding, the task's structure, its format, the time available for completing it, and the evaluation criteria that are applied. Douglas notes that these characteristics are often implicit in a TLU situation as they are part of the participants' background knowledge, but that they need to be made explicit in a test task.

2   *Input*

Input refers to the specific-purpose material that the language users process and respond to. In a text task, the input is the primary means of establishing the key features of the context. Douglas suggests that there are two aspects of the input: a prompt and input data. A prompt is used to set up a specific purpose situation where there is no separate input data or where the input data does not sufficiently delineate the context of the task. It often figures in a role-play task to provide background information concerning who and where the participants are and what the purpose of the task is. Input data consists of the visual or oral material or the physical objects that the task participants must process in order to undertake the task.[6]

3   *The expected response*

The rubric and input serve to set up the response that the test-takers hope to elicit from the testee. A key aspect of this is the nature of the language and the specific purpose background knowledge that the testee is expected to display.

4   *The interaction between input and response*

Bachman and Palmer (1996) identify three dimensions of interaction between the input and response. A task may be more or less reactive, depending on the extent to which the input can be modified as a result of the testees' response. Thus tasks can be 'reciprocal' or 'non-reciprocal' (see Chapter 2 for a discussion of this distinction). A task can also vary in terms of scope, which can be 'narrow', i.e. the input and expected response are minimal, or 'broad', i.e. the input and expected response are extended. Douglas notes that 'there is a trend in the testing field generally towards longer, richer input and responses' (Douglas 2000: 65). Finally, the task may require a 'direct' response, where the response is highly dependent on the input, or an 'indirect' response, where the testee relies more on specific purpose background knowledge.

5 *Assessment*

> This concerns the criteria that are used to evaluate performance on the task. Douglas emphasizes the need to establish 'indigenous assessment criteria', i.e. the criteria used by participants in the TLU task to establish whether the performance of the task has been successful or not. These criteria serve to formulate a definition of the construct of the specific purpose language ability that is to be assessed. Assessment criteria are considered in more detail below.

This framework provides a clear and comprehensive means for analysing TLU tasks in terms of the characteristics that must be incorporated into the design of assessment tasks. It emphasizes the need to achieve as close a match as possible to ensure that the appropriate 'internal context' (which, following Selinker and Douglas 1985, Douglas calls 'discourse domain') is activated in the testee. However, the problems of achieving a close match need to be acknowledged, as indeed Douglas does by noting that this cannot be achieved 'scientifically' but must call on the 'art of LSP testing' (ibid. 113). Precisely what this entails, however, remains unspecified.

Integrating the two approaches to task design

The two approaches to task design that we have now considered are very different, reflecting the different kinds of tests involved. In the case of tasks intended for use in system-referenced tests, a psycholinguistic approach has been adopted. That is, task design is based on some general theory of how language is stored and/or used. The emphasis here is on how tasks affect the way language is processed in production. In the case of tasks intended for performance-referenced tests, where it is necessary to target highly specific uses of language, the approach has been driven by the long-established techniques of needs analysis (see, for example, Munby 1978). We might ask, however, whether the two approaches need to be so distinct and whether each type of test might benefit from the approach adopted by the other.

Missing entirely in the psycholinguistic approach is any consideration of the content of the tasks to be used. The focus is exclusively on the design and implementational properties that affect performance. Yet, clearly, a task must have a content—an appropriate discourse domain must be activated in the testee. Of course, given that the purpose of a system-referenced test is to provide a general assessment of the learner's proficiency it will not be possible to identify specific TLU tasks for transformation into test tasks. But it will be necessary to identify what we might call 'stereotypical tasks', reflecting the kinds of context in which general-purpose learners can be expected to perform. Examples of such tasks are 'asking for street directions' or 'sharing personal information about one's family'. Such topics are precisely the ones that figure in the tasks used in oral-proficiency tests of the kind discussed by Chalhoub-Delville (2001). It would seem sensible to try to ensure that tasks based on such topics are as authentic as possible. The framework proposed by Douglas provides a means for analysing TLU tasks to achieve authenticity.

Missing from the needs-analysis approach employed in the design of LSP tests is any consideration of the psycholinguistic dimensions of tasks and how these affect performance. Douglas' specification of the 'language construct' for such tests is based entirely on analysis of indigenous assessment criteria and is framed in terms of the language knowledge, strategic competence and background knowledge that testees need to accomplish the task, i.e. in terms of the kind of model of communicative competence favoured by Bachman (1990). This framework, as Skehan (1998a) has pointed out, does not incorporate how the way language is stored affects the way it is used in real-time performance. However, it would be quite possible for designers of LSP tests, once they have identified the context they wish to sample, to attend to the kinds of dimensions listed in Table 9.2 above.

In short, the different approaches adopted in task-based system-referenced and performance-referenced testing could be usefully integrated. Norris, Brown, and Hudson (2000) illustrate how this might be achieved. They prepared 13 tasks reflecting a variety of general domains of language use (health, recreation, work, food and dining, domestic, and academic). Sample tasks are:

1   Evaluate credit card offers based on a banking 'tips' sheet
2   Order pizzas after listening to friends' preferences
3   Pay the appropriate bills using cheques.

The tasks were designed to represent six levels of difficulty according to combinations of variables representing code complexity, cognitive complexity and communicative demand, i.e. variables similar to those shown in Table 9.2. For example, Task 1 above was classified as level 6 (complex) because it was cognitively challenging in all three areas while Task 2 was classified as level 2 (simple) because it was challenging in only one area (communicative demand). Task 3 was deemed to be level 4 (intermediate) because it was demanding in two of the three areas (code complexity and cognitive complexity). However, the study designed to evaluate the predictive value of these three factors failed to find any relationship between task level and success in performing the tasks, i.e. the ability to perform a level 6 (complex) task did not necessarily entail the ability to perform a lower level (simpler) task. This failure mirrored the failure of other studies to establish the factors that influence task complexity in a testing situation (see the discussion on p. 288–9). However, Norris, Brown, and Hudson's study is important because it demonstrates how the psycholinguistic and needs-analysis traditions of direct testing might be combined.

Implementation procedures

Research on tasks has shown that what we have called 'procedures' for implementing a task in the classroom (see Figure 1.4 in Chapter 1) can have a profound effect on the resulting performance. It is, therefore, somewhat surprising to note that language testers have largely ignored this aspect of test tasks. Here we will consider two testing procedures that have received some attention.

Planning time

There is ample research to show that planning time can affect a language learner's performance of a task in a teaching or laboratory context by enhancing the fluency and complexity, and sometimes accuracy, of learners' productions (see Chapter 4). The question arises as to whether it can have a similar effect in a testing context. This is of considerable importance given that testers in general are concerned to elicit the 'best performance' from a testee (see McNamara 1997). If planning time can improve a test-taker's performance then arguably it ought to be adopted as a key implementation procedure.[7]

Three research studies have investigated planning in a testing situation. They were briefly mentioned in Chapter 4 but will be considered in detail here. Wigglesworth (1997b) examined the performances of 107 adult ESL learners performing five tasks that were part of the Australian Assessment of Communicative Skills (Access) test. The candidates performed the tasks in a planned and unplanned condition.[8] The performances were rated by two trained raters using an analytic rating scale to measure fluency, grammar (or, in one, task vocabulary), and intelligibility The performances of 28 of the 107 candidates, who were divided into high- and low-proficiency groups, were transcribed and analysed using measures of complexity, fluency, and accuracy. Wigglesworth reported no significant differences in the rating scores for the planned and unplanned conditions but significant differences in the analytic discourse measures for complexity, fluency, and accuracy, especially in the high-proficiency candidates and especially in tasks with a high cognitive load. She concludes that at least for some learners and in some tasks planning time can help to improve the performance of test-takers but that this effect is not evident in external ratings.

In a second study, Wigglesworth (2001) sought to further investigate one of the findings of the previous study, namely that the effects of planning time were not evident in the scores obtained from raters. The study examined the effect of a number of test task variables, one of which was planning, on adult

ESL learners' performance on five tasks that were routinely used to evaluate achievement in the Australian Adult Migrant Education Program. In this study an effect for planning was found on the test-takers' ratings but the effect was not as might have been expected. Planning proved to have a detrimental effect on tasks that were familiar to the candidates and on both structured and unstructured tasks. Wigglesworth notes that these results are inconsistent with previous findings and suggests that this may reflect the fact that her study used external ratings rather than discourse analytic measures. However, Iwashita, Elder, and McNamara (2001) used both analytic discourse measures and ratings to examine the effects of three minutes of planning time on the task performance of 201 ESL students and failed to find evidence of any effects on either the discourse measures or the rating scores.

The main conclusion to be drawn from these studies is the need for further research into the effects of planning in a test situation. It seems clear, however, that whatever effect planning time has on task performance it may not be reliably measured by an external rating. This is problematic where assessment is concerned, as it is not practical to calculate discourse analytic measures in testing situations.[9]

Interlocutor

Oral test tasks usually involve the testee interacting with an assessor or, in the case of the OPI, with an unfamiliar native speaker while a second native speaker assessor observes. Variability theory (for example, Bell 1984) and SLA research (for example, Tarone 1983) indicate that the addressee exerts a major influence on the L2 learner's production. Tarone and Liu (1995), for example, show that a five-year-old Chinese boy acquiring English in Australia was much more likely to manifest new developmental patterns in his speech when interacting with a familiar adult researcher than with his teacher. Thus, the question arises as to the impact of the interlocutor on a candidate's performance in a testing context.

Research undertaken from the perspective of sociocultural theory (see Chapter 6) is of considerable importance for understanding the role that social interaction plays in the performance of an assessment task. As Swain (2000b: 5) points out, 'performance is not a solo performance, but rests on a joint construction by the participating individuals'. She points to a number of implications for language testing. The first is that 'serious thought needs to be given to the most adequate and fair means of scoring linguistic activity and its product'. The second is that it is necessary to give consideration to whom the candidate is asked to communicate with. Thirdly, Swain suggests that examining the content of the dialogues elicited by tasks can provide test-developers with targets for measurement, i.e. the analysis of performance in direct, task-based tasks can serve to identify what features to assess via indirect tests, as illustrated in her own research.

However, it is not clear to what extent the painstaking work such analysis involves is practical in most test-development (as opposed to research) contexts. Finally, Swain argues that test-designers need to examine the cognitive and strategic processing test-takers engage in when performing an assessment task.

The effect of the interlocutor on task performance has also been addressed in a number of studies conducted by language testers. Brown and Hill (1998) found that the interaction between a test candidate and their interlocutors depended crucially on the orientation of the latter. They distinguish between interlocutors who functioned as 'facilitators' by accommodating to candidates and those who acted as 'gatekeepers' and did not accommodate. The different roles adopted by the interlocutor affected the way the candidates' performances were rated. Wigglesworth (2001), in the study referred to above, found that whether the interlocutor was a native speaker (NS) or an unfamiliar non-native speaker (NNS) influenced performance in role-play tasks that required the participants to engage in negotiation. The task proved easier when it was performed with a NNS. Wigglesworth suggests a number of reasons for this—the learners may have been more relaxed interacting with NNSs, the raters may have compensated when rating candidates in NNS-NNS pairs, the learners may have been pushed to use more complex but less accurate language with the NS, or they may have responded to the power differential when interacting with the NS, who was a teacher. Fulcher (1996a) investigated Berkoff's (1985) claim that asking candidates to perform a test task in groups overcomes the problems of 'artificial conversation' between a 'distant examiner' and a 'nervous examinee'. Fulcher investigated 47 Greek-speaking students' performance and personal reactions to three tasks, one of which involved a group discussion. The students reported that they were more confident and least anxious in the group task. Not surprisingly, they also found it more enjoyable. A statistical analysis of the rating scores found that the group task was the easiest. These studies, therefore, indicate that if the aim is to elicit a 'best performance' it may be preferable to set up a testing situation where the candidates interact with another NNS rather than with a NS examiner.

Another interlocutor variable that might be expected to exert an effect on a test performance is gender. However, O'Loughlin (2001) in a study that examined the effect of the gender of the examiner in the oral interview component of the IELTS was unable to find any differences in either the ratings assigned to test-takers who interacted with either a male or female examiner or in qualitative aspects of their discourse, for example, overlaps and interruptions.

To conclude, the implementation of task-based tests clearly needs further study in order to identify which procedures impact on test performance. In particular, research is needed to investigate to what extent external ratings are influenced by implementation factors (see below). Also, research is needed to examine the effect of time pressure on test performances. In this respect, it should be recalled that Yuan and Ellis (2003) found that when learners had the opportunity to plan online their productions were more accurate (see Chapter 4). If this proved to be the case in a testing situation as well it would have important implications for TBA.

Measuring performance in task-based tests

Tasks do not of themselves provide a measure of the testees' language ability. They elicit a performance, which then needs to be assessed in some way. Thus a crucial dimension of a task-based test is the method used to assess performance. There are three principal methods available:

1 Direct assessment of task outcomes
2 Discourse analytic measures
3 External rating.

Each of these is discussed below. In addition, there is the question of who undertakes the assessment—a third-person assessor or the testee him/herself. This section will conclude with a brief consideration of self-assessment.

Direct assessment of task outcomes

Closed tasks that result in a solution that is either right or wrong lend themselves to *direct assessment* in terms of the outcome of the task. Open tasks, for example, an oral interview involving a personalized conversation, do not. Robinson and Ross (1996) provide a good example of a closed task that was assessed in terms of outcome. The task, a component of their Library Skills Reading Test, involved a direct assessment of students' procedural knowledge in performing authentic tasks in a university library. A sample task is reproduced in Figure 9.1. It requires students to locate a journal article relating to a particular topic in a library. The criterion for success in this task is whether a student could locate the article independently or needed the assistance of an instructor. Performance on the task was scored dichotomously, i.e. as a simple pass/fail.

There are obvious advantages of assessing tasks directly. It affords an objective measurement, involving no judgment on the part of the assessor, and it is easy and quick. However, there are also some disadvantages. Tasks involving the direct assessment of task outcomes are relatively difficult to administer as they generally involve the tester observing each candidate as he/she completes the task. However, this difficulty might be overcome if the task requires a written product (as does the task in Figure 9.1), which can be assessed after the task has been completed. The main

objection to direct assessment is that it is not clear to what extent it measures language ability as opposed to non-linguistic abilities or general
knowledge. For example, candidates may be successful in the task in
Figure 9.1 simply because they are familiar with the procedure for finding
a journal article in a library. Thus, arguably, this task does not tell us anything about the candidate's academic language skills.[10] This, however, is
more a problem of direct performance-referenced tasks derived from a
work-sampling approach than of the direct method of assessment itself.
Construct-derived tasks of the kind used in direct system-referenced
testing avoid this problem and lend themselves to direct assessment. For
example, a spot-the-difference task could be scored in terms of the number
of differences the participants were able to identify. In this case, the valid-

---

INSTRUCTIONS

Do each step of the task in turn. Please do not consult with any other student when
doing this task. If you find that you cannot go on, please stop and tell your teacher,
or the ELI representative. Please do not bother the librarians!

Step 1 (time limit ten minutes)

Consult the hardcover abstracts in the References Section of Hamilton Library and
find out as much as you can about the competition between the United States and
Japan to develop high technology computers.

Suggestion: Limit your search to a single article. Consult the *Sociological Abstracts* for
1987 first.

Key words: computers, Japan, United States, research

a) Write down the page number in *Sociological Abstracts* where you found the
abstract you need. _____
b) How difficult was it for you to find *Sociological Abstracts*?

Very difficult   0   1   2   3   4   5   6   7   Very easy

Step 2 (time limit five minutes)

Look around the Reference Section until you find the blue or green covered Current
Periodicals List. Check immediately in the Current Periodicals List to see if Hamilton
Library has the journal you need.

a) Write down the call number of the journal you need. _____
b) How difficult was finding the journal in the Current Periodicals List?

Very difficult   0   1   2   3   4   5   6   7   Very easy

---

*Figure 9.1: Direct performance-referenced task from the Library Skills
Reading Test (Robinson and Ross 1996: 474–5)*

ity of the score is less questionable, as success in the task will clearly be dependent on the participants' language abilities.

Discourse analytic methods

Discourse analytic methods provide counts of specific linguistic features occurring in the discourse that results from performing the task. The features so measured are varied. They can focus on the candidate's linguistic competence, for example, the measures of fluency, accuracy, and complexity used in the task-based research reported in Chapter 4; on their sociolinguistic competence, for example, a measure of appropriate use of requesting strategies; on their discourse competence, for example, a measure of appropriate use of cohesive markers; or on their strategic competence, for example, a measure based on the use of strategies used to negotiate meaning. Discourse analytic measures afford a more or less objective measure of the specific aspects of the testees' performance that have been chosen for assessment. On the face of it, they also constitute a direct measure of performance. However, this is disputable, as discourse analysis is far removed from how we judge communicative behaviour in the real world—we do not, for example, generally judge how effectively someone has communicated by assessing to what extent their language is fluent, complex, or accurate.

Discourse analytic measures have been widely used in task-based research. However, they require a transcript of the task performance to be prepared—a time-consuming operation—and, for this reason, are understandably not considered practical by testers. However, although discourse analytic methods are generally not used in TBA, they have been employed in research into task-based tests, primarily as a means of comparing the assessments afforded by discourse analytic methods and external rating.

External ratings

External ratings, like the direct assessment of tasks, involve the assessor observing a performance of a task and making a judgment. They differ from direct assessment in one crucial respect—the nature of the judgment that is made. In direct assessment the judgment is essentially objective, i.e. the testee did or did not succeed in performing the task. In external ratings, the judgment is more subjective, although, of course efforts are made to ensure that it is reliable.

External ratings based on scales are the most common method of assessing performance on task-based tests of both the system-referenced and performance-referenced kinds. These scales specify (1) the competency, i.e. what is being measured, and (2) the levels of performance (often referred

Band	Descriptor
4	Route marked correctly in all details
3	Starting point and end point marked correctly but route contains one error.
2	Starting point and end point marked correctly but route contains two or more errors
1	Starting point marked correctly but fails to mark rest of route correctly including end point
0	No route drawn or unable to locate starting and finishing points on the map.

Table 9.3: Rating scale for a map task

to as 'bands'). However, an alternative kind of external rating involves a checklist of competencies, which can be ticked off according to the specific competencies the candidate has demonstrated (see, for example, the Certificate in Spoken and Written English, Hagan *et al.* 1993). Such an approach yields valuable diagnostic information.

In task-based tests the target competency can be specified in behavioural terms relating to task fulfillment or it can be expressed in linguistic terms. Table 9.3 gives an example of a rating system where the competency is behavioural. The competency is derived directly from the task, which required the candidates to read a letter containing directions about how to reach a particular location and mark the route to be followed on a map. One problem with rating scales measuring task fulfillment in this way is that the scales will need to be task-dependent, i.e. a different scale is required for each task. Norris, Brown, and Hudson (2000), in the study referred to earlier, developed a task-dependent rating scale for each of the 13 tasks they designed. It is also possible to devise scales that incorporate both behavioural and linguistic competencies. Baker (1989) gives an example of such a rating scale for a task requiring candidates to hire a car. Here the behavioural competency is whether the candidates were successful in hiring the car, while the linguistic competency concerned the smoothness of the communication with the car-hirer, for example, Band 3: 'Car hired with occasional breakdowns in communication'. The choice of a behavioural or linguistic competency raises, once again, the issue of what the test is measuring—language ability or general ability to perform the task.

Where the competency is linguistic the question arises as to how this competency should be specified—that is, which linguistic aspects of the task performance are to be measured. A basic choice is between a holistic measure of linguistic competency (as illustrated in Table 9.4) and an analytic measure, where different dimensions of linguistic ability, for example, the four language skills, are identified for rating separately. Many direct tests,

300   *Task-based Language Learning and Teaching*

Band	Descriptor
5	Speaking proficiency equivalent to that of an educated native speaker.
4	Would rarely be taken for a native speaker but can respond appropriately even in unfamiliar situations. Can handle informal interpreting from and into language.
3	Participate effectively in most formal and informal conversation on practical, social, and professional topics.
2	Able to satisfy routine social demands and work requirements, needing help in handling any complication or difficulties.
1	Can ask and answer questions on topics very familiar to him (sic), able to satisfy routine travel needs and minimum courtesy requirements. (Should be able to order a simple meal, ask for shelter or lodging, and give simple directions, make purchases and tell time).

Table 9.4: Holistic rating scale used in the Interagency Language Roundtable/Foreign Service Institute (ILR/FSI) oral interview.

such as the OPI, include both. If an analytic scale is employed, further decisions need to be made regarding the specific dimensions to be targeted. Skehan (1998) argues rightly that the dimensions chosen need to be principled in the sense that they connect to some underlying theory of language or language processing. His own preference is for linguistic competency to be specified in terms of the three dimensions that figure in his own research—accuracy, complexity, and fluency. However, many test designers prefer to specify competencies in more functional terms, for example, speaking ability at the 'expert' level in the oral interview component of the old ELTS test was specified as 'Speaks with authority on a variety of topics. Can initiate, expand and develop a theme'. Theories of communicative competence or performance (for example, Canale and Swain 1980; Bachman 1990) have also been used as a basis for determining the competencies to be measured.

Competencies are defined in terms of performance levels or checklists. The questions that arise here are 'How are the levels/checklists to be determined?' and 'On what basis is the criterion level to be chosen?' McNamara (1996) provides a detailed account of scale levels and the development of descriptors for them. He distinguishes two approaches. In the theoretically-driven approach, descriptors can be context-driven, as in competency-based language assessment, where criterion behaviours are specified and checked off, or they can be derived conceptually, where descriptors of different levels are developed in terms of the linguistic skill displayed. In this case, the highest level is typically framed in terms of 'native-like proficiency' (or, in some cases, such as IELTS, as 'expert user'). But the problem here is that native-speaker performance on the tasks has generally not been established empirically. McNamara reports a study of an EAP reading test which demonstrated that performance of native speakers taking the test was far from uniform, reflecting the educational level and work experience of the test-takers. He concludes that 'the expert user is indeed an elusive creature' (ibid. 193).

The alternative approach is to develop descriptors empirically. This can be undertaken statistically using a technique known as 'content-referencing', based on Rasch scaling procedure, which allows the relationship between different items in a test and general abilities to be deduced to form a developmental scale.[11] McNamara notes that relatively few scales have been developed following such a procedure. However, a good example can be found in North (1995). North describes the procedure he followed in developing a common framework scale of descriptors for assessing the English language proficiency of Swiss learners. This involved developing a descriptor pool by asking experienced teachers to sort and evaluate descriptors drawn from 30 scales of language proficiency and then using the descriptors so identified to construct overlapping questionnaires. These were then completed by 120 teachers, who each selected five learners to rate. The ratings were then subjected to a Rasch analysis, which identified a number of problems, each of which was then systematically addressed. North's research serves as a model for how to scale the statements that make up a rating scale. Scales can also be developed empirically using insights from discourse analysis. For example, Fulcher (1996b) recorded students' performances on speaking tests, identified the features that contributed to fluency, and used these to construct descriptors in a rating scale, which was then trialled on a new sample of students.

Defining the test criterion level in a scale is even more problematic. Clearly, the level must depend upon the performance criterion and, therefore, is necessarily relative. For this reason, it is often left up to the stakeholder and often appears to be chosen fairly arbitrarily. For example, at the University of Auckland the criterion level for entry into undergraduate courses in the faculty of Arts is 6.0 on IELTS and for entry into most graduate courses 6.5. The basis for choosing this level and the distinction between the criterion level for graduate and undergraduate students remains unstated and probably simply reflects the practice of similar universities. Bachman, Lynch, and Mason's (1995) study provides further evidence of arbitrariness. They describe a test (the Language Ability Assessment System) designed to determine which undergraduate students possessed sufficient confidence in their foreign language to enable them to engage in a full academic immersion programme overseas. In the case of the grammar-rating scale they chose level 4 (in a seven-level scale) as the criterion level. This states 'A large but complete range. Control of some structures used, but with many error types.' However, they offer no explanation for why such a level is needed or sufficient for immersion education in a foreign language.

Rating scales have to be applied. Thus, a crucial factor in tests employing rating scales is the rater. This is discussed later in the section dealing with problems in TBA.

Self-assessment

There is the question of who performs the assessment—an external assessor or the testee him/herself. Both direct assessment and ratings of task perform- ance (but not discourse analytic measurement) can be carried out through *self-assessment*. The task in Figure 9.1 provides a simple example of how candidates might be asked to assess task-fulfillment. More complicated analytic instruments (similar to the rating scales discussed above) will be needed for the self-assessment of linguistic competency.

Self-assessment has a number of practical and educational advantages. It is less time-consuming and also less expensive to carry out than methods of assessment that rely on external ratings. Crucially, also it can help fulfill educational goals in situations where one of the main purposes of instruction is to develop the ability of learners to take control of their own learning. It can serve as a means of developing a reflective attitude in the learner and can stimulate goal setting. In this respect, self-assessment is to be seen as a component of formative assessment, which is discussed later in this chapter.

The crucial issues regarding self-assessment are its validity and reliability. To what extent are candidates capable of providing accurate assessments of their own performance? A number of studies have investigated this. For example, Bachman (1990: 148) refers to two studies showing that the manner in which the self-rating questions are framed affects the test-takers' responses. Questions that refer to the test-takers' actual needs and situations rather than to abstract linguistic abilities serve as better indicators of language proficiency. Similarly, questions that ask them to judge how difficult they find different aspects of language work better than questions about how well they can use the language. Some studies, however, suggest that self-assessment lacks predictive and concurrent validity. Sasaki (2000), for example, found that self-assessment scores and objectively-measured Japanese language scores were not related and concluded that they represented 'different mental traits'. Sasaki suggests this may have been because the instrument she used (the Japanese Self-Assessment Questionnaire) had generic rather than specific specifications of the target performance, thus supporting Bachman's claim. Reliability measured in terms of internal consistency is generally high in self-assessment but test-retest reliability is more questionable, for example, Sasaki reported a very low correlation between scores from two administrations of her questionnaire. Overall, however, self-assessment appears to be capable of affording measurements that are both valid and reliable. As Oscarson (1997: 182), in a review of self-assessment studies, points out, 'although no consensus has been reached on the merits of the self-assessment approach, a clear majority of the studies surveyed report generally favourable results'.

Final comment

To conclude, the measurement of test-task performances in order to arrive at an assessment of the test-taker's ability is a crucial aspect of TBA. As Brindley (1994: 90) points out, it will involve assessments that are 'complex, qualitative, and multidimensional, rather than uniform and standardized'. The challenge is not just to develop a method that provides valid and reliable measurements, but also one that is practical and cost-effective.

Designing a task-based test

Now we have considered in some detail the various components of a task-based test we are in a position to describe the procedure for developing such a test. The procedure outlined below is a composite of proposals advanced by Bachman, Lynch, and Mason (1995), Douglas (2000) and McNamara (1996). It is applicable to the development of both system-referenced and performance-referenced task-based tests. Step 3, however, is more relevant to a performance-referenced test.

STEP 1: This involves two procedures, which need to be undertaken concurrently and interactively:
(a) Articulate the test rationale. McNamara (1996) suggests that to achieve this it is necessary to be clear about who wants to know, what they want to know about, about whom the information is required, and for what purpose information is being sought.
(b) Identify a set of theoretical principles to guide the test development, for example, one of the principles Bachman, Lynch, and Mason based their test on was 'Present test-takers with authentic materials and tasks'. Above, it has been proposed that task-based tests, whether of the system-referenced or performance-referenced kinds, need to define the construct ('language ability') that is to be measured.

STEP 2: Establish what resources there are and what constraints exist. These will need to be taken into account in all the subsequent steps.

STEP 3: Undertake a needs analysis to establish what target language use (TLU) tasks need to be sampled. In addition to observation, this will involve an approach based on grounded ethnography, i.e. describing and understanding

TLU tasks from the perspective of language users who perform them, and subject-specialist informants (see Douglas for a detailed account). McNamara includes the collection and examination of authentic texts in this step.

STEP 4: Draw up a set of test specifications. This constitutes an outline of the purpose of the test, the TLU situation that is being sampled, the characteristics of the test-takers, the construct that is being measured, the content of the test, the implementational procedures, the criterion for success on the test, samples of test tasks, and the assessment method. These specifications can then be shown to expert informants and to stake-holders for comment and revised accordingly.

STEP 5: Select and train an initial team of raters if an external rating system is to be used.

STEP 6: Trial the test. Bachman, Lynch, and Mason (1995) trialled different parts of their test with different groups of test-takers, then conducted larger group trials and finally carried out an operational field trial.

STEP 7: Analyse the data obtained from trialling the test and revise the test specifications and the test itself. Analysis will involve using appropriate statistical procedures to determine the validity and reliability of the test tasks (see J.D. Brown (1988) for an account of standard correlation procedures used in test development and McNamara (1996) for a general account of Rasch analytic techniques including multi-faceted procedures). Revision may involve changes to the content, structure, and format of the task, to implementational procedures, and to the method of assessment.

STEP 8: Select and carry out final training with a team of raters if these are required. The test is then ready for implementation. However, test development is an ongoing process and further changes may be needed as more data become available and are analysed. Thus potentially all of the steps outlined above are iterative.

Some problems with task-based assessment

In the course of our exploration of task-based teaching we have encountered a number of problems, which we will now examine in some detail. Some are common to all kinds of testing but some are specific to task-based testing. The following issues will be considered: (1) representativeness; (2) authenticity; (3) generalizability; (4) inseparability; and (5) reliability.

Representativeness

To what extent should a task-based test seek to elicit a representative or a 'best' performance from candidates? This becomes a key issue in task-based testing because of the research that has shown that implementational variables such as planning and interlocutor can have an effect on a testees' performance. Wigglesworth (1997b) suggests that there is a tension in a testing situation between the need to elicit the best possible performance from a candidate and the need to examine performance that is representative of real-world language use. She notes, for example, that in real life there is usually no opportunity to plan a task. In the case of oral interview tests a similar problem arises with regard to the role of the interviewer. As He and Young (1998: 8) point out, 'LPIs (language proficiency interviews) do not simply sample an ability that exists in the learner prior to the interview; rather they actually produce or fabricate the abilities they supposedly measure'. Clearly, then, the manner in which the interviewer interacts with candidates will influence how they perform and thereby the rating they obtain (see Brown and Hill 1998). Should the interviewer adopt a formal, distant 'test-like' stance, or a more informal, friendly, supportive stance? To what extent should the interviewer attempt to 'scaffold' the candidates' productions?

These are not easy questions to answer. One possible answer, suggested by Wigglesworth, is that the test should seek to ensure the same implementational conditions as candidates will experience in the target language use situation. In contrast, H.D. Brown (1994) includes 'giving students advance preparation' as one of the principles that need to be followed in creating 'interactive and intrinsically motivating tests'. He sees the role of the test designer as that of being an ally of the testee. Minimally, as part of the test specifications, test designers should make explicit what kind of performance they are attempting to measure.

Authenticity

Authenticity is generally discussed in terms of language specific purpose testing, i.e. in relation to direct performance-referenced tests, although it is of equal relevance to direct system-referenced tests. The discussion draws heavily on Widdowson's (1979) distinction between 'genuine' texts and 'authentic' discourse. Texts are genuine if they are taken from the real world rather than contrived for some pedagogic purpose. Discourse is authentic (or rather authenticated) when language users engage their 'language capacity' in order to interact with a text (genuine or contrived). Bachman (1990) makes a similar distinction in the context of assessment, distinguishing situational *authenticity*, i.e. do the test task's characteristics match those of the target-language task?, and interactional authenticity, i.e. is the test taker engaged in the task? Bachman argues that for a test task to be authentic it must achieve both situational and interactional authenticity. As Douglas (2001: 48) puts it, 'mere emulation of a target situation in the test is not sufficient to guarantee communicative language use'.

Establishing situational authenticity is problematic enough. In a discussion of the problems she faced in developing a direct performance-referenced test to assess teachers' ability to use an L2 as the medium of classroom instruction, Elder (2000) has pointed out that even in an area where there is a considerable literature (teacher talk), domain definition is not easy. She comments that when faced with the problem of modelling and sampling classroom genres systematically and of arriving at a test content that was capable of providing a measure of general proficiency in this domain 'we have no other option than to settle for an expedient solution to domain definition'. Thus, the test developer has to trade off the real and ideal, hoping to retain 'something of the communicative "flavour" of the TLU tasks'. Elder's account of the difficulty she encountered in establishing situational authenticity suggests that Douglas' (2000) procedure for ensuring equivalence between TLU tasks and test tasks (outlined on p. 290) may prove difficult to implement in at least some contexts.

Guaranteeing 'interactional authenticity' is even more problematic. The difficulty lies within the nature of the testing situation itself. Tests require candidates to display what they know and what they can do and thus are likely to give rise to 'a test genre construct' (Shohamy, Donitsa-Schmidt, and Waizer 1993) that differs markedly from naturally occurring discourse. Evidence for this claim comes from research that has investigated the interactional properties of discourse in the OPI. Johnson and Tyler (1998), for example, undertook an analysis of a representative sample of OPI discourse involving a level-2 speaker in order to address the question posed by van Lier (1989: 28): 'Is it really a conversation?' This is their conclusion:

> Our analysis reveals that in terms of such prototypical aspects of every-day conversation as turn-taking phenomena and topic nomination, this model OPI does not conform to normal conversation. In addition, the analysis of the interviewers' contributions reveals a distinct lack of the features of conversational involvement and shows of responsiveness that are prevalent in natural, friendly, everyday conversation. We conclude that the face-to-face exchange that occurs in this OPI interview cannot be considered a valid example of a typical, real-life conversation.

Thus, interactional authenticity in a test situation may be a chimera (Davies 1978). Of course, it may be more feasible in other forms of direct performance tests, for example, in monological oral tests or in tests of reading or writing, but this remains to be demonstrated.

What solutions are there to this problem then? Douglas (2001) offers none except the recommendation that testers strive to achieve as much situational and interactional authenticity as they can. Doye (1991: 106) argues that it is not economic to strive for situational authenticity and that we should remove the 'incidentals' that do not impact on the specific ability being tested: 'We should endeavour to employ just the amount of realism that makes it (the test) understandable but no more.' Authenticity is to be balanced by abstraction. Doye gives an example of how this can be achieved in a test designed to assess candidates' ability to ask for information. Drawing on speech act theory, he suggests that 'essential authenticity' can be achieved by ensuring that the two preparatory conditions for this act, i.e. the speaker does not know the answer and it is not obvious that the hearer will provide the information without being asked, are met. This can be done by muffling parts of a text that students are asked to listen to and thus obligating them to ask the tester questions. In effect, Doye's proposal entails an abandonment of direct testing in favour of indirect performance testing, which, by definition, does not seek to achieve either situational or interactional authenticity. Where interactional authenticity is concerned, Elder (2001) suggests that, as part of the process of test development, it is necessary to establish that the discourse that the test tasks elicit bear a reasonable resemblance to that observed in TLU tasks.

Discussion concerning the role of authenticity in language testing has taken place at a theoretical level. There has been relatively little empirical research examining such questions as 'Which characteristics are critical for distinguishing authentic from non-authentic test tasks?' or 'How important is authenticity for the various stakeholders of a test?' (Lewkowicz 2000: 51–2). The latter question seems of particular importance. To address it, Lewkowicz carried out a small scale study of 72 first-year students from the University of Hong Kong who had completed an 'English enhancement course' as part of their degree studies. They were administered two tests—one was based on a TOEFL practice test and consisted of multiple-choice items, the other was an EAP test which, in terms of the test characteristics described earlier in this chapter, was deemed to be 'reasonably authentic'. The students were asked to say which test they considered assessed what they had been taught in their enhancement course more accurately and also to identify the aspects of both tests that they considered important. Lewkowicz found that these test-takers' perceptions of the two tests varied widely and that authenticity was not universally important for them. Her findings endorse Bachman and Palmer's (1966) claim that stakeholders do not necessarily attach the same importance to authenticity as language testing experts.

Generalizability

Generalizability concerns the extent to which performance on a test is predictive of performance in situations found in the real world. It concerns the ecological validity of the test and thus goes to the very heart of assessment. How confident can we be of making decisions affecting the lives of individuals on the basis of their performance on the assessment tasks? A key element of the rationale for employing direct as opposed to indirect methods of assessment is that they are more generalizable.

Generalizability operates differently in direct system-referenced tests and direct performance-referenced tests. To understand the difference we need to distinguish two aspects of generalizability—breadth and specificity. In the case of direct system-referenced tests, as Baker (1989) has pointed out, the results cannot be extrapolated to any specific situation but rather are vaguely relevant to a wide range of needs and situations. For example, in a test involving 'pedagogic' type tasks we can measure learners' language proficiency in terms of accuracy, complexity, and fluency, and thus obtain a general picture of their ability to use the L2 in a wide range of contexts but, arguably, we will learn little of their ability to perform specific real-world tasks. In other words, direct system-referenced tasks have the advantage of breadth but are lacking in specificity.

The opposite is true of direct performance-referenced tests; they purport to provide valid estimations of candidates' ability to perform specific real-world tasks. The generalizability of such tests is, therefore, necessarily restricted to performance in a particular target task or type of target task. The question arises, however, as to what extent we can ever extrapolate from performance tasks to real-world situations. As Douglas (2001: 49), a proponent of LSP testing, acknowledges, 'It has proven very difficult to make predictions of non-test performance in the 'real-life' target situation on the basis of a single test performance, no matter how true to 'real life' the test tasks might be'. This is so, Douglas explains, because of the impossibility of adequately sampling even the most specific of target language use tasks. Douglas' solution to this problem is to ensure that the test tasks and the TLU tasks share similar characteristics (using the framework described earlier in this chapter). However, although matching test and TLU tasks may ensure situational authenticity, it cannot guarantee interactional authenticity. Ultimately the best way of demonstrating the generalizability of a test task is through research that compares performance in the test with performance in the real world and shows them to be similar.

A broad solution to the problem of generalizability might be to construct direct tests that combine system-referenced and performance-referenced methods. Note that such tests would be entirely task-based but that different types of tasks would need to be used, i.e. tasks of a 'pedagogic' nature and tasks derived from TLU tasks. Such a composite test would cater to both breadth and specificity. At this point in time, however, it is not clear what such a composite test would look like. One way forward might be to conduct research that examines the relationship between scores obtained from direct system-referenced and performance-referenced tests. This information might be used to address the need for a composite test and also the relative weighting to be given to scores obtained from the two types of test.

Inseparability

In TBA, language ability is measured in relation to some subject content. In the case of direct system-referenced tests, the tasks chosen are likely to reflect subject content of a general or personalized nature drawn from what Morrow (1979) referred to as 'ordinary situations' in order to ensure that it is familiar to test-takers. The tasks in Norris, Brown, and Hudson (2000), illustrated on p. 292, serve as examples of such tasks. In this way, it is hoped to obtain a measure of language ability that is not confounded with the test-taker's world knowledge. Of course, this is probably not entirely achievable but it is reasonable to assume that, with care, tasks can be designed that are reasonably 'content-fair', i.e. do not advantage specific groups of test-takers.

In the case of direct performance-referenced tests, however, the problem is more acute as, necessarily, the tasks used must reflect the specific purpose content of the TLU task. In other words, language ability cannot be assessed separately from subject content. As McNamara (1996) has pointed out, this can lead to an 'ambiguity of focus' about the choice of criteria for assessment. Should rating scales be framed in entirely linguistic terms, in entirely behavioural terms or in a combination of the two (see earlier discussion)? And, even if linguistic descriptors are used, to what extent is it possible to separate the test-takers' use of language from their real-world expertise, given that the task, through design, integrates the two? Douglas' (2001) answer to this question is that because language knowledge and specific purpose background knowledge are 'inextricably intertwined' separation is impossible and should not be attempted.[12] Thus he defines specific purpose language ability as comprising both types of knowledge and argues that 'until we know more about how the mind deals with abilities and knowledge, leave it at that' (ibid. 50). Interestingly, however, he provides an example where 'leaving it at that' is clearly not appropriate—when trainee medical practitioners perform poorly on a test of English for medical purposes it would obviously be desirable to know whether this is the result of poor English skills or lack of medical knowledge. In this case, Douglas suggests administering a separate test of medical knowledge to control for background knowledge but gives no indication of how such a language-free test might be designed.

Subject-background knowledge is not the only factor that can influence performance on test tasks—individual test-taker factors also play a part. Upshur (1979, cited in McNamara 1996) provides a telling example of how 'sensitivity to interlocutor' can influence success in a task. The task here was 'wooing an American teenager'. One candidate accomplished this task successfully by dint of talking little and allowing the girl to talk. A second candidate was unsuccessful as a result of talking too much! One of the obvious drawbacks of TBA is that candidates' performances are especially susceptible to variation due to individual factors such as personality and communicative style. Again, though, it might be argued that such factors do not need to be taken into account in assessing learners' ability to use language, as they are inseparable parts of real-life language use.

Reliability

We saw earlier that the early communicative language testing movement in the United Kingdom, as reflected in Morrow (1979), began by rejecting the traditional role that reliability has played in language testing. Similarly, protagonists of 'alternative assessment', for example, personal conferences, portfolios and self- and peer-assessment, have suggested that reliability is guaranteed by the form of assessment itself and does not have to be separately demonstrated (see Huerta-Macias 1995). However, as Brown and Hudson (1998) have argued, such a position is untenable if decision-making based on test results is to be responsible. Reliability remains a key issue in all kinds of assessment, including task-based testing.

Reliability refers to the extent to which a test measures a candidate's proficiency in an error-free manner. In the case of task-based assessment this is primarily evident when a repeat test or a second rating produces the same measure of proficiency.[13] There are a number of potential sources of unreliability:

1 The personal dispositions of the candidates; these are likely to be especially important in oral TBA as research has shown that anxiety is a major factor in both language use and achievement (for example, Gardner and McIntyre 1993).
2 Administrative conditions: a major concern here, especially in task-based tests that involve interaction with an assessor, is ensuring that the task is carried out consistently with different test-takers. Sociocultural theory (see Chapter 6) suggests that this is an impossibility as each performance is constructed jointly and dynamically by the participants.
3 Inconsistency in scoring procedures: as we noted earlier this is especially problematic when the method of scoring involves external ratings carried out by raters. This issue will now be considered in some detail.

The reliability problem associated with external ratings really involves two separate issues—the consistency with which a rater applies the scale when assessing different candidates and the extent to which different raters' ratings are in agreement. Intra-rater reliability is best achieved by ensuring that the raters have a solid understanding of the rating scale, for example, through training based on 'benchmark' exemplars of performances at different levels in the scale. Inter-rater reliability is more problematic and, indeed, controversial. Inconsistency stems from several sources. For example, Lumley and McNamara (1995) found that scores raters assigned to individual candidates were influenced by their assessment of whether the candidates' interlocutors were difficult or supportive. A. Brown (1993) found that the background of the raters impacted on their ratings; raters drawn from the Japanese tourist industry (tour guides) were much more severe than teachers when rating performance of a task that was seen as difficult but closely matched to the demands of tour-guiding. Reed and Cohen (2001) review the factors that have been found to result in discrepancies between raters—whether the rater is a native speaker or non-native speaker, the occupation of the rater, for example, specialist vs. non-specialist, gender, and the personality fit between the rater and the candidate. However, Shohamy (1995) has argued that it may be beneficial if raters do *not* agree, providing that they all have 'good' reasons for the rating they have assigned.

What solutions to these threats to the reliability of task-based assessments have been proposed? We will consider four here: (1) lengthening the test; (2) the use of two or more raters; (3) rater training; and (4) post hoc adjustment of scores based on statistical analysis. As in all testing, the longer the test, the more reliable the scores obtained from it are likely to be. In the case of direct tests, raters are more likely to arrive at a reliable rating of a candidate's performance if the test provides them with an extensive sample of language use. Also, averaging the scores assigned by two raters provides a more accurate judgment of the candidate's performance than relying on one. Bachman, Lynch, and Mason (1995), in the study referred to earlier, used two raters and also a third rater where the original raters' scores differed across the criterion level. In this case they used the two closest ratings to calculate the final score. However, they found that the gains in reliability from employing a third rater in this way were minimal. Asking raters to discuss their assessments when there is a major difference also enhances the reliability of the final score that is assigned (Gipps 1994). Rater-training is widely advocated but there is doubt about its efficacy. McNamara (1996), for example, reports that differences in rater severity following training may affect a candidate's chances of obtaining a given rating by as much as 40%. Post hoc adjustment of scores using the multi-faceted Rasch model allows discrepancies among raters to be compensated for, as long as they are internally consistent. This approach seems promising but involves considerable time and effort, which may not be practical in many testing situations. Overall, reliability is best ensured using a combination of these four methods.

This discussion of the problems of TBA is not intended to be comprehensive; the issue of practicality (for example, the cost of developing, administering, and scoring task-based tests is heavy in both time and money) has not been considered. Nor is this discussion intended to lead to the conclusion that TBA is undesirable. The gain in validity and the potential positive washback effect on teaching are more than sufficient to outweigh the disadvantages. The purpose of the discussion is to acknowledge the difficulties in order to provide a balanced view of TBA, for only when this is achieved can decision-making based on the results of task-based tests be safely undertaken. Also, the purpose is to emphasize the need for research in seeking solutions to the problems.

Formative task-based assessment

The foregoing discussion of TBA so far has been conducted in something of a vacuum. There has been no mention of the overall use to which assessment is to be put. Implicit in the discussion, however, has been the assumption that assessment serves as a basis for making high-stakes decisions about test-takers, for example, regarding certification, contractual accountability or admission to university. That is, TBA has been discussed in its *summative* role. Clearly, this is an important purpose for undertaking an assessment but it is probably not the most common use of TBA or the one that most concerns teachers. As Weir (2001: 121) points out:

> Teachers need to evaluate formatively, to make appropriate decisions concerning modifications to teaching procedures and learning activities and to steer their way through the syllabus in action, i.e. to shape and influence the process.

In this section we will briefly consider the role that TBA can play in *formative assessment* undertaken as part of an instructional programme for the purposes of improving learning and teaching.

Where formative assessment is concerned, TBA needs to be defined broadly. It will include the use of the kinds of testing instruments we have discussed in the preceding sections but also the on-going contextualized assessment that teachers undertake as they carry out task-based teaching. Thus, it will be helpful to distinguish two kinds of formative assessment involving tasks—planned and incidental. Both can contribute to the goals of monitoring progress and guiding instruction.

Planned formative assessment

Planned formative TBA involves the classroom use of direct tests of the system-referenced and performance-referenced kinds. The test-tasks used will be the same or of the same kind as those in the instructional programme for, as Spolsky (1992) notes, formative assessment is curriculum-driven. Brindley (2001: 131) considers that 'it is relatively easy to make the connection between teaching tasks and assessment tasks'. In planned formative assessment, though, tasks will need to be supplemented with some method for measuring the students' performance, as discussed earlier in this chapter (see p. 296) and this raises problems. Practical concerns, i.e. the availability of time and expertise in testing methods, are likely to dictate the method(s) chosen. Thus, the discourse-analytic method can be discounted. The direct assessment of task outcomes can be undertaken easily. It will be especially helpful in evaluating the task itself, for example, whether it is of an appropriate level of difficulty for the students, and thus can inform future task-selection, but it will not provide the teacher with much information about a student's language ability and how this develops over time. For this, some kind of external rating based on observation of students performing the task may be necessary. As teachers are unlikely to have the time to develop rating scales for each individual task, they may do better to make use of general, ready-made scales that have been validated for formal tests. Where possible, to assist the reliability of measurement, teachers should enlist the help of a second rater. The use of scales will make it possible for teachers to compare students' performance and arrive at estimations of their language abilities over time. They will also provide a means of offering students explicit feedback on their performance—a major goal of formative assessment. Self-assessments will also be valuable. In conjunction with external ratings, they will provide evidence of how accurately students are able to assess themselves and thus provide valuable information about their metacognitive skills. Janssen-van Dieten (2000) reports the result of a study designed to investigate the validity of self-assessment carried out by adult migrants with a low educational level. The students were trained to carry out self-assessment of their progress. The study found that training resulted in more accurate assessments and also higher scores in a writing test overall, although the differences between the groups receiving training and the control groups were not statistically significant. Janssen-van Dieten suggests that the crucial factor determining the efficacy of training for self-assessment is whether the learning environment is conducive to this form of assessment.

Regarding the procedure for conducting planned formative assessments Spolsky (1992) argues for a multi-level approach involving self-assessment, where students are given opportunities before and after units of instruction to assess their own performance, teacher-assessment, where teachers periodically assess their students' performances and discuss their respective assessments, and occasional third-person assessments that are discussed with the teacher.

To what extent do teachers actually engage in planned formative assessment? Research suggests not much. Brindley (1989) studied 131 teachers in the Adult Migrant Education Program in Australia and reported that they preferred to rely on the kind of incidental formative assessment discussed below. Weir (2001: 125) summarizes a number of studies he carried out and found a lack of a 'feelgood' factor among teachers where planned classroom testing was concerned. He concludes that 'there is a need to focus on the development of progress-sensitive performance tests for use during courses'.

Incidental formative assessment

Incidental formative assessment refers to the ad hoc assessment that teachers (and students) carry out as part of the process of performing a task that has been selected for instructional rather than assessment purposes. It is part of the online decision-making that arises in the course in performing a task in the classroom, as discussed in earlier chapters (see for example the section on Implementing Focused Tasks in Chapter 5 and the discussion of scaffolding in Chapter 6). It arises in and is accomplished through the 'instructional conversations' that tasks give rise to (see Chapter 8) and thus, as Rea-Dickens (2001) points out, this kind of formative assessment is indistinguishable from good teaching. Surprisingly, however, little attention has been paid to incidental formative assessment in the task-centred classroom. Gipps (1994: 130) comments 'describing and analyzing teachers' informal formative assessment is a complex and little attempted task'.

It may be useful to distinguish two types of incidental formative assessment; internal and external. Internal assessment occurs as part of the discourse through which a task is enacted. It takes place through teacher questioning and probing and, in particular, the various strategies for providing online feedback discussed in Chapters 3, 5, and 6. In accordance with the central rationale for task-based teaching (see Chapter 1), it contributes directly to the accomplishment of the task at hand and indirectly to L2 development. Incidental formative assessment of the external kind arises when teachers and students reflect on a task performance, either while it is taking place or on completion, and make mental or actual notes of what they notice. Rea-Dickens and Gardner (2000) provide examples of this kind of conscious, external assessment by teachers in the context of tasks performed in primary school classrooms by L2 learners. They identify four principal functions of such evaluations—as input for managing and planning teaching, as evidence of curricular learning and development, as evidence of learner attainment matched against externally prescribed targets and levels, and as evidence for evaluating their teaching. The internal assessments that teachers engage in while performing tasks doubtlessly provide a basis for their external assessments but little is known about how this is achieved.

Of particular interest is whether teachers' internal assessments are valid and reliable. Rea-Dickens and Gardner cite Harlen and James (1997: 376), who comment:

> The kind of information that is gathered by teachers in the course of teaching is not tidy, complete and self-consistent, but fragmentary and often contradictory.

The same authors argue, however, that this is an advantage because it reflects and documents the variability that arises when individual learners perform different tasks. This, as we have seen is a central problem in TBA. It is one that informal formative assessment is much better equipped to handle than more formal, 'one-shot' tests and arguably it is what constitutes its major strength. However, as Rea-Dickens and Gardner illustrate, teachers do not always record the language their students use accurately, for example, they may assign something that was said to the wrong student, and this is a potential threat to reliability.

To conclude this section, formative assessment of both the planned and incidental kind constitutes a common and important form of TBA. There is a need for both types. Brindley (1989) points out that planned formative assessment is necessary because it provides information that is explicit and systematic. Incidental formative assessment helps learners to construct a notion of the target standards towards which they strive and enables them to compare their actual performance with the desired performance. It also shows teachers how they are succeeding on a day-by-day basis. As Brindley (2001: 128) notes, 'with experience, many teachers become skilled judges and observers capable of evaluating the quality of language performances and making fine-grained diagnoses of learners' difficulties'. However, there is an obvious need for further research into the validity and reliability of the judgments that teachers make.

Conclusion

TBA (which in this chapter has been defined as direct testing) differs from task-based teaching (TBT) in two key respects. First, it requires greater attention to the choice of tasks. In testing and teaching, the tasks chosen should adequately sample the construct or domain that is to be taught/assessed. But whereas in testing this is essential for validity, in teaching it is merely desirable—teachers can afford to adopt a more hit-and-miss approach based on experience and, perhaps, their knowledge of research findings. The problem is that tasks are a source of variability in language use and 'neither the nature nor the degree of the effect of tasks on scores from tasks is well understood' (Fulcher 1997). Teachers must and do live with such uncertainty. Testers cannot do so, for, as Widdowson (2001) points out, they are in the business of establishing 'conventions of certainty'. Teachers cope with the problem of variability by varying the types of task they select. Interestingly, this is the solution also proposed for TBA—base assessment on multiple tasks. But this is simply hedging one's bets; it does not guarantee certainty. Nor is it very practical in many cases.

The second difference between TBA and TBT concerns the measurement of task performances. Again, the difference is not absolute, for, as we have seen, formative assessment is an intrinsic part of TBT. But whereas task-based tests must necessarily provide an explicit means of measuring performance, TBT is not so obligated. What we have called incidental formative assessment is undertaken 'on the hoof' as one of the teachers interviewed by Rea-Dickens and Gardner (2000) put it and is a largely implicit affair. As we have seen, developing explicit measures of task performances that are valid and reliable is a complex and time-consuming business, requiring considerable expertise. The success of task-based tests depends very much on whether such measures can be developed.

Two conclusions emerge from this. The first is that TBA has to be seen as 'a long-term rather than short-term investment' (Brindley 1994). It will require considerable research to ensure that tasks and methods of measurement are valid and reliable and, in the eyes of some (for example, Widdowson 2001), it cannot be achieved. Second, TBA need not and probably should not be used by itself but rather in combination with indirect methods of assessment, not just because reliability is easier to guarantee in such methods but because, as Brown and Hudson (1998: 657) point out 'virtually all of the various test types are useful for some purpose, somewhere, sometime.'

Notes

1 Institutional tests are often of a 'mixed' type, i.e. they contain components that belong to more than one type of testing. IELTS, for example, contains components of the direct performance-reference type, (the speaking component), and the indirect performance-referenced type (the listening component).

2 There are contexts in which a dictation can function as a direct performance-referenced test, for example, in a test designed to measure a secretary's ability to write down accurately what is dictated to him/her. Usually, however, dictation is used as an indirect system-referenced test.

3 These two types of TBA mirror the distinction that McNamara (1986) makes between performance tests of the strong type (where the tasks represent real-world tasks and performance is judged in real-world criteria) and of the weak type (where tasks can be more artificial, as in the OPI, and performance is judged in terms of the language ability manifested). Following Baker (1989), I have chosen to distinguish these two types in terms of whether they are system- and performance-referenced.

4 The OPI involves four stages: (1) a warm-up to put the test-taker at ease and to provide a tentative estimate of his/her proficiency; (2) Level Checks where the interviewer guides the test-taker through a number of topics to verify the preliminary estimate and afford the test-taker an opportunity to demonstrate what level of language can be handled confidently and accurately; (3) the Probes, where the interview raises the level of conversation to establish the limits of the test-taker's proficiency; and (4) the Wind-down, where the test-taker is put at ease by returning to a level of conversation he/she can handle easily. See Stansfield (1992).

5 Skehan (2001) acknowledges that the meta-analysis summarized in Table 9.2 is post hoc and that the conclusions drawn from it must be necessarily tentative.

6 Douglas (2000) describes in some detail the factors that need to be attended to ensure 'rich input'. Thus, the test designer needs to ensure that characteristics of the TLU input relating to the setting, the participants, the purpose for communicating, the form and content, the tone, the channel and modality, the norms of interaction, and the genre are identified and incorporated into the test task.

7 In fact, it is arguable whether a test should seek to elicit a testee's 'best performance', a point that is taken up in a later section of this chapter.

8 Unfortunately, Wigglesworth does not state the length of planning time provided in this study.

9 Elder (personal correspondence) makes another important point regarding the use of analytic discourse measures and ratings. She argues that if differences that are shown to exist at discourse level do not show up in the ratings this may be because they are not salient enough to make any difference in communication.

10 In fact, Robinson and Ross (1996) report that scores obtained from an indirect systemic placement test failed to provide an accurate prediction of students' performance on the library task. One interpretation of this result is that the students' general language proficiency was not a major factor in successful performance of the task.

11 McNamara (1996: 132–3) describes the Rasch model as follows:
    The model states that the likelihood of a particular rating on an item for a particular rater/candidate can be predicted mathematically from the ability of the candidate, the difficulty of the item and the severity of the rater.

12 Elder (2001) also points out the difficulty of separating language and content.

13 The reliability of a test can also be measured in terms of its internal consistency. This concerns, in particular, sources of error traceable to differences in test tasks and item formats. Split-half reliability estimates such as the Kuder-Richardson reliability coefficient are often used to measure the internal consistency of a test. Bachman (1990: 172ff.) provides a detailed account of the procedures that can be used. While test-retest reliability and rater consistency are arguably of greater importance in task-based assessment, internal consistency also needs to be considered.

10 Evaluating task-based pedagogy

Introduction

The previous chapters have explored the psycholinguistic rationale for the use of tasks in teaching, the empirical research on tasks that this rationale has spawned and practical considerations regarding the design of task-based courses, their implementation in the classroom, and the development of task-based tests. It is notable that, despite the disparities in the nature of the psycholinguistic underpinnings, there is a broad consensus that 'task' is a construct that can guide and shape both pedagogy and assessment. This reflects the importance that all the psycholinguistic theories we have considered attach to the centrality of meaning-making in second language (L2) acquisition and, by extension, in language pedagogy and language assessment. No matter whether the theory was based on a view of language use/learning as information-processing (as in, for example, the Interaction Hypothesis or Skehan's cognitive theory) or as constructivist (as in the case of sociocultural SLA), language learning is seen as a process that requires opportunities for learners to participate in communication where making meaning is primary. 'Task' is a tool for engaging learners in meaning-making and thereby for creating the conditions for language acquisition.

The various theories are agreed on another point—in addition to, and in the process of making meaning, learners need to attend to and become aware of linguistic form. In information, processing models this premise is reflected in the Noticing Hypothesis (Schmidt 1990). In sociocultural SLA it is reflected in the mediational roles of social interaction and private speech in enabling learners to achieve higher levels of consciousness (Lantolf 2000a). Without attention to form learners' interlanguages may stabilize and fossilization set in. Learners who use their strategic competence to overcome their linguistic limitations and who are thereby able to participate adequately in meaning-making situations may lose the motivation to attend to form and, thus, cease to learn. Thus, the goal of pedagogy is not just to provide opportunities for meaning-making but also to ensure that learners are motivated to attend to form—to notice new linguistic features in the input and to work with their interlocutors to construct new zones of proximal development. Again, 'task' is seen as the ideal tool for achieving a focus on form. By manipulating the design features of a task and/or implementational procedures, learners can be encouraged to attend to form in the context of meaning-making. Much of the discussion in the preceding chapters has concerned how this integration of meaning and form can be achieved.

Thus, there is a clear psycholinguistic rationale (and substantial empirical support) for choosing 'task' as the basis for language pedagogy. One might expect, therefore, to find task-based courses figuring strongly in current language education. However, this is not the case. As Candlin (2001: 230) points out, there is a 'comparative lack of attention to tasks within language education in the context of educational systems'.[1] Similarly, task-based courses do not figure strongly in publishers' catalogues of teaching materials. Thus, while many published courses often claim to be 'task-based', a close inspection reveals that they are not—at best they are 'task-supported'. That is, there are few courses that are organized entirely around tasks but many that utilize more traditional designs involving the presentation and practice of discrete linguistic features with tasks providing opportunities for their free production. In other words, 'task' has generally been used not as the organizing principle of courses but as a methodological device for implementing the final step of a well-established methodological sequence, i.e. PPP, in linguistically organized courses. Nor is task-based teaching (as opposed to task-supported teaching) a feature of most initial teacher training programmes. The question arises as to why this is.

To address this question, it is necessary to go beyond the psycholinguistic perspective that has informed the previous chapters. I shall do this in two ways. First, I will consider the practicality of task-based teaching from an *innovationist perspective*. Second, I will argue that there has been a lack of empirical evaluations of task-based materials, which needs to be remedied. I will examine how they can be undertaken and report the results of two such evaluations, both of which provide grounds for optimism that task-based teaching can be both practical and effective. Finally, I will summarize and respond to a number of theoretical criticisms of task-based teaching by applied linguists working from an 'educational' rather than a psycholinguistic perspective.

An innovationist perspective

In this section we will examine the extent to which task-based teaching is likely to be adopted by practitioners by taking an innovationist perspective. Task-based language teaching can be viewed as an 'innovation' and its potential for adoption examined in accordance with the factors that have been found to influence uptake of innovations in general (see Markee 1997). As I pointed out in Ellis (1997a), innovation can be conceived in two different ways. First, in the absolutist sense, it can constitute a completely new idea. There are probably very few completely new peda-gogic ideas, although arguably Prabhu's Communicational Teaching Project constituted one at the time. Second, in the perceived sense, a peda-gogic proposal can be seen as an entirely new idea by the practitioners who engage with it, irrespective of whether the proposal has already been adopted by other practitioners operating in different contexts. For ex-ample, task-based teaching would constitute an innovation for many Japanese high school teachers of English. Given that 'task' is by now a very familiar construct, it is in the perceived rather than absolutist sense that it can be considered innovatory.

An innovation constitutes a 'threat' in the sense that it may challenge existing preconceptions about teaching and require teachers to adopt new routines to replace those with which they are familiar. Four sets of factors that govern how teachers cope with these threats can be identified. These are: (1) the sociocultural context of the innovation; (2) the personality and skills of the individual teachers; (3) the method of implementation; and (4) the attributes of the proposals themselves. (1) is discussed more fully in a later section of this chapter. Task-based teaching may not be well-suited to cultural contexts where the relationship between students and teacher is based on views about their relative status. With regard to (2), task-based teaching ideally requires that teachers are sufficiently proficient in the L2 to engage easily and comfortably in face-to-face interaction. Implementation will be problematic in contexts where teachers lack or are insecure about their oral proficiency. (3) is of crucial importance but is not directly concerned with the nature of the innovation itself and so will not be addressed here. We will focus on (4) as a way of asking what the likelihood is of instruction involving tasks being adopted.

Drawing on research into the uptake of innovations in language teach-ing and education in general (for example, Kennedy 1988; Fullan 1993; Markee 1993; Stoller 1994), Table 10.1 summarizes the main attributes of innovation that have been found to influence adoption. Some of these attributes are seen as increasing the likelihood of an innovation becoming adopted, for example, feasibility, relevance, and experience, while others are likely to inhibit it, for example, complexity. Many of the factors are relative, for example, initial dissatisfaction and feasibility; that is, they can only be considered in relation to a particular group of teachers working in a particular context. However, a number of factors are more inherent in the proposal itself. We will focus on these here.

How *complex* is task-based teaching? Arguably, it is not very difficult for teachers to grasp what it is about. The principal idea, namely that linguis-tically unfocused tasks can be used to engage learners in the communica-tive processes that will foster acquisition, is essentially a simple one. However, task-based instruction becomes more complex when the idea of linguistically focused tasks is introduced, as it may not be easy for teachers

Attribute	Definition
Initial dissatisfaction	The level of dissatisfaction that teachers experience with some aspect of their existing teaching.
Feasibility	The extent to which the innovation is seen as implementable given the conditions in which teachers work.
Acceptability	The extent to which the innovation is seen as compatible with teachers' existing teaching style and ideology.
Relevance	The extent to which the innovation is viewed as matching the students' needs.
Complexity	The extent to which the innovation is easy to grasp.
Explicitness	The extent to which the rationale for the innovation is clear and convincing.
Triability	The extent to which the innovation can be easily tried out in stages.
Observability	The extent to which the results of the innovation are visible to others.
Originality	The extent to which the teachers are expected to demonstrate a high level of originality in order to implement the innovation, e.g. by preparing special materials.
Ownership	The extent to which teachers come to feel they 'possess' the innovation.

Table 10.1: Attributes of innovation (from Ellis 1997: 29)

to distinguish these from contextualized language exercises (see Chapter 5 for a discussion of this distinction). Another obvious area of complexity is the sequencing of tasks; as we saw in Chapter 8, there is no simple, algorithmic procedure for grading tasks in terms of their inherent characteristics. Also, while there is agreement that tasks need to induce attention to form as well as meaning, there is no consensus on how this is to be achieved. Overall, task-based teaching, while superficially simple, is complex. How *explicit* is the rationale for task-based instruction? While this is a matter of opinion, it is arguable that teachers may have difficulty in following the rationale if only because it draws on very different theories, which are often presented as being in competition with each other. However, if the rationale is restricted to a single theoretical perspective, for example, Skehan's cognitive theory, then it may be perceived as clear and convincing. Teaching with tasks scores highly on *triability* if it is accepted that there is no need to totally replace existing linguistically driven approaches. After all, it is relatively easy and unthreatening to try out a task or two. The *originality* required of teachers will depend on whether the innovation involves teaching a task-based course for which, as I have already pointed out, published materials are not readily available, or just performing selected tasks for which ample materials are available.

This analysis is revealing. It suggests that, from an innovationist perspective, a clear distinction needs to be made between asking teachers to adopt a task-based course and asking them to experiment with individual tasks alongside their existing practices. The former is challenging and one would predict that the innovation would run into problems. The latter is relatively unthreatening as it requires only a modification to the way teachers teach, rather than a radical change. It is likely to succeed. The difference in these two innovations broadly reflects the distinction I have made throughout this book between task-based and task-supported language teaching. An innovationist perspective suggests that the former has much less chance of being adopted than the latter. It does not follow, however, that task-supported teaching is more theoretically desirable than task-based teaching.

The empirical evaluation of task-based teaching

In the previous section I attempted an 'external' evaluation of task-based teaching, addressing its implementability in a somewhat speculative manner. However, there is an obvious need for 'internal' evaluations of actual attempts at task-based teaching. The empirical evaluations, to which I now turn, address whether task-based teaching 'works', i.e. achieves its objectives, in particular contexts. In fact, there have been surprisingly few such evaluations. In contrast to the extensive research into tasks examined in the preceding chapters there have been no more than a handful of evaluations of task-based teaching. In particular, there is a surprising lack of empirical information about complete task-based courses. We will consider two approaches to evaluation: micro-evaluation, where the object of the evaluation is a single task, and macro-evaluation, where an evaluation of an entire task-based course is carried out. Examples of both will be provided in the hope of stimulating further such evaluations.

The micro-evaluation of tasks

A *micro-evaluation* can be carried out for two main purposes. It can be used to investigate whether a task 'worked' for a particular group of learners. It can also be used to identify weaknesses in the design of a task and, thus, ways in which the task can be improved.

In Ellis (1997c), I outlined the steps that need to be followed in conducting a micro-evaluation of tasks. I argued that the decision about *what* to evaluate lies at the heart of such an evaluation and identified three types of evaluation. A student-based evaluation is aimed at identifying the students' attitudes towards and opinions of the task that is being investigated. Such an evaluation is necessary because, arguably, a task can only be said to have worked if the students found it enjoyable and/or useful. Student-based evaluations conducted by means of questionnaires or short interviews are the easiest to carry out. A response-based evaluation requires the evaluator to examine the actual outcomes (both process and product) of the task to see whether they match the predicted outcomes. For example, if one of the purposes of the task was to encourage the negotiation of meaning, a response-based evaluation would examine whether the task resulted in plentiful requests for clarification and confirmation. If the task was a focused one directed at getting learners to produce a specific linguistic form, the evaluation would examine whether the students did in fact use this form. If the product outcome of a task was to draw a route on a map, the evaluation would assess to what extent the students' routes were accurate. Response-based evaluations are time-consuming because they usually require recordings of the task performance to be made, transcribed, and analysed. However, they provide valuable information about whether a task is achieving what it was intended to achieve. Finally, a learning-based evaluation can be carried out to establish whether the task has resulted in language learning. This is the most difficult kind of evaluation to carry out. Ideally, it requires the evaluator to conduct some kind of pre- and post-test of the kinds Swain and her co-researchers (for example, Swain and Lapkin 2001) have used, although it may also be possible to obtain evidence of learning by a careful inspection of the discourse that results from the task, especially if the theoretical framework that informs the evaluation is sociocultural SLA. A limitation of learner-based evaluations is that performance of a single task may not be sufficient to bring about any measurable change in students' interlanguages, especially if the task is an unfocused one.

In Ellis 1999, I provided an example of a task-based evaluation carried out by a teacher, drawing on a report of an evaluation by Hoogwerf (1995). She sought to evaluate the use of a specific consciousness-raising (CR) task with second-year Japanese college students enrolled in an eight-month College Study Abroad Program. Her concern was to find if the task 'worked' and also how it might be improved for future use. The objectives of the CR task were to raise students' awareness of the correct use of subject-verb agreement and to enhance the students' motivation to attend to what was a common error in their writing. The data for the task consisted of: (1) a statement of the subject-verb agreement rule; (2) sentences serving as examples of the rule taken from the students' own free writing; and (3) sentences to be completed by the students using the choices provided. The intended product outcomes were that the students would underline the subjects of the sentences and supply the correct verb forms. The intended process outcome was that they would work diligently and with enthusiasm on the task.[2] Hoogwerf carried out three types of evaluation described above. Table 10.2 summarizes the results of her evaluation. She concluded that she had achieved her major objectives and thus that the task had 'worked'. But she also concluded that most learners were unable to transfer what they had learned to their own free writing. As a result of carrying out the evaluation, she decided that consciousness tasks should be used more regularly, that wherever possible they should be based on data taken from the students' own productions, and that follow-up activities were needed to 'reinforce' what the students learned from CR tasks.

Type of evaluation	Main results
Student-based	Comments in students' journals indicated that the students responded positively to the task. Many wrote asking for more such tasks. Students especially liked working with their own sentences in the task.
Response-based	The students attacked the task eagerly and completed it in less than ten minutes (whereas normally they worked much more slowly). The students' written answers to the task matched the intended outcome closely. Nearly all the students underlined all the subjects and chose the correct form of the verbs.
Learning-based evaluation	Overall the students did not show much improvement in the pre-test and post-test (both involving free writing). But the top three writers did show substantial gains in accuracy. Hoogwerf reports that these students asked more questions about subject-verb agreement during subsequent writing conferences and made more crossings out and changes in -s endings in first drafts of compositions.

Table 10.2: Results of a micro-evaluation of a task

Micro-evaluations of tasks such as the one conducted by Hoogwerf are valuable in two ways. First, they provide useful information about the design of a task, showing its strengths and weaknesses. Teachers can use the information they obtain from such evaluations to revise and improve tasks for subsequent use. Second, task evaluation, when conducted by teachers in their own classrooms (as in Hoogwerf's evaluation), serves as an effective way of carrying out action research. It serves as a way for teachers to become 'reflective practitioners' (Schön 1983).

Macro-evaluations of task-based courses

A *macro-evaluation* of a task-based course constitutes a *programme evaluation*. Weir and Roberts (1994: 4) characterize the purpose of such an evaluation as 'to collect information systematically in order to indicate the worth or merit of a programme or project'. Thus, programme evaluation, in contrast to research, is an inherently practical affair. Stakeholders, for example, teachers, administrators, aid donors, want to know whether the programme has 'worked' and whether it is worth continuing. For this reason, each evaluation is focused on a particular language learning situation, i.e. the one where the programme was executed. In contrast to micro-evaluation, there is a large literature on the evaluation of language programmes (see, for example, Alderson and Beretta (1992), Rea-Dickens and Germaine (1992) and Weir and Roberts (1994)). We will consider two examples here and then address some of the problems that exist in carrying out macro-evaluations of task-based courses.

The Communicational Teaching Project (Prabhu 1987) was evaluated by Beretta and Davies (1985) and also by Beretta (1990). The first evaluation sought to compare the learning outcomes of learners involved in the project (the experimental group) with those in 'traditional' classes, where the structural-oral situational method was followed (the control group). To avoid bias in testing, Beretta and Davies devised a battery of tests that included tests that 'favoured' the experimental group, i.e. a task-based test, and the control group, i.e. a structure test, and also three 'neutral' tests, i.e. contextualized grammar, dictation, and listening/reading comprehension. The results lend support to the effectiveness of task-based teaching. In the neutral tests, the experimental group clearly outperformed the control group. However, on the group-biased tests, while the experimental group did better on the task-based test, the control group scored higher on the structural test. Beretta and Davies conclude that the results of the evaluation support the claim that task-based instruction produces significantly different learning from traditional form-focused instruction and that this is reflected in the task-based learners' superior acquisition of structures that have not been explicitly taught and also in their ability to deploy what they have learned more readily. However, Beretta and Davies also point to a number of problems with their evaluation, which will be considered below.

Beretta's (1990a) evaluation addressed a different aspect of the Communicational Teaching Project—whether the methodological innovations proposed by Prabhu were actually implemented by the teachers involved in the project. Beretta collected historical narratives from 15 teachers and then rated these according to three levels of implementation: (1) orientation—the teacher demonstrated a lack of understanding of task-based instruction and failed to implement it; (2) routine—the teacher understood the rationale of the project and was able to implement it effectively; and (3) renewal—the teacher had adopted a critical perspective and could demonstrate awareness of its strengths and weaknesses. Beretta found that 40% of the teachers were at Level 1, 47% at Level 2, and 13% at Level 3. However, when he distinguished between regular and non-regular teachers involved in the project, he found that three out of four regular teachers were at Level 1. Beretta concluded that task-based instruction of the kind practised in the project may not be easily assimilated by regular classroom teachers in southern India. He points to these teachers' lack of English proficiency as one reason for their failure to adopt task-based teaching.[3] Beretta's conclusion raises the same issue we considered above—whether such task-based instruction is feasible in many non-western teaching contexts.

Programme evaluation is complex and problematic (see Alderson and Beretta (1992) and Weir and Roberts (1994) for a detailed discussion of the key issues). Product-based evaluations that involve the kind of method comparison undertaken by Beretta and Davies have an undistinguished history, typically failing to demonstrate any significant differences. There are several reasons for this. One is the difficulty in determining appropriate tests to measure the learning outcomes; the tests chosen need to be either 'balanced', i.e. tests that favour each of the methods being compared, or 'neutral', i.e. tests that do not favour one method over the other. Another problem is determining equivalence of the learners in the instructional groups. Random sampling is not usually possible in real-world teaching contexts. Nor is it always feasible to obtain pre-test scores, as often the instruction has started before the evaluation is planned. A third problem arises when the method comparison is conducted on the basis of external descriptions of the methods rather than internal accounts of what actually occurs in the classroom. Beretta and Davies' evaluation of the Communicational Teaching Project manifests all three of these problems, as they are careful to point out.

The key issue from our perspective here is 'What can programme evaluations tell us about the effectiveness of task-based teaching?' As Beretta (1990b) points out, evaluators find themselves between a rock and hard place in trying to satisfy the differing demands of the academic and the policy-shaping communities and frequently satisfy neither. Beretta cites his own evaluation with Davies as an example of an evaluation that was undertaken in a kind of limbo, demonstrating neither awareness of what was needed to advance theory nor with any clear understanding of how the results could contribute to the actual practice of task-based teaching. Nevertheless, despite this pessimism, there is a clear need for programme evaluations of task-based instruction. Such evaluations need to address not just what learning takes place (and whether this is more or less than that achieved through other instructional approaches) but, crucially, also whether the external precepts of task-based teaching are reflected in actual classroom practices. In this latter respect, Beretta's (1990a) evaluation shows the way, although, as Prabhu (1990) was quick to point out, he relied only on teachers' reports of their practices and did not obtain observational data on what actually transpired during the task-based lessons. The information supplied by a process-oriented evaluation can be used by practitioners to make adjustments to both the design and the implementation of task-based courses in specific instructional contexts. However, no single evaluation is likely to have much impact on the theory of task-based teaching and learning. Clearly, there is a need for more evaluations of task-based programmes.

To sum up this section, the two kinds of empirical evaluation we have considered afford rather different kinds of insights. Micro-based evaluations of individual tasks shed light on what happens when individual tasks are performed in classrooms (as opposed to laboratory type settings) and, if carried out by the teachers themselves serve as a basis for reflective practice through action research. Programme evaluations of complete task-based courses allow some of the central claims about task-based instruction to be tested (although probably not definitively) and also address the crucial question of the feasibility of this kind of instruction in real-world teaching contexts.

Theoretical objections to task-based teaching

I will now turn to theoretically inspired critiques of task-based teaching. These address: (1) the restricted nature of task-based communication; (2) the cultural relativity of task-based teaching; and (3) the impossibility of teaching language as communication. I will also respond to each of the critiques.

The restricted nature of task-based communication

The first critique does not dismiss task-based teaching but points to its inherent limitations. It argues that task-based teaching restricts the way in which language is used, causing learners to miss out on experiences that may be of crucial importance for successful language learning. The critique is based on a multi-functional view of language.

Jakobson (1960), in a widely cited article, identifies six main functions of language:

1 the referential function, i.e. the use of language to convey information
2 the emotive function, i.e. the use of language to express feeling
3 the connative function, i.e. the use of language to influence the actions of another person
4 the phatic function, i.e. the use of language to simply establish, discontinue or prolong communication or check whether it has taken place
5 the metalingual function, i.e. the use of language to communicate about the code itself
6 the poetic function, i.e. the use of language in such a way that attention is drawn to the form of language itself.

Which of these language functions do tasks cater to? The kinds of tasks discussed in the previous chapters have been largely referential in nature (Yule 1996). They require learners to listen to directions, exchange information, describe pictures, tell stories, report findings, etc. There are also tasks that give priority to the connative function; opinion-gap tasks call on learners to express their opinions and convince others of a course of action. Consciousness-raising tasks (see Chapter 5) involve the metalingual function; learners are invited to talk about language and to formulate their own grammar rules. Role-play tasks can be designed to elicit language that performs the emotive function. It can be argued that all tasks involve the phatic function to a degree, although in fact, it is doubtful whether learners feel strongly motivated to use language simply as a means of making contact, being sociable, or keeping the channel open, for example, by talking about the weather, as there is no social necessity for such talk in the context created by a task. Indeed, transcripts of task-based interactions provide few examples of this kind of language use. The poetic function, however, is entirely absent; when learners perform tasks they do not try to manipulate language in ways that draw attention to the language itself. Indeed, the nature of most tasks, which prioritize the transmission of referential content or personal beliefs, precludes the 'poetic' use of language.

One such poetic use is language play. Cook (1997: 227) defines 'language play' as 'behaviour not primarily motivated by human need to manipulate the environment and to share information for this purpose and to form and maintain social relationships—though it may indirectly serve both of these functions'. Cook argues that language play is predominant in all areas of life and is of necessity concerned with form and semantic meaning. It involves creating patterns of sound, for example, rhyme and alliteration, and of structure, through establishing patterns and parallelisms. It also involves playing with units of meaning, for example, by creating neologisms.

Language play figures naturally in the language of both children and adults—in games, riddles, literature, jokes, and conversational banter. Cook emphasizes that language play is authentic and that any approach to teaching that is based on the premise that language should be solely taught for solving problems, performing social actions, or talking about the real world is necessarily limited. In Cook (2000) he outlines the essential differences between the language of play and current pedagogic emphases, as reflected in task-based teaching. These are summarized in Table 10.3.

Cook's principal point is not that the kind of communication that tasks elicit is worthless but that it is inherently limited because it emphasizes the rational and transactional and does not contain opportunities for the imaginative and playful. He suggests this is limiting in two respects. First, it does not reflect how people use language authentically —for everyday language use is full of language play. Second, it is demotivating. He claims that catering to students' natural tendencies to use language for play would make communication not just meaningful but interesting. If tasks imply 'work' (see, for example, Long's (1985) definition in Figure 1.1 of Chapter 1), then, Cook insists, there also needs to be room for 'play'. However, his principal plea is for recognition of the complexity of language where 'it is sometimes play and sometimes for real, sometimes form-focused and sometimes meaning-focused, sometimes fiction and sometimes fact' (Cook 1997: 231). Recognizing this would guarantee a 'richer and more complex environment for learning' than that afforded by any one methodology.

Feature of language play	Current pedagogic emphases
Linguistic parallels and repetitions	Information
Indeterminate meanings	Exactitude
Vital subject matter	Mundane subject matter
Alternative reality	Actual reality
Solitude, intimacy, or large congregations	Medium-size groups
Competition or affection	Collaboration
Pleasure	Usefulness
Form focus	Meaning focus
Atomism (synthetic syllabuses)	Analytic syllabuses
Ritualistic and repetitive	One-off activities

Table 10.3: Differences between language play and current pedagogic emphases (based on Cook 2000)

Thus, Cook is not proposing that we develop a methodology where language play is central, only that it should be catered for by whatever approach we adopt. It follows that his critique can be addressed by acknowledging the need for tasks that will engage learners in the ludic uses of language. This is a challenge, although not one that Cook takes up in a convincing manner. Cook (2000) does advance some pedagogic proposals for introducing the language of play into the classroom. He suggests, for example, that pattern drills involve similar procedures to those found in language play, for example, repetition and substitution of linguistic forms, and thus have a useful part to play in language teaching. However, this proposal is unconvincing, as the underlying motives for language play and pattern drills are entirely different, making them entirely different activities. The requirement that learners 'display' correct linguistic forms is likely to inhibit any desire to 'play' with language. Maley (2001), in his review of Cook's book, suggests a more obvious way of tackling the problem would be to exploit the genre of creative fiction. Literature offers a rich source of texts that serve as the 'input' in the design of tasks. Also, tasks that require learners to produce their own literary texts serve as obvious ways of providing opportunities for learners to exercise the 'poetic function' (see Maley and Moulding (1985) for examples of such tasks).

The cultural relativity of task-based teaching

The second theoretical critique is sociopolitical in nature, drawing on accounts of linguistic imperialism (for example, Phillipson 1992) and of critical approaches to language pedagogy (for example, Pennycook 1994). From this perspective, task-based teaching is an Anglo-American creation. Irrespective of whether it is psycholinguistically justified, it must be considered in terms of the social and cultural impact it has on consumers, especially in non-western contexts, and also in terms of whether the language practices it espouses are 'transformative', i.e. enable learners to achieve control over their lives.

A critical pedagogy requires that any particular approach to language teaching be analysed to uncover its underlying socio-political messages. As Pennycook (1994) has pointed out, the way we teach a language entails the concurrent teaching of those discourses that are embedded within the chosen approach. In the case of English-language teaching, this has involved the spread of 'the discourses of development, democracy, capitalism, modernization and so on' (ibid. 53). Pennycook warns against the danger of uncritically accepting this spread as natural, neutral, and beneficial and seeks to uncover the assumptions that underlie the way English is taught. In short, Pennycook invites us to examine the often hidden socio-political messages of our instructional practices and advocates the establishment of 'counter discourses' to prevent learners from becoming passive consumers of neo-colonialist ideology.

We can ask then what the hidden socio-political messages of task-based teaching are. Clearly, the content of many of the tasks that figure in both research and language-teaching materials implicitly espouse the cultural values and norms of the western English-speaking world. For example, Ur's (1988) 'Candidates for a Job Task' (see Figure 5.1) requires students to select a teacher from a number of applicants. This task assumes that it is culturally appropriate to involve students in the teacher-selection process. Further, an inspection of the information about the four applicants reveals them all to be native speakers, thus reinforcing the stereotypical view that English-language teachers should be native speakers. This task is not unique in the hidden values it espouses. It would be possible to undertake a similar deconstruction of most tasks. From the perspective of critical pedagogy it is necessary not just to identify content that is motivating and relevant to the students, as discussed in Chapter 7, but also to examine the choice of content for the social and political messages it conveys and, more crucially perhaps to invite students themselves to undertake a critical examination of the content. This problem, then, is far from insuperable; it can be avoided by careful use of the theme generator shown in Figure 7.2 together with a critical sensitivity to the selection of thematic content.

More seriously, the classroom practices required by task-based teaching can be seen themselves as culturally loaded. For example, the requirement that teachers function as task-participants rather than as instructors is indicative of the democratic, egalitarian discourses that Pennycook warns us to be on the lookout for. The kinds of discourse processes identified as desirable for task-based teaching in Chapter 8 (see Figure 4) assume a set of relationships between teacher and students that may run counter to the kinds of relationship considered culturally appropriate in some classrooms outside the western world. Widdowson (1993), for example, cites an unpublished study by Scollon and Scollon suggesting that 'conversational methods' are antithetical to the Confucian emphasis on benevolence and respect between teacher and students in China. Task-based teaching, as a form of communicative teaching, implies a particular cultural context that may be in conflict with cultural contexts where learning is not seen as a collaborative and experiential activity. The problems that arise out of this mismatch are now well-documented. Li (1998), for example, offers an interesting discussion of why communicative language teaching was viewed as difficult to implement by Korean teachers of English.

A related issue concerns the often-voiced belief that what is appropriate for a 'second-language' teaching context may not be appropriate for a 'foreign-language' context. While there are difficulties in distinguishing teaching contexts in this way, the strength and depth of this belief is evident.[4] Two concerns seem to underlie it. First, task-based instruction is seen as impractical in foreign language contexts because of the limited class time available for teaching the L2. The need to ensure the maximally effective use of the available teaching time leads teachers to distrust an approach that is predicated on the assumption that language acquisition is a slow, gradual process requiring extensive opportunities for using the language. Second, task-based teaching is seen as difficult to implement by non-native speaking teachers whose L2 oral proficiency is uncertain. Medgyes (1994) points to several advantages of teachers being non-native speakers—they provide good models for their students, they know what learning strategies can be usefully taught, they can supply information about the English language, they can anticipate and prevent difficulties, they are good at showing empathy, and, most obviously, they can exploit the use of the students' L1. Task-based teaching, however, may not be the most obvious vehicle for maximizing these strengths.

Thus, we can see that a critical perspective on task-based teaching raises important questions. It forces us to go beyond the psycholinguistic rationale for task-based instruction in order to examine the social, cultural, political, and historical factors that contextualize teaching and influence how it takes place. Further, it requires that teachers examine how what they are teaching affects the lives of their students and how they can transform them for the better. As the previous chapters give testimony to, discussions of task-based teaching based on psycholinguistic models of language learning do not encompass this wider picture.

However, it is not impossible for task-based teaching to do so. Clearly, we need to ensure that the contents of tasks are chosen with due sensitivity to the socio-political messages they convey. We also need tasks that invite a critical response from learners. This might be achieved by developing consciousness-raising tasks that focus not just on linguistic features but on how the choice of particular linguistic forms encodes socio-political meanings in texts. Problems of implementing task-based instruction due to cultural or contextual constraints can be addressed through learner and teacher development programmes and by the obvious strategy of ensuring that the final choice of approach lies in the hands of those who will be responsible for putting it into practice. Thus, the critique that critical pedagogy offers constitutes not a rejection of task-based teaching as discussed in the preceding chapters but rather an indication of its limitations (and perhaps dangers). These limitations, once acknowledged, need to be and probably can be addressed.

Teaching language as communication

The final critique rejects task-based teaching as implausible. It attacks the central premise on which it is based, namely, that tasks serve to create communicative contexts that foster language acquisition. As we have seen, tasks do not aim to teach communication but to engage learners in communication, the assumption being that by so doing they will help learners develop communicative competence, including linguistic competence. This raises the obvious question: Do tasks result in communicative language activity of the kind that facilitates acquisition? The answer provided by the previous chapters is 'Yes'. However, there is an alternative view, which we have touched on briefly previously and will now examine more closely.

In Chapter 8 we considered the empirical evidence put forward by Seedhouse (1997) that tasks often result in very minimal, heavily elided forms of communication that do not serve to 'push' learners to advance their interlanguages. We have also noted that learners may call on their strategic competence to address the communicative demands of a task, consequentially losing the opportunity to 'stretch' their interlanguages linguistically. As Breen (2001: 128) points out:

> Interaction is embedded within the discourse of the specific task and may not enable the development of the language beyond the immediate interactive requirements of the task.

In short, it can be argued that there can be no guarantee that tasks will promote the kind of communication that they are designed to achieve and which is required for acquisition to take place.[5]

It can also be asked whether it is ever possible to achieve full situational authenticity and/or interactional authenticity. In the last chapter, we saw that it is questionable whether we can ever achieve either type of authenticity in the context of a language test. The same doubts can be raised about instructional contexts. As we have seen, the classroom constitutes a communicative context in its own right with its own distinctive patterns and rules, which supplant those that operate in the less asymmetrical contexts outside the classroom. Thus, we can never be sure that the classroom tasks we choose will successfully simulate the kinds of communicative acts that learners will experience in real-life contexts. It can be argued, therefore, that we would do better to stop trying to replicate naturalistic communication in the classroom and instead acknowledge that classroom discourse constitutes a kind of 'institutional discourse' (Seedhouse 1996) and concentrate on trying to understand how this discourse can be made to work for acquisition.

There is another reason why tasks may not engage learners in the type of communication desired. As we have seen, tasks require students and teachers to act as language users (as opposed to language learners) and to treat language as a tool (rather than as an object); in other words, they are required to play 'the communicative game'. But students are learners and, if they are cognitively mature, will quite naturally attempt to view language as an object that can be analysed and 'cognized'. Similarly, teachers are pedagogues, whose job it is to ensure that their students learn the language. To ask students and teachers to engage in the pretence that the *raison d'être* of the classroom is communication and that learning will occur incidentally is asking a lot of them. There is growing evidence (see, for example, Ellis,

Basturkmen, and Loewen 2001) that, although classroom participants do play the communicative game when they perform tasks, they do not entirely abandon the roles of teacher and student. As a result, the communication that arises may be characterized by frequent although not necessarily intrusive 'time-outs', where the participants switch roles from those of language users to those of learners/teacher. The attention to form that occurs in these time-outs is, of course, precisely what theorists (including myself) have argued is needed (see Chapter 5). But these time-outs are not 'communicative' as they are typically motivated not by the need to negotiate meaning but rather by the felt need to treat language as an object by negotiating form. In short, there are good reasons for believing that tasks do not result in what they set out to achieve—'genuine' acts of communication.

If it is impossible to simulate communication, should we bother trying? Widdowson (2001: 18) argues that it is not:

> You just cannot test the ability to communicate, and so it is pointless to try. And you cannot teach it either if it comes to that. All you can teach and test is some aspect of it.

He proposes that we would do better to focus instead on teaching that aspect of language that has 'particular saliency or implicational value'— linguistic competence. However, he suggests that this does not mean a return to square one, i.e. the teaching of the formal properties of sentences in accordance with a Chomskyan view of language, but rather the teaching of linguistic knowledge as meaning potential, guided by a Hallidayan view of language. In Halliday's theory, the form of language reflects its functional uses or, as Widdowson puts it, 'communication is immanent in the code as an intrinsic valency' (ibid. 19). Thus, by teaching functional grammar we can acknowledge the central creativity of language and, crucially, get our hands on 'something specifiable to deal with'. So, instead of trying to achieve the impossible by simulating communication through tasks, i.e. teaching language *as* communication, we should opt for the possible by teaching linguistic competence *for* communication.

According to this view, then, the goal of language teaching should be to prepare students to communicate, not to get them communicating. It is based on both theoretical reasons for rejecting task-based teaching, i.e. the impossibility of simulating communication in the classroom, and practical reasons for adopting a linguistic syllabus, i.e. a linguistic syllabus based on a functional model of language offers a systematic and manageable basis for designing courses.

This critique is more fundamental than the previous two. It attacks the central assumption of task-based teaching, namely that through tasks we can teach language as communication. However, Widdowson's claim that this is impossible seems to me fundamentally mistaken. It depends crucially on what is meant by the term 'communication'. The claim of task-based teaching (and of direct system-referenced testing) is not that it will result in *communicative acts* that mirror those occurring outside the classroom. This is indeed unlikely, as Seedhouse (1996) and Widdowson himself have convincingly argued. The essential claim is that, through tasks, we can engage learners in the kinds of *cognitive processes* that arise in communication outside the classroom. These processes have been discussed in detail in the preceding chapters from a variety of different perspectives. They include top-down and bottom-up processing, noticing, negotiating meaning, lexicalized and rule-based production, scaffolded production, private speech, and negotiating form. They involve the learner in attention to meaning and form in the context of using the L2 to achieve a communicative purpose. It is these processes, not the communicative acts themselves, that create the conditions for acquisition to take place. Thus, it is not necessary to demonstrate that task-based communication is 'natural', 'authentic', or 'conversational', only that it involves the cognitive processes that will promote acquisition. It is this claim that Seedhouse (1997) sought to challenge by claiming that task-based interaction is seriously impoverished. However, as the earlier chapters have demonstrated, this claim has no basis; task-based interaction can be complex and rich, promoting the cognitive processes through which acquisition takes place.

However, in dismissing this critique, I do not want to suggest that teaching the linguistic system as meaning potential (the alternative that Widdowson proposes) has no place in language pedagogy. My advocacy of task-based instruction is not intended to exclude other approaches. Indeed, I have argued elsewhere (see Ellis 2002 and Chapter 8) for a modular approach involving a combination of task- and linguistically-based components.

Conclusion

I began this chapter by noting that despite the clear psycholinguistic rationale for task-based teaching, there have been few attempts to adopt this kind of teaching in institutional contexts (such as high schools) and few truly task-based courses published to date. It is, perhaps, now clearer why this is the case. First, in the opinion of some applied linguists task-based teaching is limited in the kinds of language use it offers learners. Second, task-based teaching may be perceived as an Anglo-American invention not suited to cultural contexts with non-western norms and values. Third, it has been viewed as untenable because tasks do not result in 'natural communication' in the classroom. Fourth, task-based teaching may be perceived as a radical innovation that is difficult to implement. While we can reject the claim that it is not possible to teach language as communication, it is obvious that the other points constitute hefty impediments to the widespread adoption of task-based courses. However, as I tried to show, they are not insuperable. They do not require a rejection of task-based teaching but rather modification (primarily in terms of the content of tasks) and sensitivity to its implementation.

While task-supported teaching, which poses fewer problems of implementation, is likely to become part of many teachers' practice (indeed in some teaching contexts it already has), task-based teaching may not. If task-based teaching is to make the shift from theory to practice it will be necessary to go beyond the psycholinguistic rationale that this book has attempted to develop and to address the contextual factors that ultimately determine what materials and procedures teachers choose. This chapter has suggested how this might be achieved—by experimenting with task-based courses in different contexts, along the lines of the Communicational Teaching Project, and submitting them to careful empirical evaluation. If it can be shown that: (1) task-based courses are 'feasible'; (2) that they 'work'; and if (3) the conditions that make for their success can be identified, then the likelihood of their acceptance as practice will be increased. Micro- and macro-evaluations can play a major role in helping to propagate teaching with tasks. So, too, can teacher training. The case for including an introduction to the principles and techniques of task-based teaching in initial teacher-training programmes is a strong one, as this book has demonstrated. Such programmes should make trainees aware of the important distinction between task-based and task-supported teaching (or else the latter may be mistaken for the former) and should focus on the methodology of task-based teaching (as described in Chapter 8), emphasizing the importance that teacher and learner roles play in ensuring that tasks are performed as intended and in ways that can foster acquisition.

Notes

1 Candlin (2001) does provide one example of where a task-based approach has been adopted institutionally—in the 'Target-oriented Curriculum' for English in Hong Kong. It is interesting to note that the curriculum document discusses tasks not just in terms of their psycholinguistic potential but also in personal and affective terms, i.e. their ability to motivate learners, and in the terms of broad educational objectives, for example, developing the ability to experiment, analyse, and reason.

2 This objective reflects one the main reasons teachers have for using tasks. They see them as a way of 'energizing' their students by encouraging their active and willing participation.

3 In his response to Beretta's evaluation, Prabhu (1990) makes it clear that the purpose of the Communicational Language Teaching Project was 'developmental', i.e. to examine whether it was possible to identify teaching procedures consistent with the theory of learning that underlay the project, not with full-scale implementation. In this respect, the project was clearly a success.

4 On an anecdotal level, I am often questioned about the relevance and feasibility of task-based teaching in EFL contexts during question time following lectures I have given in Japan and elsewhere.

5 This is a different argument from that advanced in Chapter 6, where it was pointed out that a task can result in very different kinds of activity depending on the motives and goals of the learners. The argument here is that tasks can never elicit communication of the conversational type when performed in a classroom context.

Glossary

academic listening task A task that involves learners listening to an academic text, e.g. a lecture, and then demonstrating their understanding, e.g. by answering questions. An academic listening task often involves note-taking and can be interactive or non-interactive.

accuracy The extent to which the language produced in performing a task conforms with target language norms.

activity theory 'A unified account of Vygotsky's original proposals on the nature and development of human behavior' (Lantolf 2000b: 8). The theory accounts for human behaviour in terms of the biologically created or socially constructed motives that underlie actions.

authenticity A pedagogic task is situationally authentic if it matches a situation found in the real world and it is interactionally authentic if it results in patterns of interaction similar to those found in the real world.

automatization This refers to the process by which declarative knowledge become proceduralized through practice. Automatization results in the development of automatic processes which allow for L2 knowledge to be accessed easily and rapidly with minimal demands on the learner's information-processing capacity.

bottom-up processing This involves understanding a text by analysing the words and sentences in the text itself. It contrasts with *top-down processing*.

clarification request An interactional strategy used by speakers to try to clarify something that their interlocutor has said to them, e.g. 'Pardon?'

closed task A task that requires students to reach a single, correct solution or one of a small finite set of solutions. Many *information-gap tasks* are closed.

code complexity The extent to which the linguistic forms required to perform a task are easy or difficult to process.

cognitive complexity The extent to which the cognitive operations required to perform a task are easy or difficult to execute. See *cognitive processes*.

cognitive processes This refers to the mental processes involved in such operations as classifying and reasoning. Cognitive processes are also involved in comprehending and producing language.

collaborative dialogue The talk that enables learners to produce spoken or written texts collaboratively while performing a task.

communication strategy A strategy such as paraphrase used by learners to overcome a communication problem caused by a lack of or inability to access L2 knowledge. See also *strategic competence*.

Communicational Teaching Project The project led by Prabhu in south India. It was one of the first attempts to develop an entirely task-based course.

communicative effectiveness A term used by Yule (1996) to refer to the ability of communicators to achieve successful outcomes to a task by identifying the referents that need to be communicated and by taking their partner's perspective.

communicative language teaching An approach to teaching that is directed at developing communicative abilities in the learners either by teaching aspects of communicative competence (the weak version) or by creating conditions for learners to learn through communicating (the strong version).

communicative language testing A test that provides scores for overall task fulfillment rather than for linguistic knowledge or language skills. Thus a communicative language test is a *performance test*.

communicative stress A term coined by Candlin (1987) to refer to the degree of stress learners experience when required to perform tasks of varying degrees of complexity.

complexity The extent to which the language produced in performing a task is elaborate and varied.

comprehensible input Input that has been made comprehensible to learners either by simplifying it (see *simplified input*), by using the situational context to make the meaning clear, or interactionally though the *negotiation of meaning*.

comprehension check An interactional strategy used by speakers to check whether their own preceding utterance has been understood, e.g. 'Do you know what I mean?'

confirmation check An interactional strategy used by speakers to confirm whether they have correctly understood something their interlocutor has said, e.g. 'You cancelled the picnic because it was raining, did you?'

connectionist theories of language learning A connectionist theory claims that language learning results from the operation of general cognitive mechanisms that are sensitive to the frequency with which linguistic sequences (phonological, lexical, and grammatical) occur in a language and that store implicit information about these sequences.

consciousness-raising tasks A task that engages learners in thinking and communicating about language. Thus, a language point becomes the topic that is talked about.

content-compatible language The language that is useful or natural for the completion of a task but that is not absolutely essential.

content-obligatory language The language that is essential for the successful completion of a task.

context dependency This refers to whether the language needed to perform a task is closely linked to the input materials of the task or is supported by situational props or whether it is independent of them.

controlled processing This occurs when learners utilize conscious effort and attention in L2 performance. It is demanding of their information-processing capacity. Controlled processing involves the use of *declarative knowledge*.

convergent task An *opinion-gap task* that requires students to agree to a solution to a problem, e.g. deciding what items to take on to a desert island.

co-operative learning Learning that results from group work in which the participants engage in collaborative dialogue, i.e. each student adds to or extends his/her partner's contributions.

critical pedagogy A critical pedagogy requires that any particular approach to language teaching be analysed in order to uncover its underlying socio-political messages.

declarative knowledge Declarative knowledge is characterized by Anderson (1993) as 'knowledge that'. In the case of language it consists of factual information about the L2 that has not yet been automatized.

dictogloss Devised by Wajnryb (1990), dictogloss is a procedure that requires learners to reconstruct a short text after listening to it twice. The text is specially designed to focus attention on a specific grammatical feature so it constitutes a type of *focused task*.

direct assessment Direct assessment involves the holistic measurement of language abilities involving some kind of task.

discourse analytic method A method for analysing the language a learner produces when performing a task. It involves providing separate measures for different aspects of language use, e.g. for fluency, accuracy, and complexity.

discourse mode A discourse mode is an oral or written text that has a specific rhetorical structure reflecting its overall communicative function. Examples of discourse modes are 'description' and 'narrative'.

display question A question intended to elicit a display of language as opposed to providing information. A display question is typically 'closed', i.e. the person asking the question already knows the answer.

divergent task An *opinion-gap task* where students are assigned different viewpoints on an issue and have to defend their position and refute their partners', e.g. discussing the pros and cons of television.

dual-knowledge system Skehan (1998a) posits that linguistic knowledge is comprised of two separate systems, one that is exemplar-based, consisting or words and ready-made phrases, and another that is rule-based, allowing for the construction of novel sentences. These two knowledge systems are drawn on differentially according to the task demands.

encoding hypothesis This claims that taking notes serves as a way of organizing lecture content while listening and thus of enhancing on-line comprehension.

enriched input Input that has been contrived to provide multiple exemplars of a specific linguistic feature. The feature may or may not be enhanced, e.g. by typographical highlighting. See *structured input*.

explicit linguistic knowledge This consists of knowledge *about* language, e.g. knowledge about the rule for making nouns plural in English, and is potentially verbalizable.

external storage hypothesis This views note-taking as a record of

the content of a lecture which can be subsequently referred to and which thus promotes long-term retention and ease of recall.

fluency The extent to which the language produced in performing a task manifests pausing, hesitation, or reformulation.

focus on form The cognitive processes by which learners attend to form when comprehending or producing communicative messages. Long (1991) uses the term to refer to instruction that engages learners' attention to form while they are primarily focused on message content.

focus on forms Long (1991) uses this term to refer to instruction directed at teaching pre-selected linguistic items in activities where the students' primary focus of attention is on form rather than meaning.

focus on meaning The cognitive processes involved in comprehending and producing messages for the purpose of communication.

focused feedback Feedback that addresses specific errors, e.g. past tense errors, as opposed to feedback that it is generally focused on any errors that learners produce.

focused task An activity that has all the qualities of a task but has been designed to induce learners' incidental attention to some specific linguistic form when processing either input or output (see also *unfocused task*).

formative assessment Assessment that is undertaken as part of an instructional programme for the purposes of improving learning and teaching.

genre A genre is a class of speech events considered by a particular speech community to be of the same type. Examples of genres are a job interview, a soccer commentary, and a doctor–patient consultation.

goal-directedness A term taken from *socio cultural theory* to refer to the particular orientation learners take to a task. Goal-directedness influences the nature of the activity that results from the task.

humanistic language teaching An approach to language teaching that emphasizes tasks involving the development of human values and sensitivity to the feelings and emotions to others.

implicit learning Learning that takes place without awareness.

implicit linguistic knowledge This is the intuitive knowledge of language that underlies the ability to communicate fluently in the L1. It manifests itself in actual language performance and is only verbalizable if it is converted into *explicit linguistic knowledge*.

implicit methodological techniques Feedback techniques that teachers use to draw attention indirectly to linguistic form in the context of task-based interaction without interrupting the flow of communication. See *recast*.

indirect assessment Indirect assessment involves measuring language proficiency analytically by means of tests of discrete points of language or of specific steps in a task, e.g. a multiple-choice grammar test.

information-gap task A task where one participant holds information that the other participant(s) do(es) not have and that must be exchanged in order to complete the task.

information-processing model A cognitive theory that accounts for how information is attended to and subsequently stored in long-term memory. Different theories account for the serial and parallel processing of information.

innovationist perspective An evaluation of new pedagogic proposals in terms of the likelihood of them being adopted by teachers.

input enrichment Input enrichment involves designing tasks in such a way that the targeted feature is (1) frequent and/or (2) salient in the input provided.

Input Hypothesis The hypothesis advanced by Krashen (1985). It states that learners acquire new linguistic forms as a result of comprehending input that contains forms a little beyond their current stage of development.

input-processing instruction VanPatten (1996: 60) defines this as instruction that is designed 'to alter the processing strategies that learners take to the task of comprehension and to encourage them to make better form–meaning connections than they would if left to their own devices'.

instructional conversation Tharp and Gallimore (1988) use this term to refer to pedagogic interaction that is teacher-led and directed towards a curricular goal (e.g. enabling students to perform a structure that they have not yet internalized) but is conversational in nature (e.g. it manifests equal turn-taking rights and is unpredictable).

integrative test A test based on a unitary rather than multidimensional view of language, i.e. it assumes there is a single underlying proficiency factor. Examples are a cloze test and dictation.

Interaction Hypothesis The hypothesis advanced by Long (1980). It states that learners acquire new linguistic forms as a result of attending to them in the process of negotiating for meaning in order to address a communication problem.

interface position This claims that *explicit linguistic knowledge* can be converted into *implicit linguistic knowledge* as a result of practising specific features of the L2. It provides a clear justification for teaching explicit linguistic knowledge. See *non-interface position*.

interlanguage The term, coined by Selinker (1982), refers to (1) the system of L2 knowledge that a learner has built at a single stage of development ('an interlanguage'), and (2) the interlocking systems that characterize L2 acquisition ('the interlanguage continuum').

interpretation task Ellis (1995) uses this term to refer to tasks designed to induce learners to pay attention to specific grammatical forms while processing spoken or written input for meaning.

intersubjectivity Intersubjectivity is achieved when the task participants can agree on the nature of the activity they are engaged in by sharing a common motive and goals for performing the task.

IRF exchange A three-part discourse pattern frequently observed in classrooms. It consists of a teacher initiation (e.g. a question), a student response, and teacher feedback.

jigsaw task A task where the input material is divided between two or more participants such that they are required to exchange information to complete the task. It is a two-way *information-gap task*.

language aptitude The special ability involved in learning an L2. This is related to but is also in part separate from general intelligence.

language-related episode A term used by Swain (1998) to refer to a sequence of talk occurring during the performance of a task where the participants pay explicit attention to some linguistic form, often by means of the negotiation of form.

learning-based evaluation An evaluation of a task in terms of whether it results in students learning something.

lesson design This term refers to the structure of a lesson, i.e. the stages that comprise a lesson. In task-based teaching it entails three stages: the pre-task stage, the during-task stage, and the post-task stage.

linguistic imperialism The process by which countries such as the UK and the US promote language policies and approaches to language pedagogy in other parts of the world in order to benefit themselves and with little regard for local conditions.

linguistic syllabus A teaching programme that is constructed around a sequence of units of language, usually grammatical structures. See *structural syllabus*.

listen-and-do task A task that requires learners to listen to a text, e.g. to instructions, and then perform some action, e.g. draw a picture, to demonstrate their understanding.

macro-evaluation An evaluation of a complete language course or programme.

mediation A term used in *sociocultural theory*. It involves the modification and reorganization of genetically endowed capacities into higher order forms by the use of some material tool, e.g. a computer, through interaction with another person, or through the use of symbols, e.g. language.

metatalk The talk directed at establishing the orientation to a task and the procedures for performing it.

micro-evaluation An evaluation of a single task. See *student-based evaluation*, *response-based evaluation*, and *learning-based evaluation*.

modified output Output is modified when a participant in a task changes something initially said or written as a result of feedback from another participant. Output modification can result in more grammatical language production. See *uptake (1)*.

modular syllabus A teaching programme consisting of two or more separate components—for example, a programme consisting of a set of graded tasks and a set of grammatical structures. In a modular syllabus a key issue is the staging of the different components.

monitoring The process by which learners attend to aspects of their own production and modify it with a view to making it more grammatical or acceptable. Monitoring involves self-correction and is distinguished from *modified output* in that it is triggered by learners themselves rather than by feedback from another task participant.

needs analysis A procedure for establishing the specific needs of language learners. These needs include the situations in which the language will be used and the communicative purposes it will be put to.

negotiation of content The process by which two or more interlocutors attempt to agree on the truthfulness of factual information.

negotiation of form The process by which two or more interlocutors identify and then attempt to resolve a linguistic problem. In contrast to the *negotiation of meaning*, it does not involve any communication breakdown.

negotiation of meaning The process by which two or more interlocutors identify and then attempt to resolve a communication breakdown. However, negotiation of meaning may or may not result in mutual understanding.

non-interface position This claims that *explicit* and *implicit linguistic knowledge* systems are distinct such that implicit knowledge does not derive directly from explicit knowledge. There are two versions: (1) the strong non-interface position which claims that explicit knowledge has no role whatsoever in the development of implicit knowledge; and (2) the weak non-interface position which claims that although explicit knowledge does not convert into implicit knowledge it can nevertheless facilitate its

development by, for example, promoting *noticing*.

non-reciprocal task A task that involves learners processing information or producing language by themselves, i.e. there is no opportunity to interact with another learner. See *reciprocal tasks*.

noticing A cognitive process that involves attending to linguistic form in the input learners receive and the output they produce. Schmidt (1990) argues that noticing is necessarily a conscious process and is a prerequisite for learning to take place.

noticing-the-gap A cognitive process that involves learners comparing forms that have been noticed in the input with their current representation of these forms in their interlanguages. As with *noticing*, Schmidt (1990) claims this is a conscious process.

notional/functional syllabus A syllabus constructed around categories of meaning rather than categories of linguistic form. These categories relate to both semantic notions such as 'duration' or 'possibility' and communicative functions such as 'inviting' and 'apologizing'.

object-regulation A term used in sociocultural theory to refer to activity that is governed by the material object a person is attending to. It constitutes a preliminary step in the development of consciousness. Compare with *other-regulation* and *self-regulation*.

one-way task An *information-gap task* where one person holds all the information to be communicated and the other participant(s) hold none.

online planning The process by which learners attend to form while planning speech acts or in order to monitor their output. Online planning takes place while learners are performing a task. It contrasts with *pre-task planning*.

open task A task where the participants know there is no predetermined solution. Many *opinion-gap tasks* are open.

opinion-gap task A task that requires the participants to exchange opinions on some issue, e.g. a balloon debate. Such tasks typically involve controversial issues about which the participants are likely to hold different views.

oral proficiency interview (OPI) A test of learners' language proficiency based on an assessment of their performance in an oral interview. The assessment may be carried out during the interview or afterwards.

other-regulation A term used in sociocultural theory to refer to activity that is governed by another person. Other-regulation serves as a means of overcoming object-regulation. Thus it constitutes an intermediate stage in the development of higher-order mental activity. See also *object-regulation* and *self-regulation*.

Output Hypothesis Swain (1985) argues that L2 acquisition is promoted by learners being pushed to produce language that is accurate and precise. She sees this hypothesis as an addition, not as an alternative, to the *Input Hypothesis*.

participatory structure The participatory structure of a lesson refers to the procedures that govern how the teacher's and students' contributions to the performance of the task are organized, e.g. in terms of teacher-class or small group interactions.

pedagogic tasks Tasks designed to elicit communicative language use in the classroom, e.g. Spot-the-difference. Such tasks do not necessarily bear any resemblance to real-world tasks although they are intended to lead to patterns of language use similar to those found in the real world. See *target tasks* and *authenticity*.

performance-referenced test A test that seeks to provide information about learners' ability to use the language in specific contexts; it is directed at assessing a particular performance, e.g. the ability of a trainee pilot to understand and respond to messages from the control tower when landing an aircraft.

performance testing Performance testing involves either observing learners perform real-world tasks or obtaining samples of communicative language use by asking them to perform pedagogic-type tasks. Their performances are typically evaluated against some rating scale.

planned discourse Ochs (1979: 55) distinguishes 'discourse that lacks forethought and organizational preparation', i.e. *unplanned discourse* and 'discourse that has been thought out and organized prior to its expression', i.e. planned discourse. See also *pre-task planning*.

PPP This refers to an approach to teaching involving the instructional sequence of 'present', 'controlled practice' (by means of exercises), and 'free production' (by means of tasks).

pragmalinguistic device A linguistic strategy used to realize an illocutionary meaning. For example, a request can be realized by means of an interrogative, e.g. 'Could you close the window?', or a hint, e.g. 'It's cold in here.'

pre-emptive focus on form Focus on form that arises as a result of one of the participants in a task choosing to attend to some specific linguistic form even though no actual or perceived error has occurred. It is typically initiated by means of a query about the specific form.

pre-task planning The process by which learners plan what they are going to say or write before commencing a task. Pre-task planning can attend to propositional content, to the organization of information, or

to the choice of language. See also *online planning*.

private speech Ohta (2001b: 16) defines private speech as 'audible speech not adapted to an addressee'. She suggests that it can take a number of forms including imitation, vicarious response, i.e. responses that a classroom learner produces to questions the teacher has addressed to another learner, and mental rehearsal.

procedural knowledge Knowledge that is fully automatized so that it is easily and rapidly accessible during the performance of a task. See *controlled processing*.

procedural syllabus The term used by Prabhu (1987) to refer to a syllabus consisting of a graded set of tasks to be performed by the learners.

process syllabus An approach to the construction of a syllabus through negotiation of the aims, instructional content, methodology and methods of evaluation by the classroom participants. It consists of banks of ideas and materials that can be called on to assist this negotiation.

processing strategy The term used by VanPatten (1996) to refer to the strategies that L2 learners use to process input. An example is 'the first noun strategy', according to which learners assume that the first noun in a sentence functions as the agent.

programme evaluation An evaluation of a complete language programme, e.g. a language course, carried out with a view to determining its effectiveness and/or to improving it.

progressive discourse Interaction in which the participants work towards a common understanding by engaging collaboratively in logical and critical thinking.

psychometric testing The psychometric tradition in language testing draws on the methods used in psychological testing in the first half of the twentieth century and on structural linguistics. Psychological tests are characterized by questions of the closed type, e.g. multiple choice, and for this reason were considered 'objective' in nature.

pushed output Output that reflects what learners can produce when they are pushed to use the target language accurately and concisely. Pushed output may or may not contain *modified output*.

rating A method of obtaining a measurement of proficiency by asking assessors to provide a holistic score and/or a set of analytic scores based on learners' performance of a task.

reasoning-gap task A task that requires participants to engage in reasoning, e.g. synthesizing the information provided and deducing new facts, in order to perform it successfully. Prabhu (1987) distinguishes reasoning-gap tasks from *information-gap* and *opinion-gap tasks*.

recast An utterance that rephrases a preceding utterance 'by changing one or more of its sentence components (subject, verb, or object) while still referring to its central meanings' (Long 1996: 436).

reciprocal task A task that involves information or opinions being exchanged between two or more people. See *non-reciprocal task*.

referential question A question intended to obtain information. A referential question is typically 'open', i.e. the questioner does not already know the answer. Compare with *display question*.

reliability The extent to which the measurements provided by a test are consistent. A test is reliable if it gives the same results when administered on different occasions or scored by different people.

response-based evaluation An evaluation that seeks to establish whether the student's performance of a particular task matches that intended by the teacher, i.e. the extent to which the 'task' and the 'activity' correlate.

responsive focus on form The corrective feedback that occurs when learners make errors.

restructuring This refers to the qualitative changes that occur in a learner's *interlanguage* as a result of learning. For example, learners may first represent past-tense forms as separate items and then shift to representing them by means of a general rule for past-tense formation.

scaffolding Scaffolding involves the interactive work participants engage in to accomplish a task collaboratively. Through scaffolding the participants construct *zones of proximal development* and thereby foster learning.

schematic knowledge This consists of 'schemata', i.e. mental structures for organizing different aspects of the world. There are both content schemata for organizing information about the world and formal schemata for organizing how information can be rhetorically structured.

self-assessment An assessment that a learner provides of his/her own performance or proficiency.

self-regulation A term used in *sociocultural theory* to refer to the ability of an individual to regulate his or her own mental activity. It constitutes the final stage in the development of higher-order skills. See also *object-regulation* and *other-regulation*.

simplified input Input that has been made simpler by modifying either the linguistic features, e.g. by using simpler grammatical structures, or the discoursal features, e.g. by supplying paraphrases. Simplified input can be premodified, i.e. the modifications are made before the input is made available to the learners, or interactionally modified, i.e. the modifications arise during interaction.

skill-based theory A skill-based theory views knowledge as originating in an explicit form

and gradually being proceduralized into an implicit form through practice. See *also interface position* and *non-interface position*.

sociocultural theory of the mind A theory of learning derived from the work of Vygotsky that emphasizes the role played by mediated learning in enabling learners to exercise conscious control over such mental activities as attention, planning, and problem-solving. See *mediation*.

strategic competence The knowledge of how to use communication strategies such as paraphrase to deal with communication problems caused by gaps in linguistic knowledge and also to improve the effectiveness of communication.

strategic planning See *pre-task planning*.

structural syllabus A teaching programme constructed around a sequenced list of grammatical items and structures, e.g. verb tenses, prepositions, subordinate clause constructions.

structure-based production task A *focused task* directed at eliciting production of a specific structure.

structured input Input that has been specially contrived to provide frequent exposure to a specific linguistic feature. See also *enriched input*.

structured task A task that lends itself to the participants utilizing a ready-made schema for performing it. A structured task is considered less complex than an unstructured task, where the participants need to actively construct a mental framework for performing it. See *schematic knowledge*.

student-based evaluation An evaluation of a task based on students' views about the task.

stylistic continuum Tarone (1983), drawing on the work of Labov, suggests that learners internalize different styles of language depending on the degree of attention they pay to language choice. They shift from using a 'careful style' (involving close attention to language choice) to a 'vernacular style' (involving less attention, as in everyday conversation).

system-referenced test A system-referenced test aims to provide 'information about language proficiency in a general sense without reference to any particular use or situation'. (Baker 1989: 10).

target task A task found in the real world, e.g. making a theatre booking or filling in a cheque.

task-based assessment (TBA) Assessment based on tests consisting of tasks. Such assessment involves *direct assessment*.

task-based language teaching Teaching that is based entirely on tasks. Such teaching makes use of a *procedural syllabus*.

task complexity The extent to which a particular task is inherently easy or difficult. Different dimensions of task complexity are *code complexity*, *cognitive complexity*, and *context dependency*.

task cycle A *lesson design* consisting of three stages; pre-task, during task, and post-task.

task difficulty The extent to which a particular learner finds a task easy or difficult. Individual difference factors such as intelligence, language aptitude, learning style, memory capacity, and motivation are responsible for task difficulty.

task procedures The methodological procedures used to teach a task. These can be classified into pre-task procedures (e.g. planning), during-task procedures (e.g. limiting the time for performing the task), and post-task procedures (e.g. repeating the task).

task-supported language teaching Teaching that utilizes tasks to provide free practice in the use of a specific linguistic feature that has been previously presented and practised in exercises. See *PPP*.

teacher talk The special register that teachers use when talking to students. Teacher talk directed at language learners is characterized by input that has been simplified in accordance with the proficiency level of the students.

test specifications An outline of the test in terms of its purpose, the test takers, the tasks used, and the methods of measurement.

text-reconstruction task A task that requires learners to read or listen to a text that has been seeded with a specific structure and subsequently to reconstruct it as accurately as possible without referring back to the text. See *dictogloss*.

top-down processing Understanding a text by making use of one's existing knowledge and contextual information. See also *bottom-up processing* and *schematic knowledge*.

two-way task An *information-gap task* where the information to be exchanged is split between two or more participants.

unfocused task A task that is designed to encourage the comprehension and production of language for purposes of communication, i.e. it is not designed to elicit attention to any specific linguistic feature. It contrasts with *focused task*.

Universal Grammar (UG) The term used by Chomsky to refer to the innate abstract knowledge of language with which children are innately endowed and which constrains the acquisition of the L1 grammar. This theory underlies the various theories of grammar that Chomsky has developed over the years, including the Principles and Parameters Theory and the Minimalist Program. Universal Grammar competes with *connectionist theories* of language.

unplanned discourse See *planned discourse*.

uptake (1) The output that learners produce as a result of the feedback they receive on their preceding utterance. Uptake may or may not consist of *modified output*.

uptake (2) Allwright (1984) uses the term to refer to what learners are able to explicitly report having learned as a result of participating in a lesson.

usage Widdowson (1978) uses this term to refer to the function of an item as part of a linguistic system, e.g. when we study the definite article 'the' as part of the grammar of English. The term contrasts with *use*.

use Widdowson (1978) uses this term to refer to the function of an item as part of a communicative system, e.g. when we study the definite article 'the' in terms of how it is used in discourse to refer to a previously mentioned entity. The term contrasts with *usage*.

validity The degree to which a test measures what it was designed to measure or can be successfully used for the purposes for which it was intended. Different types of validity can be distinguished, such as 'construct validity' and 'face validity'.

washback effect The effect that a test has on teaching. The design and content of a high-stakes test may result in teachers seeking to focus their efforts on the particular types of tasks included in the test. Also known as 'backwash effect'.

zone of proximal development (ZPD) This term is used in *sociocultural theory* to explain how participants in a task interact in order to enable learners to perform functions that they would be incapable of performing independently. It refers to the learner's potential as opposed to actual level of development.

Bibliography

Ahmed, M. 1988. *Speaking as Cognitive Regulation: A Study of L1 and L2 Dyadic Problem-solving Activity.* Unpublished doctoral dissertation, University of Delaware.

Alderson, J. and **A. Beretta.** (eds.) 1992. *Evaluating Second Language Education.* Cambridge: Cambridge University Press.

Aljaafreh, A. and **J. Lantolf.** 1994. 'Negative feedback as regulation and second language learning in the Zone of Proximal Development.' *The Modern Language Journal* 78: 465–83.

Allen, L. 2000. 'Form-meaning connections and the French causative. An experiment in processing instruction.' *Studies in Second Language Acquisition* 22: 69–84.

Allen, P. 1984. 'Functional-analytic course design and the variable focus curriculum' in Brumfit, C. (ed.) *ELT Documents 124: The Practice of Communicative Teaching.* Oxford: Pergamon.

Allwright, D. 1984. 'Why don't learners learn what teachers teach? The interaction hypothesis' in Singleton, D. and D. Little (eds.) *Language Learning in Formal and Informal Contexts* (pp. 3–18). Dublin: IRAL.

Allwright, R. and **K. Bailey.** 1991. *Focus on the Language Classroom.* Cambridge: Cambridge University Press.

Anderson, A. and **T. Lynch.** 1988. *Listening.* Oxford: Oxford University Press.

Andersen, R., R. Reynolds, D. Schallert, and **E. Goetz.** 1977. 'Frameworks for comprehending discourse.' *American Educational Research Journal* 14: 367–81.

Anderson, J. 1993. *Rules of the Mind.* Hillsdale, NJ: Lawrence Erlbaum.

Anderson, J. 2000. *Learning and Memory: An Integrated Approach,* revised edition. New York: John Wiley and Sons.

Anton, M. and **F. J. DiCamilla.** 1998. 'Socio-cognitive functions of L1 collaborative interaction in the L2 classroom.' *The Canadian Modern Language Review* 54: 314–42.

Anton, M. 1999. 'A learner-centered classroom. Sociocultural perspectives on teacher–learner interaction in the second language classroom.' *The Modern Language Journal* 83: 303–18.

Appel, G. and **J. Lantolf.** 1994. 'Speaking as mediation: A study of L1 and L2 text recall tasks.' *Modern Language Journal* 78: 437–52.

Arnaudet, M. 1984. *Approaches to Academic Reading and Writing.* New York: Pearson ESL.

Artigal, J. 1992. 'Some considerations on why a new language is acquired by being used.' *International Journal of Applied Linguistics* 2: 221–40.

Asher, J. 1977. *Learning Another Language Through Actions: The Complete Teacher's Guidebook.* Los Gatos, California: Sky Oaks Publications.

Aston, G. 1982. *Interact.* Oxford: Modern English Publications.

Aston, G. 1986. 'Trouble-shooting in interaction with learners: the more the merrier?' *Applied Linguistics* 7: 128–43.

Ayoun, D. 2001. 'The role of negative and positive feedback in the second language acquisition of passé composé and the imparfait.' *The Modern Language Journal* 85: 226–43.

Bachman, L. 1990. *Fundamental Considerations in Language Testing.* Oxford: Oxford University Press.

Bachman, L. and **A. Palmer.** 1996. *Language Testing in Practice: Designing and Developing Useful Language Tests.* Oxford: Oxford University Press.

Bachman, L., B. Lynch, and **M. Mason.** 1995. 'Investigating variability in tasks and rater judgements in a performance test of foreign language speaking'. *Language Testing* 12: 238–57.

Baker, D. 1989. *Language Testing: A Critical Survey and Practical Guide.* London: Edward Arnold.

Bardovi-Harlig, K. 1994. 'Reverse-order reports and the acquisition of tense: Beyond the principle of chronological order.' *Language Learning* 44: 243–82.

Barnes, D. 1976. *From Communication to Curriculum.* Harmondsworth: Penguin.

Batstone, R. 1994. *A Scheme for Teacher Education: Grammar.* Oxford: Oxford University Press.

Beebe, L. 1980. 'Sociolinguistic variation and style-shifting in second language acquisition.' *Language Learning* 30: 433–47.

Bell, A. 1984. 'Language style as audience design.' *Language in Society* 13: 145–204.

Benson, M. 1989. 'The academic listening task: a case study.' *TESOL Quarterly* 23: 421–45.

Benson, P. 2000. *Teaching and Researching Autonomy.* London: Pearson Education.

Bereiter, C. 1994. 'Implications of postmodernism for science, or, science as progressive discourse.' *Educational Psychologist* 29: 3–12.

Bereiter, C. and **M. Scardamalia.** 1996. 'Rethinking learning.' in D. Olson and N. Torrance (eds.): *The Handbook of Education and Human Development* (pp. 485–513). Cambridge, MA: Blackwell.

Beretta, A. 1990a. 'Implementation of the Bangalore Project.' *Applied Linguistics* 11: 321–37.

Beretta, A. 1990b. 'The program evaluator: The ESL researcher without portfolio.' *Applied Linguistics* 11: 1–15.

Beretta, A. and **A. Davies.** 1985. 'Evaluation of the Bangalore Project.' *ELT Journal* 39: 121–7.

Berkoff, N. 1985. 'Testing oral proficiency: A new approach' in Y. Lee (ed.): *New Directions in Language Testing.* (pp. 93–100). Oxford: Pergamon.

Berwick, R. 1990. *Task Variation and Repair in English as a Foreign Language.* Kobe University of Commerce: Institute of Economic Research.

Berwick, R. 1993. 'Towards an educational framework for teacher-led tasks' in G. Crookes and S. Gass 1993b (eds.).

Bialystok, E. 1982. 'On the relationship between knowing and using forms.' *Applied Linguistics* 3: 181–206.

Bialystok, E. 1990. *Communication Strategies: A Psychological Analysis of Second-Language Use.* Oxford: Basil Blackwell.

Bialystok, E. 1991. 'Achieving proficiency in a second language: a processing description' in R. Phillipson *et al.* (eds.).

Biber, D. 1989. 'A typology of English texts.' *Linguistics* 27: 3–43.

Bitchener, J. 1999. *The Negotiation of Meaning by advanced ESL Learners: The Effects of Individual Learner Factors and Task Type.* Unpublished PhD Thesis, University of Auckland.

Bolinger, D. 1975. 'Meaning and memory.' *Forum Linguisticum* 1: 2–14.

Bourke, J. 1996. 'In praise of problem solving.' *RELC Journal* 27: 12–29.

Braidi, S. 1997. 'Reconsidering the role of interaction and input in second language acquisition.' *Language Learning* 45: 141–75.

Breen, M. 1984. 'Process syllabuses for the language classroom' in C. Brumfit (ed.): *General English Syllabus Design.* Oxford: Pergamon Press and the British Council.

Breen, M. 1985. 'The social context for language learning—a neglected situation?' *Studies in Second Language Acquisition* 7: 135–58.

Breen, M. 1987. 'Learner contributions to task design' in C. Candlin and D. Murphy (eds.).

Breen, M. 1989. 'The evaluation cycle for language learning tasks' in R. K. Johnson (ed.): *The Second Language Curriculum.* Cambridge: Cambridge University Press.

Breen, M. 1998. 'Navigating the discourse: On what is learned in the language classroom' in W. Renandya and G. Jacobs (eds.): *Learners and Language Learning.* Singapore: SEAMEO Regional Language Centre.

Breen, M. 2001. 'Overt participation and covert acquisition in the language classroom' in M. Breen (ed.): *Learner Contributions to Language Learning.* Harlow: Longman.

Breen, M. and C. Candlin. 1980. 'The essentials of a communicative curriculum for language teaching.' *Applied Linguistics* 1: 89–112.

Breen, M. and M. Littlejohn. (eds.) 2000. *Classroom Decision-Making: Negotiation and Process Syllabuses in Practice*. Cambridge: Cambridge University Press.

Brindley, G. 1989. *Assessing Achievement in the Learner-Centred Curriculum*. Sydney: National Centre for English Language Teaching and Research.

Brindley, G. 1994. 'Task-centred assessment in language learning: The promise and the challenge' in N. Bird, P. Falvey, A. Tsui, D. Allison, and A. McNeill (eds.): *Language and Learning*. Hong Kong: Hong Kong Institute of Language in Education, Hong Kong Education Department.

Brindley, G. 2001. 'Language assessment and professional development' in C. Elder *et al.* (eds.).

Brooks, F. 1990. 'Foreign language learning: A social interaction perspective' in B. VanPatten and J. Lee (eds.): *Second Language Acquisition—Foreign Language Learning*. Clevedon: Multilingual Matters.

Brooks, F. and R. Donato. 1994. 'Vygotskian approaches to understanding foreign language learner discourse during communicative tasks.' *Hispania* 77, 262–74.

Brown, A. and K. Hill 1998. 'Interviewer style and candidate performance in the IELTS interview' in S. Woods (ed.): *Research Reports 1997: 1*. Sydney: ELICOS.

Brown, G. 1995. *Speakers, Listeners and Communication*. Cambridge: Cambridge University Press.

Brown, G. and G. Yule. 1983. *Discourse Analysis*. Cambridge: Cambridge University Press.

Brown, G., A. Anderson, R. Shilcock, and G. Yule. 1984. *Teaching Talk: Strategies for Production and Assessment*. Cambridge: Cambridge University Press.

Brown, H.D. 1994. *Teaching by Principles: An Interactive Approach to Language Pedagogy*. Englewood Cliffs, N.J.: Prentice Hall.

Brown, J.D. 1988. *Understanding Research in Second Language Teaching: A Teacher's Guide to Statistics and Research Design*. Cambridge: Cambridge University Press.

Brown, J.D. and T. Hudson. 1998. 'The alternatives in language testing'. *TESOL Quarterly* 32: 653–75.

Brown, R. 1968. 'The development of *Wh*- questions in children's speech.' *Journal of Verbal Learning and Language Behavior* 7: 279–90.

Brown, R. 1991. 'Group work, task difference, and second language acquisition.' *Applied Linguistics* 21: 1-12.

Brown, R. and U. Bellugi. 1964. 'Three processes in the child's acquisition of syntax.' *Harvard Educational Review* 34: 133–51.

Brumfit, C. 1979. 'Communicative language teaching: An educational perspective' in C. Brumfit and K. Johnson (eds.).

Brumfit, C. 1984. *Communicative Methodology in Language Teaching*. Cambridge: Cambridge University Press.

Brumfit, C. and K. Johnson (eds.). 1979. *The Communicative Approach to Language Teaching*. Oxford: Oxford University Press.

Buck, G. 1991. 'The testing of listening comprehension: An introspective study.' *Language Testing* 8: 67–91.

Burt, M., H. Dulay, and E. Hernandez. 1973. *Bilingual Syntax Measure*. New York: Harcourt Brace Jovanovich.

Butterworth, B. 1980. 'Some constraints on models of language production' in B. Butterworth (ed.): *Language Production, Vol. 1*. New York: Academic Press.

Bygate, M. 1996. 'Effects of task repetition: Appraising the development of second language learners' in J. Willis and D. Willis (eds.): *Challenge and Change in Language Teaching*. Oxford: Heinemann.

Bygate, M. 1999a. 'Task as the context for the framing, re-framing and un-framing of language.' *System* 27: 33–48.

Bygate, M. 1999b. 'Quality of language and purpose of task: Patterns of learners' language on two oral communication tasks.' *Language Teaching Research* 3: 185–214.

Bygate, M. 2001. 'Effects of task repetition on the structure and control of oral language' in M. Bygate, P. Skehan and M. Swain (eds.): 23–48.

Bygate, M., P. Skehan, and **M. Swain**. (eds.). 2001. *Researching Pedagogic Tasks, Second Language Learning, Teaching and Testing*. Harlow: Longman.

Bygate, M., P. Skehan, and **M. Swain**. 2001. Introduction in M. Bygate, P. Skehan and M. Swain (eds.).

Byrne, D. and **S. Rixon**. 1979. *ELT Guide 1: Communicative Games*. NFER.

Canale, M. 1983. 'From communicative competence to language pedagogy' in J. Richards and R. Schmidt (eds.).

Canale, M. and **M. Swain**. 1980. 'Theoretical bases of communicative approaches to second language testing.' *Applied Linguistics* 1: 1–47.

Cancino, H., E. Rosansky, and **J. Schumann**. 1978. 'The acquisition of English negatives and interrogatives by native Spanish speakers.' In E. Hatch (ed.).

Candlin, C. 1987. 'Towards task-based language learning' in C. Candlin and D. Murphy (eds.).

Candlin, C. 2001. 'Afterword: Taking the curriculum to task' in M. Bygate, P. Skehan, and M. Swain (eds.).

Candlin, C. and **D. Murphy**. 1987. *Language Learning Tasks*. Englewood Cliffs N.J.: Prentice Hall International.

Carpenter, C. 1996. 'Peer-teaching: a new approach to advanced level language teaching' in E. Broady and M. Kenning (eds.): *Promoting Learner Autonomy in University Language Teaching*. London: Association for French Language Studies/CILT: 23–38.

Carpenter, P. and **M. Just**. 1999. 'Computational modeling of high level cognition versus hypothesis testing' in R. Sternberg (ed.): *The Nature of Cognition*. Cambridge, MA: MIT Press.

Carr, W. and **S. Kemmis**. 1986. *Becoming Critical: Education, Knowledge and Action Research*. London: The Falmer Press.

Carrell, P., J. Devine, and **D. Eskey**. (eds.). 1988. *Interactive Approaches to Reading*. Cambridge: Cambridge University Press.

Carroll, J. 1983. 'Psychometric theory and language testing.' In J. Oller (ed.). *Issues in Language Testing Research*. Rowley, Mass: Newbury House.

Carroll, J. and **S. Sapon**. 1959. *Modern Language Aptitude Test—Form A*. New York: The Psychological Corporation.

Chalhoub-Delville, M. 2001. 'Task-based assessments: Characteristics and validity evidence' in Bygate *et al.* (eds.): 210–28.

Chang, Y. 1999. 'Discourse topics and interlanguage variation' in P. Robinson (ed.): *Representation and Process: Proceedings of the 3rd Pacific Second Language Research Forum*. Vol. 1 Tokyo: PacSLRF: 235–41.

Chaudron, C. 1982. 'Vocabulary elaboration in teachers' speech to L2 learners.' *Studies in Second Language Acquisition* 4: 170–80.

Chaudron, C. 1988. *Second Language Classrooms: Research on Teaching and Learning*. Cambridge: Cambridge University Press.

Chaudron, C., L. Loschky, and **J. Cook**. 1994. 'Second language listening comprehension and lecture note-taking' in J. Flowerdew (ed.).

Chaudron, C., J. Lubin, Y. Sasaki, and **T. Grigg**. 1986. 'An investigation of procedures for evaluating lecture listening comprehension.' *Technical Report No. 5*. Hawaii: Center for Second Language Classroom Research, Social Science Research Institute, University of Hawaii, Manoa.

Chaudron, C and **J. Richards**. 1986. 'The effect of discourse markers on the comprehension of lectures.' *Applied Linguistics* 7: 113–27.

Chomsky, N. 1986. *Knowledge of Language: Its Nature, Origin and Use*. New York: Praeger.

Clapham, C. and **D. Corson**. (eds.). 1997: *Encyclopedia of Language and Education, Volume 7: Language Testing and Assessment*. Dordrecht: Kluwer Academic.

Clark, R. 1974. 'Performing without competence.' *Journal of Child Language* 1:1–10.

Clerehan, R. 1995. 'Taking it down: Notetaking practices of L1 and L2 students.' *English for Specific Purposes* 12: 137–55.

Cohen, A. 1982. 'Writing like a native: The process of reformulation.' *ERIC ED 224 338.*

Cook, G. 1997. 'Language play and language learning.' *ELT Journal* 51: 224–21.

Cook, G. 2000. *Language Play, Language Learning.* Oxford: Oxford University Press.

Cook, G. and B. Seidlhofer (eds.). 1995. *Principles and Practice in Applied Linguistics.* Oxford: Oxford University Press.

Corder, S. P. 1967. 'The significance of learners' errors.' *International Review of Applied Linguistics* 5: 161–9.

Corder, S. P. 1973. 'The elicitation of interlanguage' in J. Svartvik (ed.).

Corder, S. P. 1978. 'Strategies of communication.' *AFinLa 23.* Also in Corder 1981.

Corder, S.P. 1981. *Error Analysis and Interlanguage.* Oxford: Oxford University Press.

Coughlan, P. and P. A. Duff. 1994. 'Same task, different activities: Analysis of a SLA task from an activity theory perspective' in J. Lantolf and G. Appel, 1994: 173–94.

Craik, F. and R. Lockhart. 1972. 'Levels of processing: A framework for memory research.' *Journal of Verbal Learning and Verbal Behavior* 11: 671–84.

Craik, F. and E. Tulving. 1975. 'Depth of processing and the retention of words in episodic memory.' *Journal of Experimental Psychology: General* 104: 268–94.

Crookes, G. 1986. 'Task classification: a cross-disciplinary review.' *Technical Report No. 4.* Honolulu: Center for Second Language Classroom Research, Social Science Research Institute, University of Hawaii.

Crookes, G. 1989. 'Planning and interlanguage variability.' *Studies in Second Language Acquisition* 11: 367–83.

Crookes, G. and S. Gass (eds.). 1993a. *Tasks and Language Learning: Integrating Theory and Practice.* Clevedon: Multilingual Matters.

Crookes, G. and S. Gass (eds.). 1993b. *Tasks in a Pedagogical Context: Integrating Theory and Practice.* Clevedon: Multilingual Matters.

Crookes, G. and K. Rulon. 1985. 'Incorporation of corrective feedback in native speaker/ non-native speaker conversation.' *Technical Report No. 3.* Honolulu: Center for Second Language Classroom Research, Social Science Research Institute, University of Hawaii.

Cullen, R. 1998. 'Teacher-talk and the classroom context.' *ELT Journal* 52: 179–87.

Cummins, J. 1983. 'Language proficiency and academic achievement' in J. Oller (ed.). *Issues in Language Testing Research.* Rowley, Mass.: Newbury House.

Curran, C. 1972. *Counseling-Learning in Second Languages.* Apple River, Ill.: Apple River Press.

Davies, A. 1978. 'Language testing: Part one.' *Language Teaching and Linguistics Abstracts* 11: 145–59.

Davies, A., C. Brown, C. Elder, K. Hill, J. Lumly, and T. McNamara. 1999. *Dictionary of Language Testing. Studies in Language Testing 7.* Cambridge: Cambridge University Press.

Day, R. (ed.). 1986. *Talking to Learn: Conversation in Second Language Acquisition.* Rowley, Mass.: Newbury House.

DeKeyser, R. and K. Sokalski. 1996. 'The differential role of comprehension and production practice.' *Language Learning* 46: 613–42.

DeKeyser, R. 1998. 'Beyond focus on form: Cognitive perspectives on learning and practicing second language grammar' in C. Doughty and J. Williams (eds.).

Dewey, J. 1916. *Democracy and Education.* (1966 edn.) New York: Free Press.

Di Pietro, R. 1987. *Strategic Interaction.* Cambridge: Cambridge University Press.

Di Vesta, F. and S. Gray. 1972. 'Listening and note-taking.' *Journal of Educational Psychology* 63: 8–14.

DiCamilla, F. J. and M. Anton. 1997. 'The function of repetition in the collaborative discourse of L2 learners.' *The Canadian Modern Language Review* 53: 609–33.

Dickinson, L. 1987. *Self-Instruction in Language Learning*. Cambridge: Cambridge University Press.

Donato, R. 1994. 'Collective scaffolding in second language learning' in J. Lantolf and G. Appel (eds.).

Donato, R. 2000. 'Sociocultural contributions to understanding the foreign and second language classroom' in Lantolf, J. (ed.).

Donato, R. and D. McCormack. 1994. 'A sociocultural perspective on language learning strategies: The role of mediation.' *Modern Language Journal* 78: 453–64.

Dörnyei, Z. 2001. *Motivational Strategies in the Classroom*. Cambridge: Cambridge University Press.

Doughty, C. 1991. 'Second language instruction does make a difference: evidence from an empirical study on SL relativization.' *Studies in Second Language Acquisition* 13: 431–69.

Doughty, C. 2001. 'Cognitive underpinnings of focus on form' in P. Robinson (ed.). *Cognition and Second Language Instruction*. Cambridge: Cambridge University Press.

Doughty, C. and T. Pica. 1986. 'Information gap tasks: Do they facilitate second language acquisition?' *TESOL Quarterly* 20: 305–25.

Doughty, C. and E. Varela. 1998. 'Communicative focus on form' in C. Doughty and J. Williams (eds.).

Doughty, C. and J. Williams. (eds.). 1998. *Focus on Form in Classroom Second Language Acquisition*. Cambridge: Cambridge University Press.

Douglas, D. 2000. *Assessing Languages for Specific Purposes*. Cambridge: Cambridge University Press.

Douglas, D. 2001. 'Three problems in testing language specific purposes' in C. Elder *et al.* (eds.). (pp. 45–52).

Doye, P. 1991. 'Authenticity in foreign language testing' in S. Anivan (ed.). *Current Developments in Language Testing*. Singapore: SEAMEO Regional Language Centre.

Doyle, W. 1983. 'Academic work.' *Review of Educational Research* 53: 159–99.

Duff, P. 1986. 'Another look at interlanguage talk: taking task to task' in R. Day (ed.).

Dulay, H. and M. Burt. 1973. 'Should we teach children syntax?' *Language Learning* 23: 245–58.

Dunkel, P. 1988. 'The content of L1 and L2 students' lecture notes and its relation to test performance.' *TESOL Quarterly* 22: 259–82.

Dunkel, P. 1991. 'Listening in the native and second/foreign language: Toward integration of research and practice.' *TESOL Quarterly* 25: 431–57.

Dunkel, P. and J. Davis 1994. 'The effects of rhetorical signaling cues on the recall of English lecture information by speakers of English as a native or second language' in J. Flowerdew (ed.).

Dunkel, P., S. Mishra, and D. Berliner. 1989. 'Effects of note-taking, memory, and language proficiency on lecture learning for native and non-native speakers of English.' *TESOL Quarterly* 23: 543–50.

Dunn, W. and J. Lantolf. 1998. 'i + 1 and the ZPD: Incommensurable constructs; incommensurable discourses.' *Language Learning* 48: 411–42.

Ehrlich, S., P. Avery, and C. Yorio. 1989. 'Discourse structure and the negotiation of comprehensible input.' *Studies in Second Language Acquisition* 11: 397–414.

Elder, C. 2001. 'Assessing the language proficiency of teachers: LSP unlimited?' *Language Testing* 18: 149–70.

Elder, C., A. Brown, E. Grove, K. Hill, N. Iwashita, T. Lumley, T. McNamara, and K. O'Loughlin (eds.). 2001. *Studies in Language Testing 11: Experimenting with Uncertainty – Essays in Honour of Alan Davies*. Cambridge: Cambridge University Press.

Ellis, G. and B. Sinclair. 1989. *Learning to Learn English*. Cambridge: Cambridge University Press.

Ellis, N. 1994. *Implicit and Explicit Learning of Languages*. London: Academic Press.

Ellis, N. 1996. 'Sequencing in SLA: phonological memory, chunking, and points of order.' *Studies in Second Language Acquisition* 18: 91–126.

Ellis, N. 1998. 'Emergentism, connectionism and language learning.' *Language Learning* 48: 631–64.

Ellis, N. 2002. 'Frequency effects in language processing: A review with implications for theories of implicit and explicit language acquisition.' *Studies in Second Language Acquisition* 24 (2): 143–188.

Ellis, R. 1984. 'Can syntax be taught? A study of the effects of formal instruction on the acquisition of *Wh*-questions by children.' *Applied Linguistics* 5: 138–55.

Ellis, R. 1984. *Classroom Second Language Development*. Oxford: Pergamon.

Ellis, R. 1985. 'Teacher-pupil interaction in second language development' in S. Gass and C. Madden (eds.): *Input in Second Language Acquisition*. Rowley, Mass.: Newbury House.

Ellis, R. 1987a. 'Interlanguage variability in narrative discourse: Style shifting in the use of the past tense.' *Studies in Second Language Acquisition* 9: 1–20.

Ellis, R. 1987b. *Second Language Acquisition in Context*. London: Prentice Hall International.

Ellis, R. 1988. 'The role of practice in classroom language learning.' *AILA Review* 5: 20–39.

Ellis, R. 1991. *Second Language Acquisition and Language Pedagogy*. Clevedon: Multilingual Matters.

Ellis, R. 1993. 'Second language acquisition and the structural syllabus.' *TESOL Quarterly* 27: 91–113.

Ellis, R. 1994a. *The Study of Second Language Acquisition*. Oxford: Oxford University Press.

Ellis, R. 1994b. 'A theory of instructed second language acquisition' in N. Ellis (ed.).

Ellis, R. 1995a. 'Interpretation tasks for grammar teaching.' *TESOL Quarterly* 29: 87–105.

Ellis, R. 1995b. 'Modified input and the acquisition of word meanings.' *Applied Linguistics* 16: 409–41.

Ellis, R. 1997a. *SLA Research and Language Teaching*. Oxford: Oxford University Press.

Ellis, R. 1997b. 'Explicit knowledge and second language pedagogy' in L. van Lier and D. Corson (eds.): *Encyclopedia of Language and Education Vol 6: Knowledge about Language*. Dordrecht: Kluwer Academic.

Ellis, R. 1997c. 'The empirical evaluation of language teaching materials.' *ELT Journal* 51: 36–42.

Ellis, R. 1998a. 'Discourse control and the acquisition-rich classroom' in W. Renandya and G. Jacobs (eds.). *Learners and Language Learning* (pp. 145–171). Singapore: SEAMEO.

Ellis, R. 1999a. 'Input-based approaches to the teaching of grammar.' *Annual Review of Applied Linguistics* 19: 64–80.

Ellis, R. 1999b. *Learning a Second Language Through Interaction*. Amsterdam: John Benjamin.

Ellis, R. 1999c. 'Evaluating and researching grammar consciousness tasks' in P. Rea-Dickens and K. Germaine (eds.) *Managing Evaluation and Innovation in Language Teaching*. Harlow: Longman.

Ellis, R. 2000. 'Task-based research and language pedagogy.' *Language Teaching Research* 4: 193–220.

Ellis, R. 2001. 'Focussing on form: Towards a research agenda' in W. Renandya and N. Sunga (eds.): *Language Curriculum and Instruction in Multicultural Societies* (pp. 123–44). Singapore: SEAMEO.

Ellis, R. 2002a. 'The place of grammar instruction in the second/foreign language curriculum' in E. Hinkel and S. Fotos (eds.): *New Perspectives on Grammar Teaching in Second Language Classrooms*. Mahwah, NJ: Lawrence Erlbaum.

Ellis, R. 2002b. 'Does form-focussed instruction affect the acquisition of implicit knowledge? A review of the research.' *Studies in Second Language Acquisition* 24 (2): 223–236.

Ellis, R., H. Basturkmen, and S. Loewen. 2001. 'Learner uptake in communicative ESL lessons.' *Language Learning* 51: 281–318.

Ellis, R. and S. Gaies. 1999. *Impact Grammar*. Hong Kong: Longman.

Ellis, R. and X. He. 1999. 'The roles of modified input and output in the incidental acquisition of word meanings.' *Studies in Second Language Acquisition* 21: 319–33.

Ellis, R. and R. Heimbach. 1997. 'Bugs and birds: Children's acquisition of second language vocabulary through interaction.' *System* 25: 247–59.

Ellis, R. and H. Takashima. 1999. Output enhancement and the acquisition of the past tense. In R. Ellis 1999b (pp. 173–88).

Ellis, R., Y. Tanaka, and A. Yamazaki. 1994. 'Classroom interaction, comprehension and the acquisition of word meanings.' *Language Learning* 44: 449–91.

Eraut, M. 1994. *Developing Professional Knowledge and Competence.* London: Falmer.

Erlam, R. 2001. A Comparative Study of the Effectiveness of Processing Instruction and Output-based Instruction on the Acquisition of Direct Object Pronouns in L2 French. Unpublished paper, University of Auckland, Auckland, New Zealand.

Estaire, S. and J. Zanón. 1994. *Planning Classwork: A Task Based Approach.* Oxford: Heinemann.

Færch, C. and G. Kasper. 1980. 'Processes and strategies in foreign language learning and communication.' *Interlanguage Studies Bulletin* 5: 47–118.

Færch, C. and G. Kasper (eds.). 1983a. *Strategies in Interlanguage Communication.* London: Longman.

Færch, C. and G. Kasper. 1983b. 'Plans and strategies in foreign language communication' in C. Færch and G. Kasper (eds.).

Færch, C. and G. Kasper. 1986. 'The role of comprehension in second language learning.' *Applied Linguistics* 7: 257–74.

Farrar, M. 1992. 'Discourse and the acquisition of grammatical morphemes.' *Journal of Child Language* 17: 607–24.

Ferrier, L. 1978. 'Some observations of error in context' in N. Waterson and C. Snow (eds.): *The Development of Communication.* Wiley: New York.

Flowerdew, J. (ed.). 1994. *Academic Listening.* Cambridge: Cambridge University Press.

Flowerdew, J. 1994. 'Research of relevance to second language lecture comprehension—an overview' in Flowerdew, J. (ed.).

Flowerdew, J. and L. Miller. 1996. 'Lectures in a second language: Notes towards a cultural grammar.' *English for Specific Purposes* 15: 121–40.

Foley, J. 1991. 'A psycholinguistic framework for task-based approaches to language teaching.' *Applied Linguistics* 12: 62–75.

Foster, P. 1996. 'Doing the task better: How planning time influences students' performance' in J. Willis and D. Willis (eds.).

Foster, P. 1998. 'A classroom perspective on the negotiation of meaning.' *Applied Linguistics* 19: 1–23.

Foster, P. 2001. 'Rules and routines: A consideration of their role in task-based language production of native and non-native speakers.' in M. Bygate, P. Skehan, and M. Swain (eds.)

Foster, P. and P. Skehan. 1996. 'The influence of planning and task type on second language performance.' *Studies in Second Language Acquisition* 18: 299–323.

Foster, P. and P. Skehan. 1999. 'The influence of planning and focus of planning on task-based performance.' *Language Teaching Research* 3: 215–47.

Foster, P., A. Tonkyn, and G. Wigglesworth. 2000. 'Measuring spoken language: A unit for all reasons.' *Applied Linguistics* 21: 354–75.

Fotos, S. 1993. 'Consciousness-raising and noticing through focus on form: Grammar task performance vs. formal instruction.' *Applied Linguistics* 14: 385–407.

Fotos, S. 1994. 'Integrating grammar instruction and communicative language use through grammar consciousness-raising tasks.' *TESOL Quarterly* 28: 323–51.

Fotos, S. and R. Ellis. 1991. 'Communicating about grammar: A task-based approach.' *TESOL Quarterly* 25: 605–28.

Frawley, W. and J. Lantolf. 1985. 'Second language discourse: A Vygotskian perspective.' *Applied Linguistics* 6: 19–44.

Frawley, W. and J. Lantolf. 1986. 'Private speech and self-regulation: A commentary of Frauenglass and Diaz.' *Developmental Psychology* 22: 706–8.
Fulcher, G. 1996a. 'Testing tasks: Issues in task design and the group oral.' *Language Testing* 13: 23–51.
Fulcher, G. 1996b. 'Does thick description lead to smart tests? A data-based approach to rating scale construction.' *Language Testing* 13: 208–38.
Fulcher, G. 2000. 'The "communicative" legacy in language testing.' *System* 28: 483–97.
Fulcher, G. 1997. 'The testing of L2 speaking' in C. Clapham and D. Corson (eds.): 75–85.
Fullan, M. 1993. *Changing Forces: Probing the Depths of Educational Reform.* London: Falmer.

Gardner, R. and P. McIntyre. 1993. 'On the measurement of affective variables in second language learning.' *Language Learning* 43: 157–94.
Gardner, D. and L. Miller. 1996. *Tasks for Independent Learning.* TESOL Publications.
Gass, S., A. Mackey, M. Fernandez, and M. Alvarez-Torres. 1999. 'The effects of task repetition on linguistic output.' *Language Learning* 49: 549–80.
Gass, S. and C. Madden. (eds.). 1985. *Input in Second Language Acquisition.* Rowley, Mass.: Newbury House.
Gass, S. and M. Varonis. 1984. 'The effect of familiarity on the comprehension of non-native speech.' *Language Learning* 34: 65–89.
Gass, S. and E. Varonis. 1985. 'Task variation and non-native/non-native negotiation of meaning' in S. Gass and C. Madden (eds.).
Gass, S. and E. Varonis. 1989. 'Incorporated repairs in non-native discourse' in M. Eisenstein (ed.): *The Dynamic Interlanguage: Empirical Studies in Second Language Acquisition.* New York: Plenum Press.
Gass, S. and E. Varonis. 1994. 'Input, interaction, and second language production.' *Studies in Second Language Acquisition* 16: 283–302.
Gatbonton, E. 1978. 'Patterned phonetic variability in second language speech: a gradual diffusion model.' *Canadian Modern Language Review* 34: 335–47.
Geddes, M. and G. Sturtridge. 1979. *Jigsaw Listening.* Place of publ. Dominie Press Inc.
Genesee, F. 1994. 'Integrating language and content instruction' in R. Bostwick (ed.) *Immersion Education International Symposium Report* (pp. 44–66). Japan: Katoh Gakuen.
Gipps, C. 1994. *Beyond Testing: Towards a Theory of Educational Assessment.* London: The Falmer Press.
Givón, T. 1979. *On Understanding Grammar.* New York: Academic Press.
Goffman, E. 1981. *Forms of Talk.* Oxford: Basil Blackwell.
Goh, C. 2000. 'A cognitive perspective on language learners' listening comprehension problems.' *System* 28: 55–75.
Goldman-Eisler, F. 1968. *Psycholinguistics: Experiments in Spontaneous Speech.* New York: Academic.
Gower, R. and S. Walters. 1983. *Teaching Practice Handbook.* England: Oxford.
Gregg, K. 1989. 'Second language acquisition theory: the case for a generative perspective' in S. Gass and J. Schachter (eds.).
Gregg, K. 1993. 'Taking explanation seriously; or, let a couple of flowers bloom.' *Applied Linguistics* 14: 276–94.
Gremmo, M., H. Holec, and P. Riley. 1978. *Taking the Initiative: Some Pedagogical Applications of Discourse Analysis.* Nancy: Mélanges Pédagogiques, CRAPEL.

Hagan, P., S. Hood, E. Jackson, M. Jones, H. Joyce, and M. Mandis. 1993. *Certificate in Spoken and Written English.* Sydney: NSW Adult Migrant English Service and the National Centre for English Language Teaching and Research.
Hakuta, K. 1976. 'Becoming bilingual: A case study of a Japanese child learning English.' *Language Learning* 26: 321–51.

Hall, J. 1993. 'The role of oral practices in the accomplishment of our everyday lives: The sociocultural dimension of interaction with implication for learning another language.' *Applied Linguistics* 14: 145–66.

Hall, J. 1995a. '(Re)creating our worlds with words: A socio-historical perspective of face-to-face interaction.' *Applied Linguistics* 16: 206–32.

Hall, J. 1995b. 'A consideration of SLA as a theory of practice: A response to Firth and Wagner.' *Modern Language Journal* 81: 301–05.

Halliday, M. 1986. *An Introduction to Functional Grammar*. London: Arnold.

Hansen, C. 1994. 'Topic identification in lecture discourse' in J. Flowerdew (ed.).

Harlen, W. and M. James. 1997. 'Assessment and learning: Differences and relationships between formative and summative assessment.' *Assessment in Education* 4: 365–79.

Harley, B. 1989. 'Functional grammar in French immersion: A classroom experiment.' *Applied Linguistics* 10: 331–59.

Harley, B. 1994. 'Appealing to consciousness in the classroom' in J. Hulstijn and R. Schmidt (eds.):

Hatch, E. (ed.). 1978a. *Second Language Acquisition*. Rowley, Mass.: Newbury House.

Hatch, E. 1978b. 'Discourse analysis and second language acquisition' in Hatch, E. (ed.).

Hawkins, B. 1985. 'Is the appropriate response always so appropriate' in S. Gass and C. Madden (eds.).

He, A. and R. Young. 1998. 'Language proficiency interviews: A discourse approach' in R. Young and A. He (eds.): *Talking and Testing*. Amsterdam: John Benjamins.

Henzl, V. 1979. 'Foreigner talk in the classroom.' *International Review of Applied Linguistics* 17: 159–65.

Hoey, M. 1983. *On the Surface of Discourse*. London: George, Allen and Unwin.

Holunga, S. 1995. *The Effect of Metacognitive Strategy Training with Verbalization on the Oral Accuracy of Adult Second Language Learners*. Unpublished doctoral dissertation, University of Toronto (OISE).

Hoogwerf, P. 1995. *Evaluation of a Grammar CR Task*. Unpublished M. Ed. course paper, Temple University Japan.

Horowitz, E. 1987. 'Surveying student beliefs about language learning' in A. Wenden and J. Rubin (eds.): *Learner Strategies in Language Learning*. Englewood Cliffs, NJ: Prentice Hall.

Hosenfeld, C. 1976. 'Learning about language: Discovering our students' strategies.' *Foreign Language Annals* 9: 117–29.

Howatt, A. 1984. *A History of English Language Teaching*. Oxford: Oxford University Press.

Huerta-Macias, A. 1995. 'Alternative assessment: Responses to commonly asked questions.' *TESOL Journal* 5: 8–11.

Hughes, A. and D. Porter. (ed.). 1983. *Current Developments in Language Testing*. London: Academic Press.

Hulstijn, J. 2002. 'Towards a unified account of the representation, processing, and acquisition of second-language knowledge.' *Second language Research*. 18: 193–223.

Hulstijn, J. and W. Hulstijn. 1984. 'Grammatical errors as a function of processing constraints and explicit knowledge.' *Language Learning* 34: 23–43.

Hulstijn, J. and R. Schmidt. (eds.). 1994. 'Consciousness in Second Language Learning.' *AILA Review* 11.

Hymes, D. 1971. *On Communicative Competence*. Philadelphia, PA: University of Pennsylvania Press.

Iwashita, N., C. Elder. and T. McNamara. 2001. 'Can we predict task difficulty in an oral proficiency test? Exploring the potential of an information-processing approach to task design.' *Language Learning* 51: 401–36.

Izumi, I. and M. Bigelow. 2000. 'Does output promote noticing and second language acquisition?' *TESOL Quarterly* 34: 239–78.

Jacobs, G. 1998. 'Cooperative learning or just grouping students: The difference makes a difference' in W. Renandya and G. Jacobs (eds.): *Learners and Language Learning* (pp. 145–171). Singapore: SEAMEO.

Jakobson, R. 1960. 'Closing statement: linguistics and poetics' in T. Sebeok (ed.): *Style in Language*. Cambridge, Mass.: MIT Press.

Janssen-van Dieten, A. 2000. 'Alternative assessment: Self-assessment beyond the mainstream.' *Melbourne Papers in Language Testing* 9: 18–29.

Jauregi, K. 1990. *Task-variation in Native/Non-native Conversation*. Unpublished Master's thesis, University of Reading.

Joe, A. 1998. 'What effects do text-based tasks promoting generation have on incidental vocabulary acquisition?' *Applied Linguistics* 19: 357–77.

Johnson, D., R. Johnson, and E. Holubec. 1993. *Circles of Learning*. 4th edn. Edina, MN: Interaction Book Company.

Johnson, K. 1982. 'Five principles in a "communicative" exercise type' in K. Johnson. *Communicative Syllabus Design and Methodology*. Oxford: Pergamon.

Johnson, K. 1988. 'Mistake correction.' *ELT Journal* 42: 89–101.

Johnson, K. 1996. *Language Teaching and Skill Learning*. Oxford: Blackwell.

Johnson, K. 2000. 'What task designers do.' *Language Teaching Research* 4: 301–21.

Johnson, M. and A. Tyler. 1998. 'Reanalyzing the OPI: How much does it look like a conversation?' in R. Young and A. He (eds.): *Talking and Testing* (pp. 27–51). Amsterdam: John Benjamins.

Johnston, M. 1986. 'Second language acquisition research in the adult migrant education program' in M. Johnston and M. Pienemann, *Second Language Acquisition: A Classroom Perspective*. Place of publ. New South Wales Migrant Education Service.

Jourdenais, R., M. Ota, S. Stauffer, B. Boyson, and C. Doughty. 1996. 'Does textual enhancement promote noticing? A think-aloud protocol analysis' in R. Schmidt (ed.). *Attention and Awareness in Foreign Language Learning* (pp. 183–216). Honolulu: University of Hawaii Press.

Kasper, G. (ed.). 1986. *Learning, Teaching and Communication in the Foreign Language Classroom*. Aarhus: Aarhus University Press.

Kasper, G. and E. Kellerman. (eds.). 1997. *Communication Strategies: Psycholinguistic and Sociolinguistic Perspectives*. London: Longman.

Kasper, G. and E. Kellerman. 1997. Introduction in G. Kasper and E. Kellerman (eds.).

Kellerman, E. 1991. 'Compensatory strategies in second language research: a critique, a revision, and some (non-)implications for the classroom' in R. Phillipson, E. Kellerman, L. Selinker, M. Sharwood Smith, and M. Swain (eds.): 1991. *Foreign/Second Language Pedagogy Research*. Clevedon, Avon: Multilingual Matters.

Kellerman, E., T. Bongaerts, and N. Poulisse. 1987. 'Strategy and system in L2 referential communication' in R. Ellis (ed.): *Second Language Acquisition in Context*. London: Prentice Hall International.

Kennedy, G. 1988. 'Evaluation and the management of change in ELT projects.' *Applied Linguistics* 9: 329–42.

Kim, S. 2001. *Structured Input and Production Practice in Foreign/Second-language Learning*. Unpublished Ed.D. dissertation, Temple University, Philadelphia.

Klippel, F. 1984. *Keep Talking*. Cambridge: Cambridge University Press.

Kowal, M. and M. Swain. 1994. 'Using collaborative language production tasks to promote students' language awareness.' *Language Awareness* 3: 73–93.

Kowal, M. and M. Swain. 1997. 'From semantic to syntactic processing: How can we promote metalinguistic awareness in the French immersion classroom?' in R. Johnson and M. Swain (eds.): *Immersion Education: International Perspectives* (pp. 284–309). Cambridge: Cambridge University Press.

Kramsch, C. and S. McConnell-Ginet. 1992. *Text and Context: Cross-Disciplinary Perspectives on Language Study*. Lexington, Mass.: D.C. Heath and Company.

Krashen, S. 1981. *Second Language Acquisition and Second Language Learning*. Oxford: Pergamon.

Krashen, S. 1985. *The Input Hypothesis*. London: Longman.

Krashen, S. 1994. 'The input hypothesis and its rivals' in N. Ellis (ed.): *Implicit and Explicit Learning of Languages*. London: Academic Press.

Krashen, S. and R. Scarcella. 1978. 'On routines and patterns in second language acquisition and performance.' *Language Learning* 28: 283–300.

Krashen, S. and T. Terrell. 1983. *The Natural Approach: Language Acquisition in the Classroom*. Oxford: Pergamon.

Kumaravadivelu, B. 1991. 'Language learning tasks: teacher intention and learner interpretation.' *ELT Journal* 45: 98–107.

Kumaravadivelu, B. 1993. 'The name of the task and the task of naming: Methodological aspects of task-based pedagogy' in G. Crookes, and S. Gass (eds.) (1993a).

Lado, R. 1961. *Language Testing*. London: Longman.

Lado, R. 1964. *Language Teaching: A Scientific Approach*. New York: McGraw Hill.

Lam, W. and J. Wong. 2000. 'The effects of strategy training on developing discussion skills in an ESL classroom.' *ELT Journal* 54: 245–55.

Lange, M. 2000. 'Factors affecting communication task performance in small groups.' Unpublished MA thesis, University of Auckland, Auckland, New Zealand.

Lantolf, J. 1996. 'Second language theory building: Letting all the flowers bloom!' *Language Learning* 46: 713–49.

Lantolf, J. 1997. 'The function of language play in the acquisition of Spanish as a second language' in W. Glass and A. Perez-Leroux (eds.): *Contemporary Perspectives on the Acquisition of Spanish*. Somerville, MA: Cascadilla Press.

Lantolf, J. 1999. 'The role of inner speech in SLA: A theoretical perspective.' Plenary address, September, Annual Conference of the Applied Linguistics Association of New Zealand, Auckland, New Zealand.

Lantolf, J. 2000a. 'Second language learning as a mediated process.' *Language Teaching*, 33: 79–96.

Lantolf, J. 2000b. 'Introducing sociocultural theory' in J. Lantolf (ed.).

Lantolf, J. 2000c. 'Language play and SLA: Theorizing the private speech/learning interface.' Paper presented to the combined conferences of the Australian Linguistic Society and Applied Linguistics Association of Australia, University of Melbourne.

Lantolf, J. (ed.). 2000d. *Sociocultural Theory and Second Language Learning*. Oxford: Oxford University Press.

Lantolf, J. 2001. Personal email correspondence.

Lantolf, J. and A. Aljaafreh. 1995. 'Second language learning in the zone of proximal development: A revolutionary experience.' *International Journal of Educational Research* 23: 619–32.

Lantolf, J. and G. Appel. 1994a. 'Theoretical framework: An introduction to Vygotskian perspectives on second language research' in J. Lantolf and G. Appel, 1994. 1–32.

Lantolf, J. and G. Appel. (eds.). 1994b. *Vygotskian Approaches to Second Language Research*. Norwood, NJ: Ablex.

Lantolf, J. and A. Pavlenko. 1996. 'Sociocultural theory and second language acquisition.' *Annual Review of Applied Linguistics* 15: 108–24.

Lapierre, D. 1994. *Language Output in a Cooperative Learning Setting: Determining its Effects on Second-language Learning*. Unpublished MA Thesis. Toronto: University of Toronto (OISE).

Larsen-Freeman, D. 1976. 'An explanation for the morpheme acquisition order of second language learners.' *Language Learning* 26: 125–34.

Laufer, B. and J. Hulstijn. 2001. 'Incidental vocabulary acquisition in a second language: The construct of task-induced involvement.' *Applied Linguistics* 22: 1–26.

Lee, J. 2000. *Tasks and Communicating in Language Classrooms*. Boston: McGraw-Hill.

Leech, G. 1983. *Principles of pragmatics*. London: Longman.

Lemke, J. 1990. *Talking Science: Language. Learning and Values (Language and Classroom Processes Vol 1)*. Ablex Publishing.

Leontiev, A. 1978. *Activity, Consciousness and Personality*. Englewood Cliffs, NJ: Prentice Hall.

Leontiev, A. 1981. *Psychology and the Language-learning Process*. Oxford: Pergamon.

Leow, R. 1997. 'Attention, awareness and foreign language behavior.' *Language Learning* 47: 467–505.

Levelt, W. 1989. *Speaking: From Intention to Articulation*. Cambridge: Cambridge University Press.

Lewis, M. 1993. *The Lexical Approach: The State of ELT and the Way Forward*. Hove: Language Teaching Publications.

Lewkowicz, J. 2000. 'Authenticity in language testing: Some outstanding questions.' *Language Testing* 17: 43–64.

Li, D. 1998. 'It's always more difficult than you planned. Teachers' perceived difficulties in introducing the communicative approach in South Korea.' *TESOL Quarterly* 32: 677–703.

Lightbown, P. 1983. 'Exploring relationships between developmental and instructional sequences in L2 acquisition' in H. Seliger and M. Long (eds.): *Classroom Oriented Research in Second Language Acquisition*. Rowley, Mass.: Newbury House.

Lightbown, P. 1985. 'Great expectations: Second language acquisition research and classroom teaching' *Applied Linguistics* 6: 173–89.

Lightbown, P. 1992. 'Can they do it themselves? A comprehension-based ESL course for young children' in R. Courchene, J. St. John, C. Therrien, and J Glidden (eds.). *Comprehension-based Language Teaching: Current Trends*. Ottawa: University of Ottawa Press.

Logan, G. 1988. 'Towards an instance theory of automatisation.' *Psychological Review* 95: 492–527.

Long, M. 1980. *Input, Interaction and Second-language Acquisition*. Unpublished PhD dissertation: University of California at Los Angeles.

Long, M. 1981. 'Input, interaction and second-language acquisition' in H. Winitz (ed.): *Native Language and Foreign Language Acquisition*. Annals of the New York Academy of Sciences 379.

Long, M. 1983a. 'Native speaker/non-native speaker conversation in the second language classroom' in M. Clarke and J. Handscombe (eds.): *On TESOL '82: Pacific Perspectives on Language and Teaching*. Washington D.C.: TESOL.

Long, M. 1983b. 'Native speaker/non-native speaker conversation and the negotiation of comprehensible input.' *Applied Linguistics* 4: 126–41.

Long, M. 1985. 'A role for instruction in second language acquisition: task-based language teaching' in K. Hyltenstam and M. Pienemann (eds.): *Modelling and Assessing Second Language Acquisition*. Clevedon: Multilingual Matters.

Long, M. 1988. 'Instructed interlanguage development' in L. Beebe (ed.): *Issues in Second Language Acquisition: Multiple Perspectives*. Rowley, Mass.: Newbury House.

Long, M. 1989. 'Task, group, and task-group interactions.' *University of Hawaii Working Papers in ESL* 8: 1–26.

Long, M. 1991. 'Focus on form: A design feature in language teaching methodology.' in K. de Bot, R. Ginsberg, and C. Kramsch (eds.): *Foreign Language Research in Cross-cultural Perspective* (pp. 39–52). Amsterdam: John Benjamin.

Long, M. 1996. 'The role of the linguistic environment in second language acquisition' in W. Ritchie and T. Bhatia (eds.): *Handbook of Second Language Acquisition* (pp. 413–68). San Diego: Academic Press.

Long, M. and G. Crookes. 1987. 'Intervention points in second language classroom processes' in B. Das (ed.): *Patterns of Classroom Interaction*. Singapore: SEAMEO.

Long, M. and G. Crookes. 1992. 'Three approaches to task-based syllabus design.' *TESOL Quarterly* 26: 27–56.

Long, M., S. Inagaki, and L. Ortega. 1998. 'The role of implicit negative feedback in SLA: Models and recasts in Japanese and Spanish.' *The Modern Language Journal* 82: 357–71.

Long, M. and P. Porter. 1985. 'Group work, interlanguage talk, and second language acquisition.' *TESOL Quarterly* 19: 207–28.

Loschky, L. 1994. 'Comprehensible input and second language acquisition: What is the relationship?' *Studies in Second Language Acquisition* 16: 303–23.

Loschky, L. and R. Bley-Vroman. 1993. 'Grammar and task-based methodology' in Crookes, G. and Gass, S. 1993a (eds.)

Lumley, T. and T. McNamara. 1995. 'Rater characteristics and rater bias: Implications for training. '*Language Testing* 12: 54–71.

Lynch, T. 1989. 'Researching teachers: Behaviour and belief' in C. Brumfit and R. Mitchell (eds.): *Research in the Language Classroom*. London: Modern English Publications and the British Council.

Lynch, T. 1997. 'Nudge, nudge: Teacher interventions in task-based learner talk. *ELT Journal* 51: 317–325.

Lynch, T. 2001. 'Seeing what they meant: Transcribing as a route to noticing.' *ELT Journal* 55: 124–32.

Lynch, T. and J. MacLean. 2000. 'Exploring the benefits of task repetition and recycling for classroom language learning.' *Language Teaching Research* 4: 221–50.

Lynch, T. and J. MacLean. 2001. 'Effects of immediate task repetition on learners' performance' in M. Bygate, P. Skehan, and M. Swain (eds.) (pp. 99–118).

Lyster, R. and L. Ranta. 1997. 'Corrective feedback and learner uptake: Negotiation of form in communicative classrooms.' *Studies in Second Language Acquisition* 19: 37–66.

Mackey, A. 1999. 'Input, interaction and second language development: An empirical study of question formation in ESL.' *Studies in Second Language Acquisition* 21: 557–87.

Mackey, A. and J. Philp. 1998. 'Conversational interaction and second language development: Recasts, responses and red herrings.' *The Modern Language Journal* 82: 338–56.

Mackey, A., S. Gass, and K. McDonough. 2000. 'Do learners recognize implicit negative feedback?' *Studies in Second Language Acquisition* 33: 82–92.

Madden, C. and S. Reinhart. 1987. *Pyramids: Structurally-based tasks for ESL Learners*. Ann Arbor: University of Michigan Press.

Maley, A. 2001. Review of G. Cook's 'Language Play, Language Learning'. *ELT Journal* 55: 325–27.

Maley, A. and S. Moulding. 1985. *Poem into Poem*. Cambridge: Cambridge University Press.

Manheimer, R. 1995. 'Close the task: Improve the discourse.' Paper given at Annual Conference of American Association of Applied Linguists, Long Beach, California.

Markee, N. 1993. 'The diffusion of innovation in language teaching.' *Annual Review of Applied Linguistics* 13: 229–43.

Markee, N. 1997. *Managing Curricular Innovation*. Cambridge: Cambridge University Press.

Mathers, J. 1990. *An Investigation into Feedback in the L2 Classroom*. Unpublished MA Dissertation, Christchurch College, Canterbury.

Matthews, R., R. Buss, W. Stanley, F. Blachard-Fields, J. Cho, and B. Druhan. 1989. 'Role of implicit and explicit processes in learning from examples. A synergistic effect.' *Journal of Experimental Psychology: Learning, Memory and Cognition* 15: 1083–100.

Matusov, A. 1996. 'Intersubjectivity without agreement.' *Mind, Culture and Activity* 3: 25–45.

McCafferty, S. G. 1994a. 'Adult second language learners' use of private speech: A review of studies.' *Modern Language Journal* 7814: 421–36.

McCafferty, S. G. 1994b. 'The use of private speech by adult ESL learners at different levels of proficiency' in J. Lantolf, and G. Appel (eds.): 117–34.

McLaughlin, B. 1987. *Theories of Second Language Learning*. London: Edward Arnold.

McLaughlin, B. 1990. 'Restructuring.' *Applied Linguistics* 11: 113–28.

McLaughlin, B. and R. Heredia. 1996. 'Information processing approaches to research on second language acquisition and use' in R. Ritchie and T. Bhatia (eds.): *A Handbook of Second Language Acquisition*. San Diego: Academic Press.

McNamara, T. 1996. *Measuring Second Language Performance*. London: Longman.

McNamara, T. 1997. '"Interaction" in second language performance assessment: Whose performance?' *Applied Linguistics* 18: 446–66.

Medgyes, P. 1994. *The Non-Native Teacher*. London: Macmillan.

Mehnert, U. 1998. 'The effects of different lengths of time for planning on second language performance.' *Studies in Second Language Acquisition* 20: 83–108.

Messick, S. 1994. 'The interplay of evidence and consequences in the validation of performance assessments.' *Educational Researcher* 23: 13–23.

Met, M. 1994. 'Teaching content through a second language' in F. Genesee (ed.): *Educating Second Language Children* (pp. 159–182). Cambridge: Cambridge University Press.

Mohamed, N. 2001. *Teaching Grammar through Consciousness-raising Tasks: Learning Outcomes, Learner Preferences and Task Performance*. MA Thesis, Department of Applied Language Studies and Linguistics, University of Auckland.

Mohan, B. 1986. *Language and Content*. Reading, MA: Addison Wesley.

Morrow, K. 1979. 'Communicative language testing: Revolution or evolution?' in C. Brumfit and K. Johnson (eds.): *The Communicative Approach to Language Teaching*. (pp. 143–59). Oxford: Oxford University Press.

Moskowitz, G. 1977. *Caring and Sharing in the Foreign Language Class*. Rowley, MA.: Newbury House.

Moskowitz, G. 1982. 'Self-confidence through self-disclosure: The pursuit of meaningful communication.' *ELT Documents 113: Humanistic Approaches: An Empirical View*. The British Council.

Munby, J. 1978. *Communicative Syllabus Design*. Cambridge: Cambridge University Press.

Myles, F., R. Mitchell, and J. Hooper, J. 1999. 'Interrogative chunks in French L2: A basis for creative construction.' *Studies in Second Language Acquisition* 21: 49–80.

Nagata, H., D. Aline, and R. Ellis. 1999. 'Modified input, language aptitude and the acquisition of word meanings' in R. Ellis. *Learning a Second Language Through Interaction* (pp. 133–50). Amsterdam: John Benjamins.

Nakahama, Y., A. Tyler, and L. van Lier. 2001. 'Negotiation of meaning in conversational and information-gap activities: A comparative discourse analysis.' *TESOL Quarterly* 35: 377–405.

Nassaji, H. and A. Cumming. 2000. 'What's in a ZPD. A case study of a young ESL student and teacher interacting through dialogue journals.' *Language Teaching Research* 4: 95–121.

Nassaji, H. and M. Swain. 2000. 'A Vygotskian perspective on corrective feedback in L2: The effect of random versus negotiated help in the learning of English articles.' *Language Awareness* 9: 34–51.

Nassaji, H. and G. Wells. 2000. 'What's the use of "triadic dialogue"?: An investigation of teacher-student interaction.' *Applied Linguistics* 21: 376–406.

Nation, P. 1990. 'A system of tasks for language learning' in S. Anivan (ed.): *Language Teaching Methodology for the Nineties*. Singapore: SEAMEO.

Nattinger, J. and J. DeCarrico. 1992. *Lexical Phrases and Language Teaching*. Oxford: Oxford University Press.

Nemeth, N. and J. Kormos. 2001. 'Pragmatic aspects of task-performance: The case of argumentation.' *Language Teaching Research* 5: 213–40.

Neville, M. 1985. *English Language in Scottish Schools*. Scottish Education Department report (cited in A. Andersen and T. Lynch 1988).

Newell, A. 1990. *Unified Theories of Cognition*. Cambridge, MA.: Harvard University Press.

Newton, J. 1991. 'Negotiation: negotiating what?' Paper given at SEAMEO Conference on Language Acquisition and the Second/Foreign Language Classroom, RELC, Singapore.

Newton, J. 1993. 'Vocabulary learning and communication tasks.' Unpublished paper, English Language Institute, Victoria University, Wellington, New Zealand.

Newton, J. 2001. 'Options for vocabulary learning through communication tasks.' *ELT Journal* 55: 30–37.

Newton, J. and **G. Kennedy.** 1996. 'Effects of communication tasks on the grammatical relations marked by second language learners.' *System* 24: 309–22.

Nicholas, H., P. Lightbown, and **N. Spada.** 2001. 'Recasts as feedback to language learners.' *Language Learning* 51: 719–58.

Nobuyoshi, J. and **R. Ellis.** 1993. 'Focussed communication tasks.' *English Language Teaching Journal* 47: 203–10.

Norris, J., J. D. Brown, and **T. Hudson.** 2000. 'Assessing performance on complex L2 tasks: Investigating raters, examinees and tasks.' Paper presented at the Language Testing Research Colloquium, Vancouver.

North, B. 1996. 'The development of a common framework scale of language proficiency based on a theory of measurement.' Unpublished PhD thesis. Thames Valley University, Ealing, London

Numrich, C. 1996. 'On becoming a language teacher: Insights from diary studies.' *TESOL Quarterly* 30: 131–53.

Nunan, D. 1987. 'Communicative language teaching: Making it work'. *ELT Journal* 41: 136–45.

Nunan, D. 1989. *Designing Tasks for the Communicative Classroom.* Cambridge: Cambridge University Press.

Nunan, D. 1992. 'Socio-cultural aspects of second language acquisition.' *Cross Currents* 19: 13–24.

Ochs, E. 1979. 'Planned and unplanned discourse' in T. Givón (ed.): *Syntax and Semantics Vol 12: Discourse and Semantics.* New York: Academic.

Oh, S. 2001. 'Two types of input modification and EFL reading comprehension: Simplification vs. elaboration.' *TESOL Quarterly* 35 (1): 69–94.

Ohta, A. S. 1995. 'Applying sociocultural theory to an analysis of learner discourse: Learner-learner collaborative interaction in the zone of proximal development.' *Issues in Applied Linguistics* 612: 93–122.

Ohta, A. S. 2001a . 'Japanese second language acquisition in the classroom: What the voices of teachers and students tell us about the process of learning' in H. Nara (ed.): *Advances in Japanese Pedagogy.* Columbus: National Foreign Language Resource Centre.

Ohta, A. S. 2001b. *Second Language Acquisition Processes in the Classroom: Learning Japanese.* Mahwah, NJ: Lawrence Erlbaum.

Oliver, R. 2000. 'Age differences in negotiation and feedback in classroom and pairwork.' *Language Learning* 50: 119–51.

Oller, J. 1979. *Language Tests in Schools.* London: Longman.

O'Loughlin, K. 2002. 'The impact of gender in oral proficiency testing.' *Language Testing* 19, 2.

O'Malley, J. and **A. Chamot.** 1990. *Learning Strategies in Second Language Acquisition.* Cambridge: Cambridge University Press.

Ondarra, K. 1997. *Collaborative Negotiation of Meaning.* Amsterdam: Rodopi.

Ortega, L. 1999. 'Planning and focus on form in L2 oral performance.' *Studies in Second Language Acquisition* 21: 108–48.

Oscarson, M. 1997. 'Self-assessment of foreign and second language proficiency' in C. Clapham and D. Corson (eds.). (pp. 175–87.)

Oxford, R. 1990. *Language Learning Strategies: What Every Teacher Should Know.* Rowley, Mass.: Newbury House.

Patterson, C. and **M. Kister.** 1981. 'The development of listener skills for referential communication' in W. Dickson (ed.): *Children's Oral Communication Skills.* New York: Academic Press.

Pawley, A. and F. Syder. 1983. 'Two puzzles for linguistic theory: Native-like selection and native-like fluency' in J. Richards and R. Schmidt (eds.).

Pennycook, A. 1994. *The Cultural Politics of English as an International Language*. London: Longman.

Phillipson, R. 1992. *Linguistic Imperialism*. Oxford: Oxford University Press.

Phillipson, R., E. Kellerman, L. Selinker, M. Sharwood Smith, and M. Swain (eds.) *Foreign/Second Language Pedagogy Research*. Clavedon: Multilingual Matters.

Pica, T. 1983. 'Adult acquisition of English as a second language under different conditions of exposure.' *Language Learning* 33: 465–97.

Pica, T. 1987. 'Second language acquisition, social interaction, and the classroom.' *Applied Linguistics* 8: 3–21.

Pica, T. 1988. 'Interlanguage adjustments as an outcome of NS–NNS negotiated interaction.' *Language Learning* 38: 45–73.

Pica, T. 1992. 'The textual outcomes of native-speaker–non-native speaker negotiation: what do they reveal about second language learning' in C. Kramsch and S. McConnell-Ginet (eds.).

Pica, T. 1994. 'Research on negotiation: What does it reveal about second-language learning conditions, processes, and outcomes?' *Language Learning* 44: 493–527.

Pica, T. 1997. 'Second language teaching and research relationships: A North American view.' *Language Teaching Research* 1: 48–72.

Pica, T. and C. Doughty. 1985a. 'Input and interaction in the communicative language classroom: a comparison of teacher-fronted and group activities' in S. Gass and C. Madden (eds.).

Pica, T. and C. Doughty. 1985b. 'The role of group work in classroom second language acquisition.' *Studies in Second Language Acquisition* 7: 233–48.

Pica, I., L. Holliday, N. Lewis, and L. Morgenthaler. 1989. 'Comprehensible output as an outcome of linguistic demands on the learner.' *Studies in Second Language Acquisition* 11: 63–90.

Pica, T., L. Holliday, N. Lewis, D. Berducci, and J. Newman. 1991. 'Language learning through interaction: what role does gender play?' *Studies in Second Language Acquisition* 13: 343–76.

Pica, R., R. Kanagy, and J. Falodun. 1993. 'Choosing and using communication tasks for second language research and instruction' in S. Gass and G. Crookes (eds.): *Task-based Learning in a Second Language*. Clevedon: Multilingual Matters.

Pica, T., F. Lincoln-Porter, D. Paninos, and J. Linnell. 1996. 'Language learners' interaction: How does it address the input, output and feedback needs of L2 learners?' *TESOL Quarterly* 30: 59–84.

Pica, T., R. Young, and C. Doughty. 1987. 'The impact of interaction on comprehension.' *TESOL Quarterly* 21: 737–58.

Pienemann, M. 1985. 'Learnability and syllabus construction' in K. Hyltenstam and M. Pienemann (eds.): *Modelling and Assessing Second Language Acquisition*. Clevedon, Avon: Multilingual Matters.

Pimsleur, P. 1966. *Pimsleur Language Aptitude Battery (PLAB)*. New York: Harcourt Brace Jovanovich.

Platt, E. and F. Brooks. 1994. 'The acquisition rich environment revisited.' *Modern Language Journal* 78: 497–511.

Platt, E. and S. Troudi. 1997. 'Mary and her teachers: A Grebo-speaking child's place in the mainstream classroom.' *Modern Language Journal* 81: 28–59.

Plough, I. and S. Gass. 1993. 'Interlocutor and task familiarity effects on interactional structure' in Crookes, G. and Gass, S. (eds.)

Polio, C. and S. Gass. 1998. 'The role of interaction in native speaker comprehension of non-native speaker speech.' *The Modern Language Journal* 82: 308–19.

Posner, M. 1994. 'Attention in cognitive neuroscience: An overview' in M. Gazzaniga (ed.): *The Cognitive Neurosciences* (pp. 615–24). Cambridge, MA: MIT Press.

Potovsky, L. 1974. 'Effects of delay in oral practice at the beginning of second language learning.' *Modern Language Journal* 58: 229–39.

Poulisse, N. 1990. *The Use of Compensatory Strategies by Dutch Learners of English.* Enschede: Sneldruk.

Poulisse, N. 1997. 'Compensatory strategies and the principles of clarity and economy' in G. Kasper and E. Kellerman (eds.).

Prabhu, N.S. 1987. *Second Language Pedagogy.* Oxford: Oxford University Press.

Prabhu, N.S. 1990. Comments on Alan Beretta's paper 'Implementation of the Bangalore Project'. *Applied Linguistics* 11: 338–40.

Rahimpour, M. 1997. *Task Complexity, Task Condition, and Variation in L2 Oral Discourse.* Unpublished PhD dissertation, University of Queensland, Australia.

Rampton, B. 1987. 'Stylistic variability and not speaking "normal" English: Some post-Labovian approaches and their implications for the study of interlanguage' in R. Ellis (ed.) which Ellis text?

Rea-Dickins, P. 2001. 'Mirror, mirror on the wall: Identifying processes of classroom assessment.' Mimeograph, School of Education: University of Bristol.

Rea-Dickins, P. and **S. Gardner.** 2000. 'Snares and silver bullets: Disentangling the construct of formative assessment.' *Language Testing* 17: 215–43.

Rea-Dickins, P. and **K. Germaine.** 1992. *Evaluation.* Oxford: Oxford University Press.

Reber, A. 1989. 'Implicit learning and tacit knowledge.' *Journal of Experimental Psychology: General* 118: 219–35.

Reed, D. and **A. Cohen.** 2001. 'Revisiting raters and ratings in oral language assessment' in C. Elder *et al.* (eds.). (pp. 82–96).

Rescorla, L. and **S. Okuda.** 1987. 'Modular patterns in second language acquisition.' *Applied Psycholinguistics* 8: 281–308.

Revell, J. 1979. *Teaching Techniques for Communicative English.* London: Macmillan.

Richards, J. 1990. *Language Teaching Matrix.* Cambridge: Cambridge University Press.

Richards, J. 1996. 'Teachers' maxims in language teaching.' *TESOL Quarterly* 30: 281–96.

Richards, J., J. Platt, and **H. Weber.** 1985. *Longman Dictionary of Applied Linguistics.* London: Longman.

Richards, J. and **R. Schmidt** (eds.). 1983. *Language and Communication.* London: Longman.

Richards, J. and **T. Rogers.** 1986. *Approaches and Methods in Language Teaching.* Cambridge: Cambridge University Press.

Ritchie, W. and **T. Bhatia.** (eds.). 1996. *Handbook of Second Language Acquisition.* San Diego, CA: Academic Press.

Robinson, P. 1995a. 'Attention, memory, and the 'noticing' hypothesis.' *Language Learning* 45: 283–331.

Robinson, P. 1995b. Task complexity and second language narrative discourse. *Language Learning* 45: 99–140.

Robinson, P. (ed.). 2001. *Cognition and Second Language Instruction.* Cambridge: Cambridge University Press.

Robinson, P. 2001. 'Task complexity, task difficulty, and task production: Exploring interactions in a componential framework.' *Applied Linguistics* 22: 27–57.

Robinson, P. and **J. Lim.** 1993. 'Cognitive load and the route marked not-marked map task.' Unpublished data, University of Hawaii at Manoa, Department of ESL, Honolulu, USA.

Robinson, P. and **S. Ross.** 1996. 'The development of task-based assessment in English for academic purpose programs.' *Applied Linguistics* 17: 455–76.

Robinson, P., S. Ting, and **J. Unwin.** 1995. 'Investigating second language task complexity.' *RELC Journal* 25: 62–79.

Roebuck, R. 2000. 'Subjects speak out: How learners position themselves in a psycholinguistic task' in J. Lantolf (ed.) 79-95.

Rost, M. 1990. *Listening in Language Learning.* London: Longman.

Rost, M. 1994. 'On-line summaries as representations of lecture understanding' in J. Flowerdew (ed.).

Rost, M. and S. Ross. 1991. 'Learner strategies in interaction: Typology and teachability.' *Language Learning* 41: 235–73.

Rulon, K. and J. McCreary. 1986. 'Negotiation of content: teacher-fronted and small group interaction' in R. Day (ed.).

Rumelhart, D., J. McClelland, and the PDP Research Group (eds.). 1986. *Parallel Distributed Processing: Explorations in the Microstructures of Cognition, Vol 2. Psychological and Biological Models.* Cambridge, Mass.: MIT.

Rutherford, W. 1987. *Second Language Grammar: Learning and Teaching.* London: Longman.

Salaberry, M. 1997. 'The role of input and output practice in second language acquisition.' *Canadian Modern Language Review* 53: 422–51.

Samuda, V. 2001. 'Guiding relationships between form and meaning during task performance: The role of the teacher' in Bygate, Skehan, and Swain (eds.) (pp. 119–14).

Samuda, V., K. Johnson, and J. Ridgway. 2000. *Designing Language Learning Tasks: A Guide Volume 1: Draft.* Lancaster: University of Lancaster.

Samuda, V. and P. Rounds. 1993. 'Critical episodes: Reference points for analyzing a task in action' in G. Crookes and S. Gass (eds.) (1993b).

Sangarun, J. 2001. *The Effects of Pre-task Planning on Foreign Language Performance.* Unpublished doctoral thesis, University of Toronto, Canada.

Sasaki, Y. 2000. 'The predictive validity of SPOT and self-assessment questionnaire.' *Melbourne Papers in Language Testing* 9: 30–55.

Sato, C. 1986. 'Conversation and interlanguage development: Rethinking the connection' in R. Day (ed.)

Sato, C. 1988. 'Origins of complex syntax in interlanguage development.' *Studies in Second Language Acquisition* 10: 371–95.

Saville-Troike, M. 1988. 'Private speech: Evidence for second language learning strategies during the "silent" period.' *Journal of Child Language* 15: 567–90.

Schinke-Llano, L. 1993. 'On the value of a Vygotskian framework for SLA theory.' *Language Learning* 43: 121–9.

Schmidt, R. 1983. 'Interaction, acculturation and the acquisition of communication competence' in M. Wolfson and E. Judd (eds.). *Sociolinguistics and Second Language Acquisition.* Rowley, MA: Newbury House.

Schmidt, R. 1990. 'The role of consciousness in second language learning.' *Applied Linguistics* 11: 129–58.

Schmidt, R. 1994. 'Deconstructing consciousness in search of useful definitions for applied linguistics.' *AILA Review* 11: 11–26.

Schmidt, R. 2001. 'Attention' in P. Robinson (ed.): *Cognition and Second Language Instruction.* Cambridge: Cambridge University Press.

Schmidt, R. and S. Frota. 1986. 'Developing basic conversational ability in a second language: a case-study of an adult learner' in R. Day (ed.).

Schober, M. and H. Clark. 1989. 'Understanding by addressees and overhearers.' *Cognitive Psychology* 21: 211–32.

Schoenfeld, A. 1985. *Mathematical Problem Solving.* Orlando, FL: Academic Press.

Schön, D. 1983. *The Reflective Practitioner.* New York: Basic Books.

Schulte, C. 1998. 'Charting new paths: Negotiating contextual meanings from dictionary definitions.' Unpublished paper, Temple University, Philadelphia.

Scollon, R. 1976. *Conversations with a One-year Old.* Honolulu: The University of Hawaii Press.

Seedhouse, P. 1996. 'Classroom interaction: possibilities and impossibilities.' *ELT Journal* 50: 16–24.

Seedhouse, P. 1997. 'Combining meaning and form.' *ELT Journal,* 51, 336–44.

Seedhouse, P. 1999. 'Task-based interaction.' *ELT Journal* 53: 149–56.

Selinker, L. and D. Douglas. 1985. 'Wrestling with context in interlanguage theory.' *Applied Linguistics* 6: 190–204.

Sfard, A. 1998. 'On two metaphors for learning and the dangers of choosing just one.' *Educational Researchers* 27: 4–13.

Sharwood Smith, M. 1981. 'Consciousness-raising and the second language learner.' *Applied Linguistics* 2: 159–69.

Sharwood Smith, M. 1986. 'Comprehension vs. acquisition: two ways of processing input.' *Applied Linguistics* 7: 239–56.

Sheen, R. 1992. 'Problem solving brought to task.' *RELC Journal* 23: 44–59.

Sheen, R. 1994. 'A critical analysis of the advocacy of the task-based syllabus.' *TESOL Quarterly* 28: 127–57.

Sheils, J. 1988. *Communication in the Modern Language Classroom*. Strasbourg, France: The Council of Europe.

Shohamy, E. 1995. 'Performance assessment in language testing.' *Annual Review of Applied Linguistics* 15: 188–211.

Shohamy, E., S. Donitsa-Schmidt, and R. Waizer. 1993. 'The effect of the elicitation mode on the oral samples and scores obtained on language tests.' Paper presented at the Language Testing Research Conference, Cambridge, August 2–5.

Shortreed, I. 1993. 'Variation in foreign language talk: The effects of task and proficiency' in G. Crookes and S. Gass (eds.).

Shriffin, R. and W. Schneider. 1977. 'Controlled and automatic processing: II. Perceptual learning, automatic attending and a general theory.' *Psychological Review* 84: 127–90.

Skehan, P. 1995. 'Analysability, accessibility, and ability for use' in G. Cook and B. Seidlhofer (eds.): *Principles and Practice in Applied Linguistics*. Oxford: Oxford University Press.

Skehan, P. 1996a. 'A framework for the implementation of task-based instruction' *Applied Linguistics* 17: 38–62.

Skehan, P. 1996b. 'Second language acquisition research and task-based instruction' in J. Willis and D. Willis (eds.).

Skehan, P. 1998a. *A Cognitive Approach to Language Learning*. Oxford: Oxford University Press.

Skehan, P. 1998b. 'Task-based instruction.' *Annual Review of Applied Linguistics* 18: 268–86.

Skehan, P. 2001. 'Tasks and language performance assessment.' in Bygate *et al.* (eds.). (pp. 167–85).

Skehan, P. and P. Foster. 1997. 'Task type and task processing conditions as influences on foreign language performance.' *Language Teaching Research* 1: 185–211.

Skehan, P. and P. Foster. 1999. 'The influence of task structure and processing conditions on narrative retellings.' *Language Learning* 49: 93–120.

Skehan, P and P. Foster. 2001. 'Cognition and tasks' in P. Robinson (ed.): *Cognition and Second Language Instruction*. Cambridge: Cambridge University Press.

Snow, C., M. Met, and F. Genesee. 1989. 'A conceptual framework for the integration of language and content in second/foreign language instruction.' *TESOL Quarterly* 23: 201–17.

Spolsky, B. 1992. 'Diagnostic testing revisited' in E. Shohamy and R. Walton (eds.): *Language Assessment and Feedback: Testing and Other Strategies* (pp. 29–39). National Foreign Language Center, Dubuque, IA: Kendall/Hunt Publishing Co.

Stansfield, C. 1992. *ACTFL Speaking Proficiency Guidelines*. Washington DC: ERIC Digest. (http://www.cal.org/eroccll/digest).

Stenhouse, L. 1975. *An Introduction to Curriculum Research and Development*. London: Heinemann.

Sterlacci, P. 1996. 'A micro-evaluation of a focused-communication task for the ESL/EFL classroom.' Unpublished course paper. Tokyo: Temple University Japan.

Stern, H. 1983. *Fundamental Concepts of Language Teaching*. Oxford: Oxford University Press.

Stern, H. 1990. 'Analysis and experience as variables in second language pedagogy' in B. Harley, P. Allen, J. Cummins, and M. Swain (eds.): *The Development of Second Language Proficiency*. Cambridge: Cambridge University Press.

Stern, H. 1992. *Issues and Options in Language Teaching*. Oxford: Oxford University Press.

Stoller, E. 1994. 'The diffusion of innovation in intensive ESL programs.' *Applied Linguistics* 15: 300–27.

Storch, N. 1999. 'Are two heads better than one? Pair work and grammatical accuracy.' *System* 27: 363–74.

Storch, N. 2001. 'How collaborative is pair work? ESL tertiary students composing in pairs.' *Language Teaching Research* 5: 29–53.

Sullivan, P. 2000. 'Playfulness as mediation in communicative language teaching in a Vietnamese classroom' in J. Lantolf (ed.). pp. 115–31.

Svartvik, J. (ed.) 1973. *Errata: Papers in Error Analysis.* Lund, Sweden: CWK Gleerup.

Swain, M. 1985. 'Communicative competence: some roles of comprehensible input and comprehensible output in its development' in S. Gass and C. Madden (eds.). pp. 235–52.

Swain, M. 1995. 'Three functions of output in second language learning' in G. Cook and B. Seidlhofer (eds.). *For H.G. Widdowson: Principles and Practice in the Study of Language.* Oxford: Oxford University Press.

Swain, M. 1998. 'Focus on form through conscious reflection' in C. Doughty and J. Williams (eds.). pp. 64–81.

Swain, M. 2000a. 'The output hypothesis and beyond: Mediating acquisition through collaborative dialogue.' in J. Lantolf (ed.). pp. 97–114.

Swain, M. 2000b. 'Examining dialogue: Another approach to content specification and to validating inferences drawn from tests scores.' Mimeograph, Ontario Institute for Studies in Education. University of Toronto. To appear in *Language Testing.*

Swain, M., L. Brooks, and A Tocalli-Beller. Forthcoming. 'Peer–peer dialogue as a means of second language learning.' *Annual Review of Applied Linguistics*

Swain, M. and S. Lapkin. 1998. 'Interaction and second language learning: Two adolescent French immersion students working together.' *Modern Language Journal* 82: 320–37.

Swain, M. and S. Lapkin 2000. 'Task-based second language learning: the use of the first language.' *Language Teaching Research* 4: 251–74.

Swain, M. and S. Lapkin. 2001a. 'Talking it through: Two French immersion learners' response to reformulation.' Unpublished paper, OISE, University of Toronto, Canada.

Swain, M. and S. Lapkin. 2001b. 'Focus on form through collaborative dialogue: Exploring task effects' in M. Bygate, P. Skehan, and M. Swain (eds.). pp. 99–118.

Swales, J. 1990. *Genre Analysis.* Cambridge: Cambridge University Press.

Swan, M. and B. Smith. 2001. *Learner English.* (2nd ed.). Cambridge: Cambridge University Press.

Takashima, H. and R. Ellis. 1999. 'Output enhancement and the acquisition of the past tense.' in R. Ellis. *Learning a Second Language Through Interaction* (pp. 173–88). Amsterdam: John Benjamins.

Tarone, E. 1979. 'Interlanguage as chameleon.' *Language Learning* 29: 181–91.

Tarone, E. 1980. 'Communication strategies, foreigner talk, and repair in interlanguage.' *Language Learning* 30: 417–31.

Tarone, E. 1981. 'Some thoughts on the notion of communication strategy.' *TESOL Quarterly* 15: 285–95.

Tarone, E. 1982. 'Systematicity and attention in interlanguage.' *Language Learning* 32: 69–82.

Tarone, E. 1983a. 'On the variability of interlanguage systems.' *Applied Linguistics* 4: 143–63.

Tarone, E. 1983b. 'Some thoughts on the notion of 'communication strategy' in C. Færch and G. Kasper (eds.): *Strategies in Interlanguage Communication.* London: Longman.

Tarone, E. and G. Liu. 1995. 'Situational context, variation, and second language acquisition theory' in G. Cook and B. Seidlhofer (eds.). pp. 107–24.

Tarone, E. and B. Parrish. 1988. 'Task-related variation in interlanguage: the case of articles.' *Language Learning* 38: 21–44.

Tauroza, S. and D. Allison. 1994. 'Expectation-driven understanding in information systems lecture comprehension.' in J. Flowerdew (ed.).

Tharp, R. and **R. Gallimore**. 1988. 'Rousing Minds to Life: Teaching, Learning and Schooling in a Social Context.' New York, NY: Cambridge University Press.

Thomson, C. 1992. 'Learner-centred Tasks in the Foreign Language Classroom.' *Foreign Language Annals* 25: 523–31.

Tomlin, R. and **V. Villa**. 1994. 'Attention in cognitive science and second language acquisition.' *Studies in Second Language Acquisition* 16: 183–203.

Tong-Fredericks, C. 1984. 'Types of oral communication activities and the language they generate: a comparison.' *System* 12: 133–4.

Trahey, M. and **L. White**. 1993. 'Positive evidence and preemption in the second language classroom.' *Studies in Second Language Acquisition* 15: 181–204.

Tsui, A. and **J. Fullilove**. 1998. 'Bottom-up or top-down processing as a discriminator of L2 listening performance.' *Applied Linguistics* 19: 432–51.

Tuz, E. 1993. 'From controlled practice to communicative activity: Does training transfer?' *Temple University Japan Research Studies in TESOL* 1: 97–108.

Upshur, J. 1979. 'Functional proficiency theory and a research role for language tests' in E. Briere and F. Hinofotis (eds.): *Concepts in Language Testing: Some Recent Studies*. Washington D.C.: TESOL.

Ur, P. 1981. *Discussions that Work*. Cambridge: Cambridge University Press.

Ur, P. 1988. *Grammar Practice Activities*. Cambridge: Cambridge University Press.

Van den Branden, K. 1997. 'Effects of negotiation on language learners' output.' *Language Learning* 47: 589–636.

Van Ek, J. 1976. *The Threshold Level for Modern Language Learning in Schools*. London: Longman.

van Lier, L. 1989. 'Reeling, writhing, drawling, stretching and fainting in coils: Oral proficiency interviews as conversation.' *TESOL Quarterly* 23: 489–508.

van Lier, L. 1991. 'Inside the classroom: learning processes and teaching procedures.' *Applied Language Learning* 2: 29–69.

van Lier, L. 1992. 'Not the nine o'clock linguistics class: Investigating contingency grammar.' *Language Awareness* 1: 91–108.

van Lier, L. 1994. 'Forks and Hopes: Pursuing Understanding in Different Ways.' *Applied Linguistics* 15: 328–46.

van Lier, L. 1996. *Interaction in the Language Curriculum: Awareness, Autonomy and Authenticity*. London: Longman.

VanPatten, B. 1990. 'Attending to form and content in the input.' *Studies in Second Language Acquisition* 12: 287–301

VanPatten, B. 1996. *Input Processing and Grammar Instruction in Second language Acquisition*. Norwood, NJ: Ablex.

VanPatten, B. and **T. Cadierno**. 1993. 'Explicit instruction and input processing.' *Studies in Second Language Acquisition* 15: 225–41.

VanPatten, B. and **S. Oikennon**. 1996. 'Explanation versus structured input in processing instruction.' *Studies in Second Language Acquisition* 18: 495–510.

VanPatten, B. and **C. Sanz**. 1995. 'From input to output: Processing instruction and communicative tasks' in Eckman, F. *et al.* (eds.): *Second Language Acquisition Theory and Language Pedagogy*. Mahwah, NJ: Lawrence Erlbaum.

Varonis, E. and **S. Gass**. 1985. 'Non-native/non-native conversations: a model for negotiation of meaning.' *Applied Linguistics* 6: 71–90.

Vygotsky, L. 1978. *Mind in Society*. Cambridge: MA: MIT Press.

Vygotsky, L. 1981. 'The genesis of higher mental functions' in Wertsch, J. (ed.). *The Concept of Activity in Soviet Psychology*. Armonk, NY: M.E. Sharpe.

Vygotsky, L. 1987. *The Collected Works of L. S. Vygotsky. Volume 1. Thinking and Speaking*. New York, NY: Plenum Press.

Wagner-Gough, J. 1975. 'Comparative studies in second language learning.' *CAL-ERIC/CLL Series on Language and Linguistics* 26.

Wajnryb, R. 1990. *Grammar Dictation*. Oxford: Oxford University Press.

Wang, J. 1996. 'Same task: Different activities.' Unpublished research report, University of Pittsburgh, Pittsburgh, PA.

Weir, C. 1988. *Communicative Language Testing*. Exeter Linguistic Studies, Volume 11. Exeter: University of Exeter.

Weir, C. 2001. 'The formative and summative uses of language test data: Present concerns and future directions' in C. Elder *et al.* (eds.). (pp.117–25.)

Weir, C. and **J. Roberts.** 1994. *Evaluation in ELT*. Oxford: Blackwell.

Weissenreider, M. 1987. 'Listening to the news in Spanish.' *Modern Language Journal* 71: 18–27.

Wells, G. 1985. *Language Development in the Pre-School Years*. Cambridge: Cambridge University Press.

Wells, G. 1998. 'Use L1 to master L2: A response to Anton and DiCamilla's sociocognitive functions of L1 collaborative interaction in the L2 classroom.' *The Canadian Modern Language Review* 54: 343–53.

Wells, G. 1999. *Dialogic Enquiry*. Cambridge: Cambridge University Press.

Wells, G. 2000. 'Dialogic enquiry in education: Building on the legacy of Vygotsky' in C. Lee and P. Smagorinsky (eds.): *Vygotskian Perspectives on Literacy Research*. (pp. 51–85). New York: Cambridge University Press.

Wendel, J. 1997. *Planning and Second Language Production*. Unpublished Ed. D. Dissertation, Temple University Japan.

Wenden, A. 1995. 'Learner-training in context: A knowledge-based approach.' *System* 23: 183–94.

Wertsch, J. 1985. *Vygotsky and the Social Formation of Mind*. Cambridge, MA: Harvard University Press.

Wertsch, J., N. Minick, and **F. Arns.** 1984. 'The creation of context in joint problem solving' in B. Rogoff and J. Lave (eds.): *Everyday Cognition: Its Development in Social Contexts*. Cambridge, MA: Harvard University Press.

White, J. 1998. 'Getting the learners' attention: A typographical input enhancement study' in C. Doughty and J. Williams (eds.). pp. 85–113.

White, L. 1987. 'Against comprehensible input: the input hypothesis and the development of second language competence.' *Applied Linguistics* 8: 95–110.

White, L. 1991. 'Adverb placement in second language acquisition: some effects of positive and negative evidence in the classroom.' *Second Language Research* 7: 133–61.

White, R. 1988. *The ELT Curriculum*. Oxford: Blackwell.

Wickens, C. and **C. Carswell.** 1997. 'Information processing' in G. Salvendy (ed.): *Handbook of Human Factors and Ergonomics* (pp. 89–129). New York: John Wiley and Sons.

Widdowson, H. 1972. 'The teaching of English as communication.' *ELT Journal* 27: 15–19.

Widdowson, H. 1978. *Teaching Language as Communication*. Oxford: Oxford University Press.

Widdowson, H. 1979. *Explorations in Applied Linguistics*. Oxford: Oxford University Press.

Widdowson, H. 1989. 'Knowledge of language and ability for use.' *Applied Linguistics* 10: 128–37.

Widdowson, H. 1990. *Aspects of Language Teaching*. Oxford: Oxford University Press.

Widdowson, H. 1993. 'Innovation in teacher development.' *Annual Review of Applied Linguistics* 13: 260–75.

Widdowson, H. 1998. 'Skills, abilities, and contexts of reality.' *Annual Review of Applied Linguistics* 18: 323–33.

Widdowson, H. 2001. 'Communicative language testing: The art of the possible' in C. Elder *et al.* (eds.): (pp. 12–21).

Wigglesworth, G. 1997a. 'Task variation in oral interaction tests: Increasing the reality.' *Prospect* 12: 35–49.

Wigglesworth, G. 1997b. 'An investigation of planning time and proficiency level on oral test discourse.' *Language Testing* 14: 85–106.

Wigglesworth, G. 2001. 'Influences on performance in task-based oral assessments' in Bygate *et al.* (eds.). (pp. 186–209).

Wilberg, T. 1987. *One-to-One*. Hove: Language Teaching Publications.

Wilkins, D. 1976. *Notional Syllabuses*. Oxford: Oxford University Press.

Williams, J. and **J. Evans.** 1998. 'What kind of focus and on which forms?' in C. Doughty and J. Williams (eds.).

Willing, K. 1987. *Learning Styles and Adult Migrant Education*. Adelaide: National Curriculum Resource Centre.

Willis, D. and **J. Willis.** 1996. 'Consciousness-raising activities in the language classroom' in J. Willis and D. Willis (eds.).

Willis, J. 1996. *A Framework for Task-Based Learning*. Harlow: Longman.

Willis, J. and **D. Willis.** (eds.). 1996. *Challenge and Change in Language Teaching*. Oxford: Heinemann.

Winn-Bell Olsen, J. 1977. *Communication Starters and Other Activities for the ESL Classroom*. San Francisco: Alemany.

Wong Fillmore, L. 1976. *The Second Time Around: Cognitive and Social Strategies in Second Language Acquisition*. Unpublished Ph.D. dissertation, Stanford University.

Wong, W. 2001. 'Modality and attention to meaning and form in the input.' *Studies in Second Language Acquisition* 23: 345–68.

Wood, D., J. Bruner, and **G. Ross.** 1976. 'The role of tutoring in problem-solving.' *Journal of Child Psychology and Psychiatry* 17: 89-100.

Wright, T. 1987. 'Instructional task and discoursal outcome in the L2 classroom' in C. Candlin and D. Murphy (eds.).

Yalden, J. 1983. *The Communicative Syllabus: Evolution, Design and Implementation*. Oxford: Pergamon.

Yuan, F. and **Ellis, R.** 2003. 'The effects of pre-task planning and on-line planning on fluency, complexity and accuracy in L2 oral production.' *Applied Linguistics*.

Yule, G. 1996. *Referential Communication Tasks*. Mahwah, N.J.: Lawrence Erlbaum.

Yule, G. and **D. McDonald.** 1990. 'Resolving referential conflicts in L2 interaction: the effect of proficiency and interactive role.' *Language Learning* 40: 539–56.

Yule, G. and **M. Powers.** 1994. 'Investigating the communicative outcomes of task-based interaction.' *System* 22: 81–91.

Yule, G., M. Powers, and **D. McDonald.** 1992. 'The variable effects of some task-based learning procedures on LZ communicative effectiveness.' *Language Learning* 42: 249–277.

Zinchenko, V. 1985. 'Vygotsky's ideas about units for the analysis of mind' in J. Wertsch, (ed.): *Culture, Communication and Cognition. Vygotskian Perspectives*. Cambridge, MA: Cambridge University Press.

Zobl, H. 1995. 'Converging evidence for the "Acquisition-learning" distinction.' *Applied Linguistics* 16: 35–56.

Zuengler, J. 1993. 'Explaining NNS interactional behavior: The effect of conversational topic' in G. Kasper and S. Blum-Kulka (eds.): *Interlanguage Pragmatics*. New York: Oxford University Press.

Zuengler, J. and **B. Bent.** 1991. 'Relative knowledge of content domain: an influence on native–non-native conversations.' *Applied Linguistics* 12: 397–415.

Index

References to the Glossary are shown by 'g' after page numbers. References to the end-of-chapter notes are indicated by 'n' followed by the note number.

language play 190–1, 329–31
language production 103–39
language skill 6–7
language-related episodes 156, 344–5g
Lantolf, J. 175, 176, 178, 179, 180, 182,
   183, 184, 190, 193, 195, 198, 199,
   265, 319
   with Aljaafreh, A. 24, 191–2
   with Appel, G. 183, 185, 188–9, 197–8,
      202n3
   with Dunn, W. 180
   with Frawley, W. 178, 197
learning-based evaluation 324, 325, 345g
lectures 59–65
Lee, J. 4–5, 238, 244, 249
Leontiev, A.N. 175, 183
lesson design 243–62, 345g
Levelt, W. 25, 107–8, 110
lexicalized processing 24–5
Library Skills Reading Test 296–7
linguistic communication strategies 75
linguistic imperialism 331–3, 345g
linguistic knowledge, representation 103–7
linguistic syllabuses 207–10, 345g
listen-and-do tasks 50–9, 345g
listening, comprehension 37–67
listening-to-comprehend 38–45, 65
listening-to-learn 45–9, 65
listening-to-notice 38
Long, M. 2, 3, 4, 6, 23, 46, 70, 71, 79, 88,
   89–90, 144, 168, 208–9, 220
   with Crookes, G. 27, 86, 207–8
   with Inagaki, S. and Ortega, L. 168–9
loose tasks 123–4

Mackey, A. 82, 154–6
   with Gass, S., Fernandez, M. and
      Alvarez-Torres, M. 134
   with Philp, J. 169
McNamara, T. 33, 279, 293, 300–1,
   303–4, 309, 310–11, 316n3
   with Iwashita, N. and Elder, C. 119, 130,
      131, 132, 289, 294
macro-evaluation 326–8, 345g
macro-markers 61
meaning *see* focus on meaning; negotiation
   of meaning
meaning-focused activity 32
measurement, of language production
   115–27
mediation 175–6, 345g
medium of input 222
medium of outcome 226

mental model 44–5, 65
metacognitive focus 32–3
metacognitive strategy training 194
metalingual function of language 329
metatalk 188, 195–7, 199, 345g
methodology 205, 243–78
micro-evaluation 323–6, 345g
micro-markers 61
Minimalist Program 138n1
mistakes vs. errors 172n1
Modern Language Aptitude Battery 57
modified input 51–9, 70
modified output 99, 168, 345g
modular syllabuses 210, 236–8, 345g
monitoring 110, 345g
morphological acquisition 67n4, 81–2
morphological creativity communication
   strategies 75

nativist theories 104
Natural Approach 28
need, learner involvement 58–9
needs analysis 292, 345–6g
negotiation
   of content 72, 346g
   of form 99, 256, 346g
   of meaning 23–4, 70–3, 96–100, 213–14,
      224, 346g
Newton, J. 24, 25, 86, 87, 90, 116, 121,
   130–1, 247
   with Kennedy, G. 125
Nijmegen Project 75
non-interface position 106, 149, 346g
non-reciprocal tasks 49–50, 346g
non-understandings 70–3
note-taking 60–4
noticing 47–8, 144, 149, 261–2, 346g
noticing-the-gap 47, 111–12, 144, 149,
   346g
notional/functional syllabuses 28, 30,
   207–8, 346g
nudging 256
Nunan, D. 2, 3, 4, 7, 17, 19, 31, 35n4,
   205, 223, 246, 265, 266

object-regulation 177, 197, 346g
off-line planning *see* pre-task planning
Ohta, A.S. 178, 193, 194–5, 198–9, 274
one-way tasks 60, 88–9, 94, 96, 215, 271,
   347g
online planning 25, 110, 128–9, 133–4,
   347g
open tasks 89–91, 122–3, 126, 347g